MW01119827

TERRAIN OF
MEMORY

TERRAIN OF MEMORY

A Japanese Canadian Memorial Project

Kirsten Emiko
McAllister

UBCPress · Vancouver · Toronto

20 19 18 17 16 15 14 13 12 11 10   5 4 3 2 1

Printed in Canada on FSC-certified ancient-forest-free paper
(100% post-consumer recycled) that is processed chlorine- and acid-free.

Library and Archives Canada Cataloguing in Publication

McAllister, Kirsten Emiko
   Terrain of memory : a Japanese Canadian memorial project / Kirsten Emiko McAllister.

Includes bibliographical references and index.
ISBN 978-0-7748-1771-4

   1. Nikkei Internment Memorial Centre. 2. Memorials – British Columbia – New Denver. 3. Japanese Canadians – British Columbia – New Denver – History – 20th century. 4. Collective memory – British Columbia – New Denver. 5. Japanese Canadians – Evacuation and relocation, 1942-1945. 6. New Denver (B.C.) – History. I. Title.

FC3849.N47Z57 2010   971.1'62004956   C2010-901731-5

Canadä

UBC Press gratefully acknowledges the financial support for our publishing program of the Government of Canada (through the Canada Book Fund), the Canada Council for the Arts, and the British Columbia Arts Council.

This book has been published with the help of a grant from the Canadian Federation for the Humanities and Social Sciences, through the Aid to Scholarly Publications Programme, using funds provided by the Social Sciences and Humanities Research Council of Canada.

Simon Fraser University has provided generous financial support for the publication of this book through a Single Publication Grant.

UBC Press
The University of British Columbia
2029 West Mall
Vancouver, BC V6T 1Z2
www.ubcpress.ca

This book is dedicated to the members of the
Kyowakai Society
of New Denver, British Columbia,
and to my issei grandparents,
Yatsumatsu Nakashima and Miyuke Nakashima
who lived through the hatred and cruelty of wartime society
to transform all into generations of change.

Contents

Illustrations

Acknowledgments

Manuscripts travel. This work accompanied me as I moved across Canada to the United Kingdom and home again to British Columbia, where I now live and work. Manuscripts are never produced in isolation. Many people have contributed to making this work possible, helping me to both gain distance from the overwhelming intensity of the material and move into its most intimate spaces.

First and foremost, the members of the Kyowakai Society of New Denver must be acknowledged. With their formal permission, I began this study. I want to especially express my gratitude for the guidance, generous support, and warm kindness of Mrs. Pauli Inose, Mrs. Sumie Matsushita, Mr. Shoichi Matsushita, Mr. Tad Mori, and Mrs. Kay Takahara. I also want to thank Mrs. Sumie Matsushita and her son Masaye (Mas) Matsushita for granting permission to reproduce Mr. Shoichi Matsushita's photographs of New Denver. I especially want to thank Mas for all the time and thought he put into finding and digitizing a selection of captivating images from his father's treasure of photographs, a task that required numerous trips from Revelstoke to New Denver. Katherine Shozawa must be thanked as well. Just after the birth of Beatrice, with the help of David Hsu, she found time to select images for this manuscript from the archives of her magical 1995 New Denver memory box project. I would also like to thank Don Lyon from Nelson for providing an image of the Nikkei Internment Memorial Centre's (NIMC) garden. He is a well-known local photographer who is dedicated to the preservation of history in the Kootenays.

It was L.H. who invited me to the valley, into the space of memory that the Kyowakai Society has nurtured over the years. Her enduring support, despite her trepidations about taking an academic, even if friend, under her wing, was Herculean.

I am incredibly indebted to Alan Hunt, the senior supervisor for my PhD in the Department of Sociology and Anthropology at Carleton University, and I must also thank his partner, Ros, for her insight and generous kindness. I continue to be astonished at Alan's immoveable support for this project as it unfolded so unpredictably, especially in the last phases of writing. His patience, persistence, and the force of his honest engagement and his intellectual rigour are what propelled me forward.

Derek Smith shared his libraries of scholarship as well as imaginative textual strategies for transposing other worlds across the divides of time and place in our ongoing discussions. Audrey Kobayashi revealed conceptual routes forward and grounded me in the necessity of joining together the complex and contradictory spaces of community, activism, and academia. And Rob Shields, with his voracious mind and sense of methodological play, has also had no uncertain influence on my work.

Behnam Behnia, Wendy Larner, Julianne Pidduck, and Melanie White offered friendship and an intellectual community; it was Melanie who gave incisive feedback that helped draw out a form from the mass of raw experience I brought back with me from New Denver. Ottawa Aikikai introduced me to an embodied ethics that helped put what I had learned into words: I am grateful for what sensei Don Dickie and Gladys Manchester taught me. John Brule and Anne Marchand became dear friends who over the years of writing this manuscript provided all means of shelter and inspiration in my restless movements. Likewise, Ana Chang, Shafraz Jetha, and José Arroyo have remained stalwart friends over the long distances we have lived all these years.

From Lancaster University, where I was a SSHRC postdoctoral fellow, Annette Kuhn and Jackie Stacey were instrumental in providing new insights into the capacity of writing for memory work. Their gentle insistence that the book must be finished was crucial, more so than they likely imagined. Jackie gave me the opportunity to begin explicitly exploring questions of voice and my relationship to historical trauma in a 2001 issue of *Cultural Values* on testimonial culture. In inviting me to co-edit a book, Annette taught me about the most practical and the most imaginative dimensions of producing a book, giving me humble respect for what lay ahead.

At the University of Windsor, I was moved by scholars committed to progressive principles, and it was Jyotika Virdi who threw me the lifeline of her friendship. She also accepted no excuses for letting this manuscript, with all the work and time of countless people, disappear into a file box. For Jyotika, it was a straightforward matter of historical materialism, simply a question of labour.

On my return to Vancouver, colleagues in the School of Communication showed me the satisfaction along with what was purely practical in the most daunting of goals: they include Ellen Balka, Alison Beale, Zoë Druick, Jan Marontate, Catherine Murray, Yuezhi Zhao and, from other departments, Helen Leung, who gave encouragement and advice during long morning walks, and Eugene McCann, who provided invaluable references on the chronotope and space. Zoë Druick has stood by through thick and thin, reminding me that culture is not simply to be studied but also to be lived. Graduate students Daniel

Ahadi, Dorothy Christian, Marcos Moldes, Kjetil Rodje, Rebecca Scott, Milan Singh, and Ayaka Yoshimizu have pushed me to think in new ways about all dimensions of this work.

I can not imagine a better home than UBC Press for this manuscript. After the government lifted restrictions on "people of the Japanese racial origin" in 1949, a generation of *nisei* pursued degrees at the University of British Columbia, including my mother. The Press has published many works dedicated to the historical and contemporary worlds of British Columbia, which is the terrain of the NIMC. I was privileged to work with Jean Wilson before her retirement, learning how UBC Press deeply respects the book and its place in public life. It has been a marvel to work with my editor, Darcy Cullen, whose skill, patience, and authority of experience has brought me effortlessly through all stages of publication. I am deeply grateful to the reviewers for the time and care they took in reading my work. They made a vital difference in the resulting manuscript. I could not have wished for a more dedicated production editor. Laraine Coates oversaw the production of the book with incredible patience, meticulous care, vision in design, and knowledge of the human dynamics of book production. I must also recognize the work of Anne Marie Todkill and thank Lesley Erickson for so incisively and thoroughly copying editing the manuscript.

I relied heavily on the archives and libraries and their staff. I give tribute to the NIMC, the Selkirk College Library (Judy Deon), the Japanese Canadian National Museum (Grace Eiko Thomson, Reiko Tagami, Timothy Savage, Linda Reid, and Daien Idhe), Library and Archives Canada, and Simon Fraser University's librarian, Mark Bodnar, who, with detective-like relish, tirelessly assisted with copyright queries.

This project has received support from many funding bodies. Both the Canadian Federation for the Humanities and Social Sciences, through the Aid to Scholarly Publications, and Simon Fraser University, through a Single Publication Grant, provided generous financial support for the publication of this book. I received a PhD Fellowship from the Social Sciences and Humanities Research Council of Canada, a scholarship from the Imperial Order, Daughters of the Empire War Memorial Scholarship, an Ontario Graduate Scholarship, a Special Projects Award from the National Association of Japanese Canadians' Redress Foundation, a Canadian Japanese Mennonite Scholarship, and numerous awards, bursaries, and scholarships from Carleton University. I am greatly indebted to these organizations.

Throughout all, Roy Miki and Slavia Miki have been fundamental. I have been one of the many students, writers, and artists they have welcomed into the warmth of their home to discuss, collaborate, and receive guidance late into the night. What they shared about the ethos of creative work has made me question much about my own thinking and writing. And as this manuscript took shape over the last few years, at every stage, Roy has been there with support and advice. In the last days, as I struggled with sections that defeated rewrite after rewrite, Roy presented a way forward, to let go of what I wanted to write and instead pay attention to what was emerging in the writing itself. And also in Vancouver, as I circled around my manuscript, labouring to turn it into a book, my friendship with Glen Lowry and Elizabeth Kelson provided a place to freely muse about writing and ideas, about the processes and politics of production, about methodology and the principles of research.

Always, the contributions of Japanese Canadian redress activists, artists, thinkers, curators, and academics have made me act and think beyond the interests of any one individual or institution. In addition to Roy Miki and Audrey Kobayashi are Grace Eiko Thomson, Mona Oikawa, Cindy Mochizuki, Michael Fukushima, Katherine Shozawa, Monika kin Gagnon, and Scott McFarlane. Mona Oikawa in particular has spent long hours in discussion with me about the complexities of research and community work, giving support and insight into what is at stake in our research. She has been inspiring and supportive as a scholar and friend over the years, sharing her experience and knowledge of the challenge of researching a history that, in many respects, is still under a variety of forms of censure.

My Obaasan, Mrs. Miyuki Nakashima, my parents, Rosalie Chitose and Carey Douglas McAllister, my uncles, Frank, Rick, and Herb Nakashima, and my brothers, Angus and Murdoch, have sustained and inspired me with their sense of principle and their many pursuits. And my parents must know that their belief in my work has always been the glowing heart of what I have done and hope to do. I look to them and their commitment to the public good, to their involvement in cooperatives, credit unions, anti-racist policies, civic politics, the environment, and to their joy in their shared love of the arts.

TERRAIN OF
MEMORY

The Drive to Do Research

It was a ten-hour drive inland from the Pacific coastline of British Columbia. My destination was a remote, mountainous valley in the interior of the province. I was expected to arrive at dusk, the moment when night swallows the visual world of day. I traced my route from the network of red lines on the road map. It was not the fastest or the most direct route, but it followed the contours of the landscape I would traverse over the next several years.

Tashme, Christina Lake, Greenwood, Lemon Creek, Slocan, Harris Ranch, New Denver, Rosebery, Sandon, Kaslo ... In 1942, these places were part of another map, a field of operation aimed at countering the "quiet insidious penetration" by an "aggressive, unassimilable" race of people (Ward 1990, 107) who had made their homes along the coast. Slowly engulfed by the passing years, today all you see are derelict mining towns, overgrown fields, and serene lakes nestled in mountain valleys.

Highway 3 was the southern route through rugged valleys, over wild mountain ranges with fast, curving descents that unwound unpredictably across rolling savannah. For most travellers it was the slow, scenic route. But for those recollecting the remains of the past, it was a route inscribed with the passage of others, a route in memory of others.

I drove through the heat of the day, stopping only for gas, directions, and coffee. As the light began to fade, I cut north up Highway 6, chasing the setting sun up the Slocan Valley, a valley carved by advancing glaciers thousands of years ago. The mountains were enormous; the lake, a deep inland sea. The narrow highway climbed high, close to the pale twilight sky. Then suddenly it descended to the valley bottom: a cool rush into darkness.

The red lines could take me no further. I had reached my destination. New Denver. Over fifty years before, the bureaucratic machinery of war had transformed the surrounding mountains into "natural prison walls." This is where thousands of women, men, and children of "Japanese racial origin" were interned for four years before the government took the final step to solve the "Japanese problem" and permanently remove them from the province. This was my point of departure. (EXCERPTS FROM LETTERS TO FRIENDS, 1996)

0.1   New Denver internment camp, views looking north toward the tuberculosis sanatorium, ca. 1943-1945. *Harold Hayashi Family Collection 92/32.019. Courtesy of the Japanese Canadian National Museum.*

In Memory

In 1994, Japanese Canadian elders[1] living in the village of New Denver built the Nikkei Internment Memorial Centre (NIMC) to mark the isolated mountainous terrain with their history of persecution. From 1942 to 1946, the Canadian government operated six internment camps in this region. Little evidence of the internment of 7,250 people remains today.[2] When the war ended in 1945, the government dismantled most of the camps and forced most of the internees to leave the province (Miki and Kobayashi 1991, 31). Over time, the landscape has absorbed the physical evidence. A few durable traces remain: water lines, fragments of ceramic plates, the foundations of communal outhouses, grave markers, and service roads. Soon the landscape will reclaim even these vestiges as they are ploughed into farmers' fields, overtaken by vegetation, worn into the earth by heavy winter snow and torrential summer storms, and incorporated into the built environment by local residents and businesses.

Even as the hard evidence erodes, the experiences of internment continue to resonate in the lives of those who still live in the valley. Although the government forced most Japanese Canadian internees to leave the province in 1945, some were permitted to remain. In addition to approximately two thousand "self-supporting" Japanese Canadians scattered throughout the province, government advisors calculated that there were two thousand "persons who could not be rehabilitated to other parts of Canada ... [including] TB patients, incurables, derelict single old men, and women and old couples who [had] no younger members of their families living in Canada, people in mental homes and those serving in penal institutions" (Eastwood 1944). Concluding that they were unable to support themselves, the government gathered "the incurables," "derelicts," and "old couples" from other camps throughout the province and "congregated" them in New Denver. New Denver was chosen in part because the British Columbia Security Commission had built a tuberculosis sanatorium there for internees.[3] The government provided support payments for the "incurables," though advisors suggested that they would eventually cease to be a "problem" because they "would gradually die off over a period of the next fifteen years to twenty years" (Desbrisay 1944).

But the "incurables" did not die off. By 1947, the administrator responsible for Japanese Canadians in New Denver claimed there were 936 who were

> likely to be a Government charge for some years to come. [Three hundred] are those that would leave here if housing with their children in the east was available. In this group we must realize that a number of the daughters and children that went east are very young and unless the parents had money they would not be in a position to procure housing for their parents ... They are anxious to go when housing is obtainable ... [Another three hundred] have made definite plans for relocation ... certain areas [in British Columbia] have asked us to defer sending them until the Japanese problem is more or less definitely clarified with the Province. (Mackinnon 1947)

Poverty, illness, and uncertainty about their prospects in other regions made it difficult for some to leave New Denver. Others left as soon as they had secured employment and accommodations elsewhere and had saved enough to cover the costs of moving. Others decided to stay in New Denver, and some who left gravitated back after 1949, when the government lifted restrictions and permitted Japanese Canadians to return to British Columbia. These elders spoke about feeling adrift in other regions of Canada, at a loss without the communal bonds of their pre-war communities in a radically transformed postwar society. In 1957, when the government agency responsible for administrating "the Japanese problem" was required to dispose of its holdings, the Japanese Canadian leaders in New Denver proposed that the government deed the internment shacks and the accompanying lots to the remaining Japanese Canadians. The government agreed. Half the land was donated to the Village of New Denver for the creation of Centennial Park along the lakefront. The shacks were rearranged into a grid system. When the former internees were confident that the government would not uproot them again, they began to make small improvements to their shacks and lots (Matsushita, History Preservation Meeting, 20 August 1996).

Over the years, the lives of Japanese Canadians became integrated with other residents. They worked alongside one another as loggers, cooks, nurses' aids, and seamstresses. Some ran for political office in the village – for example, Mr. Senya Mori was elected as mayor for several terms – and others set up New Denver's first kindergarten. Their children went to the village school, married the locals, and participated in May Day celebrations and Remembrance Day ceremonies. They transformed what had been an internment camp into their home community.

When I first visited in 1995, fifteen Japanese Canadians elders remained in New Denver. Most were original members of the Kyowakai Society of New Denver. In Japanese, *Kyo* means peacefully, *wa* means together, and *kai* means society: thus, *Kyowakai* can be translated as "working together peacefully" (Kamegaya in Truly 1995). The society was established in 1943 to represent the interests of the 1,500 Japanese Canadians interned in the New Denver camp. As one of the elders wrote to me, "The Society was an important influence for the confused and stressed days of our internment years. The Kyowa Kai ... meant moral support and strength (I'm sure [like] any society, during the war years) (Mrs. Pauli Inose, Interview, 6 August 2006).

The elders were conscious that they would soon die and that there would be few left with living memories of the internment camps. And so they built the Nikkei Internment Memorial Centre (NIMC) for future generations. They built it so those unable to find resolution to the disturbing forces haunting their lives would always have a place to return. They built it so future generations would not forget the history of internment camps in Canada. As Mrs. Inose explained, the memorial reminds us how quickly "discriminatory" attitudes can be transformed into government measures targeting "minorities" (Inose, Interview, 16 August 1996).

The memorial centre occupies almost one full block in the residential area of New Denver on the river flats south of Carpenter Creek, the site of the original internment camp. It is a prominent public statement marking the sleepy village with a painful history that some residents would have preferred to have left buried. Inside the cedar post fence enclosing the grounds are four buildings dating back to the internment camp, all set within a traditional landscaped Japanese garden. Three cramped shacks show the living conditions endured by the internees, and in the Kyowakai Hall artifacts and documents tell the history of Japanese Canadians. In its first summer of operation, the NIMC received over two thousand visitors.

The Terrain of Memory

To build the Nikkei Internment Centre, people in New Denver went through a process of excavation, looking for the remains of the camp. The elders searched their memories for details about the camp's operation and their daily life as internees. They looked through their homes for wartime dishes, homemade furniture, photographs, and government documents. Many other residents joined the search, combing through photograph albums, personal records, attics, and cupboards. To determine the location of the camp, they remapped their neighbourhoods, tracing the outlines of the camp's service roads and the long-gone rows of internment shacks along the lakeshore.

Not everyone was comfortable about making this unpleasant chapter of New Denver's history public. Yet, despite the tensions in the village, the Kyowakai Society remained committed to building the memorial. When it opened, the NIMC placed New Denver on a new map, a map of return. Large numbers of visitors began to arrive from across Canada and even Japan. Some came on pilgrimage-like journeys to the site where their families had been incarcerated; others hoped to find clues about lost childhood friends. Some argued that the government's actions were justified. Others drew parallels with their own histories of persecution.

I was first introduced to the memorial by one of my mentors at the time, Teresa Takana,[4] a *sansei*[5] living in the Slocan Valley whom the elders had recently designated as the chair of their History Preservation Committee. In 1995, she asked me to travel to New Denver to assist with two projects at the memorial, and the following summer she invited me to return to help complete them. This is when I arranged to conduct research on the memorial. Thus, this study focuses on the memorial two years after it opened. Living in the Slocan Valley for just under a month in 1995 and for another three months in 1996, I worked closely with members of the Kyowakai Society on their projects, and I also socialized with them as a guest in their homes and at community events. My time in the valley provided a basis for understanding the significance of the memorial for the elders. During the course of my stay, some elders shared their astute criticisms of the NIMC with me. They warned that it threatened to "museumify" their Buddhist otera, which was now housed in the NIMC. Others spoke about the small-scale memory projects the memorial made possible. Without this time, my understanding would have been limited to a formal analysis of interview material and the memorial's layout and educational exhibits.

In writing *Terrain of Memory,* my intention was to honour the contributions of the elders from New Denver. Rather than focusing on their individual life stories, the book examines the memorial as a collective form of memory.[6] This memorial was one of many projects they have initiated over the years to unearth memories that have haunted the valley long after the internment camps closed. When they built the memorial, the members of the Kyowakai Society acted out of a sense of responsibility to a larger community living across Canada. Yet, in building it, they also transformed their own terrain of memory. Here, the term "terrain" indicates not only a tract of land but also a field of knowledge and a sphere of influence or action (*Oxford Modern Dictionary* 1996). How the elders remember the past has been profoundly transformed by the thousands of people who visit the river flats of New Denver each year, each with her or his own reason for remembering the internment camps. The elders have learned that there is a need not only for Japanese Canadians but also for everyone affected by the removal of all people "of Japanese racial origin" from British Columbia to have a place to grieve, recall, and question the past.

Not a Recovery

Unlike historical studies of Japanese Canadians that are aimed at recovering details of pre-war and wartime life, this book examines how memory shapes contemporary communities. I approach memory as a collective cultural activity. As Mieke Bal, Jonathan Crewe, and Leo Spitzer claim, "cultural memorization as an activity occurring in the present, in which the past is continuously modified and redescribed even as it continues to shape the future ... [is] the product of collective agency rather than the result of psychic or historical accident" (1999a, vii). Thus, this study examines how the practices of memory can both change and create new understandings of and relations to the past while shaping the manner in which members of cultural communities live in the present and approach the future. Using methods from the academic discipline of cultural studies, and more specifically memory studies, this book explores different practices, relations, and understandings of the New Denver internment camp through an examination of the discourses at play in the NIMC's historical displays (Chapter 2), the memorial's space of mourning (Chapter 3), the elders' oral accounts (Chapter 4), their memory projects (Chapter 5), and the responses and practices of tourists (Chapter 6).

My previous research on Japanese Canadians has entailed extensive archival research, interviewing, and fieldwork (McAllister 1994, 1998, 2001, 2002, 2006a, 2006b). While recognizing the value of historical research, my work belongs to the field of cultural studies and, more specifically, memory studies. Historical research on the past and research on cultural memory are two different enterprises. The former aims to accurately recover factual details – whether about the working class, for instance, or immigration legislation – cultural memory projects begin with the premise that recollection, which includes not only oral accounts and photographic practices but also the activity of research itself, both occurs in and affects the present (Bal, Crew, and Spitzer 1999a; Hirsch 1997a; Kuhn 1995). Memory, as well as the act of writing about memory, operates in a political field of power, desire, denial, and struggle, something that not all historical scholars recognize as a valid area of inquiry.[8]

My approach to writing and research has been influenced by Asian Canadian researchers such as Audrey Kobayashi (1994b) and Roy Miki (1998a) who, rather than "studying" Asian Canadian communities, recognize that their scholarly activities contribute to the very production of these communities (Said 1979), whether by building intergenerational relations through their interview activities or by contesting exclusionary national discourses (McAllister and Oikawa 1996). It could be argued that the difference between the two approaches can be summed up by the difference between Foucault's (1979) disciplinary knowledge and Marx's praxis (1963 [1844]).

American-trained and Canadian-trained researchers concerned with establishing a field of Japanese (and Asian) Canadian studies in many ways subscribe to the disciplinary approach.[9] This approach is especially evident in the United States, where a number of expatriate Canadians trained at American universities are trying to establish their research on Asian Canadians as a credible, recognized field of study.[10] The interest in Canada as an area of academic expansion reflects the more general nationalist-imperial drive of Asian American scholarship criticized by Canadian scholars such as Miki (1998d), Kamboureli (2005), and Oikawa (forthcoming). For instance, Miki (1998d) argues that the inclusion of Asian Canadian texts such as *Obasan* (Kogawa 1983) in the American canon "results in the erasure of the difference that 'nationalisms' make; in an act of institutional appropriation by US academics of Asian Canadian texts, the site-specific formation of the Japanese Canadian subject ... tends to become another version of the 'Asian American' example" (Miki 1998d, 155).

In contrast to research aimed at producing knowledge that fits the criteria of an established discipline, the research conducted by Japanese Canadian activists in the 1970s and 1980s was an example of praxis (Adachi 1991 [1976]); Sunahara 1981; National Association of Japanese Canadians 1984, 1985, 1988). They conducted research to provide evidence that proved the government had violated the rights of thousands of its citizens and that its use of the War Measures Act to incarcerate Japanese Canadians, liquidate their properties, and force them to leave the province of British Columbia and, in many cases, Canada had no justification.[11] Their research also laid the grounds for making a case to repeal the War Measures Act, though the Emergencies Act continues to give the federal cabinet discretionary power to target whatever segment of the population it deems to be a threat to national security (Kobayashi and Miki 1989). Thus, while their research could be categorized as "recovery work" insofar as it recovered historical facts, it was overtly political (Kobayashi 1992a). Redress activists, including lawyers such as Ann Sunahara and academics such as Roy Miki and Audrey Kobayashi, produced studies to contest established historical "truths" reproduced by the federal government and scholars, upsetting many academics who were working in ethnic studies and other fields of social science research (Miki 2004; Kobayashi 1992a, 1994a).

In contrast, disciplinary "recovery scholars" are dedicated to "objectively" increasing accurate knowledge about the past. Many such scholars dismiss research on cultural memory as postmodern and subjective and political recovery work as biased.[12] Positivist in orientation, these historians do not critically reflect on their own investments in producing knowledge that reifies the past as facts waiting to be discovered. They do not examine how their own research and writing not only constructs "the past" but also produces social, political, and psychological (after)effects. In contrast, studies of cultural memory are concerned with the *process* of recollecting, revising, and repressing past events and with how this process socially, politically, and psychologically configures contemporary communities and subjects (Langer 1991; Young 1993; Bennett 1995; Kuhn 1995; Hirsch 1997a; Spitzer 1998; Bal, Crew, and Spitzer 1999b; Radstone 2000a; Winter and Sivan 2000; Huyssen 2003; Lansberg 2004).

Investments

I have my own investments in remembering the past. My work at the NIMC made me question these investments, especially my need for a stable identity within British Columbia's fluid racial discourses. I am a sansei whose mother's family prospered in the fishing industry before they were interned during the Second World War and whose father's family were Scottish socialists who circulated as freely among White Russian fishermen, secular Sikhs, and Jewish furniture-shop owners as they did among anti-establishment writers and artists of Scottish and English ancestry. Much of the pre-war and wartime social landscape of British Columbia remains alive in their stories. Although my world has always been a confluence of these stories, the wartime landscape of internment camps has had a stronger hold on me. Whatever it was that first compelled me to reach toward the fading contours of my mother's family's past, it has never been about simply recovering what had been destroyed, reconstructing the details of a lost world. Like the work of Mona Oikawa (2002), my research has very much been concerned with the living community of Japanese Canadians.

Like many sansei, I have my own story of "return" that secures my identity as Japanese Canadian. It was the Vancouver community that literally swept me into its arms when I graduated from university. When I first walked into the Japanese Canadian Citizens' Association (JCCA) on Powell Street to ask about volunteer work, I was recognized by people I had never met before. Despite my own ambivalence as a "double" (someone of mixed heritage), they claimed me as a member of the community. Although for my mother's family there was no question that I was part of the Nakashima clan, it was not until I began to work in the Japanese Canadian community that I learned about the anxieties about the more than 95 percent "intermarriage" rate. But, at the same time, I learned that most sansei and *yonsei*[13] were double (Kobayashi 1989; McAllister 1991; McAllister and Medenwaldt 1992; *Nikkei Voice* Staff 1997, 1).

Members of Vancouver's Japanese Canadian community knew my mother's family and shared details from over the last seventy years about people I never knew and places I had never visited. I was inspired by people like Tatsuo Kage and Judy Hanazawa, who worked on the JCCA human rights committee as well as activists, writers, and artists such as Fumiko Greenaway, Mona Oikawa, Roy Miki, Slavia Miki, Tony Tamiyose, Randy Enomoto, Naomi Shikaze, Ken Shikaze, Gordon Kayahara, Mary Seki, Michael Fukushima, and Leslie Komori. I discovered that many of my mannerisms, especially those that others considered peculiar, were part of a cultural language shared with this community. Drawn by this uncanny sense of familiarity, I soon learned that I had been recruited by Frank Kameya to run the JCCA oral history project. Before I knew it, I had over fifty volunteers and was organizing community events and forums and writing articles for local and national Japanese Canadian newspapers, Vancouver's *JCCA Bulletin* and *Nikkei Voice*.

I was introduced to the community in 1989, just after the National Association of Japanese Canadians negotiated a settlement for redress with the Canadian government. I met those who feared that, without redress as a common and unifying goal, the end of the community was near. Some lived in their memories of the pre-war community. Interviewing Japanese Canadians about life in the early 1900s to the 1930s, I learned that despite the restrictive racist legislation and impoverished living conditions that many (although not all) endured, they believed that the future was full of promise. The war threw that future into question and destroyed it for some. When the internment camps were closed, little was left of their pre-war world, a world many felt they had to repudiate if they were to be accepted by other Canadians and spare their children from the racial hatred that had torn their lives apart.

Newly embraced by the Japanese Canadian community in Vancouver, I defiantly argued against "the end of the community." For me, this fear echoed what psychiatrist Robert Jay Lifton described as one of the symbolizations of death that characterized the late twentieth century. In general, death represents the annihilation of life, whether psychic or organic. It threatens what Lifton refers to as our sense of immortality, in which immortality is the symbolization of continuity, "an individual's experience in some form of collective life-continuity" (Lifton 1979, 17). For traumatized individuals, their

> individual death cannot be separated from the sense that (as Hiroshima sur-vivors put it) "the whole world is dying." This perception is truly unnatural. It is partly a product of our holocaust-dominated age ... [connected to] imagery of extinction that haunts contemporary man ... But even in the absence of holocaust, people can equate the end of the self with the end of everything ... [Here] one's own death is anticipated, irrespective of age and circumstances, as premature, absurd, unacceptable. (Ibid. 47)

I was adamant that this apocalyptic view failed to recognize the possibilities of a post-redress community. Surely, if Japanese Canadians could mobilize across Canada in a movement for redress, they could embrace a post-redress com-munity with its intercultural families and postwar immigrants (McAllister 1991; McAllister 1992b; and McAllister and Medenwaldt 1992)?

Renditions of the past filled with images of a cohesive pre-war community, embellished with swirls of nostalgia, gave the history of Japanese Canadians a mythic quality. But the past did not circulate simply as stories of a golden era (Lifton 1979). Some described their family's prosperity before the war to express the enormity of what they had lost when the government liquidated their property and forced them out of British Columbia. In families and community forums, there were also silences that slammed shut conversations. There were those who adamantly denied their families had suffered during the war, despite the fact that the government had liquidated their properties and sent members of their families to different camps. Some could not acknowledge the existence of racism and insisted they were no different from other Canadians.

There are researchers who uncritically support this position. For example, in *The Canadian Sansei* (1998), Tomoko Makabe dismisses "the hypothesis that the evacuation-internment experience may be a central component of the dis-tinctive Japanese-Canadian identity." She rejects the idea that the "evacuation-internment" had any impact, in particular, on sansei identity (Makabe 1998, 164). According to Makabe, the damaging impact of the internment and forced assimilation stopped with the *nisei*. For proof, she takes the statements of her interviewees at face value and claims they are "completely free from negative 'minority feelings'"(ibid. 165). She concludes that "overall the sansei have a positive, self-imposed [identity] of so-called ethnic pride" because "they became aware of the advantage of being a member of a 'respectable' minority" (ibid. 167).[14] Yet she does not explain why her interviewees insist that they do not experience racism and cannot identify with "the plight of others who have been subjected to racism." She does not examine some of her interviewees' racist attitudes toward other groups (ibid. 140-142). According to sociologist Donna Nagata (1993) and psychologist Amy Iwasaki Mass (1986), if victims have racist attitudes or show no empathy toward other victims, this can be a sign of pathologies such as disassociation and identification with one's aggressor.[15]

In addition to the denial of racism, there is also what I can describe only as a slow paralysis. It is as if those afflicted are unable to live in their bodies, retreating from the world around them, pulled elsewhere by an unseen struggle or undefined anguish in an unreachable place. It was this haunting presence of loss that also underlay my own ambivalent history growing up in British Columbia, struggling against what I slowly realized were the ways in which I was mapped within its racialized terrain. Attempts to avoid the disturbing presence of the past were impossible; it suffused my everyday world. Avoidance was possible only through retreat, by confining the self to a smaller and smaller space of existence, a slow suffocation, which amounted to a refusal to live in the world as it was constituted (Manganyi 1977; Herman 1992).

I began my exploration of the powerful strategies people used to make sense of the past in the 1990s. In this period, the West Coast literary and arts scene was alive with projects by racialized communities working collaboratively across their different histories.[16] Artists and writers, filmmakers and video artists launched critiques against institutions and discourses that contained histories of violence in the distant past while experimenting with new forms of representation. For me, the poet, scholar, and activist Roy Miki[17] was a key figure in this scene. He set up public venues to gather emerging and established artists and writers to discuss and debate cultural production as well as to publish work that established presses and journals had refused. Writing and research were approached as catalytic engagements with the world rather than as disciplinary studies that objectified and commodified culture. In this milieu, where artists and writers were mapping the topos of race in the everyday world of British Columbia, there was also space to explore my own ambivalent relation to the past. I became interested in forms of representation and cultural practices that transformed rather than reproduced the damaging aftermath of political violence. The present work is shaped by this milieu, which I see as the West Coast School of Cultural Studies.[18] It has shaped my approach to critically investigating how the past is remembered, revised, and forgotten.

Collective Forms of Remembering Political Violence

This study belongs to a growing body of literature on cultural memory (Langer 1991; Young 1993; Bennett 1995; Kuhn 1995; Hirsch 1997a; Spitzer 1998; Bal, Crew, and Spitzer 1999b; Radstone 2000a; Winter and Sivan 2000; Huyssen 2003; Lansberg 2004). It has its roots in Halbwachs' classic study on collective memory (1980) and Connerton's work on social memory (1989). Both of these studies investigate the role of the practices and institutions of remembering in the reproduction of society. The act of remembering provides continuity for members of a society. Rituals and social practices – whether funerals, commemorations of the war dead, or looking through family photograph albums – affirm a shared origin; they gather us together to enact our communal ties. These events, practices, and institutions selectively identify historical figures and events that shape our collective identities, symbolize the values and goals we share, and form the basis for imagining and planning for a future together.

For groups such as Japanese Canadians who have been the target of political violence, the past is not easily recollected. Their organizations have been disbanded, their rituals and practices banned, and their cultural and material resources confiscated or destroyed. If members have not been killed, they are scattered and forced to go into actual or psychological hiding. Although political violence can include acts ranging from genocide to political torture, my definition is broader: the systematic deployment of measures that damage or destroy the capacity of a community to continue to function as a social collective. This differs from, although assumes, the pathological hostilities that compel dominant groups to devalue and vilify segments of a population they view with disgust and fear, who they conclude must be controlled or destroyed (Memmi 1965; Fanon 1967; Jordan 1968; Achebe 1988; Gilman 1989; Lee 1999; Eng 2001). Political violence is organized at the level of institutions and legal apparatuses and can include programs that restrict human rights and either inadvertently or intentionally dismantle a group's socio-cultural, economic, and/or political institutions. But even "inadvertent" damage is not innocent. It typically occurs when administrators do not foresee the destructive impact of their programs. The very inability to foresee the destructive impact on another group indicates a failure to meaningfully consult with them, which points to a more fundamental failure: the inability to recognize the group's autonomy. Moreover, it demonstrates the inability to recognize and value vital elements of others' cultural-material life systems. These failures typically occur through large disparities in power, by which one group is granted the capacity to make changes that threaten the ability of another group to reproduce itself culturally, socially, and materially. Destructive measures can include uprooting a group from their settlements or forcing them to physically disperse and assimilate into the dominant population; such actions have had devastating results for indigenous peoples among others (Canada 1996; Haig-Brown 1988).

The relation that survivors of political violence have to the past is damaged. The past is marked by aggressive and hostile measures to socially or physically annihilate them as peoples. Many persecuted groups, whether survivors of the Holocaust, Palestinians, or indigenous peoples in Canada, recognize that remembering political violence collectively is a necessary aspect of rebuilding their communal life and of healing from the long-term damage that can plague survivors and subsequent generations. To collectively remember the past, whether by building memorials and archives, transmitting oral histories, producing novels and films, or pursuing human rights cases, requires members of the community to rebuild institutions and social networks, to find records, and to reconstitute rituals and public places where they can gather and create new languages, imagery, and cultural practices.[19] Remembering can also offer a means to collectively mourn what has been lost and destroyed. In recognizing the damaging effects, there is the possibility of identifying ways to transform debilitating intergenerational effects and thus assert (a new form of) continuity over time (Herman 1992, 70-71; Lifton 1967, 534-535).

In deciding to build the Nikkei Internment Memorial Centre, the Kyowakai Society of New Denver committed itself to a form of remembering that was collective, regathering and rebuilding relationships among Japanese Canadians locally and nationally. It has been a challenge to build as well as run the memorial. Everyone has had different emotional investments in recollecting and, in some cases, forgetting or revising Japanese Canadian history. This study explores the challenges of building memorials as public spaces that link together people with differing and sometimes conflicting views and emotional investments.

Here, the literature on public memorials is particularly useful. Like studies that examine memorials commemorating widely recognized events such as the Holocaust (Young 1993), the Vietnam War (Sturken 1997), and the two world wars (Winter 1996; Winter and Sivan 1999), this study examines the Nikkei Internment Memorial Centre as a public site of mourning and remembrance that contributes to the formation and reconfiguration of contemporary communities (Creef 2004). Unlike much of the literature in this field, this book does not focus on an event that has international currency, such as the Holocaust and the First and Second World Wars (Young 1993; Brandt 1994; Winter 1996). The dates, key figures, and killing technologies of the Holocaust and the world wars have all become part of world history (Bischoping and Fingerhut 1996);

their events have become iconic in the moral order of contemporary societies (Geddes 2001).

This study examines the memorialization of a smaller-scale act of political violence. Although during the 1980s Japanese Canadians activists turned their history of persecution into a national issue, today this history has drifted from public memory. Despite readily available documentary films, books, and fiction about Japanese Canadian history, the violation of their rights is no longer a national issue, and it is not unusual for Canadian university students to know nothing about the internment camps.

What is the relevance of this particular case? The violation of Japanese Canadians' rights commands less moral urgency than large-scale violence such as genocide in former Rwanda, the Sudan, or East Timor or the ongoing struggles in Palestine (see Khalili 2005). Since the Canadian government has publicly acknowledged that it violated the rights of Japanese Canadians, their wartime experiences seem even less urgent to revisit. But I would argue that it is imperative to avoid delineating acts of political violence into a checklist of solved and unsolved cases of greater and lesser import. All measures to physically eradicate, expel, or culturally erase people constructed as deviant, whether racially or sexually undesirable or biological inferior, point to the legacy of modern population management programs (Green 1984; McLaren 1990; Semujanga 2003). The alarming frequency of the smaller-scale acts of political violence within the memories of our families and the borders of our home territories show that extermination, expulsion, and assimilation as political practices are part of our "heritage." Moreover, it is these smaller-scale acts that feed into the structural violence of everyday life (Farmer 1996), making the removal of biologically and culturally undesirable people a feasible solution within the public imagination.

Although the project of remembering acts of political violence at home within the boundaries of our worlds offers the possibility of another future, at the same time, groups seeking to overcome violent pasts are not immune from reproducing reactionary forms of commemoration (Ben-Amos 1993). Historical accounts of persecution can end up constructing the survivors as helpless victims. Victimhood can be mobilized in a number of ways. Rather than being the basis for movements to seek redress or reconciliation, historical wrongs can be used to grant survivors a sense of moral righteousness that justifies imperialistic nation-building projects, as many have argued has been the case with Israel's Zionist policies against Palestine (Brunner 1997; Ram 1995). With the fear that their community is under constant threat, members can be pressured into following reactionary practices and norms, advocating a return to a mythical community based on oppressive gender roles, racial purity, and authoritarian leadership. Under these regimes, critical thought, social difference, and change are often construed as threats to the integrity of the community (Anthias and Yuval-Davis 1989; Parker et al. 1992).

This study considers the extent to which the construction and operation of the NIMC positions Japanese Canadians as fixed subjects in static configurations of community life that automatically construct others as threats and social change as the death of tradition. As the elders intended to contribute to building a just society, this book considers whether the memorial makes possible a form of community that is inclusive rather than hostile to others.

The Political Starting Point

The NIMC is one of many memory projects initiated by Japanese Canadians in the 1990s. These projects followed in the wake of the successful conclusion of the Japanese Canadian movement to seek redress from the Canadian government. I will briefly describe the redress movement because it created the social and material conditions that made projects like the NIMC and this study possible.

Throughout the 1940s and the 1950s community activists made a series of attempts to seek compensation for Japanese Canadians (Miki and Kobayashi 1991). They found little support from other Japanese Canadians, who were immersed in the struggle to rebuild their lives in unfamiliar and, in some cases, hostile environments outside of British Columbia without the support of prewar institutions such as farming cooperatives, Japanese language schools, and women's associations (Adachi 1991 [1976]; Oikawa 1986; Kobayashi 1987; Miki and Kobayashi 1991). During the 1950s through to the 1970s, many Japanese Canadians, especially the nisei, had little contact with other Japanese Canadians now scattered across Canada. There were some who avoided other Japanese Canadians, not wanting to be reminded about their humiliating and painful wartime experiences. Having learned the perils of being marked as racially "other," some tried to protect their children, the sansei, by encouraging them to assimilate into mainstream Canadian society. Few sansei were encouraged to learn Japanese Canadian cultural and aesthetic practices, such as the Japanese language, an appreciation for the salty and pungent tastes of Japanese cuisine, or the respectful bodily comportment implicit in the etiquette practised by their grandparents, the *issei* (Adachi 1991 [1976]; Sunahara 1981; Takata 1983).

Mobilizing Japanese Canadians to seek redress was a formidable task. Activists brought Japanese Canadians together in private meetings and public forums. They published pamphlets and articles on the case for redress (Miki 2004). It was also necessary to "write" Japanese Canadians into Canadian history as citizens (McAllister 1999). Faced with the destruction of most of the community's records, activists turned to the recollections of issei and nisei, who gave accounts demonstrating that they were loyal citizens who had contributed to the economic development of Canada in fishing, farming, mining, and forestry and willingly served Canada during the world wars (Adachi 1991 [1976]; Ito 1984; Takata 1983). Activists also extensively used government records in the national archives to prove that the cabinet of Prime Minister Mackenzie King had violated their rights (Sunahara 1981; Ketelaar 2002).

As Roy Miki explains in *Redress: Inside the Japanese Canadian Call for Justice* (2004), the movement to seek redress was complex. Different factions vied to represent the community, and public support depended on local and national media coverage. Although support and guidance were given by First Nations leaders and civil organizations, there was also opposition from, for example, a number of war veterans groups. In 1988, after eight years of political struggle, the National Association of Japanese Canadians negotiated a settlement for redress with the Canadian government. The settlement included a public apology, financial compensation for individuals, and funds for community development.[20]

The movement can also be credited with laying the foundation for a postwar community. But the postwar community is fundamentally different from the pre-war community, which had political, economic, and socio-cultural institutions that interconnected the lives of Japanese Canadians from geographically bound settlements along the coast of British Columbia (Kobayashi 1994b, 1992b; Adachi 1991 [1976]; Takata 1983). Racist legislation and social attitudes, on the one hand, forced Japanese Canadians to form close networks of support and, on the other hand, became the impetus for activists to challenge discriminatory laws in court and through lobbying (Adachi 1991 [1976]; Sunahara 1983; Takata 1983).[21]

For Japanese Canadians, forming a collective identity based on the violation of their rights was a powerful method to mobilize individuals dispersed across Canada (Laclau and Mouffe 1992; Boggs 1986; Carroll 1992). But, as I have argued elsewhere (McAllister 1999), political movements can also homogenize a group's history, obscuring internal political conflicts, hierarchies of power, and social differences. While recognizing the importance of mobilizing people to demand changes to repressive political structures, it is important to also recognize that reconciliation requires more than this (Mamdani 2004; Scheper-Hughes 2004; Soyinka 2004). Moreover, once a movement has accomplished its goals, as many nisei had feared, it is possible for individuals to lose their purpose for working together, especially if they are dispersed across a country and share very few cultural, economic, and social institutions. A new purpose as well as affinities and relations of interdependence are needed if a group is going to sustain itself as a collective. This is how a community differs from a single-issue social movement: a community has the capacity to reproduce itself over generations.[22]

But, more to the point, in the case of historically persecuted groups, framing political violence primarily in terms of human rights violations overlooks the need to develop *multiple* cultural narratives and practices to explore the meaning and impact of past events on contemporary communities.[23] This multiplicity is needed because political violence does not have a uniform effect on any one community.[24]

If communities do not develop new narratives and practices – new forms to rework what happened in the past – their accounts can become repetitive. Repetition can produce a static conception of the past. It can drain events of complexity and give them a mythic quality by turning persecution and victimhood into fate and destiny and by overlooking the more subtle and insidious dynamics of power and politics. Repetition can also trap individuals in one account of what happened, making it difficult to perceive the effects of violence from other vantage points (Lifton 1979; Herman 1992; Caruth 1995; McAllister 2001).

I am not arguing that the human rights narrative developed by redress activists is no longer relevant. My point is that their studies were never intended to explore the range of social, cultural, and psychological effects of the government's actions on different groups within the community. Although their studies drew on personal accounts that described the social and psychological impact of the government's actions, they were used primarily to provide evidence to demonstrate that the government had violated their rights as Canadian citizens.

The government's apology for this violation of rights was essential for redressing the past, but it did not and could not fully resolve the damaging impact. Twenty years after the settlement for redress was secured, Japanese Canadians continue to initiate memory projects to resolve the impact of wartime events on their lives today. As one of these memory projects, the NIMC shows the need to recollect the internment camps as part of an ongoing process in the formation and transformation of the Japanese Canadian community.

The Road Ahead

This project underwent profound changes during my stay in New Denver and again as I attempted to write up my results. The topic, however, did not change, nor did the research question. I had identified four clear research tasks: to reconstruct the phases of the NIMC's development, to describe the administrative structure and daily operation of the NIMC, to document its physical layout and historical displays, and to interview members of the Kyowakai Society and the contractors who had been hired to construct the NIMC. However, soon after I arrived in New Denver, I realized that the sociological methods at my disposal were hopelessly inadequate for observing, documenting, analyzing, and reporting what I faced in the field. Conscious of my own internalized sociological gaze, I underwent a "dissolution of identity" (Kondo 1986) or what I call a "necessary crisis" in identity. Although emotionally confusing, this crisis made it possible for me to begin to prise open not only my reductive social scientific methods but also my defensive stance as a cultural activist. At the same time, writing an account of my experiences in the Slocan Valley was terrifying, for it required me to move into a space of trauma that continues to haunt my family and the Japanese Canadian community. The entire process of writing this account has been shaped by tensions that arose at a methodological level, by what at times seemed to be an impossible movement between academic knowledge and the knowledge of a living community, a movement between the flat maps of my theoretical framework and the complex, temporally layered landscapes of experience, a movement between my own prescriptive political position and the infinitely more nuanced and caring ways of transformation practised by the elders. I was confronted with my inability to see the NIMC as anything other than the appropriation of a community project by contractors who turned it into a tourist site. The elders, with infinite patience, gently pulled me into their world and presented me with something much more astonishing, an "other" field of activity in which they had transformed a site of racial erasure into a constantly changing valley of remembrance.

As I attempted to write this manuscript, I strove awkwardly to create a narrative that showed readers the difficulty of shedding one's disciplinary training, without reducing my project to a self-indulgent self-exploration. Even more challenging was the task of creating a language to present what the elders shared with me, to find ways of writing that did not reduce their accounts into evidence for my own arguments. I had to let go of the need to legitimize their accounts by drawing on theory and sociological studies and instead try to generate another universe of meaning, one in which the power of their accounts could touch the readers as they had touched me. Likewise, when I described the so-called tourists, I had to resist the urge to present them as annoying camera-toting caricatures who exoticized Japanese Canadians as Orientals. I had to question my own rigid narratives of self and other and open myself to acknowledging that visitors moved in complex ways within their own memories and histories. As I discovered over the summer of 1996, for many who travelled to New Denver, including myself, the memorial was not only a space to commemorate the past, it was also a space where the irresolvable after-effects of political violence could surface unpredictably, a space where individuals sought encounters, whether conflicts or happy reunions, and a place to work through deeply embedded feelings of guilt, no matter how distanced individuals were from the historical events of the persecution of Japanese Canadians during the 1940s.

CHAPTER ONE

A Necessary Crisis

On the second floor there is a room with a small window facing north. Each evening, this is where I type out the events of the day in amber Courier, lines of glowing pixels moving across the black screen of the old PC with the steady tick-tack of the keyboard. The hum and whirl of the hard drive is comforting. With no phone connection, no Internet, with only the company of resident mice, I try to make sense of each day. Since arriving in the valley, I've found myself floundering amid confusing social negotiations, unspoken divides and allegiances, and shifting layers of contentious history.

I struggle to let go of how I interpret the world, to resist incorporating what I see and hear into my already established way of understanding the world, a predefined interpretive system imported from elsewhere. I need to somehow open myself to others as they guide the course of inter/action.

But it is difficult to let go ... to pry myself open, to relinquish control. It's unnerving. To let go requires trust, a sense of security. I am an outsider, a stranger, someone no one quite knows. What will happen if I let go, if I open myself, a stranger, to their terms of determination? (EDITED EXCERPTS FROM LETTERS AND FIELD NOTES, AUGUST 1996)

Conflicting Positions

I was in no way prepared for the months ahead, living in a valley with the remains of nine internment camps.[1] I met elders who had vivid memories of my maternal grandparents and the places where they had lived and worked before the government stripped them of their rights, liquidated their properties, and sent everyone to internment camps, sugar beet farms, and prison-of-war camps. Nor was I prepared for the continual flow of visitors, each with her or his own conflicted emotional investments in the Nikkei Internment Memorial Centre (NIMC). Some wandered through the memorial in silence; others came to express feelings of guilt. Some were rigid with suspicion and quick to accuse. Many came in remembrance of a childhood friend or schoolmate who had suddenly disappeared in 1942. Some shared their own family's tragic experiences of persecution during other wars. And, among those who sought the joy of happy reunions with old acquaintances they might meet at the memorial, there were others who questioned the authenticity of everything from the Japanese garden to those working at the site, myself included.

I also had to deal with my new status as an outsider. Previously, I had worked as a member *of* the Japanese Canadian community on projects *for* the community.[2] I was now discursively positioned as an outsider who had travelled to New Denver to ostensibly study the elders and their memorial. I had become the intrusive researcher of my graduate student nightmares. I feared I would be trapped within my field of knowledge, unable to learn anything outside of what my theoretical framework already dictated. Like Audrey Kobayashi (1992a, 1994a), Roy Miki (1998b, 2004), and Mona Oikawa (2002b, forthcoming), I was committed to aligning my research with activism but worried that my study would amount to no more than a textbook example of how academics reproduce discursive regimes of knowledge, as Smith (1990) and Foucault (1979) have so exhaustively argued.

In preparation for fieldwork, I had read about the emotional and social trials that ethnographers face in communities they do not really understand, especially when driven by agendas that fail to take into account the political and historical circumstances that made their research possible in the first place. These studies follow the descent of ethnographers into turmoil, clinging to their identities as well-meaning academics, while their research subjects approach them in unfamiliar and alienating terms as suspicious outsiders, ill-mannered guests, naive Westerners, surrogate relatives, and personal confidants (e.g., see Briggs 1970; Crapanzano 1972, 1980; Rabinow 1977; Myerhoff 1980; Kondo 1986). During my first visit to New Denver in 1995, it became obvious that reading about the complexities of negotiating identity in the field is far different than the actual struggle one actually undergoes.

What was at stake in this struggle? I was undergoing what I later realized was a "necessary crisis" in identity. The longer I stayed, the more my way of knowing the world started to lose validity. I became distrustful and critical of my academic field. But without my theories and analytic skills, how was I to make sense of what I saw and experienced? It was only when my institutionalized worldview really began to unravel that I was able to realize that another distinct mode of knowing and ordering the world existed: the world of the elders. And it was this realization that allowed me to view their memorial in new ways, rather than as I initially saw it: a tourist site that also functioned as an educational centre. By working with the elders, I learned that the memorial was one of many memory projects through which they had transformed the valley's terrain of memory over the years.

I had not initially planned to include my own messy subjective struggles in this study; for one thing, they involved my relationships with people living in

New Denver, people who were members of my own community. Although feminist scholars have reflexively turned to the self and the body as a productive site for the analysis of intersecting discursive, psychic, affective, and technological forces (Kuhn 1995; Hirsch 1997a; Stacey 1997; Sedgwick 2003; Sobchak 2004), in the field of cultural studies, there appears to be decreasing interest in subjective struggles and breakdowns. Especially over the last decade, researchers have increasingly turned to visual and digital media and away from more material questions of identity and the politics of representation – which some have argued can easily slide into moralistic "victim discourses" (Brown 2001). With increased investment in virtual media – which involves disembodied, multi-situated subjects – research in cultural studies has moved away from ethnographic, community-based studies, which are found now in specialized area studies rather than in the foundational streams of the field (see Hall et al. 1980).

For my part, I found it necessary to turn to ethnographic practices to track the methodological and epistemological issues that arose from the inter-subjective dynamics that shaped what I was able to perceive in New Denver. Ethnographers from the 1970s onward have argued that the subjective struggles faced by fieldworkers have significant epistemological implications (Marcus and Fischer 1986). In the past, the conflicts and frustrating emotional dynamics of field research was left out of research reports, especially when the researcher's field notes revealed not very admirable feelings of irritation and disdain for her or his research subjects (Rosaldo 1989, 175-179). But ever since the posthumous publication, in 1967, of the diaries of Bronislaw Malinowski (Geertz 1983, 56), the myth of the distanced anthropologist who objectively observes the lives of "Natives" has been thoroughly revised with, on the one hand, the anti-colonial criticisms of ethnography (Clifford and Marcus 1986; Harrison 1997 [1991]; Smith 1999) and, on the other, the turn to hermeneutics in the 1970s (Marcus and Fischer 1986; Rosaldo 1989). It is now widely accepted that examining the views, social positions, and changing relationships between anthropologists and their subjects is an essential component of ethnographic scholarship.

While being wary of the "navel gazing" of confessional writing, interpretive anthropologists such as Geertz (1973), Clifford and Marcus (1986), and Rosaldo (1989) claim that subjective struggles can demonstrate how the cultural worlds of others cannot simply be translated into the formulaic theories of a paternal-istic anthropologist. Numerous anthropological field studies from the 1970s and 1980s onward show that it is not possible to slide seamlessly into another cultural world and gather whatever information is needed for one's research. This work questions the authority of anthropologists and other social scientists and reveals their value systems, hierarchies, and vested interests. It makes evident that these researchers are limited by their cultures, emotional capacities, and ability to establish equilateral human relations, in addition to raising questions about who benefits from studying "other" cultures. In fact, ethnography has been one of the few disciplines that systematically critiques the ethical and political legacy of its neocolonial relationship to *otherness* at the most intimate level of the self.

Although my study is not strictly ethnographic – it focuses on the memorial rather than, more widely, on the community – ethnography has informed my methods of research as a participant-observer and my hermeneutic approach to interpretation (see Rosaldo 1989). My analysis of many components of the study, including the elders' memory practices as well as the visitors' use of the memorial as a tourist site and place of mourning, rely on ethnographic participant observation. Even though the analysis in Chapters 2 and 3 uses a cultural studies framework – examining an array of materials, including archival records, the NIMC's exhibitions, maps, tourist literature, and images of the everyday landscape of New Denver – it has been informed by participant observation and what I learned from the elders during my stay in the valley. In other words, this study is not restricted to a formal discursive analysis of the memorial; it situates the memorial in the everyday world of New Denver.

This study was influenced by feminist and ethnographic practices that challenge the conventional power relations of academic research, for instance, by requiring researchers to make contributions to rather than simply taking away data from the community.[3] But I was also interested in ethnographic writing devices that would reveal the more subtle power dynamics both in the field and in my final text (see Jacobs-Huey 2002; Ulysee 2002; Cruickshank 1990; Cruickshank et al. 2005). To make power dynamics evident, ethnographers often write themselves into their texts as characters among other characters in the field. They purposely include their annoying value judgments and transparent desires, which they can never fully purge no matter how earnestly they attempt to see the world through the eyes of others. As Rosaldo (1989) claims, the social failings and floundering of anthropologists in the field, their descent into emotional turmoil as well as their obnoxious behaviour and arrogant misconceptions, reveal the fallacy of both the objectivity and superiority of researchers trained in the Western university system (also see Briggs 1970).

Ethnographers' turmoil can also signal being at "the brink of loss of the self," especially the loss of the "analytic self," as I will discuss next in relation to my own study (Briggs 1970; Kondo 1986). Previously, "going native," whereby anthropologists lose distance from their subjects and begin to assimilate their version of reality, was considered one of the dangers of fieldwork (Rosaldo 1989). But more recent writings recognize the insights gained when ethnographers start to question the meanings and values that order their worldviews and become open to the possibility of other realities. Likewise, my turmoil began when my version of reality began to collapse. Distancing myself from my totalizing version of reality, one I viewed with increasing repugnance, made it possible to realize that the elders had a distinctive worldview. This worldview was shaped profoundly by their experiences of internment and their ethos of collectivity that made it possible for them to transform what had been an internment camp into their home community. As I was pulled into the dimensions and rhythms of their way of seeing the world, into their lifeworld, my understanding of exactly what the memorial "was" and what it "did" were radically transformed.

An Outsider

There was no way of avoiding the fact that I was an outsider in New Denver, a village with approximately five hundred residents. Although the old-time logging and mining families with close ties to the elders would occasionally chat and greet me with a friendly wave, there were other locals who regarded me with suspicion, particularly some of the back-to-the-land community, which included artists, tofu makers, homesteaders, and the like. The fact that I was a sansei researching the aftermath of a history that affected my own family did not seem to count for much. Nor did it make a difference that my mentor in New Denver, the person I refer to as Teresa Takana, was a member of their community.

Takana was an established member of the New Denver Japanese Canadian community. As the chair of the Kyowakai Society's History Preservation Committee, she had invited me to New Denver to assist her with a number of projects at the NIMC. During my first visit, I came as her research assistant. When I returned the next year to help finish the projects, I also arranged to conduct my own research.

Given my close working relation with Takana, I was taken aback when I realized she regarded me with suspicion, sharing the cautious regard of her back-to-the-land compatriots. She was critical of the assumptions I had as an outsider with little knowledge about life in the valley. Because I respected her political principles, I struggled to be more conscious of my assumptions. Although we never discussed the dynamics of our interaction in much detail, she took time to explain the caution displayed by some of her back-to-the-land friends. Takana explained that over the last twenty years they had seen many outsiders arrive with research projects, dreams about going "back-to-the-land," newspaper assignments, and big ideas about helping the local community. In many cases, they came with their own agendas, stayed for a brief period, and then departed, never to be seen again. Typically, they would end up misrepresenting the community in embarrassing ways, aggravating local politics, or exhausting everyone with their attempts to set up projects that required excessive time and resources.

Also, some residents had been involved with local movements to protect the local watershed from powerful industrial interests and to monitor the plans to blast highway infrastructure through the region to make a high-volume corridor for trucks to transport wood chips twenty-four hours a day. Thus, they were careful about who they brought into their confidence. On top of this, the fact that the Royal Canadian Mounted Police (RCMP) had undercover cops who kept the area under surveillance did not help. I inadvertently met one in a local store who was posing as a young, hip, long-haired guy riding a motorbike through the Kootenays. When he found out I was not a local but rather a student visiting the valley for the summer, he asked if I knew about any illegal activities. The most radical things I had seen were an experimental dance company and an organic tofu factory. As for the elders, the strongest substance I had seen them use was cayenne pepper, which they liberally sprinkled on their garbage to ward off bears. In any case, given the experience that some back-to-the-landers had with security forces during the Vietnam War, this surveillance would have made them even more cautious about newcomers like myself.

In regard to my relations with Takana, even though I was her friend and protégé, she never overlooked the fact that I had my own agenda as a researcher. In her constant company, I began to internalize her suspicion, compounding my discomfort about being in New Denver. I had no idea how to bridge what seemed like two incommensurable positions. On the one hand, I was a nosy researcher driven by an academic agenda; on the other hand, I was a member of a fragmented postwar community that bore the burden of a traumatic history still alive in the constant flow of strangers, all connected yet disconnected through the internment camps. Caught between these two positions, I literally froze in the field. Repelled by my internalized sociological gaze, I avoided even the most basic research tasks while I was working at the NIMC, whether jotting down observations or collecting documents about the memorial. Even the most mundane descriptions of my life in field notes and letters are imbued with anxiety about the implications of my presence in the valley:

> I write late into the night, turning inward, marvelling at the lamp's flutter-
> ing halos of insect life, tickling skin, becoming tangled in eyelashes. As I
> write, I hesitate to turn the page for fear that these delicate creatures will
> be crushed, to lay down a line of ink for fear that they will become mired
> in my words. Yet I continue. (FIELD NOTES, ROSEBERY, AUGUST 1996)

Yet, as my compulsion to write about my experiences demonstrates, I was desperate to find a way to give meaning to what I was undergoing. At the same time, I felt a responsibility to share what the elders were teaching me. But, associating my analytic skills with my internalized sociological gaze, I did not know how to proceed. This confusion did not end when I left the field. Language failed me months later as I struggled to find the words – a voice – to translate everything into a meaningful account without reducing it to the terms set by my discipline.

Caught between my position as outsider and insider, it could be argued that I was what anthropologists conventionally (and problematically) have called the native anthropologist. The native anthropologist supposedly has enough cultural knowledge to understand her or his research community but lacks the social distance required for objective analysis (Narayan 2003 [1997]). But, as Narayan argues, the dichotomy between insider and outsider is reductive. The operation of power is complex. She states that all researchers, whether insider or outsider, "[exhibit] what Rosaldo has termed a 'multiplex subjectivity' with many crosscutting identifications ... Which facet of our subjectivity we choose or are forced to accept as a defining identity can change, depending on the context and the prevailing vectors of power" (ibid., 291).

In New Denver, "a multiplex subjectivity with many crosscutting identifications" described my situation well. I was a member of the broader Japanese Canadian community in British Columbia but was also an outsider in the village of New Denver. I was conducting research as an academic but was also assisting the Kyowakai Society with their History Preservation Committee's projects. Each position involved different sets of responsibilities as well as different expectations, degrees of social distance, and levels of formality and informality. Narayan argues, however, that as soon as members of a community position themselves as researchers, they step out of their social role and formally become "outsiders." Their agenda becomes defined by terms set by their research institutions rather than by the social dynamics or politics of the community. Yet, as Narayan writes, increasing numbers of anthropologists studying their communities question how to negotiate the conflicting obligations, agendas, and identities entailed in their outsider/insider roles and, in particular, the power dynamics these roles entail (2003 [1997], 285).

Like Narayan, I was uncomfortable with my identity as an academic outsider. It was the most objectionable cross-cutting strand of my "multiplex subjectivity." I had the authority but not the knowledge to make conclusive statements about the other realities of those living in the valley. Takana constantly made me question my authority. I sought a position, an identity, that did not place me primarily in authoritative relation to whatever I observed, automatically fitting data into predefined categories, reordering everything according to established theories and ideologies (Todorov 1987; Comaroff and Comaroff 1992). I struggled to release the grip my discipline had on the way I understood and wrote about what I saw and heard. Thus, my first struggle was over the insidious power dynamics of my disciplinary knowledge. Only subsequently, as I struggled to write about New Denver, did I realize the difficulty I had bearing the confusing and painful memories of incarceration (McAllister 2001, 2006b; Hirsch 1997b).

In many ways, Takana took up the classic position of gatekeeper, monitoring and questioning my research activities. Although this was intimidating at times, it also meant that all my activities were double-checked and discussed with someone knowledgeable about the community. I could also ask Takana as well as Katherine Shozawa, a researcher-artist with close ties to New Denver, for critical feedback on the drafts of my dissertation (see Greenaway 1995). Ironically, it was especially because I knew Takana so well that I understood her ambivalence about my status as an academic outsider. My experience with the controversial debates about politics of representation in the 1990s made me hypersensitive to Takana's views on outsiders. In the 1990s, Vancouver and other Canadian cities were alive with protests about the domination that hegemonic institutions had over representations of racialized communities in the public arena. Cultural activists and artists mobilized to challenge demeaning (mis)representations of their communities and demanded equal access to funding, venues, and infrastructure so they could represent their own histories and explore images and abstractions that did not reproduce Orientalist and colonial imaginaries (Bannerji 1993, 2000; Miki 1998d; Gagnon 2000; Lowry 2001; Gagnon and Fung 2002; Razack 2002). Thus, through the lens of the politics of representation, I could understand Takana's identification of me as an outsider with the institutional power to misrepresent her community (or communities).

My relationship with Takana as a gatekeeper was complex because, as mentioned, she was also one of my mentor figures. She shared insider information with me. Before even arriving in New Denver, she told me that community activists from the valley and elsewhere had concerns about the contractors' design for the memorial. Some claimed the contractors had ignored the community's vision for the memorial and instead constructed a tourist site that would generate revenue for local businesses. At the same time, Takana pointed out that it was unfair to criticize the contractors since, from the start, the Kyowakai Society had not specified that the memorial was a community-based project. Moreover, the contractors had experience in historical restoration, not with racialized communities coming to terms with historical traumas.

Ironically, as will become evident in Chapter 6, I rather dogmatically adopted a defensive insider position and was critical of what I concluded was the appropriation of the elders' memorial as a tourist site. It could be argued that I reproduced the moral discourses that rigidly divided the world into outsiders and insiders, making me excessively vigilant about what I deemed appropriate behaviour. As Hunt explains, "moral discourses impute blame and assign responsibility. Most importantly, moral regulation acts upon" subjects, impelling them take responsibility for "constant self-monitoring and self-supervision" (1999, 411). Cloaked in the language of protection and cultural self-determination, when taken to an extreme this discourse can become a way to assert authority over others, and it fails to recognize the complex intersubjective and discursive constitution of communities. I had to question my emotional investment in this position, as I will discuss in Chapters 4 and 6, if I was to learn about how the elders found ways to work with the contractors and also turn the memorial into a site for their own memory projects, as discussed in Chapter 5.

Working with a Gatekeeper

Takana introduced me to the elders, whom she had known since the 1970s, when she and her former husband had gone "back to the land" in the Slocan Valley. They were among the many politicized young Americans who came to Canada, escaping the Vietnam War draft. She explained how, given her Nikkei background, she was drawn to the valley because of the resident Japanese Canadian community. Her own mentor was the widely respected Mrs. Kamegaya, the president of the Kyowakai Society who initiated the memorial project.

When the NIMC was opened to the public in 1994, two projects still needed to be completed: the NIMC's historical collections and the NIMC's public displays. The Kyowakai Society decided to make Takana the chair of their History Preservation Committee, placing her in charge of the projects. She asked me to assist her with the projects because I had some experience with community-based work of this kind. She offered funding to cover my travel expenses as well as an honorarium. We had worked together on other projects when I lived in Vancouver, and so in this respect I was an insider. She knew I shared similar principles and would support her plan to design the historical collections in a way that would allow the elders to access and manage them without relying on external expertise.[4]

As a video artist with experience in political theatre troupes, Takana had an acute awareness of the political implications of a project's aesthetic form, design, and operation. Working on the projects with her was challenging. She did not hesitate to quickly dissect one's ideas, pointing out their practical consequences and ethical problems. Notes from my diaries give an example of these dynamics.

> My eager urge to make suggestions to improve the memorial has been met with disapproval. Takana does not hesitate to question, for example, my assumption that making the memorial more accessible to Japanese Canadian artists and researchers from other regions would be a good thing. This idea fails to take into consideration the needs of the members of the Kyowakai Society – the elders living here in New Denver. Already the elders find the large number of researchers travelling to New Denver to interview them and take photographs exhausting. Why encourage an even larger influx of researchers and artists, especially if their visits might begin to influence the operation of the NIMC?
>
> Takana pointed out that, while plans to expand might be suitable for a memorial centre in a large urban centre with ample resources and volunteers, this was not necessarily the case for New Denver. Before jumping forward with plans to expand, introduce new programs, increase the accessibility of the NIMC's historical collections, and make commitments to set up annual events for researchers and artists, it is necessary to consider what each will entail, not just in terms of financial resources but also in terms of the impact on elders. Despite Takana's efforts to make me understand the context, I continue to find it difficult to resist my urge to introduce expansion. (FIELD NOTES, 6 AUGUST 1995)

I was always on my toes. Takana could be taciturn at the best of times, but now our conversations seemed to be a minefield. I never knew what might trigger an explosion of disapproval. Still, I was drawn to work with Takana precisely because of her critical awareness and extensive experience. At heart, she wanted to ensure that the elders' needs were at the centre of our design of the NIMC projects. Her careful attention to their daily routines and social interactions meant the projects would dovetail with the elders' lives rather than forcing them to reorganize their routines around the NIMC projects. As I would later learn, a number of other sansei working with elders in New Denver, including Katherine Shozawa, Tsuneko Kokubo, and Ruby Truly, shared this approach.

Takana must have found me a handful, always bursting with poorly conceived ideas. Nevertheless, she requested that I return the following year to assist in finishing the projects. Fixing the signage in the exhibits was a priority. Before the memorial opened, local Japanese Canadians and visiting researchers had criticized the signage designed by the contractors. They said it Orientalized

Japanese Canadians and used language that justified the government's actions in the 1940s. In response, most of the signage had been removed before the memorial opened to the public, and visitors frequently asked why there was no text explaining the history of New Denver.

When Takana asked me to return to New Denver in 1996, I told her that this was not feasible because I was in the middle of my PhD program at Carleton University in Ottawa. I planned to begin my research that summer on documentary films about Japanese Canadians and would have neither the resources nor the time to spend a second summer in New Denver. She was insistent. We discussed the idea of shifting the focus of my research to the NIMC. I was wary because of the complex community politics, and Takana was not keen to have an academic poking about New Denver. But something compelled both of us to compromise, and soon we were writing grant applications to fund a summer project. Thus, when I returned to New Denver in 1996, I came as both a graduate researcher and as a project worker for the NIMC.

In her capacity as chair of the History Preservation Committee, Takana initially oversaw my relations with the elders. I appreciated the advice and guidance she offered. At first she was mainly worried about whether my research activities would overtax the elders. They were exhausted. Over the last two years they had dedicated most of their time and energy to building the memorial. And following the opening of the NIMC in 1994, the director Anne Wheeler arrived in New Denver to film *The War between Us,* a television drama about the internment. She hired many local Japanese Canadians as extras, actors, interpreters, and consultants, re-enacting what many had undergone during the war years. Although working on the film was exciting, replaying scenes from the past was emotionally wearing.

Working closely with Takana on the NIMC projects every day left little time to reflect on our dynamics. I was also a guest in her home. During my first visit in 1995, since there was a shortage of short-term accommodations available in the valley, Takana and her partner offered me the "coal shed," a small yurt-like sleeping hut for guests. Dark and filled with comforters and blankets, it wasn't a place to do much more than sleep, though I was welcome to use their kitchen and living room.

Without a car, I was dependent on Takana for transportation. We would drive into New Denver together each morning to work on the projects. Then I discovered an abandoned railway bed that internees had used to travel from the Rosebery internment camp to New Denver. I began walking the five-mile route every few days, retracing the paths of the internees through the overgrown brush, luxuriating in the space for much-needed reflection. Takana did her best to ensure a good working relationship, despite what must have been the tedious responsibility for her younger and often annoying urbanite friend. She even left New Denver and stayed a few days in her house in Nelson, no doubt to regain some much-needed personal space, giving me time to settle into a routine.

When I returned in 1996, I ensured I had my own transportation, purchasing my brother's old Toyota pickup truck. As in the previous year, there wasn't much housing available in this economically depressed, sparsely populated region. Takana suggested I rent "the mansion" from her and her partner for a low monthly cost. Once a rather grand Victorian home built during one of the mining booms in the early 1900s, the mansion was, when I moved in, a gutted two-storey wooden shell surrounded by the encroaching forest. Takana's partner had installed electricity and plumbing before I arrived, and so, with borrowed dishes, sheets, a lopsided table, and a good supply of firewood, it became my makeshift home. The mansion was in Rosebery, where Wilson Creek's icy waters spill into Slocan Lake. During the mining boom over seven hundred men lived there. Most worked in the local mill, processing silver and lead ores. It was also a transportation hub where the railway line from Nakusp connected with the steamship and barge that served mining towns up and down the length of Slocan Lake (Turnbull 1988). Today, Rosebery is a series of empty fields with a scattering of residents. The only employment is the log yard on the edge of the lake and the Wild Rose Mexican Restaurant. It was also the site of the Rosebery internment camp, although almost nothing is left to indicate its presence. But, like most of the other internment sites in the Slocan Valley, such as Lemon Creek and Popoff, there was something disquieting about the place, especially after dusk. Although I was relieved to have my own place where I could retreat, I was never quite at ease, as letters to friends and daily field note entries indicate.

The mansion's wooden structure expanded with the moist coolness of the evening, creaking and trembling with echoes of life. Among "the living" were my rarely seen cohabitants, nocturnal creatures living in the walls. I could make out families of mice, flying squirrels, and also a bird or two from their annoyed squeals, chirping lullabies, and determined gnawing. The most ornery creature was the packrat. At midnight it would thump on the living room floor in a menacing manner, as if to shoo me upstairs, reminding me that my shift downstairs was over. Unfortunately, it took to peeing under the sofa, prompting Takana to take swift action. She asked her son to set a trap, sealing its fate. When it was finally captured, it stared angrily at me from the depths of the cage, its delicate, pink, human-like hands clasping the wire door. Then it let out one last defiant pool of acrid pee. Clearly, the packrat didn't have any doubts about who was the rightful occupant of the mansion: it certainly was not me. (FIELD NOTES, JULY 2006)

Looking back, I see that my descriptions of daily life are overwritten with metaphors that express anxieties, as in the case of the poor packrat that was displaced from the mansion and met its fate soon after. The unseen presence of other entities, living and dead, was also a recurring theme, as I will suggest in Chapter 3. These field notes point to my unease in New Denver, my inability to define a space of living where I felt secure, an inability that led to, as I will discuss, an existential crisis, or what I call "a crisis in identity."

Renting the mansion in Rosebery meant that I worked and lived, not quite under the same roof, but nevertheless in close proximity to Takana, whose house was within walking distance. There's no doubt that I relied on Takana for guidance and company. When we went for evening walks, Takana would share her reflections on her own history in the valley.

Earlier in the evening, we walked north up the highway. It was just on the other side of dusk. She told me this was the new highway – that it cut right through an old cougar trail. When the road was blasted, cutting a massive trench through the bluff, the animals stood along the edge of the gapping cut, looking down in disbelief. She has a video shot of this image ... When they settled in the valley, they had a teepee up on a meadow behind the bluff. They'd walk down along the cougar trail since it was padded down by all the animals using it. Sometimes, there'd be rabbits and dead deer along it. (FIELD NOTES, 25 JULY 1996)

Given our respective projects and obligations to various organizations and funders, it was not always easy to always coordinate our work.[5] There were times when I felt that Takana was overly possessive of my time. This raised questions about the extent to which overseeing my research turned into control. For example, when Mrs. Inose and Katherine Shozawa, who was the NIMC administrator at the time, asked me to come with them to the Doukhobor's Peace Conference in Castlegar, Takana stated,

"I don't necessarily feel it is necessary for you to go – I only thought you may want to go – but as far as the project is concerned, I don't need you to go ... [though] you may enjoy seeing the event." Trying to retain some autonomy, I replied that I would determine whether or not I wanted to go. I then hesitated and added that since I was planning to go to Nelson on

Saturday, perhaps it was not a good idea. In the end, I stayed in New Denver, chagrined about what I had missed when Mrs. Inose told me about Katherine's moving speech and the proceedings. When I asked Takana for clarification about the scheduling for the projects, she stated that she was concerned about whether I could complete her projects while conducting research for my PhD. I reminded her of our initial agreement. I would spend the first three weeks on her projects and then focus on mine. Annoyed, I added that if I failed to complete whatever it was she expected, she could keep the honorarium, which, of course, she didn't. (FIELD NOTES, 25 JULY 1996)

There were also subtle battles of control over the material I documented. For instance, on another occasion I mentioned how beautiful I found the elders' singing and told Takana that one of the elders had asked me to record them. Takana raised questions about my interest in their singing. She suggested that I was privileging traditional cultural practices over more significant regular everyday activities, such as bingo. I was taken aback by the suggestion that I was more interested in what Japanese Canadians refer to derogatorily as "Japanesy" activities. I underlined

that I had been asked to record the singing by an elder and, since she [Takana] was the chair of the History Preservation Committee, she might want copies for the collection. I added that I thought singing was important to the elders. Mrs. Hoshino told me that she used to sing frequently in the Kyowakai Hall when it was filled with people, probably in the 1950s or 1960s. That was when her husband, a well-respected man, was the president of the Kyowakai Society. (FIELD NOTES, 25 JULY 1996)

Takana considered what I said and clarified her point, emphasizing the importance of activities that have historic value to the community, and she stated that she would be interested in the story behind the singing.

Feeling increasingly defensive, over time I unconsciously adjusted my behaviour, for the worse. Rather than risk a flurry of disapproval, I found it easier to show no initiative whatsoever, letting Takana determine everything from scheduling to when and if she would consider my input. I became increasingly passive and lethargic. It was only once I established my own independent relations with the elders and other residents, and my own perspective on community dynamics, that I began to reassert my boundaries.

Every researcher has her or his own way of situating her- or himself in a new place. As a newcomer with little knowledge of local life, I initially relied on the one person I knew: Takana. Entering this social space with her support helped me to become sensitized to the complex interpersonal dynamics in the valley. But it also meant a loss of autonomy. When I began to establish relationships with local residents on my own terms, my relationship with Takana began to shift. Rather predictably, I began to feel irritated when she questioned my activities and assumptions. At the time, I did not take any responsibility for my own complicity in creating a situation in which Takana oversaw my activities. I was too preoccupied with trying to break out of my own straightjacket to be self-reflexive. I became argumentative and ill-tempered around her back-to-the-land friends, waiting for a chance to point out that they were, after all, Americans, the *real* newcomers, unlike those of us with several generations of family history in British Columbia. My field notes went through a Malinowski-esque phase. I was even more cantankerous with family and friends who came to visit.

> I am far from a hospitable host. What should be a welcome respite is not. They arrive in New Denver in the midst of the slow process of my unravelling identity: the reorientation and reconfiguration of self around a character not yet developed. I resist prying myself out of this state and push my visitors away, argumentative, moody.
>
> It has taken such exhausting emotional energy to do all the work to leave my former self. I'm still not there – incomplete – somewhere in transition. When family and friends arrive, with our shared histories and understandings, I feel my old world pulling me back to my old self. I am resentful, impatient. I am ill-behaved with my parents, rolling my eyes and becoming comatose in their company.
>
> When a close old friend visits, I make a point of disagreeing with (almost) everything he says. But thank goodness the remnants of hospitality did not completely leave me. As is proper for a travel-weary senior friend, I give him the bedroom, not confident he could survive the packrat on duty downstairs or deal with the cobwebs in the study, where I sleep on the floor. Mice ping-pong off my face all night. My mood in the morning is not pretty. (BASED ON FIELD NOTES FROM DIFFERENT DATES IN AUGUST 1996)

Rereading this material on returning to Ottawa gave me a chance to reflect on what were at times my ridiculous moods and my own hyperbolic constructions of social dynamics. Anthropologist Vincent Crapanzano offers his reflections on retrospectively reading notes from his research in Morocco.

> As I look back over my notes, and as I attempt to recall my meetings with Tuhami some ten years ago, I am immediately struck by the impoverished quality of my

emotional response. My questions seem frequently cold, unemotional ... It was at such times that I took refuge in my difficulties with Arabic and exploited, I suppose, the presence of Lhacen [my assistant and translator] ... [making use of] "ethnographic distance" ... and theoretical positions ... to distance and defend myself from an onslaught of presumably intolerable emotions ... Even today, as I write, such defensive manoeuvres ... come into play ... The ethnographic encounter, like any encounter, however distorted in its immediacy or through time never ends. It continually demands interpretation and accommodation. (Crapanzano 1980, 139-140)

Likewise, rereading sections of my field notes, I continue to be taken aback by my judgmental views, irritation, and inability to appreciate what a burden I must have been for Takana. Read as defensive manoeuvres, whether in the field or in my written descriptions, this behaviour shows internal resistance to giving up my investment in a particular self – a strand of authoritative subjectivity that I had tried to repress – as it contradicted my conscious desire to respect the caution of those living in New Denver about researchers like myself.

A Dissolution of Identity

Before I began to redraw boundaries and negotiate a new identity in New Denver, it could be argued that I underwent what Kondo describes as a "dissolution of identity" (1986). As a Japanese American conducting fieldwork in Japan, Kondo had internalized enough Japanese cultural codes to feel a compulsion to please the family with whom she was staying. Trying her best to be respectful, she embraced the protocols for a good Japanese daughter, serving the father at dinner, for example. The more approval she received from the mother and father, the more she conformed to these protocols. Ironically, she became much more obedient than the daughters in the family. In contrast to the compliant role she assumed in the field, at home in the United States Kondo saw herself as an independent career woman. She was shocked when she finally grasped the extent to which her identity had been refashioned. This realization occurred by chance, when she failed to recognize her reflection in a street window. What she saw, looking back at her from the reflection, was a docile young Japanese woman.

Like Kondo, I was complicit in refashioning my identity in an attempt to become a unobtrusive, agreeable visitor. I accepted what I thought was an expected role, suppressing my critical and analytic habits. My familiarity with the basic social protocols of Japanese Canadians led me to believe that everything from my haphazard housekeeping to how I addressed the president of the Kyowakai Society must be carefully considered in order to reflect well on my host, Takana. Thus, like Kondo, I understood enough to know what was expected but lacked the cultural skill to distance myself from my host without appearing to be ignorant of social proprieties. In this instance, I felt locked into my role as a Japanese Canadian visitor invited by Takana to assist her on NIMC projects. Kondo claims that this ambiguous lack of distance between researchers and their research participants can lead to a "collapse of identity" (1986, 75). Rather than viewing this process as a failure to assert one's boundaries, however, Kondo explores the epistemological implications and concludes that this process "may open anthropological inquiry to the possibility of other, more experiential and affective ways of knowing" (ibid.).

Although Kondo recognizes that she was complicit in modifying her behaviour to seek the approval of her hosts, she also argues that this was a typical example of how research subjects can "[seek] to dominant the anthropological encounter through control of the ethnographer's behaviour. This in turn [helps] them to preserve their own sense of identity" (1986, 80). Rather than simply viewing people in the field as powerless, Kondo reminds us that "one's informants are also subjects who possess certain understandings of the ethnographer and the power to shape and control the ethnographer and the ethnographic encounter" (ibid.). Likewise, it could be argued that Takana sought to dominate the research encounter. Perhaps she wanted to ensure that I would not be an intrusive outsider. So rather than moulding me into a clearly defined role (as daughter or apprentice, for example), she seemed more concerned with setting up protective boundaries around the elders, her projects, and her personal life. I was an outsider who had to be managed.

Yet the boundaries were confusing. By sharing her concerns about the memorial and the elders, Takana suggested I was to be trusted. On some occasions it was as if I was serving an apprenticeship, training for my future life in New Denver. For example, rather than pay for the last month's rent, she asked me to arrange to get the winter's supply of firewood for the mansion, explaining that this would be an important skill if I were to live in the valley in the future.

In New Denver, I felt that my social identity was constantly under negotiation, whether with Takana, visitors who questioned my authenticity as a Japanese Canadian, or the local residents who treated me with cool suspicion. At the same time, the president of the Kyowakai Society related to me as a sansei doing research that would benefit his community. In my daily encounters with people visiting the memorial, I met some who knew my mother's family and greeted me with warm familiarity. Many of the elders extended themselves to me, welcoming me into their homes as a younger person or student from the community.

Amid these conflicting strands of identity, during the first several months I lost a sense of who or what I was *there,* in that village and valley. At an abstract level, I tried to interrelate my roles as academic researcher, project worker, and community member. But there was little to guide me through conflicting sets of responsibilities and the various levels of exclusion and inclusion that each position entailed, never mind the confusing rush of conflicting emotions. In one situation, someone might grant me a great level of trust (as a younger community member); in another, the same person might regard me with ear-scorching suspicion (as a researcher from the city). As a newcomer with no established identity in New Denver, confronted with different expectations from a range of people, I began to undergo a dissolution of, or as I came to view it, a "necessary crisis" in identity.

Anthropologists such as Rosaldo (1989) and Kondo (1986) have argued that it is precisely the dissolution of identity that makes it possible to apprehend the existence of other cultural worlds. Especially if the work requires moving to an unfamiliar place, the researcher will begin to realize at a certain point that the systems of meaning, habitual practices, and emotional sensibilities that configured her or his self have little coherence. The old sense of self begins to unravel, while a new self configured through relations in the field begins to form. When the researcher begins to rely on local meanings and sensibilities to make sense of her or himself in this new habitus (Bourdieu 1991), when these meanings and sensibilities begin to make sense emotionally, not just in abstract terms, shaping one's behaviour and inclinations, this is when she or he begins to have some insight into the other world (Geertz 1973; Shields 1991). My situation in particular, as I have explained, involved a crisis. My sense of self did not merely dissolve; rather, strands of my identity were viewed suspiciously, and many of my assumptions were regarded as objectionable. This is what accounted, I believe, for my temporary state of paralysis in the field.

In cultural studies, especially for many scholars working primarily at a theoretical level and/or conducting visual and textual analyses, field research consists of descriptive observations concerned with localized events that lack relevance beyond the place and time in which they occurred. My point is to underline that fieldwork has much to contribute at a hermeneutic level. As Kondo notes, the experiences researchers undergo when their identities dissolve "may open anthropological inquiry to the possibility of other, more experiential and affective ways of knowing" (1986, 75).

Reading theoretical texts or even studies of particular groups cannot provide the understanding made possible by fieldwork. Nor can the necessary crisis in identity that some researchers undergo be achieved through a set of cognitive exercises, for example, reading complex theories that promise to rearrange one's conceptual order of the universe. The crisis is existential. Although reading theory can be experiential, reading about a radical form of ethics that challenges your way of understanding the world does not translate readily into an artful enactment of this knowledge, especially when one is confronted by an unco-operative other who is resistant to your theories and refuses to adhere to your idealized conceptions and instead draws out your deeply ingrained emotional reactions. Undergoing this crisis helps loosen the relentless grip of one's disci-plinary framework as well as ideological and psychological investments in relat-ing to the world in particular ways, making it possible to recognize the existence of other realities: ways of ordering and understanding the world in terms distinct from one's own.

This occurs most profoundly when working with others, when the researcher becomes emotionally confused and uncertain of how to respond. Feelings of warmth might be rejected as patronizing; indignation over a perceived injustice might be viewed as egotistic. Judgments about what constitutes a topic of con-cern in a caring relationship might be viewed as meddling and controlling. When others reject or fail to recognize the terms by which one understands the world, it becomes increasingly difficult to maintain an identity based on that knowledge. That knowledge is now inadequate for negotiating relationships with others. Researchers who find themselves in this situation might retreat to more rigid articulations of their identity or, depending on the safety and ethics of giving themselves over to their participants' world, might allow themselves to undergo a crisis of identity.[6] In this case, relating meaningfully to others entails a desire to be recognized by them as a social subject.[7] Their recognition becomes important to the researcher's continuing sense of self, even if only for the sake of emotional stability during the period of research. It takes time to build relationships as well as to learn the gestures and symbolic acts that make it possible to become a social subject in a new community (Geertz 1973, 11-14). The belief that studying local habits in the abstract will make it possible to pass as an insider often leads to ridiculous mistakes. Only over time, as the researcher develops relationships with members in the community, does meaningful en-gagement, across differences and through commonalities, become possible. Rosaldo argues that only through "full engagement and involvement in the meaningful order of everyday life [can one open] oneself fully to Otherness, with a willingness to change one's perceptions through this intimate contact (Gadamer 1979, 152). Only then [can] difference be truly realized" (Rosaldo 1989, 82).

Opening oneself to otherness, on the one hand, also entails attempting to shift the power relationships that typically regulate the interactions between ethnog-raphers and others. It is not simply a matter of being willing to adjust one's perceptions; rather, it entails letting go of how one makes sense of the world as well as the security, control, and authority associated with this worldview. The suspension or shifting of power relationships is always temporary (if it is possible in the first place) because the ethnographer always returns home, where she or he can reassert the authority of her or his knowledge. Conventionally, the ethnographer then writes about "her or his subjects," representing them and rendering them meaningful according to terms set by the field of anthropology. But anthropologists have also questioned the problems of representation and the authorship of their texts. Several decades ago, ethnographers concerned with challenging the reproduction of colonial and disciplinary knowledge in their work began to critically discuss these issues (Clifford 1988; Clifford and Marcus 1986; Marcus and Fischer 1986). It is important to emphasize that realizing difference can not be equated with fully understanding the other. This is impossible. According to Kondo,

> most ethnographies, even the reflexive kind, are products of contexts in which the observer/ethnographer is a visible outsider. Perhaps as a consequence (and perhaps as a gender difference ...), these ethnographies end up depicting the Other as ineffably alien ... The best we can do, they say, is to engage a reasoned dialogue with the Other, thereby achieving a "fusion of horizons" (Gadamer 1982), where discourse constitutes threads tenuously connecting two monads (e.g., Rabinow 1977; Dwyer 1982). (Kondo 1986, 74-75)

Working with the Elders

It was with the elders that I felt the most secure. Through familiar formalities and practices of hospitality, they positioned me as a younger Japanese Canadian visiting their community. The members of the History Preservation Committee – notably Mrs. Inose, Mrs. Takahara, Mr. Matsushita, and Mrs. Matsushita – made special efforts to ensure that I felt welcome, offering their company when I was lonely and advice when I needed direction. I accompanied them to community events, where they always ensured I felt included. They shared their playful sense of humour with me. For example, at a community meeting, I caught the eye of Mrs. Inose just as she plucked a tissue out of her sleeve to dab her brow. She looked at me and said mischievously, "This is a great technique for pickpockets, you know ... You'd be surprised what one can fit up one's sleeves!" She then took the arm of Mrs. Takahara and, with a flourish of her tissue, sashayed out of the Centennial Hall.

Although the elders had busy schedules, many insisted on taking me out to restaurants or invited me to their homes, where they made all sorts of delicacies, including *matsutake gohan,*[8] *manju,*[9] or grilled chicken with secret sauce. When I visited my Obaasan's household after I left New Denver, she exclaimed, "Kausty, so round and healthy!" It became apparent that the elders had a relationship to

Obaasan through me. They wanted to be certain that I was sent back to her household looking well-fed (about ten pounds heavier in fact). This demonstrated to Obaasan that they had taken care of me and that their households, and especially their larders, were plentiful. For my Old World Japanese Canadian hosts, if I returned home looking as if I had lost weight, it would be an embarrassment, reflecting poorly on their hospitality.

In addition to nurturing me with hospitality, the elders saw that I was on a social learning curve and offered guidance, often with great patience, as this account of my visit to Mr. Senya Mori for an interview indicates.

Mr. Mori was a well-respected man of stature in the Village of New Denver and the Buddhist community. He had been president of the Kyowakai Society in the past as well as the mayor of New Denver. The morning of the interview, I rushed to the local store to find an appropriate *omiyage,* a symbolic gift of gratitude for the hospitality of his household. I would rather be late than arrive without a gift. I could not bear arriving empty-handed. When I finally arrived at his house, I was faced with another dilemma. His entire house appeared to be surrounded by an immaculately cut carpet of green grass. I couldn't see any walkway. So I stood at the edge of the lawn – panicked by my tardiness and, even more, about how I was to reach his door without treading on his lawn.

Mr. Mori finally saw me and bellowed in the fashion of my Ojiisan, "You're LATE!" I called out, "How do I cross your lawn?!" In a begrudging manner he pointed the way. After I gingerly made my way to his doorstep, I handed him my gift, a bag of large sweet fruit: "Peaches! For you!" Just as quickly, he replied in a deep voice, "Ohhhh – how nice!" Focusing on the gesture before him, rather than my late arrival, he brought me inside and arranged some in a bowl as an offering for his wife's *butsudan,*[10] explaining that she had recently departed. He gestured me down the hall to see her most beautiful butsudan, a delight to the senses so delicately carved it made one sigh. So, unforgivable lateness, a faux pas when visiting one of the community's respected leaders, was soon softened by the exchange between issei and sansei, though no doubt my lateness had been noted and would be discussed with other elders.

He beckoned me to the living room, where he brushed aside the formalities of the consent form, impatiently nodding to my description of the project, and then launched into his life story as I scrambled to set up the tape recorder. There was little chance to ask questions as he strode forward with his account. Shaking his head, with a dismissive laugh, he recounted how his family had made an agreement with a *hakujin* woman to take care of their property on Fairview slopes when they were forced to leave Vancouver in 1942. By their agreement, the woman could live in the house and rent out the rooms, but she instead quickly sold the property with all the contents, leaving the Moris with nothing. He continued with his account, weaving family history into the history of New Denver and his role in the Buddhist church. Halfway through, he stopped to make us both steaming bowls of ramen. Then he continued, inexhaustible. When we ended the interview, it was hard to say goodbye. I wasn't sure why. It felt as if we both lingered, not wanting to depart. He showed me the wooden tub he had made for the family *ofuro*, steaming hot soaks, and we visited a little while longer. Finally, politeness required me to leave, as it was getting close to the dinner hour. (Field notes, 5 September 1996)

The elders very much reminded me of my Obaasan and the formalities of her household. I recognized that Mr. Senya Mori, like the other elders, was very graciously extending his hospitality, sharing his life history and opening his home to me. The kindness and consideration of the elders were acts that called for recognition through a show of deep appreciation, respectful regard, and honorifics. But, at the same time, these formalities were not rigidly prescribed, as was evident with my tardy arrival at Mr. Senya Mori's home. There was also room to recover from clumsy missteps without being dismissed as ill-mannered and disrespectful.

When I first met the elders, one of my greatest concerns was that my position as a sansei visitor would camouflage my position as an academic researcher. But I quickly realized that I had overlooked the elders' experience with researchers. A month after my arrival in New Denver, they began to ask why I had not started my research. They observed that I was neglecting my own project and seemed to have noted my discomfort about my position as a researcher. Finally, a number of elders pulled me aside and indicated in no uncertain terms that my time was running out; if I did not start interviewing them, it would be too late. They basically told me: "Get going with your project!" They had read the documents that I had sent to the Kyowakai Society months earlier to explain my project and expected me to conduct my research. In fact, in some cases, the elders initiated the interviews. In other cases, they spoke with me about their histories in the course of conversations during social events.

Mrs. Hoshino chatted in Japanese with one of the new residents. When the new resident smiled at me and then looked the other way, I thought, uh-oh, they are chatting about me ... Then Mrs. H. leaned over the table and pulled one of my research proposals off the stack toward her. I felt kind of embarrassed because my title had "political violence" in it. But she didn't bother with the title. She underlined my name with her finger and said "Emiko." Then she told me how her grandchildren's first names are Japanese – they don't use their middle names, which are English. "Ohh ... " I replied, a little embarrassed by the way the Japanese component of my name was hidden.

She mentioned how there was a Nakashima, like my mother's family, just down the road from New Denver during the war, "though, no, probably not related." She was very physical, her hand on my shoulder, leaning close. So warm.

An energetic, fit woman in her early sixties, tall and lanky with short, cropped hair, wearing a T-shirt and shorts, came by. She scooped up the pink lemonade and began to pour herself a second cup. "Can I have another cup? This is very tasty stuff!" As she plonked the container down on the table, I replied, "Please, help yourself ... " then shrunk a few inches, realizing that my formality probably made me sound like a sarcastic smartass. Who could she be? The seniors chatted pleasantly with her, not seeming to notice anything. Then off she went, in another gust of energy.

Mrs. H. leaned over again and confided in me. The woman was the daughter of a local property owner. She said the government put internment shacks on their ranch during the war; Mrs. H. and her family were interned there in 1943. She made a gesture indicating that the woman was a small girl then. There was a look on her face – disbelief? – that said: it is always surprising to see little children grow up and become adults.

Mrs. Hoshino explained that in the camp, at first, they had no water, so they had to use buckets to retrieve water from the creek. No electricity, either. She had to walk with two buckets (she laughed in amazement, shaking her head) on a pole over her back – "Like this," she gestured. Later, when I visited her home, she told me she had had to wash their clothes in the creek. She couldn't haul all that water back to the shack – with their one-year-old son, there was a lot of laundry. She said that the family who owned the ranch was really nice. Very nice. She warmly recalled when the woman was a little girl. I asked if the family visited the interned Japanese Canadians, and she said "No [laughing], people would go visit them." This family was so different from the nearby Silverton residents, who were anti-Japanese. There were signs telling the Japanese to keep out of Silverton.

I asked where she was before the war, and she said, "Vancouver." I said, "Powell Street?" She replied that they had a drug store kitty-corner to what "was then called Powell Grounds." I said, "Oppenheimer Park?" She nodded. And she said that their house – they owned their own house – was in Kitsilano. But they lost everything during the war. (FIELD NOTES, 26 JULY 1996)

Like other elders, Mrs. Hoshino reached out to me as a younger Japanese Canadian visiting New Denver by telling me about her history and linking me to her grandchildren. In addition, this was a way to link the people she knew and the places where she lived before the war with me, creating new community bonds across the generations.

Other elders also approached me, indicating that they had information to share. This was my cue to ask them for an interview. Once I began interviewing, social courtesy required me to ask all the elders so that no one would feel overlooked. I then conducted interviews more broadly with the sansei president of the Kyowakai Society and some of the contractors who had worked on the NIMC. In many ways, it was the elders who initiated this last phase of research. No longer was I a participant-observer working in the community during the day and writing copious field notes in the evenings and early mornings. I knew residents well enough to directly ask them questions about the NIMC without feeling that I was approaching them instrumentally simply as sources of data. I now felt a responsibility to share what I learned from them.[11] I understood that the act of sharing their accounts with me entailed trust. Their trust came with an expectation. As I learned over time, this was not simply the expectation that I would record their accounts for future generations but also that I would find my own way to put into writing what they shared with me that summer.

Between working on the NIMC projects and interviewing the elders, I collected local publications, including maps, postcards, newspapers, tourist brochures, and published histories. I squeezed in time to photograph and take notes on the NIMC's layout and historical displays. Near the end of my research visit, the president of the Kyowakai Society decided that he could trust me enough to give me access to the NIMC's files.

It was through spending time with the elders, rather than simply interviewing them, that I became sensitive to their distinctive way of knowing and organizing the world. Their worldviews were present in the way they had continually transformed the site of the internment camp over the years, making it into a space of living. It took me several months before I realized the significance of the memorial to the elders. They located it in a field of activity different from (while still articulated with but not reducible to) the discourses that constituted it as a public place of mourning, a museum, or tourist site. This other field of activity was a world with its own temporality and spatiality and with many layers of nuanced meaning.

Their worldviews became apparent only as I interacted with them and as they continually unravelled my preconceptions with humour and patient explanation. I recall Mr. Matsushita's gentle manner as he showed me his photograph albums. Without thinking, I commented, "What a cute boy!" and "That teenager certainly shows a talent for art!" Mr. Matsushita quietly explained: "Oh, that is sad story; the boy drowned shortly afterwards" and then, "Well, she had problems with depression and ended up committing suicide." The elders' regard of me as someone cognizant of the implications of what I said and did was important for my sense of self. I had to reflect on my enthused commentary about the boy and the teenager in the photographs. I had an impulse to idealize life in New Denver, imposing stereotypical ideas about happy children and villages. I had failed to recognize that New Denver was a village in an economically depressed area with a history of incarceration camps.

I had no pretensions of ever being able to fully know the way elders perceived and inhabited their worlds (Geertz 1973; Marcus and Fischer 1986; Merleau-Ponty 1994 [1962]). Only those who *lived* in these worlds could have this knowledge. In New Denver I was an outsider but, as the elders showed me, not necessarily an objectionable one. As members of the Kyowakai Society, they regarded me as someone interested in the memorial who might share their principles of justice. As issei and nisei, they looked to me as a younger Japanese Canadian who wanted to learn about transforming the burden of the past carried by our community. I hoped to learn from them, beginning with how to engage in a manner that respected the terms of their existence rather than imposing my own. Through our interchanges, I realized they, too, hoped for the possibility of creating a new zone of knowledge together. The elders had the finesse to work with me as a relative stranger, inviting me into their homes. They offered a sense of security in circumstances in which I was insecure; they had the skill and generosity to teach me to persist and trust what was there, even if I did not yet have the language to articulate it.

Writing

I returned to Ottawa in the fall. Winter came and went. In March, cold sheets of rain washed the grit and icy debris from the grey city streets. In my apartment were stacks of boxes with NIMC records, newspaper and magazine articles, photographic records, and field notes. What I needed to write seemed evident, but I had no idea how to do it. Language failed me. I tried to sum up my research with a background chapter on the history of the internment camp in New Denver, a chapter on the development of the NIMC, a third chapter on the memorial's representation of the internment camp, and a fourth chapter on the ways the memorial integrated the local community into a larger national community commemorating the Japanese Canadian internment camps. But this failed to convey what I had experienced. It flattened everything into manageable facts and descriptions that simply illustrated the well-established conclusions of already published studies. A ten-day research visit would have sufficed. Had I spent significant amounts of time in New Denver over two summers, working with elders and the chair of the History Preservation Committee, to achieve only this?

Rosaldo (1989, 82) claims that to transform fieldwork into an ethnographic text it is necessary to draw away from the immediacy of the ethnographic encounter.

> Writing ... becomes a way of freezing the disturbing flux, encapsulating experience in order to control it. Writing ... offers the author the opportunity to re-encounter the Other "safely," to find meaning in the chaos of lived experience through retrospectively ordering the past. It is a kind of Proustian quest in which the ethnographer seeks meaning in events whose significance was elusive while they were being lived. The writer, then, addresses, her/himself in an attempt at self-reconstruction.

The process of imposing distance after the ethnographic encounter has also been described in the language of violence (Kondo 1986; Narayan 2003 [1997]). Imposing control and laying down structure can reduce the complexity and rich ambiguity of experience. Perhaps unconsciously, I resisted controlling the disturbing flux. Retrospectively, I realize that I feared that reordering the experience would mean imposing my interpretation, which is what I attempted to avoid during my stay in New Denver.

I wrote listlessly and endlessly, unable to find the words to connect with what I had experienced in New Denver. I could not bear reading academic texts. I viewed them as reductive and monolithic, using data, whether observations or accounts, to illustrate theories rather than engaging productively with the material in context. I turned to novels, completely consumed by their fictional worlds. There are many ways to avoid facing oneself in the struggle of writing. I immersed myself in aikido, a rather ascetic martial art, training as often as twice a day, five to six times a week, going to seminars in Canada and the United States, reading martial arts literature, and adhering to a strict training regime that included the gym and water running. Even as I wrote draft after draft, I poured all my analytic and emotional energy into aikido training.

But aikido was not simply a diversion, at least at first. After returning from my 1995 visit to New Denver, I felt overwhelmed by the valley's emotional currents and turned to the only practice I knew that might help. This was martial arts. As an undergraduate student, I had studied karate for a brief two-year period with Sam Wong, a very strict and tough teacher. I never learned how to fight effectively (despite Sam's efforts to show us where to hit all the vital organs). Instead, karate helped me learn that it is possible to withstand being swept away by powerful emotional forces, whether fear, anger, indignation, or shock. I learned that an over-reliance on cognitive thought can be a barrier to learning. Sparring, an arena of staged conflict in which powerful emotional forces can overwhelm one, can, with the right teacher, become a way to learn how to release oneself from the emotion's overwhelming power and develop other ways to engage with them. If I was to return to New Denver, I knew I would have to find a way to live in the intense emotional landscape.

In Ottawa, Wendy Larner, a friend in the PhD program at Carleton University, introduced me to Ottawa Aikikai, the dojo where she trained. For the next four years, I trained almost daily, exploring what would be entailed in an embodied ethic in one's often troubled relations with others and oneself. Whereas karate requires moving in relation to others at a hostile distance of kicking and punching, aikido emphasizes moving with the other to transform the aggression and fear into harmonious interdependence. Only later did I realize that my immersion in aikido was a way to work through traumatic post-memories (Hirsch 1997b) of internment. In the short span of four years, of course, I could only learn a little. And as Alan Hunt, my PhD supervisor, noted, it was as if a cult had claimed me. At the right moment, as no one else could have, he took it upon himself to deftly force my attention back to the real struggle, which I had clearly begun to replace rather than transform with aikido. A frank and unnerving lecture forced me awake, using what I likened to a stick of dynamite in a calm pond in which I was in fact drowning.

The question of how to write about what I learned in New Denver was really a question of how to render experience into a meaningful form (Rosaldo 1989). To render experience meaningful one must interpret, enforcing a level of control over the material. I feared doing this because imposing order seemed to be a violent act. But my refusal to interpret, to impose meaning, was a refusal to take a subject position and acknowledge my presence in the world: to have a voice. The problem I faced was trying to determine *how to take on a subject position* in a non-reductive, non-monolithic manner – how to situate myself in a mutual relation with others – which entailed interpreting and organizing experience and rendering it meaningful. Only later did I realize that representing what the elders had taught me was difficult to bear (McAllister 2001). The material was potent. The experience at some level was terrifying. I did not know how to work with the intangible residues of memory, the aftermath of loss, fear, and hatred.

I did not know how to put it into a form, to respectfully present it, keeping what remained alive.[12]

This is when Derek Smith, one of my other academic supervisors, met with me frequently. I would walk several times a week over the Alexandra Bridge to the Museum of Civilization in Hull where he was working on a project involving First Nations mapping. He would take time to talk me through the complexities of encounters with other worlds, fear, and death and to explore different novelistic forms of writing. Audrey Kobayashi, my other supervisor, kept me grounded with her guidance and the example of her own work. Her clarity about the politics of research reminded me about my responsibility to move beyond my personal struggle. Retrospectively, I can see that through my obsessive novel reading and aikido I was searching for a narrative form, a way of moving, a rhythm with a principle of mutual engagement that could bear, while transforming, what I had experienced.

Narayan argues that we need to adopt narratives with an ethical stance that does not efface our complex subject positions as researchers or deface the "vivid humanity of the people with whom we work" (Narayan 2003 [1997], 297). I have thus made this book a composite text, drawing on multiple types of material, whether field notes, quotations from interviews, and excerpts from public exhibits and archival documents. Without wanting to make myself the centre of the narrative, I have written myself into the text, especially in this chapter and Chapter 6. Following the ethnographic tradition, I constructed myself as a character, sometimes, as Alan Hunt noted, a very irritating and opinionated character. The intention was to make the basis for both *what* has been written and the *form of writing* evident. That is, I disclosed the way the constitution of my complex subject position has played into the way I render the memorial and portray the "vivid humanity of the people with whom [I worked]."

When I began reading academic texts again, Jackie Stacey's *Teratologies: A Cultural Study of Cancer* (1997) demonstrated that it was possible to create a sociological text that brought together and analytically deconstructed the different voices and disciplinary discourses that seek to contain the organic flows and ruptures of, in Stacey's case, the living body and, in my case, what would be the social body. Annette Kuhn's *Family Secrets: Acts of Memory and Imagination* (1995) revealed that it was possible through "imaginative acts" to breath life into what we too often sweep aside as the everyday clutter of our lives, what in this study are remnants of internment camps embodied in social gestures, fading letters, and stories. From these remnants, Kuhn shows that it is possible to give texture, weight, and emotional force to undocumented, untold worlds of people and places that have passed on.

In this book, I use lengthy descriptive passages to locate readers in New Denver as a site of memory. Rather than approaching the memorial in the singular, I write about its multiple forms as the memorial is constituted through different fields of activity: as a memorial marking the site of the New Denver incarceration camp; as part of the ongoing transformation of the Kyowakai Society as an organization founded by internees to represent their interests to the camp administrators; as a site for small scale-memory projects; and as a tourist site for a range of visitors travelling to New Denver, whether on personal pilgrimages or seeking education about human rights violations.

CHAPTER TWO

Mapping the Spaces of Internment

New Denver, 1996

When the Kyowakai Society of New Denver built the Nikkei Internment Memorial Centre (NIMC), it reconfigured the village around the history of internment, discursively transforming the southern flats of Carpenter Creek from a residential area with its complex layers of history into a site that over a thousand visitors travel to each year to remember, mourn, and educate themselves about the internment. The memorial uses discursive techniques such as historical displays and maps to help visitors identify the remains of the camp in the contemporary landscape, laying the past over the present. It has thus transformed what Doreen Massey refers to as "the identity of place – the sense of the place" (Massey 1993, 64) in New Denver into what I refer to as a "space of internment" for the postwar community.

As I will discuss in Chapter 4, the identity of New Denver as a former internment camp has changed over the years. During the 1980s, for example, when activists mobilized Japanese Canadians in the movement to seek redress from the Canadian government, it became a site of persecution where the citizen's rights were violated. The identity of New Denver changed again after the National Association of Japanese Canadians negotiated a settlement for redress with the government. In this period, it became a site that nisei began to reclaim through reunions organized for former internees, making the village an important place in the community's geography (McAllister 1994).

When I arrived there in 1996, I thought New Denver looked like any other small town in British Columbia. Known until the end of the Second World War as "the Orchard," it now seems an odd place for a memorial centre. It sits amid modest wooden bungalows scattered over an alluvial delta that fans out from a river valley cut by glaciers through the massive mountains thousands of years ago. Now, on a typical summer day, the occasional dog trots by, and children on bicycles zigzag around the neighbourhood in their worlds of mischief and mystery.

Upon closer inspection, the homes are remarkably similar. Many are shacks from the internment camp. This is where most Japanese Canadians in New Denver have lived since the camp closed in 1945. Over the years, they have

2.1 Housing in the Orchard: A renovated internment shack, New Denver, 1996.
Photo by the author.

modified the flimsy, leaking shacks, refashioning and extending walls, adding windows, and digging gardens. Some are picture-perfect, gleaming white, sitting amid tidy flowerbeds and lawns. Others are tucked behind sprawling vegetable gardens, peering reclusively from overgrown fruit trees strung with hammocks. Others have neatly cut hedges that create backyard parlours where guests are invited for dinner and evening conversation. Some show an artistic bent with intricate rockwork set amid fanciful flowerbeds and scarlet runners joyously twirling above sturdy tomato plants. And then there are the other shacks. Tar-paper peels off the weathered wooden skin of their walls. Their porches crumble into the surrounding thickets of dry wild grass and gnarly rosebushes. Brambles scramble over their yards. They stand empty, their inhabitants long gone.

The Nikkei Internment Memorial Centre is on Josephine Street, in the centre of what had been the internment camp from 1942 to 1945. It is a block or two from most of the elders' homes and one block from Centennial Park. There is no signage to indicate that the park was part of the internment camp. Although the large sports field is usually empty, belonging to the era when organized sports were more popular, the campground along the lakeshore remains busy. In the summer months, it becomes a city of tents, trailers, and motorhomes,

2.2 Internment shack in the Orchard, New Denver, 1996. *Photo by the author.*

with barbeques and the smell of scorched hamburgers and hot dogs, strangely reminiscent of the temporary shelters of many of the internees when they first arrived in the camps. Today, though, instead of disoriented and distressed women, children, and men, the site is filled with the happy rumble of families, many of whom amble over to visit the NIMC or the nearby Kohan Reflection Gardens. To the south is the Pavilion, its steep A-frame evoking images of an alpine lodge and healthy mountain air. It is now a long-term care facility for the elderly, but its history is less benign. As the historical displays in the NIMC reveal, it was the tuberculosis sanatorium for interned Japanese Canadians.

When I first arrived in New Denver, the historical displays in the Centre helped me to identify the remains of the camp in the village. The longer I stayed, the more I realized that the Centre provided only the barest outline of what the camp had looked like and what had happened to the internees. Many records about the internment camp have been lost. The elders often expressed anxiety about records that had "gone missing." Mr. Senya Mori told me that the government took many of the Kyowakai Society's historical records when one of the former presidents died in 1960. Because he had no next of kin, his estate passed to the provincial government. Mr. Mori wrote down the name of the president,

"Misaka Jiro, 1960 died, Nov. 21," on a small lined piece of paper from his notepad and gave it to me, hoping that I might be able to find his records in the government archives. Mrs. Inose worried that the new staff at the Pavilion had thrown out the sanatorium's extensive records on its former patients, now all valuable historical records.

Many of these records would have revealed the other histories that New Denver residents rarely speak about, which are intimately intertwined with the history of internment. It was during everyday conversations with the elders that I heard occasional references to these other histories. One day, as I chatted with Mrs. Hoshino she mentioned the "disturbed boys" who were held in the sanatorium after the tuberculosis patients were discharged. Who were these boys? She did not have many details to share. I wondered if the sanatorium had kept any records about them. She told me that "the San" was also used to incarcerate Doukhobor children (Hoshino, Personal correspondence, 1996).

Over the last thirty years, although a number of histories about the persecution of Doukhobors in British Columbia have been published (Rak 2004), New Denver has not made its role in their history public. When the Doukhobors refused to register their children in public schools, the provincial government removed the children from their families and impounded them for the duration of their "education" in the camp's former tuberculosis sanatorium. Mrs. Hoshino recalled working there as the head cook:

The children were kept in the San from when they were six to until they were fifteen years old. Visiting days were Sunday, and the parents could visit only through the fence. The detention centre was in operation for six years. Imagine going in when you are six, coming out when you are twelve, or going in when you were ten, coming out when you were sixteen! Mrs. Hoshino said that when the parents finally agreed to send their children to the province's schools, they were set free. In the San, the children had chores. Because there were so many people to feed, two girls helped her peel potatoes. She said the government hired a couple initially, one as a janitor and the other as a cook, but they fired the cook. That's when the administrator approached her and asked if she would consider cooking. She replied, "Me? I am not a cook!" But he pushed her, and she ended up being head cook. I asked what she cooked. Mrs. Hoshino looked at me, and replied, "They are vegetarians. No meat! I cooked meat for the staff. Borscht and perogies. Do you know what perogies are? Little pastries." Then she did a tiny, delicate pinching motion, and I imagined the light pressing of fingers pinching the perogies shut. I asked her how she learned the recipes. She asked two older girls; they were fifteen years old. They told her, "Oh, there is something missing from the borscht – dill." So, when their mothers came to visit, they asked for dill. They brought lots of dill, and the girls told her, "Just like our mother's cooking!" (FIELD NOTES, 10 SEPTEMBER 1996)

In Julie Rak's in-depth study, she writes about the New Denver "dormitory" and describes the hostility of anti-Doukhobor sentiment in the 1950s. She notes that children were held for up to six years and that it was only after the first few years that parents were permitted to visit every two weeks through the wire fencing (2004, 116-118). The few times the elders mentioned the Doukhobor children, I was taken aback. With the exception of Mrs. Hoshino, the comments were always made in passing amid other memories of the valley. Did anyone, at the time, draw parallels to their own incarceration? Or, still uncertain of their fate, devastated by the forced removal of thousands of other Japanese Canadians to unknown destinations throughout the rest of Canada and Japan, did those remaining in New Denver simply accept or even agree with the government's treatment of the Doukhobors?

Over time, as I settled into the everyday routines of valley life, more details of these disturbing histories surfaced. They were still part of the living memory of the residents, but my attempts to probe deeper were always ineffectual. My questions always became entangled in uneasy interconnections and wordless absences. As I will discuss in Chapter 6, one of the most eerie absences in the valley was indigenous people. I only met a few members of the First Nations passing through New Denver. There was the time I was jogging north along the highway, huffing and puffing up a hill, when a van pulled over. They informed me that I might want to know that there was a bear about 300 metres behind me. I thanked them, and as we looked back to survey the situation, we saw the bear run across the highway and disappear into the forest. I assured them I was safe but took their advice and turned back. There was also a man at the local gas station who told me about his people, the Sinixt Nation, who once prospered in the region with settlements dating from 6,000 BP (Pearkes 2002, 11) and are now fighting the government's classification of their people as extinct (as of 1956) and therefore without any right to land (*Valley Voice* 1996a). It was only after I returned to Ottawa and read more widely that I learned that they had set up an encampment north of New Denver to protect their burial lands from highway development. Given my own uneasy feelings about the absence of First Nations in this region of the province, I wondered why I had failed to know about their encampment and had not heard anyone in New Denver refer to them.

2.3   North of Carpenter Creek, Sixth Avenue, New Denver, 1996. *Photo by the author.*

The town proper, where most New Denver residents live, is separated from the Orchard by the wandering, rocky riverbed of Carpenter Creek. The creek once formed a clear racial divide between residents and internees, but this changed sometime after the war, when a number of Japanese Canadians purchased homes on the north side. To reach the town from the Orchard, one must walk north along the highway. Among the trailer homes, ranch-style 1960s bungalows, and two-level 1970s "Vancouver special" suburban houses are a few quaint gingerbread-like houses with steep roofs and deep window sills enclosed by low stone walls and dainty hedges. Small-scale Arts and Crafts inspired homes, they were probably built in the 1920s or 1930s, in the period when the world market for mineral ores began to drop and the mining industry in this region began to lose its significance. But there are still a number of testaments to the wealth that mining brought to the valley from the 1880s onward. Shabby Victorian houses originally built for the local elite, now sit at the far end of narrow lots surrounded by fences. To approach these houses, visitors must follow long walkways that pass once well-tended plots of now rather scruffy perennials, recalling the days in the early 1900s when New Denver was the "most famous mining region in British Columbia" (Turnbull 1988, 80) and was serviced by trains and a sternwheeler boat and had electricity, a waterworks system, and an opera house (Butler et al. 1995, 47-48).

Walking down Sixth Avenue toward Slocan Lake takes the visitor past typical small-town services. In addition to three gas stations, there is a credit union, a provincial liquor store, a post office, a diner, and a laundromat. Like most small-town grocery stores, the shelves of the Eldorado say something about the residents. Although one typically finds Chinese ingredients in small grocers throughout rural British Columbia, hinting at the extensive role they played in developing the province's hinterlands, in the Eldorado there is a large section for Japanese food, including *hikijiki*,[1] gohan, and miso. In local homes, these ingredients become delicacies, whether manju with artistic pink swirls or tasty Japanese versions of chow mein. I learned that a number of these dishes were inspired by recipes learned in cooking classes at the internment camp. For locals who want to dine out on formal occasions, there is the motel that, since the New Market burned down, has the only bar in the village. Mrs. Inose took me and Katherine Shozawa, a visiting sansei artist who has worked extensively with the elders, to dine there one evening in a very generous gesture of welcome. As the waitresses eyed my casual jeans and running shoes, I self-consciously realized that the Cordon Bleu menu, cloth napkins, and candles called for more formal attire. Dining here was an extravagance in this economically depressed valley, underlining even more the hospitality of Mrs. Inose.

Bed-and-breakfast businesses and an outdoor clothing store mark the turn away from logging (which replaced mining as the main industry after the Second World War) toward tourism and wilderness recreation. Organizations such as the Valhalla Wilderness Society reflect the green politics of the newer inhabitants, especially those who share the ethos of the back-to-the-land community, established in the 1960s and early 1970s when Americans escaping the Vietnam War draft settled in the region. I suspect today's urbanites would feel right at home with the health food store selling locally made tofu and natural soaps and the funky restaurants catering to those hankering for grilled eggplant, goat cheese, and espresso.

But, despite what appears to be its green politics and the harmonious coexistence of Japanese Canadians, old-time residents, and cosmopolitan back-to-the-landers, there are political and social divides, clearly stated by the rocks thrown through the windows of the Valhalla Wilderness Society when it campaigned to turn vast tracts of forest into a park. Local residents, logging companies, and government officials also stand divided over the fate of second-growth forests that hold fragile watersheds in place (*Valley Voice* 1996b). It is not clear who the employees at the new artisan bakery thought I was, with my skin brown from the sun, wearing what in Vancouver would be identified as "grunge" clothing, when, ignoring my indignant protests, they refused to serve me before the white women standing behind me. And, despite the well-established community of lesbians and gays in the Kootenays, when I arrived in the valley, I heard about the brutal beating of a gay man. When he returned from the hospital, the perpetrators lay in wait at his cabin and viciously attacked him again. But the social divides and allegiances are not easy to decipher. Most residents have friendships and family relations that cross what an outsider might assume to be unbridgeable differences. One cannot make assumptions about the residents' politics or loyalties, regardless of whether they frequent the once-exclusive golf club founded in the 1940s, participate in Remembrance Day events, volunteer at the Kohan Gardens, or attend avant-garde art shows at the Silverton Art Gallery.

Sixth Avenue ends at the lake. The green strip of grass at the foot of the avenue is a village park, the site of the local war memorial. Not far away stands a commemorative stone erected in 1977 to mark the centennial of the arrival of the first Japanese immigrant to Canada. Japanese Canadians across the country took part in the celebrations. This makes for a strange juxtaposition. During the 1980s, many veteran organizations refused to recognize Japanese Canadians as fellow citizens and lobbied against granting them redress, claiming that they were enemy aliens, like the Japanese across the Pacific. Yet I learned about both commemorative markers from one of the elders, Mr. Shoichi Matsushita, New Denver's unofficial photographer from the 1960s to the 1980s. His vivid Kodachrome slides record both sombre Remembrance Day ceremonies and the festive 1977 Japanese Canadian centennial celebrations. And so, where Sixth Avenue ends, these two commemorative markers stand side by side with their different visions of Canadian society.

The visitor who walks back up Sixth Avenue, past the village stores and services, some housed in buildings where the wartime British Columbia Security Commission and welfare services had set up their offices, will reach a junction past the graveyard where, Mr. Senya Mori told me, a crematorium was built in 1943 for the internees in New Denver who were Buddhists. Japanese Canadian internees from the Sandon camp, many of whom were Buddhists, also used it for their dead. Mr. Senya Mori told me that no Buddhists were cremated in Sandon, whereas in the Slocan camp they used pyres. When I asked about the resting place for Buddhists, he told me that ashes were kept with families, sent to Japan, or to Buddhist churches in Canada (Field notes, 13 August 1996; also see Yasui 2006).

Walking south along the highway, over the cold torrents of Carpenter Creek, which cuts through the mountain corridors to the east, descending from where the Sandon internment camp was once perched high above the valley, will take the visitor back to the NIMC. In the summer months, tourists arrive daily with their brochures, road maps, and guidebooks. They have integrated New Denver into a new network of activity as they come in search of a place that no longer exists. The memorial stands in for the muddy flats of the internment camp, with its rows of squalid shacks and tents inhabited by confused and fearful internees. The memorial eclipses the transformation of New Denver over the years into this one moment; it transforms what Doreen Massey refers to as "the identity of place – the sense of the place" (Massey 1993, 64) into what I call the space of internment for the postwar community.

As a place of identity for the postwar community, New Denver has been produced as much by acts of collective imagination as by wartime government policies, the Japanese Canadian movement for redress, and postwar reunions. In this chapter, I examine the space of internment that has been produced discursively by the Nikkei Internment Memorial Centre. Although the memorial uses historical displays to place the New Denver camp in a broader political history with details about activities, people, and housing in the camp, it relies primarily on a map of the original camp to orient visitors in the space of internment. The map locates visitors in relation to landmarks from the original camp. In the effort to make the presence of the internment camp visible to visitors, though, there is a danger of reducing the complexity of the site's meanings not only to a single history but also to a single moment in time, to an identity that Massey argues is "constructed out of an introverted, inward-looking history based on delving into the past for internalized origins ... This conception of place ... [requires] the drawing of boundaries ... This problematical necessity of a boundary [entails] a frame in the sense of a concave line around some area, the inside of which is defined in one way and the outside in another" (1993, 64). Massey argues that it is not merely boundaries that define a place:

> What gives a place its specificity is not some long internalized history but the fact that it is constructed out of a particular constellation of relations, articulated together at a particular locus ... where a large proportion of those relations, experiences and understandings are actually constructed on a far larger scale than what we happen to define for that moment as the place itself, whether that be a street, a region or even a continent. (Ibid., 66)

Following Massey, in this chapter I argue that the map, as the memorial's main discursive technique for orienting visitors in the space of internment, ends up reifying the site, erasing the presence, the histories, the movements of whatever cannot fit into its schematic logic. The map was made by the contractors who designed the memorial. As I will explain, it helped them understand the layout of the camp. They used it in the blueprint for designing the memorial as well as in their application for funding. Since little had been published about the New Denver camp, they used an array of historical sources – including government records, historical studies, personal documents, and interviews with the elders – to help them conceptualize the camp. The map is a distillation of this process.

To understand how reductive this space of internment is, I return to three of the sources used by the contractors to reconstruct the internment camp: archival government records and historical studies, maps of internment camps, and the elders accounts of New Denver. In this chapter, I reveal how each of these sources effectively maps distinctive spaces of internment and transcends the spatial and temporal boundaries that the memorial's map enforces. In constituting different spaces of internment, these sources also position whomever reads them in different relationships to the internment camps. They construct their readers as particular types of subjects who, for example, view the camps in terms of the infrastructure needed to run them or, like the interned children, know where to find the beaches and ski hills. Reading how these documents map the space of internment from different positions, it becomes possible to gain insight into the changing constellation of relationships, places, experiences, and understandings that contribute to the production of New Denver over time (Massey 1993). Reading these sources to discover their "maps" is thus also an exercise in excavation, an exercise in tracing the lines of movement, the connections, and the acts of imagination that the NIMC's map removes from its abstracted space.

The last section of this chapter presents accounts of the elders who conceive the space of internment as a space of loss and displacement that is as much about the present as it is about the past. Their oral accounts provide rich, detailed maps: oral memory maps that create lines of movement between places and across time. They capture what cannot be delineated through mapping exercises or even my own descriptions. Their space of internment is something that is potent and powerful that the elders have continued to transform over the years through their stories and "acts of memory" (Kuhn 1995).

The Spaces of the Archive

Library and Archives Canada has the most extensive collection of government documents on "the Japanese problem." These documents were part of the bureaucratic machinery that officials used to remove Japanese Canadians from British Columbia and expel thousands from Canada. Masses of documents, many now frail and faded, stored in boxes catalogued according to the government departments, committees, and officials that produced them, were opened to the public, most by 1979, thirty years after the camps closed (Sunahara and Wright 1979). Although staff at the archives created a catalogue for researchers working on the case for redress during the 1980s, the extent of all the documents pertaining to Japanese Canadians is still unknown.

The files contain everything from lists of building supplies to letters written by Japanese Canadian women requesting the release of their husbands, sons, and fathers from prisoner-of-war camps, minutes of various government meetings, monthly Royal Canadian Mounted Police (RCMP) reports on the health and conduct of internees, and petitions submitted by Japanese Canadians to protest the sale of their properties. There are also notable absences. For example, the RCMP reports on the camps rarely included lists of the internees who died, were born, left the camps, were married, or were hired, fired, or laid off by the British Columbia Security Commission (BCSC).

Visiting the archives is a strange experience, somewhat like a pilgrimage into the catacombs of what was once terrifying power.[2] I conducted research for this project in the pre-digital age and had to consult the archive's directories to identify the government offices responsible for administrating "the Japanese problem." After selecting what looked like a promising set of records from a particular department or parliamentary committee, I needed to fill in a form to order them. It could take the archive staff several days to retrieve and declassify the files, which were stored in government buildings throughout the Ottawa-Hull region.

I always felt as if I were following the path of Japanese Canadian redress activists, who were the first to search through the masses of records, piecing together evidence for their case in the 1980s. I thought of them, having no time to ponder the small bits of illumination they found buried among these files as they forged onward, looking for the evidence to prove that Mackenzie King's cabinet had violated the rights of Japanese Canadians, not for the sake of national security but because of racist conceptions of Canadian citizenship.

In my search of the archives, I found documents scattered across the records of different departments and government offices that placed New Denver within a larger geography of interrelated sites and activities. For the BCSC, one of the significant features of New Denver was its geographic relation to the other camps in British Columbia. The government reconfigured the province's isolated mountainous terrain into a series of "natural prisons" for Japanese Canadians. At the same time, the isolated mountainous terrain was the province's economic hinterland: the source of fuel wood, lumber, and mineral ores. Sawmills, logging companies, road construction operations, and orchards in these regions were experiencing labour shortages. Government reports indicate that Japanese

Canadian internees were sent to this hinterland not only because it was geo-graphically isolated but also because they could fill labour shortages (BCSC 1942, 18; see also Oikawa 1986).

The New Denver camp was one of eight internment camps for "dependent Japanese." Most of the camps, including New Denver, were located in old mining towns built in the West Kootenays. The BCSC used the old buildings in former mining towns to house some internees. In other cases, the BCSC hired crews of Japanese Canadian men to build "housing centres" – rows of flimsy shacks on leased farmland (BCSC 1942, 12).

Each government-run camp had a town supervisor who was responsible to the head office of the BCSC. The BCSC's duties included organizing the removal of Japanese Canadians from the coastal area, implementing programs to provide them with employment and housing, and administering social welfare pro-grams (Sunahara 1981, 53). When the "evacuation" was completed, the com-mission's powers reverted to the minister of labour on 5 February 1943. On this date, a commissioner of Japanese placement was designated to administer "the Japanese problem" in Canada (BCSC 1942, 13). In addition, "Occidental" welfare officers were located in each camp with a staff of Japanese Canadian social workers. Employment offices were set up to find work placements for Japanese Canadians. Only those who were considered unemployable or unable to obtain employment were given maintenance payments (ibid.). In 1943, the employment officers increasingly sought to find placements outside of the province, for example, in Ontario, increasing the movement of Japanese Can-adians, especially those in their early twenties, out of British Columbia (see Oikawa 1986).

The operation of the camps was a massive task. With over twelve thousand Japanese Canadians living in the camps, "thousands of cords of fuel wood were required. It was necessary to install or repair lighting systems and waterworks, and to build and equip schools and hospitals." Internees were hired as construc-tion and maintenance workers, nurses, cooks, clerks, and doctors (Canada, Department of Labour 1978, 10-11).

The RCMP as well as the British Columbia Provincial Police carried out various duties connected to the internment camps. Orders first from the BCSC and then from the Department of Labour were enforced mostly by the RCMP. The commissioner of the RCMP authorized several permanent detachments at strategic places to monitor Japanese Canadians. Strict observations were kept on their movements by issuing travel permits, on the grounds that it was "not deemed desirable that the Japanese shall be permitted to wander at will throughout the country" (BCSC 1942, 16). Since the "settlements are situated in mountainous valleys from which the only outlets are by a few roads ... the Royal Mounted Canadian Police established road blocks at which special guards check all passersby" (Canada, Department of Labour 1978, 11). Yet, given the proximity of the camps to one other in the Slocan Valley, the RCMP occasionally gave internees permission to visit nearby camps to see relatives and friends or attend special events such as funerals and baseball games. RCMP officers made monthly reports for each camp, documenting the fluctuation in the number of men, women, and children in the camps, reflecting the numbers of deaths, births, and transfers in and out of the camps. The officers also recorded statistics regarding the employment and health of the internees and made notes about incidents such as fires, "delinquent behaviour," or large social events (RCMP 1944).

What follows is the government's description of the New Denver camp. This is an excerpt from the report "Removal of Japanese from the Protected Area" (1942).

Interior Housing Projects
New Denver
Japanese Population: 1505

New Denver is situated in the east side of Slocan Lake, midway between the Kootenay and Arrow Lakes in the Upper Columbia River Basin. It has an altitude of 1,700 feet, with temperatures ranging from 90 degrees in the summer to sometimes 20 degrees below zero in the winter. It is well adapted to mixed farming, gardening and the cultivation of berries and fruits. Of the original white population of several thousand, only 350 remain and the place of the former residents has now been taken by Japanese evacuees.

A well equipped local hospital serves the needs of the whole adjacent district and the Commission is building a sanatorium for the hospitalization of TB cases which will accommodate 100 patients.

The New Denver Evacuation Area extends from the Harris Ranch on the south, to the old town of Rosebery on the north, a distance of about 16 miles. The 80-acre Harris Ranch has been leased by the Commission and 27 acres have already been put under cultivation. A total of 275 homes have been built for the Japanese, of the type of construction mentioned previously [14 × 28, built of rough lumber and tar paper], 31 of them being designed for two-family groups and 244 for single families only. Bath houses (an important item in Japanese life) have been erected to serve the needs of the whole community and water connections are in the process of being laid to all sections of the area controlled by the Commission ...

When it is completed, all Japanese will get their water supply from conveniently situated stand pipes. Electricity is being supplied as quickly as possible and this work, together with that of laying water mains and cutting and hauling the very large supply of firewood necessary for the fairly severe winter, will keep the male Japanese population busy for some time to come (BCSC 1942, 22-23).

Few government documents list the difficulties of living in internment camps. But descriptions of harsh living conditions sometimes surface in documents such as the "Report of the Royal Commission to Enquire into the Provisions Made for the Welfare and Maintenance of Persons of the Japanese Race Resident in Settlements in the Province of British Columbia." This document responds to concerns made by Japanese Camp Committees, the official representatives of the internees in each camp. Although the report does not include the names of the members of the committees, it does provide insight into living conditions by listing the following concerns raised by the Camp Committees:

1 That the maintenance rates for indigent Japanese are insufficient to buy adequate food at prevailing prices;
2 That houses are overcrowded, unsafe during winter weather, and unsuited to severe climatic conditions;
3 That the supply of fuel is inefficiently distributed and of inferior quality;
4 That there is unreasonable delay in supplying needed clothing and shoes to families on maintenance;
5 That the health of the people is adversely affected by inadequate housing and insufficient food and that this has resulted in increased illness and malnutrition of children;
6 That there is a lack of facilities for indoor recreation during winter months, especially for children. (Jackson et al. 1944, 3)

To assess living conditions in the camps, the report compares the conditions in the camps to Japanese Canadians' "pre-evacuation" living conditions, health, and employment opportunities. The report suggests that the conditions in the camps did not differ greatly from their pre-war living conditions; it ignores the loss of liberty, the liquidation of property, and the separation of families, never mind the poor food, the inadequate shelter, and the province's initial refusal to provide schooling for the children. The report concludes that, given wartime shortages and the fact that the camps were a "temporary means of meeting an emergency," the BCSC should be commended for its accomplishments and recommends only minor improvements to the camps. To support its conclusions, the report notes that numerous Japanese Canadians made unofficial submissions that disputed the claims made by the Camp Committees and claimed that living conditions were satisfactory. There are no records of these submissions or of the identities of the individuals said to have made them.

With the distance of years, we can view such unofficial submissions in another light. If they did in fact exist, they revealed stresses and conflicts between internees in a situation of extreme uncertainty and fear. Although Camp Committees and other groups managed to reach a consensus on the strategies for addressing their situation, not everyone agreed. Some feared that any request, no matter how reasonable, would have detrimental results (as it did for the Nisei Mass Evacuation Group who asked the government not to separate the men from their families in the camps). Others refused to cooperate at any level. *A Man of Our Times: The Life-History of a Japanese-Canadian Fisherman,* the biography of Ryuichi Yoshida, a fisherman and labour union activist, is one of the few accounts by an issei man that provides descriptions of some of these schisms, conflicts, and breaches of trust. Yoshida recounts that

each camp had troubles among the Japanese themselves. We had a Japanese fore-man for each camp. Foremen understood English and followed the supervisor's advice on managing each camp. In Roseberry [sic; a camp five miles north of New Denver] the foreman was hated and there was a continuous change of fore-men. Some people thought it was better if they didn't follow any advice from the government. They even declined to do things that were beneficial to them [e.g., building a water system or cutting wood]. I was the foreman in charge of cutting down trees for firewood ... But these people insulted me all the time, so I quit. (Knight and Koizumi 1976, 78)

Conflicts increased when the Canadian government started the "repatriation plan," whereby people remaining in the camps had to choose between being sent to eastern Canada or to Japan. Because Yoshida and ten other Japanese Canadians in Rosebery believed that Japan would be defeated, they tried to dissuade people from leaving Canada.

I was called a betrayer and a traitor. People threw rocks at our house and insulted us on the street. It is impossible to describe the amount of hate there was toward us. [When Japan was defeated, we] ... tried to convince them not to sign [the repatriation papers]. We said that Japan would be in very hard times and it would be better if they stayed here. Some still did not believe that. Others were so angry with all the discrimination that they would not listen. I think most issei signed those repatriation papers at first. The nisei, not very many signed ... After the war ended, there was a big turmoil. People began to think more clearly and there were many people who wanted to cancel their signatures for repatriation. So we hired two influential white lawyers and started a cancel movement ... At New Denver and Roseberry over half those who signed ... finally cancelled. In the meantime, most of the younger people – most of the nisei – were sent to the east. (Ibid. 1976, 81-82)

Many people chose Japan because they feared the discrimination would be worse in central Canada and, having no economic or social connections there, felt that the prospect of rebuilding their lives in unknown, predominantly French- and English-speaking environments was too daunting. Many others, after three years of internment, with all of their assets liquidated, felt betrayed by their government and were confused, angry, scared, and desperate. TB Pickersgill, who was selected to coordinate the repatriation survey, noted in correspondence to Mr. A McNamara, deputy minister of labour, that

> one of the principal factors encouraging repatriation [shipment to Japan], seems to be that voluntary repatriates will be kept in British Columbia. Another [factor] ... encouraging repatriation has been the reaction in the other provinces to our announcement. They have repeatedly raised the question of the unfavourable reaction in other provinces to permanent settlement in those provinces ... I stated to [concerned Japanese Canadians] quite frankly that this bad reaction was fairly universal across the country and undoubtedly it would make conditions more difficult for the Japanese taking employment in those provinces (Pickersgill 1945b).

According to Sunahara, Pickersgill supposedly disapproved of the repatriation policy but thought it was better that someone such as himself take the job rather than someone who was "sadistic" and "carried it out to the letter" (1981, 118). But his correspondence illustrates how administrators such as Pickersgill also fed the anxieties of Japanese Canadians, making their removal from Canada seem like the safest option.

Those who chose to "voluntarily repatriate" were allowed to continue working or to take up new positions in British Columbia until they were shipped out of Canada, in contrast to those waiting to be relocated elsewhere in the country. Many assumed that, even if they signed up for Japan, they would eventually be permitted to stay in BC and so given the opportunity to continue working, especially since many feared becoming destitute, this is what they did. Another incentive for those who signed up to be shipped to Japan was free transportation and repatriation grants that ensured they had funds up to a maximum of two hundred dollars per adult and fifty dollars per child (Canada, Department of Labour 1947, 14).

There are now many romanticized images of internment camps as places of identity where internees shared a collective life (see, for example, Watada 1997 and Shimizu 2008). But documents in Library and Archives Canada as well as historical studies reveal the actual instability of the camps, from which young single female and male nisei flowed to work placements in central Canada. The government constantly separated, reunited, and separated internees yet again from their families and kin groups as they were transferred between camps and work placements. One of the biggest disruptions occurred when the government began to reorganize the camps in preparation for the shipment of "repatriates" to Japan and the removal of the rest to other provinces in Canada. The government "segregated" "the repatriates" from the "loyal" Canadians. As described in the Introduction, those who remained in British Columbia – the "incurables" – were moved to New Denver. The government sent those who were moving to central Canada to Kaslo. Those who were being shipped to Japan were sent to Rosebery, Slocan, Lemon Creek, and Greenwood (Pickersgill 1945b). Like the earlier separation of women and men, family members, kin and social groups, and community leaders, this segregation had a devastating social impact. Families were again split apart. Members going to central Canada were separated from those being shipped to Japan (or who were signed on with their parents). The decision to segregate "repatriates" in different camps was politically motivated. In response to a request from Mr. Collins, the commissioner of Japanese placement, for advice on the removal of Japanese Canadians from British Columbia, R.A. Davidson stated that segregation "will break these Japanese up, preventing them from gathering in groups and discussing the pros and cons of the War and of the affairs of Japanese in Canada, thus avoiding much unrest and dissension" (Davidson 1944).

Although government records and historical studies outline the implementation of policies that crossed provincial and national borders, as well as providing some insights into the impact of these measures on internees, they say little about the damaging psychological and social effects, especially across generations. Here, Yoshida's account is informative. He makes seemingly incidental references to his and Mrs. Yoshida's increasingly troubled daughter, their only child. His references are noteworthy insofar as one would not expect an issei man to make extensive references to his children, especially a daughter, as he presents his life history. Nor would one expect him to make comments about what might seem like the small details of growing up. But to read his text is to realize that these comments register a loss of connection to his daughter and, subsequently, the loss of his daughter's control over her own life.

Throughout the text, the daughter appears as a source of anxiety, first as a child who liked "to play more than study." Later, in the Rosebery camp, where "it was a carefree life" for young men and women, Yoshida and his wife "used to worry about her association with boyfriends." He recollects that when she used nail polish for the first time, he was very angry and threw the bottle away because he thought it was "too sultry." He reflects, though, that "it was not even red polish, it was natural colour" (Knight and Koizumi 1976, 80). Finally, at the conclusion of his life history, we realize that his anxiety foreshadows the sad life of his daughter in Vancouver after the war. He notes she had a miscarriage and, later, that her twenty-year-old son died of an unknown cause. He states that his daughter was "very shocked" and "lost for a little while." Although he states that they feel she "has recovered herself," he describes her as very nervous and notes how "she goes to the horse races and spends all the money she earns" (ibid., 94). Typically, Japanese Canadian families try to hide members who have "vices" such as gambling or who suffer from long-term illnesses, especially mental illness. The fact that the Yoshidas' only progeny was a daughter who lost her children and subsequently her wits represents a tragic end.

My analysis of government records in this section, alongside historical studies that register some of the intergenerational after-effects, especially Yoshida's life history, outlines a space of internment that was produced discursively by government bureaucracies in the 1940s. It presents a radically different space of internment than what is imagined today as a space to be reclaimed as, on the one hand, a site of remembrance and mourning and, on the other, a space of identity for postwar generations. This space was orchestrated to segregate and control the interpersonal and political relations of internees and their movement and communication across a series of places normally under local, provincial, national, and international jurisdiction. To remove all people of Japanese "racial descent" from British Columbia, the federal government reconfigured these jurisdictions into a series of interconnected sites to isolate and break apart the social and institutional bonds of pre-war life. Rather than static spaces, the internment camps were spaces of movement and, in particular, sites of transit, through which individuals were transferred as they were forced out of the province and the country (see Oikawa 1986). In these documents, it is difficult to find out much about how Japanese Canadians experienced and viewed these events. But it is possible to read historical studies analytically in the context of wartime documents written by Japanese Canadians and camp committees, government reports, and accounts by internees such as Yoshida who were adults in the camps. As these former internees pass on, their recorded oral accounts, diaries, photographs, letters, and publications in community newspapers become one of the few means to gain insight into their views and experiences as well as the damaging after-effects that have been transmitted across generations.

In the next section, I examine how the Nikkei Internment Memorial Centre constitutes the space of internment.

The Space of Maps

What remains of the massive deployment of government resources to remove thousands of Canadians of "Japanese racial origin" from British Columbia? The Canadian government swiftly removed the evidence. As soon as the Department of Labour closed the camps, it dismantled the rows of leaking shacks built to house the uprooted women, men, and children. It returned whatever it appropriated from local residents, including buildings and tracts of land, in its "original condition" to the "original owners." The special committees, commissions, and departmental divisions established to administrate the "Japanese problem" were dissolved, and their documents disappeared into the vaults of the national archives under the protection of the Privacy Act for the next thirty years.[3]

But not all documents were sent to the National Archives of Canada (now Library and Archives Canada). Many were lost or destroyed, such as the records in the former Sanatorium that Mrs. Inose feared had been thrown out by the new Pavillion staff. In the national archives, every so often one comes across hastily written memos that indicate the extent of what has been destroyed. A memo typed on 19 February 1948 from Commissioner J.F. MacKinnon to E.R. Adams in New Denver briefly states: "Don't you think that about 99 percent of the material you have in your files in Slocan could be destroyed? I would appreciate your comments on this." One wonders what made it necessary to destroy these files. Was the information viewed as superfluous or perhaps, by 1948, when civil rights groups started to protest the treatment of Japanese Canadians, potentially incriminating? What made the 1 percent worthy of being saved? Would it be possible to extrapolate the contents of the 99 percent from the 1 percent? Was the 1 percent practice a policy for all records? Many of the records made by internees – lists of internees in each camp, minutes of meetings, diaries, letters, and photographs – have also been lost or were left behind as the internees were forced to move between camps, provinces, and countries. Moreover, censors restricted what they could record. "The Details of Information and Instructions To Internees' Family [sic]," stated:

> Letters must not be long, must be legibly written ... Do not have suspicious or objectionable drawings or pictures. Must not have reference to the operation of war. Should be written in English where possible ... PROHIBITED ARTICLES: Cigarette papers, all medicine, printed matter and photographs, money ... stationary and stamps, pen and ink, radio, inflammable materials, liquor ... books dealing

with politics, wireless, explosive weapons, chemistry lithography, spying, geography or maps. Second hand books except those donated by recognized charitable organizations. (Canada n.d.)

In the face of this massive loss of material, former internees and members of the postwar generation, including artists, writers, and filmmakers, have returned to New Denver in an attempt to re-imagine the camps, to make inventories of the infrastructure and daily operations, to understand the indignities and humiliation, to learn about the inventive cultural tactics that were used to create temporary home spaces: to map the space of internment. They are all involved in different forms of mapping: delineating the borders of containment and freedom, drawing the routes of movement between camps, and identifying the different zones of activity and the hierarchically arranged spaces of power. Mapping, then, can be viewed as a trope for the broader process of "memory work" (Kuhn 1995).

Maps conceptually organize the world as a space that is to be traversed, a world of paths, passages, routes, dead ends, detours through and around zones coded as accessible and inaccessible, safe and dangerous, for consumption and for production.[4] They create a space conceived in terms of potential movement: destinations and points of departure, a "here" and an "over there." The space is abstracted from complex terrains of shifting, dissonant, and intersecting layers of econo-geological, bio-historical, socio-ecological activities. Relevant features are selected, transfigured into symbols, and then reordered and reproportioned to fit into a coherent scheme: a "systematically organized design ... [or] classification" (*Penguin English Dictionary*, 1982).

Through mapping, space becomes inhabited: inculcated with habitual actions, habits of mind, and habits of measurement (Bourdieu 1991). This process enacts a space as a circumscribed set of movements. It is not only a practical terrain but also an imaginary one active in the body-memory of those who have inhabited that place, even if it has long since changed, as will be evident in the examination of George Doi's memory map of internment camps presented later in this chapter. For the reader of the map, it is a terrain imagined even as it has not yet been inhabited in the manner prescribed by the map, as I will argue is the case for the tourist reading the NIMC's map of the New Denver camp. To read a map is to be situated in that space, to move along its paths, passages, and routes. For all of this activity, the map does not feature people. Yet they are not absent. Their presence, as I will argue, is not only evident in the travel routes and settlements coded into its cartographic plane but also implied in its perspective or vantage point. Maps organize their readers around vantage points. In this section, I examine the vantage point of different maps of internment camps, exploring how they situate the reader in their scheme of things: the way the reader is to inhabit the camp according to its "systematically organized design."

Using the terms set out by the map, to locate oneself in or to move between zones involves difference/differentiation: the spatial relationships distinguish each location from the rest. Although these relationships are abstractly conceived in the map, the difference is never based on purely abstract measurements. It is based on the underlying scheme: an organized design with parameters set by the technologies and territories of its making, whether it is a recent geological survey map, a map of a sixteenth-century battlefield or, as I will discuss, maps of mid-twentieth-century internment camps. Within these schemata, the movement of a subject from one location to another either conforms to the order imposed by the map or transgresses the hierarchical organization of space, reconfiguring the imposed order, which can eventually result in a new map, like George Doi's memory map.

As long as there is a drive to order constantly changing multi-layered terrains into new schemata, new maps will be made, incorporating temporal changes, whether registered at socio-political, geomorphological or metaphysical levels. As new maps are made, earlier ones typically lose their utility or are transformed into other types of documents. While there are highly specialized maps that track the passage of geological and political time, in most maps, time remains static. The time of most maps is "empty time": its passage leaves no traces (Bakhtin 1981, 110). It characterizes the chronotope that Mikhail Bakhtin associates with the literary genre of Greek romance.

> The homogenization of all that is heterogeneous in a Greek romance ... a homogenization that results in a huge, almost encyclopedic genre, is achieved only at the cost of the most extreme abstraction, schematization and a denuding of all that is concrete and merely local ... The most abstract of all chronotopes is the most static. In such a chronotope the world and all individuals are finished items, absolutely immobile. In it there is no potential for evolution, for growth, for change. (Bakhtin 1981, 110)

Empty time is the temporal order of a map in use. To inhabit a terrain in the manner prescribed by a map requires the reader to enter a kind of empty time: the unchanged time of whatever "now" the map circumscribes. It is an imagined order that eludes the passage of time – notably organic time, which entails a change in the space itself as well as the transformation of the self. This is what makes maps intriguing, although in some cases it makes them destructive technologies used to engineer new social orders. To sustain the space of this imagery order, maps attempt to lock the reader in one temporal vantage point, producing a very particular type of subject.

In the modern regime of cartography, this subject is inculcated with the standardized language of maps (see Blackmore 1986a, 42-43). If a particular map fails to cohere with that standardized language, a dissonance or "noise" creates "confusion or misunderstanding" for this subject, as will be evident in the following discussion of the NIMC map (Blackmore 1986b, 43). But the relation between the language of maps and its subject is not simply a matter of (in)coherence. As instruments designed to (re)order a terrain into a coherent scheme, modern maps are one of many apparatuses that constitute particular types of subjects. Because subjects are predominantly organized around one scheme rather than others, they might be confused by a map's attempt to reconfigure their relation to a terrain. They might be puzzled by lacunae and by what is relegated to the margins of the map. They might marvel at or be perplexed by how the map integrates their land in a foreign network of activities: in peculiar forms of movement needing foreign technologies and knowledge, for instance, of star navigation, a GPS, or a gas-fuelled car, that knit them into new emotive and practical ways of moving within space between places they would never otherwise view as destinations or points of departure and through zones they would never have considered traversing.

Despite the effort to impose a singular scheme, every map is full of temporal ambivalences. Routes, nomenclature, and sites of settlements recall others no longer present. Even if forcibly removed, they can never be completely erased from the landscape (Crosby 1991). Traces of their worlds can be read even in contemporary maps: settlements that began as trading posts with long-gone inhabitants, towns that resonate with the memory of labour camps, the geo-cultural time-marking terrain formed by the movement of glaciers (Cruickshank 2005; Hirsch and Spitzer 2006). These other worlds and their inhabitants must be managed so that they do not disrupt the coherence of the dominant scheme. The ability to minimize their presence depends on the skill of the cartographer versus the will of an undisciplined reader. The ghostly presence of inhabitants of worlds consumed by the changing landscape is most pronounced in out-of-date maps. These maps present a temporal disjuncture, like the maps of the internment camps from the 1940s that I will examine here, since the way they order the landscape is distinct from how we order our contemporary terrains. But maps of no-longer-existing places can nevertheless still be used to fix contemporary landscapes in static, idealized forms as sites of origin, whether homeland or holocaust. "Noise" that introduces unwanted complexity and confusion is removed.

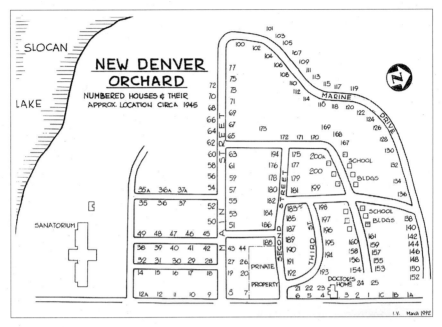

2.4 "New Denver Orchard": The Nikkei Memorial Internment Centre's map of the internment camp, 1992. *Courtesy of the Nikkei Internment Memorial Centre.*

The NIMC map (see Figure 2.4) attempts to fix the space of internment in a static, idealized form, removing noise that will distract those who are assumed to be its readers. It removes traces of the ways in which different subjects have ordered, inhabited, and imagined the site over time. Because I am interested in exploring the internment camp's changing terrain of memory, I am interested in this noise and have thus turned to maps produced at various times for different purposes by different map-makers, each with distinct schemata.

For visitors who were not incarcerated and know little about Japanese Canadian history, the remains of the camp in the Orchard are not evident. To make their outlines visible to these visitors, the NIMC presents them with a map of the camp when they enter the memorial. This map authenticates the Orchard as the site of the New Denver internment camp. "Yes, the site where we are now standing was where over 1,500 Japanese Canadians were interned. Here we are." The NIMC attendant traces her finger over the map, locating where the NIMC would be in the former internment camp. It reorients visitors, locating them in the space of internment. The map delineates the dimensions of the camp within a rectangular piece of white paper with neat lines tracing roads and administrative buildings. It locates landmarks, still visible today, such as the

Pavilion and service roads, fixing the camp in place. This is a particular version of the space of internment, one that I will argue evacuates the remains that are still potent and alive, whether rotting in internment shacks, buried in gardens, still growing in old gnarled fruit trees, and proliferating in the poppies of Mr. and Mrs. Matsushita's fanciful garden.

In what follows, I provide a critical analysis of the space of internment that the NIMC map produces. First, though, I will examine other maps that present the vantage points, routes, and activities of the internees and administrators who drew and requisitioned them during and after the war. Their rich detail shows how the NIMC map, by contrast, reifies the site. The NIMC map presents a neat, abstracted space of internment within clearly delineated borders. Positioning the visitor in this space produces her or him as a particular type of subject: what I will argue is a tourist, a subject who seeks to consume easily identifiable evidence.

At the NIMC, I came across photocopies of five maps produced during the 1940s: the "Map of Rosebery," "F.C. Harris Ranch: New Denver, BC," "Nelson's Ranch: New Denver, BC," "Map of Greenwood," and "Japanese Residential Area: The City of Sandon." They are displayed in the historical exhibit in the Kyowakai Hall with an array of black-and-white photographs presenting panoramic views of the internment camps. The memorial had little information in their acquisition records about who made these maps or their original purpose, other than to suggest they might have been made for the BCSC. Their labels indicate that the maps were copies from the library at Selkirk College in nearby Castlegar. When I contacted Judy Deon, one of the librarians at the college, she informed me that they had large-format photocopies of the maps, not the originals. She spent several weeks searching for information, but even with the help of former librarians who were familiar with earlier acquisitions she was unable to find anything about the donors or map-makers. After consulting other local archives, she discovered that the Nelson City Archives had copies of the same five maps, as does the Japanese Canadian National Museum in Burnaby. None had the originals. The archivist in Nelson also wondered if they had been made for the BCSC.

As is frequently the case with archival documents, the information that would have rendered the maps more precisely meaningful has been lost. When the maps were donated, someone might have failed to record this valuable information, or the donor might have known little about the maps, perhaps finding them in a rummage sale or inheriting them from a distant relative. Whoever made copies of the maps for the NIMC in the early 1990s recorded only the barest sketch of the information available at Selkirk College, not even noting whether the original donor was known. With the passage of time, institutional knowledge about the existence of the originals has faded. For all the searches I have made through government records in the national archives, I have never come across these maps, although I recall finding a large map of the Tashme camp. Perhaps another researcher will recognize them and identify where they are located in Ottawa's labyrinth. But, rather than waiting in the hope of finding details that might definitively reveal the identities of the map-makers and their purpose, it is important to write about the maps. While these details, as far as we know, did not survive, the fact is that the maps did. This is the reality of many archival documents. While we should not give up the search for more information, we can still examine what these documents can tell us by using a method of analysis that takes advantage of the questions arising from the missing information. It is a method that constantly problematizes whatever dares announce itself as the final, concrete conclusion about the past. This uncertainty keeps open the possibility of other ways of understanding the past and, in this case, spaces of internment.

With this approach in mind, it is possible to inspect these maps for clues about their production and use. Tiny trembles in the calligraphic titles and the slightly rumpled contour lines betray traces of the penmanship of the map-makers: two Japanese Canadians. Ichiro Roy Matsui is identified as the map-maker of the Greenwood and Sandon maps, and Ken Saito is identified as the map-maker of the Harris Ranch and Nelson Ranch maps. Similar stylistic details suggest that Saito also made the Rosebery map. I was able to find only one reference to the map-makers: Roy Yasui mentions a Ken Saito who was interned in New Denver and told children frightening campfire stories (Yasui 2006). The care the map-makers have taken to design the titles in large, stylized block lettering, prominently placed either at the top or, in the case of the Rosebery map, in the centre, obscuring part of the camp itself, betrays an attachment to the camps. The titles embellish the camps' identities, especially those on land leased from private owners, such as the Harris Ranch camp, which is lettered in an Old English style. This suggests that, for the map-makers, these sites had identities linked to that of the owners (the Harris family, for example) or, perhaps more broadly, to the province as a former British colony and Canada as part of the Commonwealth. In addition to their ability to write in flawless English, this shows they were fluent in the meanings of the province's cultural landscape, making it likely that both were either born or raised in Canada.

Matsui and Saito could have traced and enlarged the maps from pre-existing contour maps. But perhaps not. The way they precisely located the newly constructed internment buildings using formal mapping conventions such as scales and compass orientations suggests that five of the maps could have been surveyed. These maps share similar design features such as symbols and characters as well as layouts, suggesting they were made for the same purpose and, thus, organization, which, as the Nelson archivist and the NIMC records suggest, is likely the BCSC. Although only the Sandon map has a date, October 1942, because the maps were made by the same map-makers and share a similar style and design, it is possible to assume that they were all made in the same period. In 1942, the BCSC would have completed the construction of most of the camps, although there were still a number of internees living in tents (Yasui 2006). Thus, it makes sense that the BCSC decided to map the camps' facilities and locate them on the land the government had leased from private owners.

The speculation that the maps were produced for the BCSC is supported by a number of facts. First, the government prohibited Japanese Canadians from possessing and making maps. Even if Saito and Matsui managed to produce these large-scale maps secretly, what would be the purpose? It would have been a risky as well as expensive hobby. Government fears about espionage were untenable since the time, space, and resources required to make the maps would hardly allow them to be secretive. In fact, it would have been difficult to produce the maps without support and resources from the BCSC. They would have needed not only time and large, smooth surfaces in well-lit, dry rooms but also access to local information about, for example, private property lines. In addition, they would have needed specialized supplies, such as large sheets of paper and cartographic instruments. Thus, it is likely that the BCSC hired the map-makers along with the other nisei it employed to run the camps.

A close inspection of the Rosebery map (there was no BCSC map of the Orchard in New Denver in the NIMC's historical collection) shows how the camp was situated in relation to geographic features (see Figure 2.5). The largest section of housing is positioned along the shoreline of Slocan Lake on an alluvial plain, south of Wilson Creek and west of the railway. The other, smaller section of housing is located north of the creek and parallel to the highway. This layout would have made it possible for RCMP officers, administrators, and staff to quickly locate each section of housing as well as the transport routes that could not only deliver shipments of supplies and enforcement officers but also bring internees in and out of the camp.

The housing along the lakeshore is divided into "Field no. 1" and "Field no. 2," with a straight line drawn between that suggests a property line. Segments of land titled "private property" in the camps, along with "old buildings" such as the "Rosebery Hotel" situated north along the railway, identify the presence of other residents and local activities. The clearly demarcated property lines and the identification of old buildings on the map indicates that the government operated the camps in coordination with privately owned land as well as the activities of the local population. In other words, the camps were

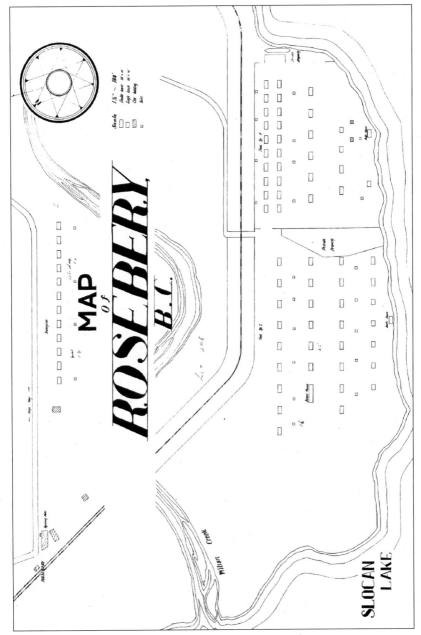

2.5 Map of the Rosebery internment camp, British Columbia, n.d. *Ken Saito. Courtesy of Selkirk College, BC.*

integrated into the ongoing economic activities and movements of local inhabitants rather than being strictly isolated from them.

The map presents the camp as an ordered space by identifying where internees slept, ate, and bathed, so that anyone who was unfamiliar with the camp, such as a new RCMP officer or government official, would have been able to quickly find the location of the camp and identify the location and activities of its subjects. Small rectangles identify "double houses" and "single homes," which are laid out uniformly in straight lines, parallel to the lakeshore and the railway. Small squares that identify toilets are regularly distributed in lines between every two housing units. A school/house is also included in Field no. 2. This layout allows the map-reader to identify the infrastructure necessary for running the camp: housing, human waste disposal, training and (re-)socializing children, and so on. Again, this suggests a map reader who is responsible for managing the population, rather than someone who is living in the camp.

In contrast to these BCSC maps, the other map I found in the memorial's historical collection was a sketch of the Slocan Valley. With its wavering lines and notes, it is clearly hand drawn. George Doi, a nisei, reconstructed the map from memory in March 1993 (see Figure 2.6). The NIMC had a copy from the Japanese Canadian National Museum in Burnaby. To identify each camp in the Slocan Valley, Mr. Doi has drawn wooden signposts on short stakes, hammered into the ground, which give a folksy, country-style feel. The map includes an insert that features a detailed three-dimensional view of the camps at the south end of Slocan Lake: Popoff, Bayfarm, and Slocan City. Mr. Doi roughly sketched in landscape features such as forests and bluffs. These features situate the map reader in the valley, as if on a hill looking northward, up the valley toward the distant lake. The map reader can imagine her- or himself in the camp, as she or he looks up at the steep cliffs of "Mickey's Bluff." With details such as "Taishoda's Drug Store," "Fuki Plants," and "Kids Ski Hill," the map reader is introduced to the identities and activities of people in the camp as members of a community. The camps are spatially organized around the activities of these people, whether it is the ski hill where kids play in the winter, the drugstore run by Mr. Taishoda where essentials like soap could be purchased, the sawmill where some of the internees likely worked, or "the Johnson's Farm" and "Johnson's Apartments," both of which the government seems to have leased.

In some cases, the significance of the features will be evident only to internees. For example, I remember my first trip to visit the internment camps with a bus tour of former internees (McAllister 1994). As we approached Slocan, everyone rose, exclaiming, "The fuki! Look at the fuki!" Like a wild herd of green-blue mythical creatures, the plants emerged from the edge of the forest, their large leaves waving whimsically in unison with each gust of wind. Clearly, the fuki

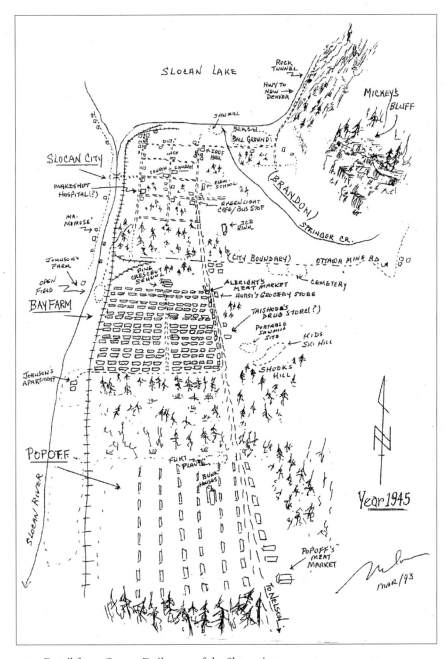

2.6 Detail from George Doi's map of the Slocan internment camps, 1993.
Courtesy of the Japanese Canadian National Museum.

was meaningful for them, not just as an edible plant but also as a plant they remembered gathering, cooking, and turning into meals. The fact that the plants were flourishing fifty years after the internees left seemed to suggest that more than their memories survived: the fuki embodied the communal life of the camp, which had, like the bonds between former internees, survived.

Thus, by including details such as "Fuki plants" as well as specific names of buildings, such as "Pine Crescent School" rather than simply "School House," as per the BCSC map, Mr. Doi's map suggests that the intended map reader might be a former internee who is familiar with these places. Moreover, written in English, many of the places on this map suggest a nisei child's or youth's perspective: "Beach" and "Ball Ground" suggest a nostalgic longing for places that no longer exist along the shores of Slocan Lake. The space of internment in this map is now one that is imagined, but not just as a fleeting image. It is one that is shared by other Japanese Canadians who remember their youth in the camps. They now live across Canada and, in some cases, in Japan, many regularly returning to the sites where they were interned to enact this nostalgic "sense of place" (Massey 1993).

There is one other map in the memorial's historical collections: a detailed map produced by Mr. Senya Mori, an elder who lived in New Denver for over fifty years. Unlike former internees who return to the sites where they were interned, Mori never left New Denver. He continued to live there over the years. Mr. Senya Mori was a community leader both for the Japanese Canadian community and for the Village of New Denver. His map is very large, at least one metre square. He taped together many sheets of heavy paper and carefully drew in all he could remember, expanding its size as necessary. I was not granted access to this map. He had loaned it to the Kyowakai Society's History Preservation Committee, and the terms of use had not yet been specified. Even a preliminary peek was not possible since the chair of the committee did not want to risk damaging the original before she had devised a way to copy it for researchers to use.

Mr. Senya Mori's map, to my knowledge, was the only original map in the memorial's historical collections. All but Mr. Senya Mori's map are copies. As black-and-white photocopied images, they tell us nothing about the marks of inscription, the quality of the ink, the force with which the lines were pressed into the paper, the texture and smell of the paper. In contrast, Mr. Senya Mori's map – in view of its large size, non-standard measurements, and the way it is taped together – is difficult to photocopy without damaging it. And, given its dimensions, if one were to shrink it down into a size that could be easily displayed along with the other maps, the details would be too small to read. Reproduction could be accomplished only by copying its sections and then reassembling and taping them back together. Because his map is incompatible with the standardized terms of reproduction as well as display, it was unclear whether, under the protective care of the history preservation chair, researchers would ever be able to view the original. It promised a rich body of information especially because its creator was still alive at the time and could have explained the details. But it had not yet been prised from its social context of use and turned into research data and so, while its meanings are alive and potent, it remained, at least to me, inaccessible, unless I was willing to breech the protocols of both the local community and the History Preservation Committee (Sekula 1999, 183). So, paradoxically, while the elders worried about the disappearance of important historical records that in many cases only they knew about, historical information was being lost because of the desire to protect the original and to respect Mr. Senya Mori's yet-to-be-determined terms of use.

Today, I read both Mr. Doi's and Mr. Senya Mori's maps as acts committed to the past and the future. As an act committed to the past, Mr. Doi's map embraces happy moments of childhood and adolescence that the adults, parents, young teachers, and elders tried to secure for young internees amid the fear, uncertainty, and hopelessness of the camp (Yasui 2006). While I have not seen Mr. Senya Mori's map, I know it presents the camp from his perspective as an adult in New Denver. From the history preservation chair's descriptions of the map, I learned that it captures the social order that men and women attempted to impose onto the unstable space of internment. As acts committed to a future, both maps were made to ensure the camps would be remembered. They add flesh to the grid of everyday living organized by the scheme found in the BCSC maps: the imposed order of the regularly spaced, identical fourteen by twenty-eight rough-plank "double" family shacks (Murdy 1992, 30); evenly distributed outdoor communal "toilets" and bathhouses; zones marked "private property" and, always, the highway into and out of the camps. They give life to the space of internment, achieving a communal (re)organization of the camp by including food stores, cemeteries, and the buildings that housed makeshift churches and schools where community dances and meetings also took place. Mr. Doi's map, and very likely Mr. Senya Mori's, does not conceptualize the camps as isolated spaces. There are directions to the next camps, where undoubtedly cousins, aunts, former neighbours, girlfriends, boyfriends, or members of pre-war debating clubs or prefecture associations were interned. The inclusion of transportation routes – such as highways and railways or geographic features such as Slocan Lake that stretch beyond the margins – suggests a connection to other jurisdictions and links at least some of the internees' activities (the "Sawmill" and "Albright's Meat Market," for example) to economies beyond the borders of the map, suggesting integration into fields of activity not in the camp, including the activities of the RCMP, the Department of Labour, and the wartime economy, even if they are neither explicitly written into Mr. Doi's map or suggested by the way it orients the map reader.

Contrasting the BCSC maps to the memory maps of Mr. Doi and Mr. Senya Mori, it is possible to compare the way the maps orient the map reader in and produce different spaces of internment. Each assumes the reader should have a different relation to the space: whether managing the interned population or nostalgically re-imagining the social life of the camp. With this in mind, I will now examine the map the NIMC uses to orient visitors in the space of internment. But first I will discuss the conventions of mapping in order to more explicitly describe the techniques this map uses to position the map reader.

The Space of the Tourist

The map shown to visitors at the NIMC is not a government map or a memory map. The map shown to visitors was made by someone with the initials I.V. in 1992, most likely someone hired by the NIMC contractors with an employment grant from the federal government (see Figure 2.4). No doubt the map-maker used details from the existing maps and accounts of Japanese Canadian elders. But, even though it was recently made, it is not a memory map. As I will discuss below, its lines were not drawn in an attempt to inscribe the space of internment with the worlds of the internees: it was not an act of memory committed to the past or the future.

As a map made for visitors to the memorial, the NIMC map selects and orders what is necessary for its own scheme. Essentially, the map leaves out what the map-maker considered noise: what for the other map-makers were the intersections and paths that ordered the daily lives of internees, inscribing these places with meaning (Augé 1995), including directions to the next camp and the location of the communal toilets. For the size of the map, it seems strangely empty compared with the densely detailed map made by George Doi. The map centres on the housing in the New Denver internment camp, much like the BCSC maps. It leaves out the town proper. There is no reference to its existence. Yet half a mile from the camp, across Carpenter Creek, the town proper was a central place in the internees' daily lives. In the early days of the camp, over 1,500 internees walked there three times a day for meals at the old skating rink. Once stoves were installed in the shacks and a regular supply of wood was secured, they went to town to purchase food. Among other things, essential services such as the post office, the welfare office, and the administrative offices for the BCSC were located in town.

Unlike the BCSC maps, the NIMC map does not trace the shapes of the shacks in a way that differentiates the various types of housing. Rather, it identifies the shacks by numbers designated by the commission. The map-maker traces the shape of only the following institutions: the Sanatorium, the doctor's house, school buildings, and a section of private property. The numbers of the shacks are arranged around a network of access lanes. Abstracted, the way space is organized does not reflect the internees' orientation and movements in relation to the camp. If it did, it would have identified significant natural landscape features such as the lake and the river, where the internees fetched their supply of water until outdoor standing pumps were installed, one for every four shacks. Nor is there any indication that the shacks were arranged in relation to collectively used buildings such as bathhouses, school buildings, or toilets, leaving out any reference to the social structure of the camp.

The network of access lanes is the main system of organization in the camp, although only four of the twelve are named: Main Street, Second Street, Third Street, and Marine Drive. The network stands out. It is the largest feature, with a heavily marked continuous border. The "numbered houses," also made prominent in the title of the map, are arranged around the network. Note that the "streets" are given more significance than the highway, which is drawn as a discontinuous, narrow, and thus minor street that passes by the eastern border of the camp. It is not named, either as a street or as a highway. The insignificance of the highway creates an internal perspective. It focuses the reader on the internal system of lanes within the camp, with few references to anything beyond the margins. It circumscribes movement along the lanes, from shack to shack, to and from the Sanatorium and school buildings. There is no indication of the possibility of moving in and out of the camps to other camps, cities, provinces, or countries. Implicitly, then, one is left with a sense of the inability to leave: of being contained within an isolated space, even though the camps were integrated into local economies that, for example, supplied other regions with fuel wood and belonged to a series of sites through which Japanese Canadians were transported as they were moved out of the province.

It is difficult to identify this as a map of an internment camp, or even a map of institutional government housing. Its title is simply "New Denver Orchard: Numbered Houses & Their Approx. Location circa 1945." It could easily be a residential area. There is an emphasis on the network of "streets" connecting what the map-maker calls the "houses" together with even and odd numbers on opposite sides of the streets. Like most residential areas, although there are social institutions such as the "school buildings," there is a lack of reference to commercial activities. It is the anomalies that are revealing. For instance, like the BCSC maps, there is a lot designated as "private property." But if this were a residential area, all lots would be private property and there would be no need to identify the lot as such. Except for a few such details, the map appears to be modelled after a residential area, suggesting rather disturbingly that the map-maker was unable to differentiate a site where individuals were incarcerated by the government from a normal civilian space.

To read the map as it was intended, it is important to place it in its context of use, which includes not only the practices of the map-maker but also the intended map readers and the institution for which the map was made. It is possible to infer the intended map reader through the design of the map. At a functional level, the map places the reader on the eastern fringe of the map facing westward, not in the typical cartographic orientation toward the north. This orientation matches that of someone driving off the highway toward the NIMC: making it evident that the map was made for visitors to the NIMC. Other evidence suggests this as well. There is a wide border of empty space on the left margin of the map, leaving out geographic landmarks such as the lake-front and river, key reference points for locals, internees, and even the BCSC staff. But, on the left border, the shoreline of the lake has been drawn in. This provides a landmark that helps the reader locate the largest building on the map: the internment camp's tuberculosis sanatorium. Providing a landmark helps visitors trace the no longer existing camp onto the present site.

As mentioned, this map was originally part of a funding proposal for the NIMC. It provided a visual description of the camp in a section titled "Con-textual History." Now the map is used by the NIMC's Visitors' Centre, where visitors pay entrance fees and are given instructions as to how to proceed through the NIMC along with a brochure with a written description of the NIMC ex-hibitions and the Centre's physical layout. The NIMC map helps visitors locate the objects, events, and people they see in the NIMC's exhibits in the local landscape. For example, the map uses internment camp nomenclature such as "the Orchard" and "the Sanatorium," which are also used repeatedly throughout the Centre's historical displays and by the books and pamphlets in the Visitors' Centre. Thus, visitors can turn to the NIMC map to locate where these build-ings and places are in the contemporary landscape.

The NIMC map assumes the perspective of a map reader intent on making a connection to the internment camp: it draws out the remains of the camp in the changing terrain, making them recognizable, something tangible that can be experienced and taken away as a concrete affirmation of the past. Although I will discuss in Chapter 6 how the experience of returning to the Orchard is not something all visitors find easy to bear, at a discursive level the NIMC map attempts to make the past accessible as safely reified details, shorn of their specificity, that can be easily identified in the abstracted language of the map. The simple layout and language makes the space of internment universally accessible for all to touch, for all to partake. No one needs specialized knowledge or previous experience to access the camp. The map thus operates to decrease the distance between the visitors and what happened on this site, which for many has remained unspeakable (Benjamin 1985). But by removing the routes and zones of activity as well as the other histories and the presence of today's residents, it threatens to drain the site of potency, to reduce the site to easily consumable evidence for the tourist (ibid.). Contained within the temporal and spatial borders of the NIMC's map, the space of internment is "constructed out of an introverted, inward-looking history based on delving into the past for internalized origins" (Massey 1993, 64). It erases "the constellation of relations articulated together in [New Denver] ... where a large proportion of those relations, experiences and understandings are actually constructed on a far larger scale than" what is delineated by the temporal order of the map (ibid., 66).

The Spaces of Stories

If the space of the internment discursively constituted through government records in the national archives marginalizes the voices of the internees, and if the space of internment in the NIMC's map cleaned up the noise of the activities and routes of internees and local residents within and between camps, then it was the elders' accounts that produced the most spatially, temporally, and imaginatively complex space of internment. Rather than focusing on the internment camps, their accounts situate the internment camps in geographically more extensive spaces, sites of transit that were designed to remove all people of "Japanese racial descent" from Canada. In their accounts, the elders bring together the places where they formerly lived along the Pacific coast with the internment camps and war-torn Japan. The devastation Japanese Canadians underwent can not be confined to the space of the camps but rather, as I argue above, must be understood as part of a series of sites in the government's reconfiguration of the nation's geography over time.

The elders' accounts capture something intangible about New Denver, a sense of place that cannot be depicted in either the memorial's mapping exercises or the government records used by administrators to run the camps. I began to become aware of this sense of place once my daily life began to revolve around the elders, and I started to see how they transformed the remnants of the past into stories. Some stories were told eagerly; others were told selectively. There were stories that surfaced in conversations over lunch, in a meeting, or when we were chatting during community events. Then there are the stories not yet told or that will never be told. The shape of these stories can sometimes be imagined, but they disappear as soon as they come into focus, lodged somewhere between the edge of a word and a carefully preserved photograph of, for instance, a sombre-looking man in his late forties in a once-stylish suit that now looks battered on his weathered, thin body as he stands, suitcase in hand – leaving for where, leaving whom, and left behind by whom, we'll never know.

What follows are excerpts of some of these stories. One finds silences here, even in the most descriptive stories. There is a sense that each story bears much more than can be told in words alone. In their stories, the elders nevertheless provide a sense of what they suffered and the losses they endured. As narratives that have been told and retold, these stories have become part of the elder's everyday lives, their telling reworking the traces of pain and the humiliation while ensuring that feelings of compassion and stolen moments of happiness will be remembered.

Most of the accounts are excerpts from the interviews I conducted with the elders. I reconstructed Mr. Matsushita's descriptions of his experiences in the Hastings Park "Clearing Station" from one of our discussions. It is difficult to sense the nuances of these stories without hearing the rhythm of the elders' voices, the way they pause or emphasize words. It is hard to capture these nuances without seeing the way the elders embellished phrases with gestures or made references to photographs, letters, or items in their homes that bear witness to the past.

To provide a setting for the first account, I provide a descriptive context. I have laid out the accounts to produce an accumulating context of meaning from which to read the next account; after a certain point, it becomes unnecessary to write a full descriptive context for each account.

Mrs. Matsushita: We were some of the last people to leave Vancouver, my grandparents and myself. Everything was so quiet. You don't see anyone, you walk the street but you don't see, you know, your friends, the people you know, your family, your relatives. They are all gone this way or that way ...

The RCMP came and said, it was a Thursday, and they said you go such and such a day, which was the following Monday. Because my grandfather was sort of, not bedridden, but a semi-invalid, he had stroke a couple of times ... and there would be a bed on that day so he could travel on the train lying or sitting. Otherwise you'd have to travel sitting up all the way ...

Beforehand, you sort of prepare because you don't know when, when you, we were just told three days beforehand: ... Friday, Saturday, Sunday. It was just – I was just going in circles. My grandmother had a lot of things, everything ready, but even so. Even trying to get a friend to help, [my grandparents] being older people, a friend to help bundle up the belongings, it was very hard. There were not a lot of young people left [in Vancouver] ...

You just keep wondering from week to week. You hear so and so has already gone, and so and so ... from week to week or day to day, the RCMP will come around and say you have to go. Such and such a day, such and such a place. (Sumie Matsushita, Interview, 15 August 1996)

Mrs. Matsushita describes the period before she and her grandparents were ordered to leave Vancouver. They lived on Powell Street in Vancouver, which was once a busy commercial and residential area with fish stores, bakeries, and dry goods stores beside bathhouses, barbers, restaurants, and tailors. Every morning the streets were swept clean. Japanese Canadians lived in the houses and rooming houses lining the surrounding streets. Today, among the now run-down buildings, it is hard to imagine the busy tofu shops next to fish stores, bakeries exuding the fragrance of sweet bean, the heavenly smell of freshly baked bread, and soothing soaks in public baths. There would be arrivals and departures of many people. There would be groups of men arriving from or leaving for seasonal work, perhaps logging in central British Columbia. There would be women from Japan who had travelled by ship across the Pacific Ocean to join husbands they had met only through letters. They would arrive bewildered to what appeared to them to be a brutish, uncivilized town. You could also see fashionable young nisei women in stylish heels with hair coiffed in the latest perms along with young men in loose-fitting trousers, their hair slicked back as they sauntered along the streets, ready for the horizon of possibilities out of their parents' reach (see Kobayashi 1992b).

In this context, each of Mrs. Matsushita's words are dense with the imagery of a world that is no longer lived today. Loaded into the word "quiet" in the statement "everything was so quiet" is the eerie silence that prevailed in Vancouver's once bustling *nihonmachi* along Powell Street, when the RCMP began to deliver "evacuation" notifications to residents in Vancouver. In interviews I've conducted for the Japanese Canadian Citizens' Association in Vancouver, the same eerie feel is described by other Japanese Canadians as their friends, neighbours, and the shop owners along Powell Street began to disappear. One day you would walk past a house that was filled with the bustle of kids and the clutter of gardens; the next day, they would be empty.

Those waiting for their orders to leave were usually no longer employed. They had lost their jobs as Japanese Canadian businesses closed or had been fired by their employers. This meant that they were running out of money to pay for food and rent. They also had to venture out to hostile non-Japanese Canadian neighbourhoods for supplies. Once Japanese Canadians left for the internment camps, Powell Street turned into a desolate area with boarded-up stores, empty boarding houses, and vacant parks.

> *Mrs. Matsushita:* My mother and father, they were first in Popoff. They were living in the tent until toward the end of November. There was a mess hall for people when they first came to have their meals. Father was working there. But it was really hard for my mother because she wasn't really well. Because she had rheumatism and arthritis. And the cold weather. Because November of '42, we saw the snow – snow already. By the end of November, they were able to get the house in Bayfarm. But my grandparents and myself, we had, I think they used to call it a bunkhouse. They had rooms and in the middle of the building [there was] a big kitchen. There were quite a few people. Everyone had to take turns cooking on the big stove ... There was a big table where all the people could eat, but we ate in the room with our bunk bed. (Sumie Matsushita, Interview, 15 August 1996)

It is difficult to imagine what was involved in living in the bunkhouses and internment shacks. Mrs. Matsushita provides an image of the depressing conditions when she recounts how she ate her meals with her grandmother and semi-invalid grandfather in the tiny, dark room where there was just enough space for a bunk bed. She presents an image of them quietly eating their food in the cramped, dark space as the noise of strangers sharing the bunkhouse passed through the thin walls, filling their ears as they self-consciously finished their meals.

> *Mrs. Matsushita:* With so many people, and the little store we had in Popoff, there was always a lineup. You'd hear about vegetables coming to the store. It's the first time you have just half a cabbage, a quarter or half of a celery. In '42, there use to be some Doukhobors who would sell vegetables, which helped a lot. And then when you hear, "Slocan City, there's something's coming in." Someone would say it, and we'd all rush. And you'd have a good half an hour's walk from Popoff to Slocan, yes a good half hour. It was so difficult getting things at the store. There were so many people there, and the store was a small general store or grocery store. You'd hear someone say there was such and such a thing. But a lot of the time, by the time you rush there, it'd be gone. (Sumie Matsushita, Interview, 15 August 1996)

The lineups Mrs. Matsushita describes involved waiting with other distraught women and children – sometimes for an entire afternoon for half a cabbage. If they were lucky enough to get half a cabbage, it would have to be shared with three to seven other people over a week. What sort of adrenaline rush would cause each internee to dash with all the others two miles through the winter snow or through mud and clouds of insects in the late spring along the rough tracks to the next camp on the chance that he or she would be able to purchase maybe half or a quarter of a vegetable?

Mr. Matsushita lived in Steveston before the war. He was the oldest son of a very large fishing family living in the canneries. His family was sent to different camps. He spent several months in Hastings Park before being shipped to New Denver.

Mr. Matsushita: Finally, I had to go into Hastings Park. They had me working as a carpenter in there before I got sick. One day, some officials asked me to come with them. They took me to a stall, a stall for animals, and there was this young mother. She couldn't understand English, not a word. They had put her in isolation, in this horse stall, because they suspected that she had scarlet fever. She was crying and crying; she was beside herself, in a panic. They had taken her kids from her. She didn't know what was happening, what they had done to her kids, what they were doing to her. She didn't know anyone, no relatives or friends, no one in Hastings Park, and there was over two thousand people. It was like she was all alone in the world.

So they asked me to come interpret. I felt so helpless. There was nothing I could do. I wanted to help her, to find a way to comfort her. I would have done anything to help her, even gone out to find whether there was someone who knew her. Maybe there was someone still in Vancouver who hadn't been sent to the camps yet. I cried. But once they made the rule, it was hard to get permission to leave Hastings Park. Her husband, maybe he was in a road camp or a prisoner-of-war camp in Ontario. She didn't know where he was. She was all alone in the world. It sort of made a man out of me. (Shoichi Matsushita, Personal correspondence, 21 July 1996)

Mr. Matsushita: Later, I got sick. I started coughing up blood. Yes, TB. It was really bad. And as I told you before, I was left outside in a large doorway where there was a draft. They figured I wouldn't be living by the morning. But I sort of came back. Somehow and I was able to live through it. Always, always, no matter how bad things got. Each time I remembered what I promised my dad. To take care of all of my sisters, my mum. How would they survive if I died. The youngest one was only four. But making it through, still, at that time it was quite depressing for myself. My mother and sisters were in Kaslo. I couldn't cry to them. At the same time, I lost my grandmother. My favourite grandmother. Couldn't attend the deathbed. That made me ill. More so. (Shoichi Matsushita, Personal correspondence, 21 July 1996)

Mr. Matsushita: There was always tension, an underlying unbearable tension. When you walked through the camp, the shack walls, they were so thin, with all of that tension; the husband and the wife, yelling at each other. You'd hear the screaming, crying, all the angry words. Everything about their personal life was out in the open. There was no privacy. There was so much anxiety; people were tense; there were conflicts. Anger. It was hard. No one knew if they were staying or going. The next day or the next week the RCMP could come and tell them to pack up and leave for eastern Canada. So, no one had the heart to really fix up their shacks and make them nice. They would just have to leave it all behind again, just like on the coast, except this time they knew they would never come back. (Shoichi Matsushita, Personal correspondence, 21 July 1996)

Mrs. Inose: My best friend in the San, her TB was bad. She couldn't sit up, so they had her lying flat on a bed. We were young then, both of us in the San with TB. She was always so cheerful and happy-go-lucky. There was a social at the San where the staff paired the guys and girls, sort of like double dates. The men came to visit us in our ward because we [were too weak; we] couldn't move. It was when I first met Sho [her now deceased husband]. Celia and I were paired together with him and another fellow, and she kept talking, getting me to overcome my shyness. She was so kind and thoughtful, so full of life.

At the end of the war, her parents decided to go to Japan, war-torn Japan. They didn't know it would pretty well be a disaster area with bandits, blackmail, starvation, towns levelled by bombing. They carried her away on a board, lying flat, onto the ship that took them down the lake, where a train took them to the coast, [to Vancouver] one more time to the coast, and then a ship to Japan. Didn't hear much more from her after that. I don't know what happened. (Inose, Interview, 16 August 1996)

Mrs. Takahara: In Hastings Park, there was dysentery and food poisoning. Everyone was running to the bathroom. I think it was two or three times we had dysentery. I was there five months, and then I had a notice to go to New Denver. But that night my little boy Richard came down with chicken pox. All that time! He missed it the first time.

I was detained for two weeks [in the isolation ward]. I was scared. My parents and everyone were going. [Richard and I were going to be left behind in Hastings Park.] So my mother stayed behind with me. We were in an isolation ward, but it was just plywood, with a bunk bed inside. Whenever the kids would get up in their bed, they'd talk with the kids in the [next stalls, who were also in isolation], so chicken pox, whooping cough, measles, and mumps. It was all over. I tried to stay away from everybody.

And every so often there would be this smell, this fecal smell, and I looked down under my bunk and there was a trough there. Every fifteen minutes they flushed the toilet. It was a building for animals, so all the waste was thrown in there and run through: human waste [just below us].

But after two weeks we were ready to come to New Denver. [When we got there, it was all mud and shacks. I thought what is this? Where did they drop us!] Richard still had spots but was okay. We went over to Nelson Ranch. We didn't even have a stove yet. Two houses down, Mr. Niwa said, "Because you have a little boy – we'll give you our stove" ... because we were making our food outside in a little fire, like camp. And then two days later Richard had meningitis. He had a convulsion, and we rushed him over to the hospital. Doctor said he was one in a million that came through. (Takahara, Interview, 23 August 1996)

Mr. Tad Mori: I [remember looking] at the clothesline [in Steveston before the war and seeing] all those white shirts. We used to wear white shirts, you know. I thought, look at what mum has to go through every day [washing all those clothes, making them white]! So one day, I said, "I would like to have a sweatshirt, a grey one." [She asked,] "Why's that?" I said, "Oh, I'd like to have one." She says, "Okay, you go get it." So I tried to get a sweatshirt whenever I could. Less work for mum. I was nine years old! All that work for eight children, cooking, washing – Oh my god.

And I haven't seen her since 1946.

She passed away in 1966.

Because in 1946 the government gave you a choice – either you go east or west. Mum says I got nobody out east, so I am going back to Japan. She wants me to come home [to Japan] too. I said, "No way! I got job here and I am I going to work here. If I get any money, I'll send it back to you." But I never did. Because I can't, I was working for $37.50 a month! Yes?

I said goodbye to her at Slocan Terminal, somewhere. And that was it. I haven't seen her since.

All the rest of my brothers and sisters came back. Three brothers and another sister went back with her to Japan. But I didn't ...

She was eighty-eight when she died, I hear. My brother Sam, he told me one day, he says, "I would have never have said this to anyone but today." He was living in Osaka with our uncle, who was a minister. Everyday he comes from work, and aunty asks, "Have you had enough to eat?" He says, "Oh yes." He tells me, "I thought I would never tell anyone, but today I have to tell you. One potato. [That's all I had to eat each day]." (Mr. Tad Mori, Interview, 23 August 1996)

Another elder described her experiences after the war and her complex relationships with other residents in New Denver over time. She was one of the many women who remained in New Denver after their husbands died in the camp. Her husband died when he became infected with tuberculosis in 1945 when the war ended. One afternoon, when I visited her at her home, she shared her memories of her husband near the end of his life, recalling how he was overcome by worry and anxiety.

"He was worrying too much. He had wanted to return to Japan but knew that there would not be enough food. There wasn't even enough to feed their own people." I asked how she managed to stay in British Columbia after he died, when the government forced so many Japanese Canadians to leave. She replied, "there was nowhere for me to go!" She was in New Denver for a little while, but then there was a missionary – Miss Gillespie – who wanted her to live with her. When the war began in 1942, they called in all the missionaries living in Japan and sent them to the camps. But Miss Gillespie loved Japan and wanted to go back to die, and after the war, she did. She was a Pentecostal. So Mrs. A. bought her house, the big one on the corner that the Swansons now live in.

When her children grew up, the house was too big, so she bought this smaller house. It's a nice house full of light, one level with many rooms, and there is a large lawn for her apple and plum trees plus her three gardens. The living room is filled with pictures of her family and collections of Japanese dolls. She went to the cabinet and brought out a tiny wooden barrel – one centimetre in diameter – and opened it, shook it, and out rolled a tiny, tiny wooden doll, two millimetres in length. She said her granddaughter had always wanted these dolls, but she had told her they were too small and too easily lost. She laughed as she touched one with her finger to roll it over, "See, see the face; it's the boy." And then she exclaimed, "Oh! Where's the other one?" She looked inside, shook the barrel again, and out rolled the tiny girl: a tiny wooden head attached to a tiny wooden body with tiny bright strokes of paint, pink and red with girlish facial expressions. It was amazing.

A world of such joy and marvel fit into such a tiny space. The granddaughter recognizes its magic, but it is something so dear to the grandmother that she is not ready to give it up. What might this space hold for

Mrs. A., with its tiny couple, forever together? The elders were always surprising me with the worlds they fit into both the smallest and most unexpected spaces in their everyday lives in New Denver. (FIELD NOTES, 10 SEPTEMBER 1996)

The fear, loss, and confusion, the distrust and desperation, the humiliation, all of this is reworked and remade over the years, sediments of grief and hope, of determination and loss, permutating over the years, through the lives of this village, along the gravitational flow of the watershed. These stories, told and retold again and again, sometimes change with every account, sometimes remain steadfastly the same in tone, word, and gesture. There are events too harsh to tell directly face to face and so are half-told, given a softer, more open shape, under another guise, not as an analogy but as a parable of sorts. Then there is what remains, left out of words but still present in a glance or stuttered word, only to be taken into the palms of their hearts and spun into a story that transforms it, capturing its yet unexplored possibilities.

CHAPTER THREE

The Chronotope of the (Im)memorial

I dread the nights. When the sun sinks below the towering mountain ranges, it's as if the valley enters a nether world. There's a disturbing presence I can't see, that my senses strain to touch. I bolt the doors and secure the windows, turning on all the lights, turning the empty wooden house into a monstrous, glittering concoction visible from miles away.

When fatigue (or common sense) defeats me, I climb the stairs to the second floor to the room where I sleep. But rarely do I sleep. I lie horizontal in the darkness, often with shoes on, and sometimes my glasses as well, all this so I can swiftly hurtle myself off the rotting second-floor balcony to safety if need be. It is not clear what the lurking threat is. If I manage to drift asleep, more often than not I violently shake myself awake – out of my murky dream state – aware that someone or something is in the room. Haunted. I can't explain it any other way. The entire valley is haunted.

And while I would not want it any other way, I am always eager for each morning to arrive ... the morning when everything wakes up from ... night dreams, anticipating the sun, waiting for its heat to soak into the earth and radiate its baked warmth back. (FIELD NOTES, COMPILED FROM NOTES IN JULY 1996)

Reclaiming Sites of Political Violence

In the 1970s, Japanese Canadians began to symbolically reclaim the geographic sites where the government had interned them during the war. In this period, the sites of internment camps, as well as the sugar beet farms where many families were sent as labourers during the war, became tropes in the community's cultural imaginary. Japanese Canadian artists, filmmakers, writers, and researchers such as Joy Kogawa and Ken Adachi gave the internment camps and beet farms a presence in their work, in literature and poetry,[1] political histories,[2] biographies, oral histories, academic studies and community reminiscences,[3] experimental and documentary films and videos,[4] as well as art installations and visual art.[5] In many cases, their work was produced independently, sometimes with the support of community organizations rather than with the support of established publishers, galleries, or museums. In some cases, these artists, writers, and filmmakers sought to recover the details of the worlds of Japanese Canadians before and during the war, worlds now lost to the postwar generations (Watada 1997; Fukushima 1992; Ohama 1993); in other cases, they have attempted to trace how the camps continue to haunt the present (Kogawa 1983, 1992; Onodera 1987; Goto 1994, 2001; Sakamoto 1998; Miki 2001; McAllister 2002; Mochizuki 2006). In addition to making the camps a trope in their cultural imaginary, Japanese Canadians have also begun to reclaim the physical sites of internment, whether by including them in pilgrim-like rituals of return (Kobayashi and Miki 1989; McAllister 1994) or, as in the case of New Denver, by dedicating land for a memorial.

Building memorials on the sites of persecution is a way for surviving community members to reassert their presence in social terrains where they were either forced to leave, denied the right to practise and pass down their cultural beliefs to younger generations, or exterminated. It takes authority to reclaim these sites. Authority is based not only on the ability to make a compelling case but also on sufficient support, which in turn requires resources to mobilize people, produce evidence, and publicize the group's case. Building a memorial thus indicates that a significant number of survivors and members of younger generations have organized as a political force.

Reclaiming sites of persecution requires residents and governments to recognize the claims of the survivors and to agree to take steps to provide access to land where a memorial can be built. This can result in conflicts not simply because it involves property and ownership: governments and residents might also prefer to forget rather than make public the ugly histories that took place in their city squares, stadiums, and neighbourhoods.[6] The residents might claim they have no memory of internment camps, residential schools, or labour camps or argue that they are not responsible for the past (Hirsch and Spitzer 2006). If they remember, they might refuse to recognize the emotional significance of reclaiming these sites for survivors and their children, for this would entail acknowledging the pain that was endured and perhaps complicity in inflicting it.

When the Nikkei Internment Memorial Centre (NIMC) was built in New Denver, it made public a history that was primarily absent in local museums in the Kootenays.[7] Until the redress movement turned the internment of Japanese Canadians into a national issue in the 1980s, most local museums in this region were dedicated to recounting the role of mining and logging in the economic development of the area. Tourist brochures, local maps, government publications, and tourist centres guided visitors to landmarks and townscapes from the late 1800s and early 1900s that presented an adventure-filled frontier history of men seeking their fortunes in mining as well as logging. The NIMC disclosed another history, a history of racial hatred in which thousands of children, women, and men with Canadian citizenship were persecuted because they were of "Japanese descent." Although the New Denver Village Council endorsed the memorial, and numerous businesses and residents made generous donations and volunteered their labour, there was also resistance. Residents did not openly oppose the memorial but indirectly voiced their anxieties about building a permanent reminder of the camp. Some were uncomfortable about revisiting a painful and controversial period in the village's history. Others, notably Second World War veterans, claimed the memorial should not be built. They believed that the government's actions against Japanese Canadians were justified. Others worried that the memorial would stigmatize New Denver with its ugly past. Despite the opposition, the NIMC has not been vandalized, unlike the property of other controversial organizations, such as the Valhalla Wilderness Society, suggesting the close relations that residents have with the Japanese Canadian members of their community and the way their lives have become socially intertwined over the years.

At a broader level, memorials such as the NIMC are also controversial because they challenge the history celebrated by national memorials and monuments that configure landscapes through ritualistic reiterations of a nation's official history (Ben-Amos 1993; Bodnar 1992; Nora 1989; Rowlands 1996; Winter 1996; Sturken 1997; Winter and Sivan 2000; Foote 2003). According to Young (1993), memorials are an integral part of a nation's rites, functioning as historically significant sites that its citizens visit in pilgrimage-like tours. Invested with "a nation's memory and soul ... traditionally, the state-sponsored memory of a nation's past aims to affirm the righteousness of a nation's birth, even its divine election. The matrix of a nation's monuments emplots the story of ennobling events, of triumphs over barbarism, and recalls the martyrdom of those who ... died so that a country might live" (ibid., 2).

Memorials built by persecuted groups challenge the "state-sponsored memory of a nation's past" by presenting the violent acts on which it is founded. These memorials offer counternarratives to the "triumph over barbarism," presenting instead the barbarism of modern states: whether the incarceration of political "dissidents," the expulsion of ethnic and religious minorities, or the expropriation of the land of indigenous peoples (Anthias and Yuval-Davis 1989; Balibar and Wallerstein 1991; Goldberg 1993; Smith 1999). Memorials that mark sites where governments instigated programs to incarcerate or extermin-ate undesirable sectors of the population not only reassert the living presence of survivors in the social terrain, they also contest their erasure from national memory, disrupting the nation's ritualized enactment of ennobling events and martyrdom.[8]

The NIMC provides a place to mourn the losses that all Japanese Canadians have suffered. It is a place for survivors and subsequent generations to perform their own rituals and regather as members of the postwar community now living in scattered locations across Canada, giving them a presence in the sites from which they were forcibly removed. Like other memorials that commemorate suffering, the NIMC marks New Denver as a site of violence – in particular, as a site of political violence. As the only internment camp in Canada that has been marked by a memorial, it has symbolically come to represent all fifteen camps, drawing Japanese Canadians who were interned not only in New Denver but also in camps such as Tashme, Lillooet, and Greenwood. Like national war memorials, the NIMC functions to incorporate this site into the history of the living community, making it a foundational moment in their postwar formation.

But an analysis of the memorial needs to go beyond a description of how it contests the erasure of the internment from national memory and turns New Denver into a site for the postwar community to regather and remember how the government tried to destroy its community. It is necessary to examine the narratives as well as the practices through which the memorial reconfigures our relation to what happened, to the victims, and to those who violated their rights. The way the NIMC shapes the manner in which we remember the past affects how we relate to events, actions, places, and people in the present. Even if memorials commemorate events omitted from official history, they can still draw on reactionary conventions and myths that reproduce "us" versus barbaric "them" narratives that typify reactionary national discourses. As memory scholars have argued, even memorials commemorating horrific and morally complex events such as the Holocaust and the Vietnam War can reproduce problematic myths about individuals who heroically sacrificed their lives either in the name of a higher cause or to protect god-given territory (Young 1993; Sturken 1997).

In his well-known studies on memorials of Holocaust, James Young provides examples of how memorials can challenge the temporal and spatial assumptions of conventional memorials that reproduce national and, specifically, fascist forms of memory. In his analysis of memorials that he refers to as "counter-monuments" commissioned by civic governments in Germany during the 1980s, he discusses the work of artists and monument makers, such as Jochen and Esther Gerz and Norbert Radermacher, who were from a generation of Germans deeply distrustful of monumental forms because of their exploitation by Nazis

(1993, 27). This generation has explored both "the necessity of memory and their [own] incapacity to recall events they never experienced directly"(ibid.). Aesthetically, through the innovative use of "self-effacing" or "negative" forms (ibid., 28, 45), these memorials "disperse" rather than "gather" memory, even as they gather the "literal effects of time in one place" (ibid., 46). For example, the Gerzes designed a twelve-metre-high, one-metre-square pillar of hollow aluminum plated with dark lead in Harburg, a suburb of Hamburg. An inscription in several languages invites citizens of Harburg to write their names on the surface as a commitment to remain vigilant against fascism. Thus, the memorial does not ask for the remembrance of heroic victims or liberators from the past. Instead, it encourages the viewer to make a personal commitment, joining others who have also written their names. As the names cover the pillar, it is gradually lowered into the ground. The inscription explains that "one day it will have disappeared completely, and the site of the monument against fascism will be empty." Rather than permanently occupying a space, remaining untouched by the forces of change, this countermonument will disappear over time; it will transform each time someone inscribes her or his name or thoughts on its surface. As the creators stated, "In the end, it is only we ourselves who can rise up against injustice" (ibid., 30).

They wanted to build an anti-fascist monument without the "fascist tendencies in all monuments ... [that presume] to tell people what to think" (Young 1993, 28). They wanted the countermonument to provoke rather than console and to change rather than remain pristine over time by inviting people to "violate" it with their own writing as it sinks into the ground and literally disappears with the passage of time. Thus, in terms of the temporal assumptions of conventional memorials, while countermonuments "stimulate memory no less than the traditional everlasting memorial [they point] ... explicitly at [their] own changing [faces and also make explicit] the inevitable – even essential – evolution of memory itself over time" (ibid., 48).

The NIMC is a much more modest enterprise than the countermonuments commissioned by civic governments in Germany. Even though Japanese Canadian artists and writers have explored different forms and media of memory, there has been very little discussion of the social, political, and psychic repercussions of how the past is represented within the community (McAllister and McFarlane 1992; McAllister 1994, 2001; McFarlane 1995; Miki 1998a, 2004; Oikawa forthcoming). Moreover, constructed by local contractors with expertise in restoring historical buildings, the NIMC was not designed to deconstruct the temporal and spatial assumptions of conventional memorials. The NIMC is the project of a small community with few resources living in a settlement of approximately five hundred people in an economically depressed region of the province. Like other locally run cultural institutions in small towns in British Columbia, it is a composite of different functions: memorial, historical centre, and community centre.

Yet just because the NIMC was not designed as a countermonument does not mean it simply reproduces the reactionary spatial and temporal dynamics of conventional memorials. The rest of this chapter examines the spatial and temporal dynamics of the NIMC and their implications for how the internment is remembered. At a formal level, the Centre draws on a number of established memorial and museum conventions: it includes restored internment shacks, historical displays, artifacts, documents to educate visitors about the camp, and a memorial garden for "reflection" (see Gagnon 2006). To dismiss the memorial for using these standard conventions would be to assume that every deployment results in the same outcome: it privileges structural form over the particularities of the context within which the NIMC is set. This chapter examines how the NIMC has used these conventions to turn New Denver into a site of remembrance. I first examine the convention that imposes a temporal order that removes the site from everyday time, placing it in what Bakhtin refers to as the chronotope of "empty time," a temporal order of the "ever lasting" and "never to be forgotten," which I refer to as the "chronotope of the immemorial" (Bakhtin 1981). I then consider the extent to which the chronotope of the immemorial fails to control the material and social dynamics of the site where the memorial is located: to stop time, to stop the decay of the material remains of the camp and the effects of disturbing memories. Decay, and with it the transformation of material remains and social and psychic relations to the past, I argue, eludes the immemorial. It is impossible to freeze what happened in the past in an unchanging "ever lasting" form that preserves its significance for generations to come. While there is nothing inherently transformative about memory, as the multiple memories of people visiting memorials change, come into conflict, dissipate, and resurface, they can form what Bakhtin refers to as the Rabelaisian chronotope of organic growth, decay, and death: for life.

The Chronotope of the Immemorial

Mikhail Bakhtin's notion of the chronotope (1981) offers a detailed way to conceptualize the temporal and spatial dynamics of memorials that I refer to as "the chronotope of the immemorial." Bakhtin uses the chronotope to conceptualize "the intrinsic connectedness of temporal and spatial relationships" (ibid., 84). Although Bakhtin is specifically concerned with the chronotope in literature, he also refers to chronotopes in "other areas of culture" (ibid.). As geographers Julian Holloway and James Kneale argue, as a concept the chronotope is not restricted to the analysis of literary texts (Holloway and

Kneale 2000, 82-83). Anthropologist Kathleen Stewart (1996) provides an example of the use of the chronotope and other Bakhtinian concepts in her ethnographic study of cultural spaces in a coal-mining region in the Appalachians, as does Paula Pryce (1999) in her study of the Sinixt Nation. Geographer M. Folch-Serra (1990) formulates how concepts like the chronotope can be used in ethnographic research on space.[9] To analyze the operation of chronotopes in non-literary media, whether a building or a graveyard, it is necessary to consider the conventions specific to the medium under consideration: its production, the material used in its construction, and the rituals and customs of its use and maintenance.[10] Bakhtin writes that the chronotope is an artistic expression of the way that "[time], as it were, thickens, takes on flesh, becomes artistically visible; likewise space becomes charged and responsive to the movements of time, plot and history" (Bakhtin 1981, 84).

As Lynne Pearce argues, Bakhtin privileges the temporal dimension of the chronotope, focusing more on the manner in which time is materialized than on how space becomes "responsive to the movements of time" (Pearce 1994, 67). An analysis of non-literary forms, especially my analysis of the memorial, requires a consideration of how space becomes "responsive to the movement of time, plot and history."

Bakhtin conceives the movement of time, plot and history, specifically the movement or, more specifically, the movement of the narrative of official history, as a linear progression of chronological events, propelled by the logic of cause and effect, whereby humans are the agents of their own fate. But Bakhtin is concerned with different types of history, which I refer to as "temporal orders," which is not just concerned with "official history." Each temporal order has its own "logic of movement," which I refer to as a "modality of happening," that sets the terms for when and how different sorts of events and actions happen.[11] As *the representation* of how these temporal orders are materialized in space, chronotopes bear the logic of the metaphysical and ideological orders within which they operate.

The chronotope characterizing ancient Greek literary texts, which Bakhtin refers to as the "chronotope of the Greek romance," bears some resemblance to the chronotope of the immemorial. The chronotope of the Greek romance is organized around a modality of happening based on chance and fate, which is predetermined by a metaphysical rather than human order (Bakhtin 1981, 94-95). Initiative does not belong to human beings; instead, things *happen to* them (ibid., 95). The plot is propelled by "simultaneity," whereby characters meet simply because they happen to be in the same place at the same time, and by "chance rupture," through which unexpected events prevent them from meeting. In this chronotope, a minute later or earlier is decisive in determining the fate of the characters rather than their ingenuity or determination. When the normal course of predestined events is interrupted, non-human factors – fate, gods, villains – intrude (ibid.).

Bakhtin describes the temporal order of this chronotope as empty time because its passage leaves no marks on the characters and terrain where the spectacular adventures occur. For example, between the beginning of the adventure, when two lovers meet, and the end, when they marry, neither their desire nor their ages alter (Bahktin 1981, 90). In this chronotope, space is an abstract expanse. Because specificity and concreteness would limit the absolute power of chance and fate, this chronotope excludes them. Bakhtin explains that every concretization – or detail that is specific to a place, person, or event – introduces its own rule-generating force (a modality of happening) that the characters would be bound to take into account. Each detail would tie the nature and outcome of their actions, whether their movement across geographic space or the characteristics of their adventures, to the particularities of local places. This would be even more the case if the adventure took place in the characters' "native world," where their knowledge of rivers and cities and their relation to inhabitants would shape their activities. Thus, the space must be not only abstract but also alien to the characters. For chance and fate to dominate, space must be indefinite, unknown, and foreign (ibid., 100-101).

In so far as the space of conventional memorials is ordered according to the chronotope of the immemorial, it is likewise abstract. Ideally, all particularities are removed from the space of the memorial, except for the fact that it is the site of an event of great significance. Even local features pertaining to the event, such as a river where people drowned, are abstracted from their contingent, changing existence and endowed with symbolic meanings that exceed their specificity, much like the corpses of unidentified soldiers that have been taken from battlefields and placed in tombs of the unknown soldier in war memorials.

The temporality of the conventional memorial is precisely the opposite of what, as I will explain below, Bakhtin identifies as the Rabelaisian temporality of decay and growth, whereby traditional hierarchies are broken down and reassembled into "one dynamic living grotesque image" (Bahktin 1981, 175). In conventional memorials, empty time dominates. Like the passage of empty time in the Greek romance, the empty time of the immemorial leaves no marks. Whatever is inducted into the memorial's timeless temporal order ideally endures the passage of time unchanged. But, in contrast to the Greek romance, events do not *occur* in the temporal order of the memorial. In Greek romance, even though events in a sense have already happened and always will happen (except where the gods intervene, etc.), insofar as they have been already predestined, they still, nevertheless, occur. In the temporal order of the memorial, they have already happened; they are forever completed. We are positioned in the present, retrospectively looking back toward them.

Unlike literary texts, the temporal order of memorials is not enacted primarily through a narrative that, for example, charts a series of events leading to the fate of various characters. Memorials engage us at a bodily level, beckoning us to stop, to enter a space outside our everyday temporal zone and reflect on people or events that had cataclysmic impacts on the worlds in which we live. The memorial has been erected to elevate the losses and sacrifices of these people and the impact of these events to a level of profound greatness. The memorial seeks to preserve them for generations to come. Entering the space of the memorial, a visitor is presented with a vista, a vantage point that places her or him in a particular orientation toward the past. The orientation is not to survey the past objectively as a historian. Rather, the proper attitude is awe in the face of the enormity of an event and/or the bravery and perseverance of the memorialized individuals, sorrow for their suffering and losses, and gratitude and indebtedness for their sacrifices. These feelings open us to a presence, to forces, beyond our mortal lives. We are inducted into the realm of the metaphysical everlasting: the immemorial.

Memorials attempt to constitute us as particular types of collectives, asserting the nature of what constitutes our "we" by identifying key elements in our collective foundations. They recover great acts, persons, deeds, and events from the morass of the past, where most disappear into anonymity with the passage of time. Placed beyond the reach of the transformative forces of growth and decay (Bakhtin 1981), these acts, persons, and events are preserved as exemplars of a good or heroic deed, a terrible suffering, or a loss. As exemplars, they also orient us toward the future. Memorials therefore attempt to structure our changing worlds in relation to the noble deeds of the past and to direct us toward what we should aspire to in the future. Placed outside of the temporal zone of the everyday, the space of the memorial works to make the event or persons it commemorates impervious to the forces of change.

For Japanese Canadians visiting the NIMC, remembering the internment camps binds them into a collective "we." Although the internment led to divisions, enflaming conflicts within families, between social classes, and among political groups, forty years later, in the 1980s, the movement for redress used the injustices that were suffered to unite Japanese Canadians, constructing the internment as a key element in the collective foundation of the postwar community, even if the redress movement was itself fraught with divisions and conflicts (Miki 2004). Yet, while the NIMC focuses on these injustices, it does not address only the members of the Japanese Canadian community. Since visitors are not necessarily familiar with the events being memorialized, the NIMC has taken on the task of educating the public by means of an interpretation centre that features exhibits of Japanese Canadian history. The relatively small amount of descriptive text in the exhibits, as I will discuss in Chapters 4 and 5, interprets the way the Canadian government stripped Japanese Canadians of their rights, incarcerated them, and forced them to leave the province. As a memorial, the NIMC makes the internees' case an exemplar of the injustice and tragedy that could happen to other unsuspecting innocents in the future. This positions all visitors as part of a "we." Everyone's families and communities become potential targets as well as potential perpetrators, thus placing each visitor in a position of responsibility. This is how the NIMC works as a memorial to evoke a particular comportment or attitude that is not exclusive to Japanese Canadians.

Memorials invoke a form of remembering that can be understood as an attitude. They must be carefully tended and maintained so that this attitude, this comportment, the configuration of self as part of a "we," does not erode, wear down, or change. The effort to ensure that this "we" does not change is precisely where the tension between the chronotope of the immemorial and the actual material and social dynamics of the memorial become evident. Unlike the empty time of literary forms, the chronotope of the immemorial must be imposed on the fabric of the everyday world. The temporal order of the everyday is unruly, characterized by conflicting forces, including local, national, and international discursive regimes of regulatory control, the daily and seasonal activities of local inhabitants, and the dynamics of ecosystems and geological forces. Human energy and resources are needed to "keep time still," free from the momentum of decay (Young 1993, 47). He argues further that time mocks the rigidity of monuments, the presumptuous claim that in its materiality a monument can be regarded as eternally true, a fixed star in the constellation of collective memory" (ibid., 47).

The energy and resources to keep time still and ensure that the design of the memorial or monument as well as its landscaping do not appear dated require the constant labour of the individual workers, communities, and organizations that maintain the memorials. Paradoxically, then, the immortality of the memorialized events and people depend on mortal, transitory, and constantly changing bodies. It is through the expenditure of labour that memorials can appear to be free from the erosion of everyday time. If memorials are not kept free from the forces of everyday time – as their polished surfaces begin to dull with dust, laying nutrients for mosses to spread over their stone surfaces, and as the boundaries between the street, plaza, and parkland erode so that pedestrians, litter, and hedges begin to envelop memorials into their various orders – they will be engulfed, assimilated into the everyday world. The discussion that follows examines the tension between the immemorial and the dynamic forces of change in New Denver, examining the extent to which the NIMC succeeds in imposing the chronotope of the immemorial. First, though, I introduce the memorial, following the route visitors follow as they tour the site.

A Tour Inside the Gates

Passing under the NIMC's gateway, through the sturdy cedar post fence, the visitor steps across a threshold, leaving the busy neighbourhood to enter the calm of the Japanese garden: the Heiwa Teien (peace garden).

Hei-wa Tei-en

This traditional Japanese garden was designed by Mr. Roy Sumi, a gardener of international reputation. Mr. Sumi, a former Rosebery internee, envisioned the gardens as "Kare-sansui" (dried-up water scenery).

Following the traditions of the Kamakura style, which dates from the 12th century, the pebble river symbolizes flowing water and incorporates many natural features. From the headwaters located north of the Old Community Hall, the river winds through rapids, under two footbridges, gradually becoming more tranquil before emptying into the lagoon.

Mr. Sumi has taken an artist's care in placing the "Standing Stones" in the garden. These represent the skeleton of the garden. Careful consideration is used in their selection, placement and orientation.

The harmony between the gardens and other elements of the site: the fence, gates, sidewalks, footbridges and buildings is in careful accord with the mood, sentiment and Japanese temperament of the site.

Japanese gardens are intended as a retreat for secluded ease and meditation. In this spirit, we invite you to ponder and reflect upon the subtle beauty of these Gardens.

(NIMC Signage 1996)

The view opens to a large garden with an array of local flora nestled among ornamental bonsai and rhododendrons, gifts from the master gardener, Mr.

Sumi. The handsome bonsai and local flora mingle, bringing together ancient Japanese traditions and life from the forested slopes of the nearby mountains to create a new home place for the internees' memories. A wide riverbed of gravel lined with stones and small boulders sweeps the visitor's gaze around the site, from the restored internment shacks along a boardwalk to the large Kyowakai Hall, which sits beside the Centennial Hall, then over a series of footbridges back to the point of entry. A pebble path guides the visitor through the site. Along the way, thick benches hewn from massive fir trees, centuries old, offer places to rest with various vantage points over the garden.

The path leads first to the Visitors' Centre, which was once an internment shack.

Visitors' Reception Centre

The exterior of this building is typical of British Columbia Security Commission constructed dwellings for Nikkei internees. Although the fir shiplap siding has been weathered over time, the initial shrinkage which resulted from the use of "green" lumber is clearly evident.

The interior of the structure has been completely renovated and modernized to serve the needs of the Visitors' Reception Centre.

(PLEASE DO NOT TOUCH THE FRAGILE EXTERIOR SIDING)

(NIMC Signage 1996)

Inside, bright white walls and a tiled floor with access to public bathrooms make the reception centre a clean, utilitarian space. Here, workers greet the visitor and offer brochures with a layout of the site and a description of its buildings. Visitors pay the entrance fee, ask questions, and purchase postcards and books on topics ranging from Japanese Canadian history to cooking and Japanese culture. An array of origami crafts are on sale as well. The members of the Kyowakai Society fold colourful paper into these three-dimensional constructions to raise funds for the Centre.

From here, the path leads through the garden to a series of restored internment shacks, frozen in time. Standard three-room shacks were fourteen by twenty-eight feet, while smaller two-room shacks were fourteen by twenty feet. The brochure and signs indicate that Shack 1 depicts the conditions from 1942 to 1944. The visitor enters through a central room, where the small, dark rudimentary kitchen is located: wooden sink, wood stove, table, chairs. To the left and right are sleeping rooms. The standard shack housed two families with a minimum of six occupants, but usually more. The first room shows

3.1   Internment shacks on display in the Nikkei Internment Memorial Centre, 1996. *Photo by the author.*

how the shacks looked when the families first moved in. It is dark and bare: finished with bare planks and containing a double plank bed with two woollen blankets. A small window lets in a tiny square of daylight. It is hard to imagine a mother and father and two, three, or four growing children and adolescents sleeping in this room each night. The next room shows how Japanese Canadians refitted the rooms. Like a carefully crafted storage box, wall shelves and bunk beds reorganize the small room into separate spaces crammed with all manner of everyday things: jars of dried beans, bedding, books, clothing, small pictures, needles, and spools of thread.

The walls are insulated with layers and layers of paper, whatever paper that could be found: newspapers, magazines, envelopes, discarded cards. In the first year, the green lumber used to build the shacks shrank, leaving wide cracks through which the wind and cold blasted. "More paper, we always collected more paper, whatever could be used to fill the cracks" (Senya Mori, Interview, 5 September 1996). But no matter, in the deep of winter, with snow piled soft and thick, it was not possible to keep the icy cold out. The cold would creep through, spreading frost along the inside walls. Shack 2 is an example of the living conditions from 1945 to 1957, although the memorial's brochure notes that it was occupied in this state until the mid-1980s. This shack is even more crammed with stuff – the stuff of living, accumulated and worn down by years of use.

One could spend hours in these small dark spaces, within the wooden walls leached of colour by years of living in impoverished conditions, poring over the details of long-gone internees. But the dim light and cramped space begin to close in. One thinks of the two families, eight to fourteen people, crammed into this fourteen-by-twenty-eight foot space, sweltering hot in the summer and freezing cold in the winter. Soon the visitor will want to leave, to stumble out into the garden into open space and fresh air.

Next, the path leads onto a boardwalk past a vegetable garden.

The Vegetable Garden

Vegetable gardens were planted by the Nikkei soon after their internment. The vegetables seen here display a variety of foods that were grown in typical gardens. The family garden provided fresh, nutritious and affordable food in a time of rationing. Internees also picked wild mushrooms "shitake"[12] and fiddleheads from the surrounding forest.

(PLEASE DO NOT PICK THE VEGETABLES)

(NIMC Signage 1996)

And at the very back of the compound, over a double-gate entrance way, is the peace arch.

The Peace Arch

The original Peace Arch, built by internees circa 1945, was situated at the entrance to the former Tuberculosis Sanatorium, present-day Slocan Community Hospital and Health Care Centre.

The Arch and the fence work together to represent peace and harmony. While the Arch offers a bridge of welcome, the fence speaks of the links between the people of all nations.

(NIMC Signage, 1996)

You keep walking past a white plaster building, the Centennial Hall, where the Kyowakai Society meets and holds its various functions.

Centennial Hall

This building was constructed in 1978 to serve the needs of the Kyowakai (working together peacefully) Society.

The exterior design of the building is reminiscent of traditional Japanese architecture. It was funded, in part, by the Province of British Columbia to commemorate the 100th anniversary of the arrival of the first Japanese in Canada, Manzo Nagano.

It now serves as a meeting place and is the hub of social and cultural activities for New Denver's Nikkei community.

(NIMC Signage, 1996)

This building is off limits to the public. It is where members of the Kyowakai Society meet and hold their events. As can be expected, visitors do not always realize this is a community building and rattle the doors, trying to gain entrance. If someone forgets to lock the doors, tourists sometimes saunter into meetings, observing the proceedings with curiosity.

The next building, the Kyowakai Hall, is open to the public. A large, barn-like building nailed over with tar paper, it is a long wooden shell with no insulation.

Kyowakai Hall

Constructed in 1943 by Nikkei carpenters, the Kyowakai Hall has long been the religious, political, social and cultural centre of the New Denver Japanese Canadian community.

3.2 Kyowakai Hall *(left)* and Centennial Hall *(right)* on the site of the Nikkei Internment Memorial Centre, 1996. *Photo by the author.*

Kyowakai Hall is a long serving Buddhist Temple. Locals practiced the "Jodo-Shinshu" form of Buddhism. The shrine features altar pieces from Vancouver's original Kitsilano Buddhist Church. The temple is still used on occasion.

The hall also served as the meeting place for the Kyowakai (working together peacefully) Society. The all-men organization met regularly to discuss issues like living conditions and how to improve them.

This hall has seen many passages: Buddhist weddings, funerals and traditional Japanese festivals. Community gatherings such as theatrical and musical productions, dances, silent movies and banquets were also held here.

Kyowakai Hall now houses the Nikkei Internment Memorial Centre Museum.

(NIMC Signage, 1996)

This is where the historical exhibits are housed. One moves from the micro-details of everyday living in the shacks to exhibits that place everything in the larger framework of Canada's history. Archival photographs, artifacts, and historical documents lead the visitor through a history of Japanese immigrants in Canada, focusing on the New Denver internment camp. This is primarily a photo exhibit, although it includes documents and artifacts that illustrate the minutiae of the internees' daily life: rough blankets, travelling clothes, luggage, small school desks, paper decorations, cloth dolls, notices to "Enemy Aliens," a wood stove. Many of the photographs are familiar, iconic images of the internment shown in almost every book published in the 1970s and 1980s on the history of Japanese Canadians. They present the well-documented aspects of the community's history, such as the confiscation of hundreds of fishing boats tied together in a mass of white hulls or the sea of bunk beds for hundreds of Japanese Canadians confined in the livestock buildings at Hastings Park, waiting to be sent to camps in the interior of British Columbia.

At the entrance, the double doors open to an enlarged photograph of a young woman with her children, a girl of perhaps four years and a boy of maybe six, amid piles of luggage and lines of people. The woman, her head and shoulders bent forward, rumpling her tailored coat, seems to be desperately intent on pulling out what looks like identification or tickets as a white man inspects their parcels. The girl with a tiny purse, princess coat, and dainty city shoes stands back to back with the boy in a tweed cap and coat. They clutch each other's hands. The only face you see is that of the girl: uncertain and distressed. She looks away from the scene of her mother anxiously searching through her purse for the required documentation as the white man, a stranger, looks through what remains of their life's possessions. The title block reads: "Intern: to Confine."

The next sections are organized into a linear chronology of pre-war, wartime, and postwar events, loosely following the human rights narrative that activists wrote to mobilize Japanese Canadians in the movement to seek redress during the 1980s. The narrative challenges the wartime construction of people of "Japanese descent" as threats to national security by presenting them as loyal Canadian citizens who immigrated to the country in the early 1900s and embraced Canada as their new homeland, despite legislated racism. In this context, the government's actions against them become a violation of their rights.[13] The chronology of events begins with the arrival of "The Pioneers," followed by "Nisei: Establishing Roots." The war-time period includes "Pearl Harbor," which presents newspaper articles and photographs that identify, incorrectly, Japan's attack on the United States as the event that forced the federal government to remove Japanese Canadians from British Columbia's coastline. The great losses incurred by Japanese Canadians are presented under the titles "Confiscation of Property" and "Moved." Then there are a series of sections that describe life in the various camps. "The West Kootenay Valley" shows photographs and maps of various camps in this region. Next is a large map of Canada identifying all of the locations where Japanese Canadians were interned.

"First Home" is an ironic title for the section on internment camps in the Slocan Valley. A photograph illustrates the accommodations where the first internees stayed before the shacks were built: collapsed snow-covered tents. The sections titled "The Buddhist Temple" and "New Denver Tuberculosis Sanatorium" include photographs of what were among the most important institutions in the New Denver camp. Off in a side room is a Japanese-style wooden bath, a reference to the fact that this building was originally built to be a public bathhouse. "Survival" has several walls of photographs depicting camp life, mostly group pictures of various occasions such as graduations, community dances, and entertainment and sports events. This seems like an odd way to illustrate "survival," but, as former internees have told me, no one wanted to take photographs of the poor living conditions and the plight of their families.[14] It would be too humiliating. Instead, photographs were taken of events that could be mementos that friends and family members could keep (McAllister 2002, 2006a, 2006b). This section also includes images of sawmills and logging operations, local industries that hired internees at low wages to fill local labour shortages. By contrast, there are only a few photographs in the section "Uprooted Again," many taken by Tak Toyota, one of the Japanese Canadians who managed to produce photographic records of the places on internment (McAllister 2006b). This section depicts chaotic scenes of the Japanese Canadians' final removal from British Columbia after Japan was defeated in 1945. Rather than being permitted to return to what remained of their homes along the coast of the province, they were loaded onto trains and buses and shipped off to face unknown fates in war-torn Japan or locations scattered across the rest of Canada. The postwar period is covered in the section titled "The Struggle for Redress," which briefly describes the redress movement and the final settlement the National Association of Japanese Canadians negotiated with the Canadian government. The exhibit ends with an oval mirror titled "Reflection." A conventional technique to encourage viewers to consider how they are implicated, it could also be argued that the mirror functions to add the visitor's image to the conclusion of the history of Japanese Canadian internment as someone who is interested in learning about Canada's history of racial discrimination.

To walk through the NIMC would take a matter of minutes. But if a visitor follows the signs, reading the text that explains the displays and examining the items on view, the visit is supposed to take anywhere from forty-five to ninety minutes. However, the visitor who intends to read all the facts and figures and view every artifact and image will find there is too much to absorb. I can only

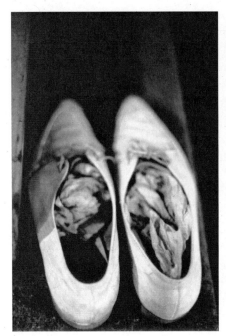

3.3   Shoes worn by a sanatorium worker and other items on display at the Nikkei Internment Memorial Centre, 1966. *Photos by the author.*

spend so much time onsite. It is not the information that is overwhelming; rather, there is something about the material remains that overwhelms me.

De-tours

The buildings intensify the weather. On a hot August day, the heat in the buildings is stifling. As winter approaches, it seemed colder inside these buildings than outside. As you enter the darkness, there is the musty smell of old things that were once alive with the activity of everyday life. With each breath you now inhale their disintegrating airborne particles.

The interior of the Kyowakai Hall feels cavernous. There is no ceiling, just an endless open space that drifts up through the exposed wooden rafters. Track lighting and hanging light bulbs cannot fill this building with light. In the dimness, the wooden plank walls emanate a slightly amber glow, giving the photographs a surreal quality.

I am drawn especially to the personal snapshots of smiling youths, so much hope gleaming from their faces, lined up for their graduation photos in the midst of the muddy squalor of the camps. There are the shots of women performing snappy dance routines and actors caught in caricatured poses in the midst of traditional Japanese theatre pieces; stylish shots of New Denver's Big Band and baseball stars. All creating a semblance of their now-destroyed communities along the coast. Especially eerie are the rows of tiny girls in kimonos, heads ensconced in ornate head pieces, intensely looking at the camera, not a smile on their tiny painted lips. They stand in front of elderly male dignitaries by the rough, barn-like Buddhist church. So little documentation, so few stories about life in the camps are accessible. And here, we are finally given a glimpse into this world. Although many of these moments have been lost to words, the light they emitted was imprinted on film. Somehow they become immortalized, outside the changes of time.

The artifacts are different. They rot with time. Yet they convey a visceral quality that cannot be conveyed by the photographs. The thick metal plate of the wood stove, now cold, is piled with a display of cooking utensils, wooden boxes, and pots. The metal once expanded with the heat of burning fir, split outside with the swing of a well-sharpened axe. Imagine the fire, roaring as it crackled through dry tinder, then maturing into the hum of glowing embers. Those dusty iron pots were once filled with steaming, fragrant gohan, glowing white in the dark squalid shacks. They were scrubbed every day, as a central part of whatever remained of family life.

Two pairs of tiny white nurses' shoes sit in front of a photo display of the sanatorium. Scuffed, a little soiled, one pair has been carefully filled with tissue and the other set on shoetrees so they will keep their shape. They lie on each side of a metal medical kit, on which there is an arrangement of small, thick, glass vials, some with pills, and one in particular with one last dose of yellow liquid. Neither the shoes nor vials are pinned down: there is no adhesive or protective Plexiglas to stop curious hands, the clumsy knock of an elbow. Instead, they are open to being touched. The shoes are especially curious. Somehow their very tininess, the way they have been so carefully placed, toes neatly in line, emanates an aura. One dare not touch them. Once they were laced up every working day and eased off at the end of a shift, pliable from the moisture, heat, and oils of feet, feet that once whisked briskly over the polished floor at the sanatorium.

The Kyowakai Hall also houses the Buddhist shrine. But it is not displayed. Instead, text and photographs describe the shrine and present the history of the Buddhist Church in New Denver. But there it sits, behind sliding panels, beyond the view of visitors. (LETTERS AND FIELD NOTES, 1996)

The Remains

On entering the memorial, visitors enter the chronotope of the immemorial, where buildings, photographs, and artifacts from the internment have been removed from the overgrown lots in the surrounding neighbourhood, from photograph albums stored in living room bureaus, and from kitchen cupboards filled with coffee mugs, rice bowls, and dinner plates. Removed from the everyday world, from routines and rituals, and presented as artifacts and archival documents, they are protected from the eroding forces of voracious vegetation and autumn rain, the oil of curious fingers, and clumsy elbows that accidentally knock glasses and plates to the floor, leaving white shards to be swept away into garbage bins, along with whatever else is to be forgotten. On display, they become the remains of the camp, of the hundreds of people interned in New Denver, giving them an auratic quality.

As James Young argues, we are not just drawn to but "venerate" the remains of significant events and people. He argues that the veneration of ruins and artifacts in part "stems from the nineteenth-century belief that such objects embody the spirit of the people who made and used them ... [They are] not only remnants of the people they once belonged to, but also traces of the values, ideas and character of the time" (1993, 127). We thus stand respectfully before the remains of the internment camp, looking back to the cataclysmic events that tore apart the vibrant pre-war Japanese Canadian community. In the space of the memorial, the presence of the hundreds of internees is invoked, their ghostly dreams of democracy and trust in the Canadian government dashed. In their absent presence, we face their loss and the suffering; some of us feeling sadness, some shame, and others, nothing at all.

Yet Young is circumspect about the veneration of remains, especially in contemporary contexts. He is critical of the "fetishization of artifacts by curators, and of ruins by the 'memory tourists,'" arguing that "we risk mistaking the piece for the whole, the implied whole for unmediated history" (Young, 1993, 127). According to Young, "the archivists' traditional veneration of the trace is tied directly to their need for proof and evidence of a particular past. But too often they confuse proof that something existed with proof that it existed in a particular way" (ibid.). He argues that archivists are used to naturalizing particular versions of history and warns that historical sites and remnants in museums and archives threaten to displace "our memory work" with claims of "material evidence and truth" (ibid.). Young is not alone in his concern. Over the last two decades, anthropologists and art theorists have criticized the reification of material remains in museums, art galleries, and archives (Clifford 1988; Krauss 1999; Gordon 1997; Sekula 1999; Taylor 2003;

Bennett 2004), and sociologists have problematized the way that memorials have been commodified as tourist attractions (Kugelmass 1996).

Has the discourse of evidence reduced the material remains of the New Denver camp to mere proofs, robbing them of their auratic quality and defiling the chronotope of the immemorial with this secular, scientific fetishization? Over the last decade, numerous scholars of memorials for the Holocaust and the Vietnam War have argued that remains of these horrific events cannot be so easily reduced to controllable facts that serve as tourist attractions or evidential truth (Sturken 1997; Hirsch 1997a; van Alphen 1997; Foote 2003; Williams 2007). So, rather than dismissing the material remains on display in the NIMC as reified evidence, this chapter examines other ways to read and, in particular, *encounter* the material remains of the camp, reflecting on the effects this material can have on visitors.

In "Performing Memory in Holocaust Museums," Richard Crownshaw argues that it is possible to find ways to critically engage with even the most reified nationalistic exhibitions, such as those in the United States Holocaust Memorial that present "an idealized and liberal American identity" and "[displace] foundational indigenous historical traumas" (2000, 18). He argues that "the meaning of an artifact is not determined only by its placement in a narrative matrix, its textuality, but [is] also conferred by its spectators ... [Their] gaze might reinterpret artefactual meaning, loosening artifacts from their exhibitional anchor and metaphysics of presence" (ibid., 19). Thus, while heeding Young's caution that ruins and artifacts can be turned into material proof, I explore the power of material remains as they are loosened from the narrative matrix of the NIMC exhibits. The material remains have a power beyond the linear narrative that uses them as evidence to illustrate the history of internment in New Denver.

In the NIMC, the remains, such as photographic images of people and events from other eras, are embedded in realities that have long since disappeared (Kracauer 1995, 56). Remains beckon us, hinting at the possibility of "[conjuring] up anew, [these] disintegrated unities" of once-intact modes of living (ibid.). To conjure suggests a magical act that calls forth what is not present. The shadowy presence of what no longer exists appears before us in what remains. Remains belong to another world that is now beyond our reach. Surviving the vagaries of time, they can seem out of place, a disturbance, disrupting our everyday sense of order. But in the timeless temporal order of the memorial, if they can be transformed into otherworldly objects of veneration, they have a place. Yet, whether the remains can be contained by the narrative of the museum or of the practices and rituals of the immemorial, as Crownshaw argues, depends on the relationship that visitors, worshippers, and the like have to the material.

The memorial, as I will describe, is a place to encounter the potent, disturbing remains of the past.

The residents of New Denver donated most of the objects and documents on display at the NIMC. They were not simply artifacts. They made up the material of living in the everyday world of the camp. Local residents found letters that had been tucked into walls and photographs of the camp discreetly pasted among family portraits in their albums; they pried open the doors of old leaking shacks, finding buckets of human hair and a barber's chair.

The employees and contractors hired to construct the NIMC sorted through the masses of old clothing, furniture, photographs, books, plates, and magazines to select items for the historical displays, with the plan of creating an archive with the remaining material. The first time I visited the NIMC in 1995, I worked with Takana, sorting through the half-catalogued piles of objects, letters, documents, and photographs left by contractors in the Centennial Hall. There were also boxes and boxes of reproduced and carefully organized photographs, but very little information about the donors, locations, events, and people in the images had been recorded. This was a great loss for the Japanese Canadian community. Our plan was to assess everything and then formulate a comprehensive proposal for how the Kyowakai Society would conduct the accession, cataloguing, and storage of the artifacts and documents of historical significance to the NIMC. While coordinating the Oral History Project for the Japanese Canadian Citizens' Association in 1990, I had gained some experience working with artifacts and archival documents from community-based historical collections, in addition to spending many hours in public archives. But I was not prepared for my reaction to the collection at the NIMC. I was overwhelmed by the mass of material. As I read, touched, and smelled, I felt as if I were being pulled by a powerful undercurrent into depths I could not navigate.

An Encounter

In the summer of 1995, the rain was constant. Heavy clouds rolled in from the west over the Valhalla mountain range, filling the valley with cool saturated air. Most days were spent inside the Centennial Hall, knee-deep in documents, wading through the details of daily life in the internment camp that was located on this site over fifty years ago.

As I sorted through these records, rain melodically pattered outside, filling the garden with glistening teardrops. Locals, oblivious to my presence, went about their daily business. The occasional tourist wandered by, peering out from the protection of mushroom-like umbrellas.

Inside the dark, slightly dank smelling hall, another world unfolded. Like debris caught in the changing of tides, the documents and material objects were the flotsam and jetsam of a long-past storm, its destructive fury still evident: bits and pieces from distant places, now adrift together in a jumbled mess. There were small bundles of personal letters written with the elegant flowing penmanship of the 1940s; odd scraps of paper with outlines of vegetable gardens plotted with colourful bursts of flowers; and sewing plans for fitted suits with impossibly tiny and impossibly large waistlines scribbled on the margins. Packets of mysterious letters sent from addresses in Japan filled with flurries of small incisive kanji[15] were stored next to makeshift length-of-the-wall scrolls listing personal donations made to New Denver's Buddhist Church on one of many special occasions.

This peculiar assortment spoke of a new configuration, a rearrangement, a reordering. Together, not only the contents of these documents but also their inscriptions – the indecipherable but familiar kanji, the elegant English writing, piercing the different textures and weights of paper, the paper soaking up the density of ink – they all embodied styles of movement and thought from another era. It was a world generated from a fusion of different habits and crossing the Pacific, a world enjoined through the process of expansion: through travel, new technologies, and imaginary projections of what lay yonder.

These letters, the gardening and sewing plans, and the Buddhist scrolls were thread-like tendrils of a life in the process of becoming, grasping toward a new environment, new conditions, new circumstances. But when Canada declared war, this life began to unravel, tear apart. It was ripped out of the new land where it had begun to flourish.

An estranged yet obsessive relationship to the destruction of their world surfaces in the careful records miraculously saved over the years. There are the masses of photographs recording the living conditions in the road camps. One wonders what drove the unknown photographer to record everything in such detail. How did he envision the records might be used in the future? And then there are the scrapbooks full of carefully clipped newspaper articles reporting everything from the bombing of Pearl Harbour to the confiscation of their fishing boats. It is difficult to imagine someone with their scissors, snipping articles as if they were recipes or stories about royalty and pasting them with precision into large scrapbooks. I was most taken by the insistent, briskly typed correspondence with the British Columbia Security Commission, protesting the way the government had sold their properties and suspended their rights. Although they followed the proprieties of the day, the letters nevertheless contained a restrained mixture of disbelief and outrage.

I looked with incomprehension at the items someone had brought to New Denver: piles of sheet music for piano with stylish 1920s Art Deco covers that belonged in a parlour with velvet upholstery. Didn't they realize there would be no pianos to play in the camps? There were also now-musty copies of the *Illustrated London News* with articles on the 1953 coronation of Queen Elizabeth II. How could they continue to so devoutly "stand on guard for thee, oh Canada" after the war?

Every now and then, a Japanese Canadian elder dropped by the Centennial Hall, startling me into the present. Alone or working silently with the chair of the History Preservation Committee, it was easy to be pulled toward the long-gone places that emanated from the wispy writing of old notes and letters, the typewriter trails of letters pounded onto bonded paper, the click of a camera shutter capturing youths posing stylishly amid the squalor of the camps. Whenever I was introduced to an elder, I was reminded that these documents were now located in the present. It was disconcerting to read a set of personal papers and then, several days later, to recognize their owner, standing before me, fifty years older, no longer the young woman or man I had imagined. (FIELD NOTES AND LETTERS, JULY 1995)

The weight of all that was not there clung to the recovered fragments of everyday life. They were impossible to put together into a coherent picture of what had happened in New Denver (McAllister 2001): the terrifying chaos, the masses of panicked, confused strangers uprooted from their homes and thrown together for an indeterminate time in cramped, leaking shacks in what was for them a desolate, wild location. What was it about these remains that gave them the capacity to evoke such a powerful response? Facts read in books, documents found in archives – none of these had ever had such an overwhelming effect on me.

As Crownshaw argues, the significance of material on display depends on our relation to it and, I would add, our encounter with it. For someone who belonged to a community haunted by the world of the camps, these fragments had an auratic quality. Each document and object had its own individuated history inscribed into its musty, fading surface, whether through ink spatters or creased corners (Benjamin 1985, 220-221). Unlike facts read in books, these objects were significant precisely because they were "inseparable from ... imbedded in the fabric of tradition" (ibid., 223). As Benjamin argues, "this tradition is thoroughly alive and extremely changeable. An ancient statue of Venus, for example, stood in a different traditional context with the Greeks ... Originally the contextual integration of art in tradition found its expression in the cult. We know that the earliest art works originated in the service of a ritual – first the magical, then the religious kind" (ibid.).

The fabric of tradition for the remains of the camp clearly differs from the pre-modern cults or rituals described by Benjamin. The objects and documents donated to the NIMC were mundane objects of everyday life in pre-war communities and the New Denver camp. But inducted into the space of the memorial, they have gained a status akin to a relic, being the remains of a cataclysmic event that profoundly changed the lives of Japanese Canadians. At the memorial, viewed by streams of visitors, they have been incorporated into a new fabric of tradition, they have become "ceremonial objects destined to serve in a cult" (Benjamin 1985, 224-225), in this case, a cult of memory. But again, the camp and its remains are not strictly "magical" or "religious," belonging to an other-worldly cosmos. Devotees do not arrive hoping for transformation or guidance as they follow carefully observed rituals that allow them to safely present themselves to the presence of divinities or the divine (Marion 1991).

Yet, like those who observe the rites of the magical and the religious, the return to the site of persecution points to a need to address the metaphysical aspects of human experience. Here, like the chronotope of the Greek romance, the metaphysical involves forces that we experience as if they were outside of the human realm of action, achievement, and reason. There are events, forces, and figures that we cannot subject to our individual control. They appear to operate through powers beyond the realm of human capacity. It is through rituals and observances that we attempt to mediate their unpredictable and powerful effects on our lives. Likewise, the psychic and somatic after-effects of political violence for survivors, persecutors, and the next generations – whether "flashbacks" of persecution, irresolvable guilt for surviving, the projection of one's violent impulses onto others, the collapse of one's system of belief, or the cautious retreat from the social world (Herman 1992, 46) – can at many levels be experienced as beyond human control. In this way, they parallel that which belongs to the metaphysical, outside what we believe to be the realm of our individual control in the supposedly predictable domain of modern life.

For those whose lives are permeated with the after-effects of political violence, the remains of one's community and the sites where they were violated, much like relics, can be experienced as having the potency of the metaphysical. This potency, as Benjamin and Marion argue in relation to cult objects, gives them the quality of "unapproachability" (Marion 1991; Benjamin 1985). In Benjamin's words: "Unapproachability is indeed a major quality of the cult image. True to its nature, it remains 'distant, however close it may be.' The closeness which one may gain from its subject matter does not impair the distance, which it retains in its appearance" (Benjamin 1985, 243).

Likewise, the site of the internment camp and its remains are unapproachable. We can never fully grasp the ways in which the past seeps into and transforms the present. Nor can we prise all its secrets from what remains, making it impossible to fully recover the past in the intensity and complexity of its entirety. But the unapproachability is not simply attributable to the impossibility of factually recovering the past. For many, much of what happened in the New Denver internment camp, as in other internment camps, remains largely "unspeakable" (Lifton 1967, 500; Caruth 1995, 152-153): the pain and enormity are impossible to recall and fully capture in words and images.

The remains embody what is unspeakable, unrepresentable. As psychiatrics working with survivors of traumatic events explain, when victims of persecution are violated, it defies their (modern) understanding of the world as a meaningful place where there is justice, where laws are upheld and rules of social conduct are respected, ensuring a sense of who we are in relation to others as valued social beings (Herman 1992, 214-215).[16] Acts of persecution – including violent attacks, torture, and captivity – destroy our understanding of the world as a meaningful place. In a world that is meaningful, such events would not be acceptable – it is hard to even imagine that they could happen. They defy meaningfulness: the values and meanings that shape how we organize our world and relate to others who belong to that world. A world in which such events would be acceptable would be a world in which those targeted would be denigrated, disposable, without human value or worth (ibid., 215; Langer 1991, 84).

To present their persecution as wrong, survivors must find ways to represent what happened, which requires giving the unspeakable events meaning. To draw these events into the realm of meaning, it is necessary to profoundly change their understanding of the world: they now must recognize that, at any time, life can be violently and ruthlessly violated (Herman, 1992, 50). Drawing the events into the realm of meaning, the drive and logic of the violent acts become more evident. Their disturbing effects can begin to loosen their grip on us as they become explicable, and perhaps even predictable, and thus more manageable. This is similar to what Benjamin refers to as the decay of aura (1985, 222), although it is never possible to completely be free of damaging effects of political violence (Herman 1992, 193, 235). But, by drawing these events into the realm of meaning, whether sociological explanation, legal discourse, or biography, we gain some control over them, drawing them "closer" to us. Yet even as we attempt to impart them with meaning, to "make credible otherwise incredible events," there is no guarantee that their disturbing effects will dissipate (Young 1990, 9). As Young argues, for example, in order to present incredible events as credible, victims must present themselves as objective and their experiences as factual. But objective factual discourses, never mind the "normal" social discourses that assume a meaningful, just world, do not have the capacity to represent disturbing events in their systems of meaning because the events violate the very principles of *social* discourse (ibid, 9-11; Langer 1991, 6-9).

In New Denver, nightmares are not laid to rest with time. The psychic debris of the camp continues to accumulate, growing with the memories of visitors and the photographs, documents, and mementos they bring. Building and visiting the memorial triggers unexpected memories, conflicts, and anxieties, as will be shown in the next chapters. Even as we dig through the layers of the past, retrieving clues and piecing them together in new explanations, examining the NIMC exhibits of carefully arranged glass vials, shoes, trunks and stoves, we are unable to recover the past, to decipher its disturbing effects, to master them and force closure.

Of great significance for memorials of political violence, then, is how the potency of "unrepresentable" effects is harnessed. Some memorials invoke the metaphysical and mediate its powerful presence through collective rituals that bind people together in imaginary communities. Others, like Young's countermonuments, gather people together even as they "disperse" their memories, working to dissipate the effects of violence over time.

The Rabelaisian Chronotope

With their power to exceed the reifying discourses of historical evidence, the material remains in the NIMC defy the chronotope of the immemorial. Although the chronotope of the immemorial enacts empty time and is impervious to the forces of change, almost everything about the NIMC is impermanent, including the social body responsible for its maintenance: the Kyowakai Society. The society is composed of a small number of elders. Although in more recent years they have invited the younger Japanese Canadians living in the area to join, this was not enough to increase the membership significantly. If the Kyowakai Society folds, the control over the NIMC will revert to the New Denver Village Council. If this happens, it is not certain whether the NIMC will continue to function primarily as a memorial, a museum, or a tourist site.

The construction and materials of the NIMC are perishable. The fence surrounding it and the walkways are built from fragrant cedar and fir planks. The restored internment shacks and community buildings are weathered wooden structures. The displays are composed of paper documents, musty wool coats and worn-in shoes, wooden buckets, dolls, and photographs. There is insufficient funding for the expertise or equipment necessary to preserve anything in sealed cases with humidity and temperature controls. Everything is exposed to the eroding forces of the seasons – winter snows, the dry crackling heat of summer, and heavy autumn rains. And the garden, a small ecosystem unto itself, constantly changes with human labour and the seasons.

This material enacts what Bakhtin refers to as the Rabelaisian chronotope. Bakhtin explains that initially the Rabelaisian chronotope artistically represented profusive growth of the "real world," challenging representations that reproduced the restrictive religious hierarchies of medieval society. This chronotope emerged in response to the disintegration of the medieval eschatological world-view, in which time was a force that destroyed rather than created (Bakhtin 1981, 205-206) and the human body was perceived as "decay and strife" rather than a source of life (ibid., 171). With residues from an older folkloric form of time based on organic growth measured by events in the agricultural labour cycle (ibid., 207), the temporal order of the Rabelaisian chronotope is materialized in space as it blossoms and ripens by multiplication and increase. Everything, including death and decay as well as consumption, is presented as part of growth.

In the Rabelaisian chronotope, the life of humans and the life of nature are inseparable. They are placed in the same categories and measured by the same scale: the seasons, nights and days, copulation, old age and death plot the course of both a person's life and the life of nature (Bakhtin 1981, 208). By opposing the profusive organic life of human corporeality to the otherworldly ideology of the church, Rabelais returned the basis of language as well as meaning to the body (ibid., 171). He drew on the body in its "anatomical, physiological and *Natur-philosophie* aspects alone [stripped of religious symbolism and demonstrated] ... the whole remarkable complexity and depth of the human body [–] its life [– in order] to uncover a new meaning, a new place of human corporeality in the real spatial temporal world" (ibid., 170).

In terms of the emerging interiority of bourgeois time, in which whatever perishes is individualized and isolated (Bakhtin 1981, 207), the spatialization of Rabelaisian temporality frees bodily functions, objects, and ideas from traditional matrixes and hierarchies so that they can touch one another in their living corporeality (ibid., 169). The "process of digestion, curative machinations, everyday household objects, phenomena of nature, farm life and the hunt are ... united in one dynamic living grotesque image. A new and unexpected matrix of objects and phenomena is created" (ibid., 175).

The perishability of the NIMC, the disintegrating material remains of the camp that visitors witness disappearing before their eyes as they inhale their particles – dust to dust – can not be immortalized by the chronotope of the immemorial. It is the perishing, the decay, that is potent. My encounter with the remains in their various stages of disintegration brought me in touch with a Rabelaisian loss: a form of transformation, of letting go rather than of preserving and fixing, that characterizes the chronotope of the immemorial.

It is the garden that remains part of the background, a setting for the historical displays that seems to most obviously enact the basic principles of a Rabelaisian form of memorialization. It does not rely on the physical durability of materials such as stone and metal, which over time will erode, nor does it rely on technologies that control the environment, for example, by removing excess humidity or ultraviolet light. In the garden, time is spatialized as a force that creates rather than destroys. It blossoms and grows, spreading roots with the wild forest plants introduced by Mr. Sumi; some bonsai die while others flourish. It does not belong to an order strictly separated from other biological or social systems. Its very life depends on the collective life of local Japanese Canadians. It requires the ongoing care of the Kyowakai Society, which has changed over time and might one day disappear as members age or pass on or as younger members introduce new mandates.

The way the garden as well as the fences, river of stones, and walkways settle into their environment as each year passes depends not only on human labour but also on the weather, plant diseases, worms, and weeds. This suggests how a memorial can become embedded in and responsive to the living world. Rather than freezing the site in time, time is materialized in Rabelaisian growth, whereby living and dying biological and social systems make the garden possible or lead to its demise. Combined in a matrix of life forms, they give us a garden that has its own integrity (Lifton 1979, 38-40).

In contrast to the living garden, the remains of the internment camp are vulnerable to the forces of decay. In the memorial's museum-like displays, where items have been saved from the movement of time and preserved for future generations, decay is viewed with alarm. It signals a failure to protect material from the organic process of decomposition. When the remains were placed within the NIMC, they were inducted into a chronotope distinct from that from which they were extricated, rotting in vacant lots, gathering dust in attics, or displayed in someone's china cabinet. Although in the everyday world these items would be of little significance, on display they are elevated into an order of meaning that supposedly preserves forever a semblance of the camp for future generations. But this semblance is slowly unravelling. As the material loses its form, it merges with the indistinct matter of earth, air, and water. Given the fluctuating temperature and humidity, it is only a matter of time before these items will disintegrate. As this material falls apart, it defies the chronotope of the immemorial. It will not last as an eternal reminder of one static version of the past.

The encounter between the visitors and the remains is generative precisely because the chronotope of the immemorial is defied. The remains still give the past body and shape: the dimensions of the bodies that wore those shoes, the gnarled fingers that grasped the tiny glass vials of medicine, the tired bodies that carried the luggage. But, as the remains disintegrate, so do the shapes and images of the events they embody. As they disintegrate, they offer potential to literalize the dissipation of their disturbing effects. Although the NIMC attempts to preserve the potency of the past in eternity, the remains give it a form in which it can fade, dissipate, and transform.

As the suffocating heat inside the dark sunless shacks deadens the senses and we inhale disintegrating particles of blankets, coats, and musty books, we are brought into a new matrix of growth and change, where death and rot are generative and where past and present "can touch each other in their living corporeality." In this way, the past in the Rabelaisian chronotope is not laid to rest and forgotten but rather is transformed and is transformative at a somatic, metaphysical and, as I have suggested, psychic level. Likewise, the elders offer an approach to death, in which death is neither something that destroys and annihilates nor something that is to be frozen in the abstract space of the immemorial. It lives with us, even as it belongs to another order.

The Return of the Dead

> *Obon: the festival for the dead. A Buddhist ritual held in either late July or early August to guide the spirits of ancestors back to their homes.*
>
> – Mrs. Takahara, 23 August 1996

Every summer the New Denver Buddhists hold Obon in the Kyowakai Hall, opening the panel doors that cover the beautiful-to-behold shrine, ornate, lavish with it gold and red carvings, its drapes of deep purple. The shrine's brilliance exudes its own light in the dim hall. Every year a minister comes to conduct the service. The first year after the passing of Mrs. Kamegaya was 1996. In addition to Buddhist and Christian members of the Japanese Canadian community, Mrs. Kamegaya's close friends from the village came to the service. On this day, the NIMC was closed to the public. We shut the gates and cleared out the Kyowakai

Hall, removing the historical displays, setting up chairs as the members of the Buddhist Church prepared the otera.

> *Mrs. Kay Takahara:* Mr. Mori and Mr. Oda said that the [Buddhist] church itself is not a museum yet. It is still alive as long as the members are here. And that was the original agreement: when there is a church service, everything, all the displays [for the NIMC], are moved aside. (Takahara, Interview, 23 August 1996)

So I have tried to always remember as I set forth, "it is alive." With the living community in New Denver it remains potent and present even if it eludes my words. So how to clear out the artifice, to make room, to prepare what is beautiful to behold for the ancestors as they return home each year?

CHAPTER FOUR

Continuity and Change between Generations

A chill blast

strips every leaf and reveals

three apples overlooked

– KAMEGAYA CHIE (1994)

Constructing an Account

Problems with History

When I left New Denver, I had boxes filled with field notes, photographs, tape-recorded interviews, clippings from local newspapers, and copies of documents from the Nikkei Internment Memorial Centre's (NIMC) files. With all this material, I presumed that one of the easiest tasks I would face on returning to Ottawa would be reconstructing a short history of the NIMC. It would be a matter of selecting the relevant information and fitting everything into the sequence of events that led to the creation of the NIMC. But as I sifted through this material, I realized that there were many different versions – my own included – of events. Each version conceived the NIMC differently: as a tourist attraction that brought revenue to local businesses, as a museum that preserved local history, as an educational centre that informed the public about human rights, as a memorial for Japanese Canadians scattered across Canada, and as a community venue for the elders.

The most obvious way to read the NIMC is as a tourist site, specifically, as a museum. But I wanted learn what the elders had envisioned when they decided to build the NIMC. I knew it was not simply a tourist site to them. I wanted to learn about their role in its development, how developing, constructing, and operating the NIMC had affected their community and how this changed over time. By making the object of my study the NIMC rather than the local Japanese Canadian community, I aimed to learn how building the memorial changed not only the terrain of memory but also the community itself.

To learn about the NIMC from the perspective of elders, it was obvious that I should ask them for their accounts. But when I began to piece together the history of the NIMC's development, I found that it was easier to acquire what

I assumed to be the necessary facts from the NIMC's files. In contrast to my interviews with the elders, funding proposals, blueprints, minutes of meetings, and contract agreements provided dates, names of donors, the criteria imposed by funding agencies, and descriptions of the responsibilities of, for example, the project manager and archivist. Eventually, though, it became apparent that these sources were limited. They provided information about the operation of the NIMC as a museum, reproducing the idea that this was its main purpose. There was very little about its significance for the community of elders in New Denver. When I finally turned to the elders, they offered quite a different history of the NIMC's development, one that revealed both the continuity and transformation of their community. For the elders, the NIMC has been one of many memory projects that they have initiated over the years to transform the site of the New Denver internment camp.

But first I will review what the NIMC files can tell us. In the early 1990s, the Kyowakai Society decided it needed a professionally written proposal to apply for funding. Members hired a local historical restoration contracting company, Robert Inwood and Associates, to write their proposal. With Inwood's proposal, they secured the majority of the $500,000 in funding that was required to construct the NIMC. Funds came from the Japanese Canadian Redress Foundation, the provincial government's British Columbia Heritage Trust, the Vancouver Foundation, private donations, and donations in kind. Government employment programs, including the BC 21 Program and the Social Services Employment Initiative Program, provided most of the wages for the employees.

Once the major funding bodies approved the proposal, the Kyowakai Society hired Ken Butler to manage the project. Drawing on his extensive experience in local historical restoration projects, Butler implemented the blueprint produced by the consultants for the NIMC's funding proposal. He was responsible for coordinating everything from fundraising, hiring employees, and installing the Centre's electrical system to creating the historical displays and assisting Mr. Roy Tomomichi Sumi, the master gardener, in his creation of the Centre's Japanese garden (see Gagnon 2006). Butler hired a construction crew and carpenters to construct the Centre and restore the NIMC's historical buildings. He hired an archival consultant and several assistants to research the history of the internment camp in New Denver and create the NIMC's historical displays. At an administrative level, Butler reported to the Kyowakai Society on a monthly basis, presenting a progress summary and financial report. The Centre took two years to construct. After its completion, the Kyowakai Society assumed control over its administration and operation. With government grants, two or three students run the Centre from May to September each year.

4.1 Nikkei Internment Memorial Gardens before the grand opening in May 1994. *Courtesy of the photographer, Don Lyon.*

The NIMC files show that the contractors integrated the Centre into broader networks of activity throughout the Kootenays that were aimed at preserving the region's past.[1] Funding agencies required the NIMC not only to demonstrate the historical value of its exhibits but also to enter formal agreements with other local museums to coordinate their operations. For example, the NIMC and the Langham Cultural Society in Kaslo entered into an agreement to be supportive of each other and to ensure that "their respective projects would not detract from each other in terms of fundraising and/or duplication of public service" (NIMC 1992). This situated the NIMC in the same field of activity as the other local museums in the West Kootenays with mandates to preserve and exhibit the local history of primary industries like mining and logging. This field of activity includes the installation of plaques and signs marking historical points of interest and the restoration of turn-of-the-century commercial buildings, town sites, and infrastructure such as sternwheeler ships and forest fire lookout towers. It also encompasses publications on the history of the region, including tourist pamphlets, postcards, maps, books, and oral histories. In addition, there are groups who have built cultural centres, like the Doukhobors who sought to preserve their history and, specifically, their experiences of persecution by building the Brilliant Cultural Centre in Castlegar.[2]

The increasing prominence of history preservation in this region has been propelled by a shift in economic activities. Over the years, as the demand for timber and ores fluctuated on the world market, and as the methods of extracting resources increasingly depleted their supply and sustainability, there has been a shift away from logging and mining in favour of service industries such as tourism, outdoor recreation, and holistic healing. This shift is not simply market-driven. Local environmentalists and village councils have joined together to protest, for example, logging methods permissible under provincial legislation that destroy local watersheds, threatening the water supply and the stability of the mountain slopes surrounding their homes. As well, the economic shift reflects the interests of various groups who have settled in the area and are committed, variously, to New Age lifestyles, skiing, rock climbing, and green politics. Provincial and federal grants, employment creation programs, and regional bylaws have also supported cultural projects, including historical preservation, events at local art galleries, festivals, and the restoration of commercial buildings with historical value.

Examining the documents in the NIMC's files in this context – including media reports, transcripts of interviews with contractors, funding applications, and correspondence with Japanese Canadian organizations – it became evident that these documents were premised on the assumption that the NIMC was a museum for the general public. The overview of the development of the NIMC that I produced from these documents did not provide insights into the effect that building and running the NIMC had had on the community. They said little about the significance of the memorial for the Kyowakai Society and whether it offered a means for them to collectively remember the past. I realized I had to write another account, but this time from the perspective of the elders.

Working with the Elders

Before I arrived in New Denver, a number of people had warned me about conflicts that had arisen between the contractors and some of the sansei over how to interpret the community's history in the NIMC's public displays. Clearly, then, individuals involved in the NIMC had very different views about the purpose of the NIMC. This made me think carefully about how I was going to give an account of the NIMC. As Jonathan Potter (1996) argues, individuals or organizations that give an account of events invariably have an agenda in doing so. They selectively solicit, record, and then assemble details to construct an explanation that reinforces or challenges prevailing views. One of my main aims here is to challenge the idea that the NIMC is just a museum, an idea that, initially, I had inadvertently reproduced. My agenda, then, is to show how the NIMC is something quite different for the elders.

My account of the NIMC is constructed primarily from interviews with three elders, although I also draw on interviews with sansei and project workers as well as from History Preservation Committee meetings and my discussions with the chair of that committee over a two-year period. These elders were the only surviving internees who were directly involved with building the memorial. Two were also members of the Kyowakai Society's History Preservation Committee and were thus responsible for overseeing the committee's research activities and the operation of the NIMC. The other elder with direct knowledge about the memorial was a prominent elder who had opposed its design.

My first challenge was to find a way to learn from the elders in their own terms, rather than using questions based on my criteria. Although I had already conducted interviews with a number of elders, they were loosely structured as oral history interviews, a familiar mode of interviewing Japanese Canadian elders. This conventional format has limitations. It orders the lives of the interviewee in a chronological narrative, following what are considered key phases of life: childhood, schooling, marriage, work, retirement.[3] The autobiographical narrative assumes an "individual and autonomous" rather than "communal or relational" notion of self; therefore, the narrative produced by this form of interviewing can value decisions that promote self-interest rather than the welfare of the group (Sweet Wong 1998, 169). In this regard, imposing an autobiographical narrative on wartime Japanese Canadians, many of whom did not pursue their individual interests or follow the normative phases of development, is not appropriate. For example, many older siblings gave up career or marital aspirations in order to support their younger siblings and older parents. For someone who, for example, "failed" to marry, the interview can end up using normative expectations that overlook the decisions they made on behalf of their extended family or other Japanese Canadians.

Yet, despite its limitations, because both the elders and I knew the autobiographical narrative well, it was possible to use this script as a starting point and then rework and alter it. Rather than asking, "When did you get married?" one can ask "Then what happened?" The interviewer can pick up the threads of the storylines in the account presented by the interviewee and ask questions to fill in descriptions of the events and places discussed, to trace out their feelings, their reasoning, their hopes, and their fears while respectfully navigating the silences. But, as a means of learning about more recent history, specifically the process of building the memorial centre, I still found this approach inadequate. The NIMC was a collective community process, not the story of an individual or family. Even when I applied Mona Oikawa's concept of relational identity from her exploration of how Japanese Canadian mothers and daughters intergenerationally remember their families' experiences during the war years (forthcoming), it was difficult to generate a narrative or "script" for the NIMC. I realized that this was in part because I had no idea what the NIMC "was" to the elders, which made it difficult to ask the right questions. Obviously, I was having trouble letting go of my assumption that the NIMC was a museum. But I was also anxious to represent the elders respectfully and to convey the complexity of their accounts. I was worried about misreading or misrepresenting what they shared with me, especially their views on the NIMC. Some of this information was sensitive, especially that concerning the conflicts between contractors, employees, and Japanese Canadians (Pamesko, Interview, 6 September 1996). At the same time, I realized that in my hesitancy to interpret their accounts, I was failing to recognize their agency. They were skilled in the interviewing process. They were clear about what they wanted me to record and how they wanted it to be documented. They would instruct me to turn off the tape recorder when they wanted to tell me something off the record. Before starting, they would forewarn me about what types of questions were not appropriate and signalled when they wanted to stop the interview for breaks. They had well-developed narratives and incisively crafted stories that identified what was important and should be noted. The elders had developed these skills over a long period. From the beginning of the redress movement in the 1980s, the elders had been interviewed frequently by journalists, oral historians, schoolchildren, filmmakers, and researchers. In addition, some regularly gave public presentations on their wartime experiences.[4]

When the elders spoke about the NIMC during interviews, they made it clear they were speaking in a formal capacity, conveying information they deemed appropriate for the public record. This did not include, for example, their personal views about other individuals. On one occasion, when I inadvertently asked an indiscreet question and the elder answered, we rewound and erased that section of the tape. During the interviews, I thus came to understand that the elders were speaking in a representative capacity, making public statements that they knew I planned to use in public forums.

To ensure I presented their views properly, I sent them my first draft, highlighting the sections in which I referred to them, and invited corrections. When they approved the first draft, I felt relieved. But I also had to make decisions about revealing their identities. Although everyone, with the exception of one elder, had signed a consent form giving me permission to do so, I still had to consider whether it was appropriate. The broader context of the Japanese Canadian community informed my decision. Starting with the grassroots activism

4.2   Mrs. Takahara, the Buddhist minister, Mr. Tad Mori, and Mrs. Okura *(left to right)* in the Kyowakai Hall, 1996. *Photo by the author.*

of the 1970s, oral histories became one way to rebuild intergenerational relationships.[5] Elder members of the community shared their knowledge with younger members, helping them understand the community's past while collaboratively producing historical records for future generations. In New Denver, several elders, notably the men, invited me to their homes to record their life histories and recollections. I understood that they gave me the responsibility to document their accounts. In this context, it was important to record their names, identifying their role in the history of the community. Nevertheless, I asked the elders for permission once again. After I left New Denver, two elders had passed away, and so I informed their families that I understood they wanted their accounts to be published. The families as well as the other elders promptly responded, confirming I had their permission to publish their accounts and their names.[6]

When I asked the elders how the NIMC was formed, very few gave a detailed account. Here, I must admit that I did not press them if they seemed reluctant to discuss the Centre. I tried to be attuned to the way they organized their trajectories, their tropes and themes, and encouraged them to elaborate using their own modes of storytelling, whether parables that illustrated life principles, political commentary, or detailed recollections of living conditions. I wanted to hear how they made sense of their worlds rather than imposing my own organizing structure. No doubt, what they presented was framed in ways they thought would make sense to me as someone who did not speak Japanese or live in New Denver and was a happa sansei.

Thus, my account of the NIMC draws on the main themes that recurred throughout the interviews, informal discussions, meetings, and visits. Although some elders gave detailed answers to my questions about the NIMC, others made only passing reference to various NIMC events. This does not mean that they saw the NIMC as insignificant. Perhaps I asked the wrong questions. For example, I may have focused too much on details about the design and construction of the NIMC. The project manager, not the elders, was responsible for these details. Or perhaps they felt it was inappropriate to convey this information to me because I was an outsider. Yet, in most cases, the elders gave their views on recent social changes associated with the NIMC, including extending membership in the Kyowakai Society to the sansei. All the elders referred to the implications of this change. In particular, they noted it had become increasingly difficult to participate in meetings because they were conducted in rapidly spoken English rather than Japanese.

To construct my account, I draw directly from my interviews with Mrs. Pauli Inose and Mrs. Kiyoko Takahara. I worked closely with them, as well as with Mr. Shoichi Matsushita on the Kyowakai Society's History Preservation Committee. Both Mrs. Inose and Mrs. Takahara had been active members of the Kyowakai Society. Mrs. Takahara was also a member of the Buddhist Church in New Denver. Mrs. Inose was a member of the Japanese Canadian United Church and the Kohan Garden Society. Both were directly involved in recent initiatives to improve the NIMC's historical displays.

I also draw on my interview with Mr. Senya Mori, a prominent figure both in the Japanese Canadian community and in the village of New Denver. He was the lay minister for the Buddhist Church and a past president of the Kyowakai Society. He was also an elected member of New Denver's Village Council, serving several terms as mayor. He was not involved in the construction and operation of the NIMC but was an active critic, strongly disagreeing with the NIMC committee's decision to turn the Kyowakai Hall, a community venue, into a display area for photographs and artifacts. In his interview, he offered a critical assessment of the implications of the NIMC for the local Japanese Canadian community.

All three elders described the NIMC in relation to changes in the local Japanese Canadian community. Overall, Mrs. Inose and Mrs. Takahara identified similar events, but they placed different emphases on their significance. They did not identify one isolated reason or event that caused the Kyowakai Society to build the Centre. Instead, they described how different events converged at various moments and culminated in the NIMC. As Mrs. Inose said, "we did not have a clear idea from the start" (Inose, Interview, 16 August 1996). According to Mrs. Takahara, "the project just got bigger and bigger." She recalled how they "didn't intend to expand like this" (Interview, Mrs. Takahara, 23 August 1996).

Accounts are complex (Bakhtin 1981; Bourdieu 1991). The social positions of the listener and speaker shape the interchange and what the speaker communicates, (Bourdieu 1991). Moreover, accounts have multiple purposes and modes of address. At one moment, the use of a particular word or tone may draw the listener into a position in which she or he listens respectfully to what will be revealed as life principles (Bakhtin 1981). At another juncture, the account may switch to a tribute to a deceased member of the community. Here, the listener participates in honouring the dead. The nature of the account can also change with the issue discussed. For example, some topics elicit a sense of camaraderie, while others prompt respectful regard or polite disagreement.

Illocutionary acts need to be read in relation to their context. Thus, when I present the elders' statements, in some instances I provide a broader context for the exchange, which includes my social position in relation to the elder. My multiple roles in New Denver changed from one interview context to another. Being a visiting student, a female, and a sansei positioned me as a particular type of guest. As a younger member of the community, I elicited the elders' protectiveness and guidance. I was also an outsider and an academic researcher. Aware that their accounts would become public records, I recognized the need for carefully worded presentations. But at the same time, I was working for their History Preservation Committee under the direction of one of their sansei, who was my mentor. With so many different roles, I had to be attuned to the obligations of each. Because of my close relationship to my Obaasan, who was very formal, I was also sensitive to the fact that the different roles entailed different types of boundaries, comportments, and emotional expressiveness. This helped me to be more attentive to my manner of communicating with the elders in specific circumstances and in my different roles. But I also knew enough to realize that my mannerisms were clumsy and my understanding of protocol sometimes inaccurate.

An Account of the NIMC

Mrs. Kamegaya and the Importance of the Past

Mrs. Takahara highlighted the role of Mrs. Kamegaya in her account of "how it all started." She began her account by identifying Mrs. Kamegaya as the individual responsible for initiating what is known today as the NIMC.[7] From 1983 to 1987, Mrs. Kamegaya was the first and the only woman to become

4.3 Mrs. Nancy Mori, Mrs. Takenaka, Ruby Truly, and Mrs. Matsushita *(left to right)* at a community event at the Nikkei Internment Memorial Centre, 1996. *Photo by the author.*

president of the Kyowakai Society. Innovative, elegant, and visionary, she was well respected in New Denver.

As Mrs. Takahara claimed, "She knew how to lead!" She planned for changes the community was about to undergo before anyone else realized that change was afoot (Takahara, Interview, 23 August 1996). She challenged the established male order in the local Japanese Canadian community, for example, by taking leadership roles typically occupied by men and by changing membership rules for the Kyowakai Society.

I understood Mrs. Takahara's recognition of Mrs. Kamegaya as a public tribute to a well-respected community leader who had recently passed away. Yet this recognition of Mrs. Kamegaya was more than a simple tribute. For members of the Kyowakai Society, Mrs. Kamegaya has come to represent the need to transform, to constantly adapt to changing circumstances while retaining a sense of what was essential to who they were: the tenets of continuity and change. This allowed community members to orient themselves toward a collective future, despite their dwindling numbers. To facilitate this adaptation, Mrs. Kamegaya revised values that threatened the continuity of the community. For example, she put aside the complex values that shaped the rules restricting the membership of the Kyowakai Society to older Japanese Canadians. Given that many of the old-timers were passing on or in failing health, they adapted the Kyowakai's rules to reflect the changing demographics of the community, or the Society would die out. At the same time, Mrs. Kamegaya respected the values essential to the older members' sense of self, which allowed them to meaning-fully engage with the world in which they lived. This was evident in their sense of responsibility to others. On the one hand, Japanese Canadians in New Denver saw their unique experiences of internment as something beyond themselves that they were obliged to share. On the other hand, they saw the areas where they lacked experience not as inadequacies but as opportunities to work with others who had experience in these areas. The idea of building a memorial for the internment camp in New Denver embodied these values.

With regard to how it all happened, Mrs. Takahara's account was not limited to Mrs. Kamegaya's role. She also identified factors that influenced Mrs. Ka-megaya. She described how Mrs. Kamegaya was moved by the stream of Japanese Canadians who began to visit New Denver in the early 1980s searching for a connection to their past. This past houses painful memories that many Japanese Canadians tried to "leave behind" after the war. Mrs. Takahara described how Japanese Canadians from "all over" began to visit New Denver. "There were busloads from the Buddhist church in Alberta who would come to New Denver. [This was] before the NIMC" (Takahara, Interview, 23 August 1996). She noted how New Denver's Buddhist church was a big attraction: "Without the church, that big building where it was housed [the Kyowakai Hall] was nothing; [there was] nothing to see in there" (ibid.). As well, she explains that when nisei began to retire and their children grew up, they had "lots of time" and so would organ-ize buses and "drop in here because a lot of people lived here [during the war] and [they] wanted to see the place again" (ibid.).

Her account concurs with other events that compelled Japanese Canadians across Canada to visit New Denver. In the mid-1970s, the Asian Canadian move-ment inspired younger Japanese Canadians to research their past and become involved in grassroots politics (Takasaki, Interview, 15 July 1990). This led to nationwide centennial celebrations in 1977 to mark the arrival of the first Japanese immigrant, Manzo Nagano, to Canada (Japanese Canadian Centennial Project 1978). Photographic records made by Mr. Matsushita, one of the elders, document the celebrations that took place in New Denver (Matsushita, Slide Show Commentary, 21 August 1996). Japanese Canadians from different regions of Canada travelled to New Denver to participate. Today, a simple obelisk (minus the brass ball that once balanced on its peak) marks the centennial in the local village park, just south of the memorial for war veterans.

Just after the 1977 celebrations, sansei and *shin-ijuusha* (recent Japanese immigrant) activists had planned to tour the Japanese Canadian communities
scattered throughout the interior of British Columbia (Kobayashi and Miki
1989) to perform cultural shows and collect information about the different
internment camps. This plan gave way to efforts to mobilize Japanese Canadians
across Canada in the movement to seek redress for the injustices they suffered
during the Second World War. To politically mobilize Japanese Canadians,
activists from different urban centres travelled to almost every Japanese Canadian community across Canada, including New Denver. Records of these activities can be found in articles published in Japanese Canadian newspapers
documenting individual journeys back to internment camps, such as Grayce
Yamamoto's 1974 "Reminiscences of Slocan: Then and Now" in *The New Canadian* and George Tanaka's 1979 "To What Lies Buried Deep," also in *The New
Canadian*. There are books that refer to camp life in New Denver, such as Shizuye
Takashima's *A Child in Prison Camp*, originally published in 1971, and there are
films that use scenes of New Denver, such as Jeanette Lehrman's problematic
documentary *Enemy Alien* (1975) and Midi Onodera's autobiographical *Displaced View* (1988).

Bus tours that take Japanese Canadians and their families to the sites of former
internment camps are a more recent trend. A group of redress activists organized one of the first bus tours in 1987 to remotivate themselves after a difficult
period of negotiation with the government (Kobayashi and Miki 1989). This
started a trend that took off after the National Association for Japanese Canadians successfully negotiated a redress settlement with the Canadian government in 1988. Soon, bus tour groups as well as families and individuals were
visiting the remains of the camps in something that resembled a cross between
a pilgrimage and a tourist trip (McAllister 1993).[8]

Under the leadership of Mrs. Kamegaya, the Kyowakai Society began to host
this stream of visitors, especially the organized group tours who pre-arranged
their visits. The Kyowakai Society formally greeted each group of visitors. Their
generosity and sense of responsibility to visiting Japanese Canadians was extraordinary. The members of the Kyowakai Society greeted hundreds of Japanese
Canadians returning to find a way to deal with a painful and humiliating past.

New Denver as a Destination

According to Mrs. Takahara and Mrs. Inose, New Denver became a key destination in these tours. It is one of the few internment sites where Japanese Canadians continued to live after the war. And it was the only site where the
government had not dismantled the internment shacks. Moreover, many

Japanese Canadians were drawn to New Denver because they had personal associations with the camp. The government interned over 1,500 Japanese Canadians in New Denver during the war, and hundreds of others were briefly held there as the camps in the surrounding area were closed and the government transported the internees out of British Columbia to Japan and other areas in Canada (NIMC displays 1996).

To welcome returning Japanese Canadians, the members of the Kyowakai Society began to prepare potluck meals. The women in the community would cook special dishes such as matsutake gohan, manju, and the local version of Japanese Canadian chow mein. The Centennial Hall and Kyowakai Hall were set up to welcome the visitors. After speeches and socializing, visitors would walk through the Orchard to view the remains of the camp.

But, as Mrs. Takahara explained, as the older members of the society grew older and passed on, it became increasingly difficult to "keep it up": "It is hard because people from all over would come ... and we would serve meals ... [But] we are getting tired ... Forty people come and ... we serve them goodies. [We can't do this all the time, now] that we are getting old. Maybe just serving tea. Serving meals would be a chore for us now ... [and] tea eventually [will be] too much for us" (Takahara, Interview, 23 August 1996).

Mrs. Inose also expressed this sentiment after she returned from a peace conference hosted by the Doukhobor community in Castlegar. She described the huge hall and the "big spread of home-cooked food" that the Doukhobors had prepared for the participants. She recalled that the Japanese Canadian community had once been able to put out a spread for visitors (although, she modestly insisted, not as big). But no more. She pointed out that they were now so few and so much older (Inose, Personal correspondence, 1996). Yet, whenever a group visited New Denver, the elders' sense of hospitality made it difficult for them not to graciously receive them with speeches and trays of delicacies.

To ease the requests to visit them, Mrs. Takahara described how Mrs. Kamegaya began to write diplomatically to Japanese Canadian newspapers and organizations to describe how they were becoming "older and fewer in numbers," suggesting that it was increasingly difficult for them to host visitors. Mrs. Takahara underlined how Mrs. Kamegaya was always thinking of ways of "bettering" or improving things. From Mrs. Takahara, I surmised that Mrs. Kamegaya wanted to build a memorial so that, when they passed on, it would stand in for the elders in their absence. Mrs. Takahara explains how Mrs. Kamegaya was inspired to "preserve all the artifacts ... so people would know what happened [to Japanese Canadians] ... She wanted everyone to know. You know, in [the] Lemon Creek [camp just south of here], nothing is left" (Takahara, Interview, 23 August 1996).

It has been the presence of the Japanese Canadian community and the remnants of the camp that has made New Denver a special place.

Unfolding from Other Projects

Mrs. Takahara described how Mrs. Kamegaya's initiatives to improve their community led to the involvement of organizations and people from outside the local Japanese Canadian community. This changed the parameters of the initial plans. As Mrs. Takahara noted, from the initial proposal for a memorial, the project kept expanding until it turned into the NIMC. When I asked about how the NIMC "began," Mrs. Takahara reflected and then started to recount how Mrs. Kamegaya had written to the Sony Corporation in Japan and even Canadian politicians "in her broken English [to explain their] predicament: 'so many old people left after the war, [so] could you help us with this video?'" Mrs. Takahara's description of Mrs. Kamegaya writing in "her broken English" poignantly underlines that even though Mrs. Kamegaya – a formally educated woman – wrote with difficulty in her second language and was aware that her English made her appear uneducated, she put aside her sense of decorum and public face to pursue a community goal: the improvement of the community's social life. The response was immediate: Sony arranged to send a VCR. The Kyowakai Hall was the only place where they could gather to view their Japanese videos. The hall was "black ... with the wind coming in, so every time we used [the VCR] we had to bring it home. We had a video going every week or second week ... in the old hall" (Takahara, Interview, 23 August 1996).

She explains that they planned to attach a smaller, unused internment shack to the hall to use for society meetings and social events. It would be easier to heat, making it more comfortable during cold weather. But when New Horizon, a provincial agency that funds projects for senior citizens, came to inspect their plans, they were shocked to see "the wind coming in, the lack of windows" (Takahara, Interview, 23 August 1996). Instead of giving a grant for renovations, New Horizon awarded a grant for the construction of a new building. Mrs. Kamegaya directed the project to build what became referred to locally as Centennial Hall. Completed in 1977, it stands out among the wartime shacks with its white plaster walls and varnished wooden beams fashioned from large tree boughs. As Mrs. Takahara exclaimed, "that was Mrs. Kamegaya's baby" (ibid.).

Whereas the Kyowakai Hall must be heated with a wooden stove hours before it is used in the winter, the Centennial Hall has electric heating as well as a modern kitchen and plumbing. Although the Centennial Hall is much more comfortable to the society's aging membership, the elders still use the Kyowakai Hall, which houses the Buddhist shrine. This is where ceremonies such as funerals and the annual Obon are conducted. After the completion of the Centennial Hall, the Kyowakai Hall was still in need of repair. Mrs. Inose recalls that the Kyowakai Hall was finally "condemned and we didn't have the funds to go ahead [and repair it]. So at a meeting we [looked over what] we could get a grant for" (Inose, Interview, 16 August 1996).

We Didn't Mean to Expand Like This

To find funding to repair the Kyowakai Hall, the Kyowakai Society approached Bob Inwood, a resident of New Denver with a consulting company specializing in historical restoration projects. He suggested that they inquire into grants for heritage sites. At first, the provincial funding agency, the Heritage Trust, claimed that the hall was not a heritage site. But then the agency discovered that, in view of the presence of the Buddhist otera, Kyowakai Hall could be considered a church. Mrs. Inose explained that

> some people suggested that we should [pursue] this ... [And] then we just couldn't stop at fixing the hall and [the plans] got bigger and bigger ... A fellow from Victoria, [the head of Heritage, came to New Denver and provided us with different ideas about what would make their project eligible for a heritage grant] ... If it was going to be a heritage [site], we would need other buildings ... Usually, heritage buildings are not moved [from their original site]. But because [the internment shacks] were going to be demolished, we were able to get permission to make them part of our heritage site ... [But before that, we] hired a project manager [Ken Butler] and [work crews]. (Inose, Interview, 16 August 1996)

Mrs. Takahara recalls how the new president of the Kyowakai Society, Sakaye Hashimoto, or "Sockeye" as he is known locally, said, "it's a good idea to preserve [the buildings]." [He said], "let's have it big ... bring all these houses in ... get donations from outside, ask for a large sum [and not be modest], because the [funding agents will] cut [what we ask for] anyway" (Takahara, Interview, 23 August 1996). Mrs. Inose explained, "both shacks were donated. In fact, all three were donated. And at one point we needed more property. Couldn't fit all three [shacks with the Kyowakai Hall on the property we already had]" (Inose, Interview, 16 August 1996). Buying the property was Sockeye's idea. "The Society members all chipped in and were able to buy [the] property next door ... [All the] property was [then] handed over to the village, so [all] the ... grounds belong to the village"(ibid.). Because the Kyowakai Society did not have much money, the members "pitched in" three hundred dollars from the funds granted to them from the settlement for redress.

I asked why the property was given to the Village of New Denver. The elders explained that, while many members of the Kyowakai Society did not want to give control over their property to a body outside of their community, some elders decided to proceed with the plan because the Kyowakai Society would not have to find extra revenue to pay property taxes each year. This continues to be a source of concern. Mrs. Inose explained that although "it's on village land ... we are allowed to use it as long as the society can carry on, and if the society can't carry on, then the village will have to take over" (Inose, Interview, 16 August 1996). I asked about what this meant for the artifacts and the buildings on the property. She replied, "I don't know how that works. Possibly we have the rights to those things – and possibly we have the right to give them to our own heritage [organizations in the larger Japanese Canadian community]" (ibid.).

The Next Generation

One of the key themes that Mrs. Takahara and Mrs. Inose discussed in relation to the NIMC was the transfer of leadership to the next generation. Mrs. Takahara explained, "We have no younger ones up here, so we dragged Sockeye in and made him president right then and there. He had no knowledge [of how the Kyowakai Society operated ... or anything!] ... so Mrs. Kamegaya took him into her place and explained everything to him. That's how it began" (Takahara, Interview, 23 August 1996). She recalled how Mrs. Kamegaya "used to say, I made a man out of him. Because Sockeye [didn't] know much about his background up here or Japanese culture, [in part] because [he was] third generation and never mixed with the Japanese, [so Mrs. Kamegaya] wanted him to read the books [on Japanese Canadian history and culture] so he [would] know more what's to be expected" (ibid.). When I asked about his response she replied, "Well, he had no choice. We are getting old and we need the younger ones. He said he'd join, and we made him president" (ibid.). Sockeye or, more formally, Sakaye Hashimoto, president of the Kyowakai Society, chuckled when he recounted the story of how Mrs. Kamegaya recruited him. He admitted he knew little about Japanese Canadian history and, with respect and warmth, described her patience and clear vision of the future (Hashimoto, Interview, 23 August 1996).

Mrs. Takahara continued:

Then we tried to recruit other younger ones, changing the bylaws so the Occidentals married to the Japanese could join. Before, members of the Kyowakai Society were all Japanese ... [But we needed to change our bylaws] because there was no one else anymore. Our first generation were sick either one day or another, so they couldn't come to the meetings or they had no transportation anymore, so we had to have the younger ones. But they are all intermarried, so we also [had to] invite their spouses too. Gayle's Melvin, Sockeye's Bronwin. (Takahara, Interview, 23 August 1996)

Mrs. Takahara recalled how this change occurred "just a couple of years before we started [working on Mrs. Kamegaya's idea of] preserving the history" (ibid.).

I had heard from local sansei that expanding the membership to include Japanese Canadians who were not "the original members," never mind their non-Japanese Canadian spouses, represented a significant change in the organization of the community for the elders. From what I understand, the Kyowakai Society functioned originally to meet the needs of the pre-war generation. Decision making worked by consultation and consensus rather than by mainstream practices such as Robert's Rules of Order. Ann Sunahara describes the way pre-war issei organizations functioned. Until the 1980s, it seems that the Kyowakai Society of New Denver followed similar practices.

[Leaders] were not selected by competitive election, but by a longer and more complicated process in which the members of an association would reach a consensus on who could best lead them. Similarly the role of the Japanese Canadian leader was different from that of an elected official ... Selection did not give the ... leader the right to act unilaterally on behalf of those he led. Rather, his role was to advise the group, to lead them to consensus on the matters facing them and, after consensus has been reached, to speak on behalf of the association when necessary ... The qualifications for leadership, therefore, were those most conducive to the determination of consensus within the group. Ideally the leader would be the head or scion of the most prestigious family – a mature, experienced, successful and preferably educated man capable of generating respect for himself and his association ... [He also needed] great sensitivity and tact in order to quietly influence the group in the attempts to reach a consensus. (Sunahara 1979, 3)

The elders realized the younger generations did not understand the established way of operating the Kyowakai Society because they were not familiar with pre-war values and systems of governance. Mrs. Takahara underlined how her generation "[respects] the elders very much and, no matter if they are wrong, we get along with them. Gradually, we tell them what's the wrong part. But we never criticize what the elders tell us. We never criticize what the elders tell us [especially in front of everyone else!]. This is the way we were taught" (Takahara, Interview, 23 August 1996). Mrs. Takahara's detailed description of what is expected from a leader suggested to me that it might be useful for the younger generations to pay more attention to these details. It could also have been a way of instructing me, as a member of the younger generation, about leadership. Although I was a temporary member of their community, the instruction also might not have been directed at me as much as through me to the sansei living in New Denver. As a member of the Japanese Canadian community, I would have been able to appreciate the importance of what I was being told and follow the protocol of diplomatically transmitting the elders' concerns to the sansei in their community.

As the original members of the Kyowakai Society had predicted, the inclusion of the third generation in the society changed how it operated. As Mrs. Takahara pointed out,

> It is mostly in English now. And then [the sansei are] well educated. We have only been to high school, then, after that, it has been nothing but Japanese since then, [so in my case] I haven't had a chance to speak English much ... After I graduated from high school – then I got married – then the war started. [I was sent here,] and then I was sent to Japan, then came back here [to live] among the Japanese community. Unless I talk to the [non-Japanese] people, I don't speak much English. (Takahara, Interview, 23 August 1996)

By expanding the membership beyond the original members, the elders dealt with their changing demographics: the addition of non-Japanese Canadian spouses, happa children, and shin-ijuusha. In the larger Japanese Canadian community across Canada, attitudes toward familial relationships with non-Japanese Canadians have changed, but it has always been a complicated and usually emotional issue (McAllister 1991; McAllister and Medenwaldt 1992). At the time of this study, the intermarriage rate was over 95 percent (*Nikkei Voice* Staff 1997, 1). Especially for issei and older nisei parents in the period just after the war, intermarriage was a difficult issue. This was when many of their children first began to marry out.[9] Unless the issei and older nisei disowned their children, they had to find ways to accept their foreign sons and daughters-in-law. It was not simply a matter of accepting a new person and that person's family into one's own family, it also meant incorporating unfamiliar forms of emotional expression, body practices (whether eating, hygiene, or grooming), and ways of relating to in-laws into the intimate domain of the family.

Today, most issei and nisei in Canada have non-Japanese Canadian in-laws and happa (great)grandchildren. But, at an abstract level, the idea of including non-Japanese Canadians – *hakujin* – into their political organizations, where they would influence the priorities and future direction of the entire community, is another matter. This concern cannot be read simply as the racial "othering" of non-Japanese Canadians; it must be read in the context of pre-war and wartime experiences in which administrators dismantled their political institutions and sent many of their community leaders to prisoner-of-war camps. There were many stories about white neighbours and friends who promised to take care of their properties while they were incarcerated but sold them for profit. In New Denver, some elders express a sentiment shared by many older Japanese Canadians in the larger community across Canada:

> When the hakujin start coming over here and taking over, it is not going to be
> the same. And there are no younger Japanese over here ... So I don't know what's
> going to happen after we're all home bound and that ... We are kind of worried
> about that (Elder, correspondence, New Denver 1996).

In New Denver, the abstract hakujin differs from individuals who have become close friends or family members. This includes non-Japanese Canadian spouses of either the elders' children or the local sansei. In New Denver, these spouses are involved in the community through their Japanese Canadian partners. They have taken on supportive roles, for example by offering skills in areas such as accounting, construction, organizing public events, and artistic productions. With their sansei spouses, some have accepted positions on the executive committee of the Kyowakai Society. Here, they follow the lead of their Japanese Canadian spouses. From what I observed, they question only those decisions that either seem impractical or run counter to the society's principles. They refrain from undermining or taking over the decision-making process itself.

Two of the sansei who were on the Kyowakai Society's executive committee became more involved in the society's affairs during the last phase of the NIMC's construction. They were alarmed when they learned that the NIMC committee did not heed the elders' opposition to turning their community venues into historical displays at the NIMC. Thereafter, to ensure that the elders' concerns and insights were addressed by the executive committee, these sansei set up consultation practices. For example, with regard to hiring, rather than holding one meeting to decide on the candidates, time was now taken to enable the elders to look over the candidates' curriculum vitae and discuss the potential candidates among themselves. If possible, the elders arrived at a consensus and then informed the sansei on the executive. In some cases, the sansei did not agree with some elders. In other cases, the sansei recognized that the issue under consideration was under the jurisdiction of the elders. This was the case with respect to whether and how the Buddhist shrine would be displayed to the public. The sansei on the executive committee recognized that the elders were the foundation of the Japanese Canadian community in New Denver and that the Kyowakai Society was one of the key institutions for fostering the collective life of Japanese Canadians in the village. This was reflected in the way the sansei wonder what will happen to the community when the remaining elders pass on.

The expansion of the Kyowakai Society's membership also extends to the shin-ijuusha. This is significant, given that many Japanese Canadian communities tend to be uncertain about how to include shin-ijuusha in their community organizations. There are cultural and linguistic differences between pre-war issei and nisei and their sansei children and postwar shin-ijuusha and their descendants. The issei who immigrated to Canada before the war as well as nisei who grew up during this period speak in older dialects and most sansei do not fluently speak Japanese. Japanese Canadians from the prewar community sometimes stereotype shin-ijuusha as arrogant, individualistic, and competitive. These feelings are based in part on class differences. Many shin-ijuusha have higher levels of education than the issei and nisei, and as a result some older Japanese Canadians believe that the shin-ijuusha disdain them as old-fashioned, uneducated fishing or peasant-stock pre-war immigrants. At the same time, some believe that modern Japanese lack traditional values and etiquette. All these generalizations point to anxieties about the pre-war generation's sense of self. It is important to note that numerous organizations founded by prewar Japanese Canadians have not hesitated to include shin-ijuusha in their activities. For example, in centres such as Ottawa and Vancouver, shin-ijuusha have been elected as the presidents of local chapters of the National Association of Japanese Canadians and as chairs of committees such as the Human Rights Committee in Vancouver and are an integral part of artistic communities.

This is the context for concerns that the expansion of the membership to shin-ijuusha could result in a complete transformation of the Kyowakai Society, a structure that has developed over the years to coordinate the elders' activities, resolve conflicts, deal with crises, and represent their interests. This is, understandably, a source of anxiety. Yet Mrs. Takahara and Mrs. Inose discussed the changes in leadership not only in terms of the "end of the community." When, at the end of our interview, I asked Mrs. Inose if she had anything to add, she speculated on the future in positive terms:

A lot of [the original members of the Kyowakai Society] that are still here were here right from the very beginning. So there is continuity. Our Kyowakai Society still continues, and it probably will even with the younger ones. They're here. Like ... Sakaye, he probably will carry on ... And from now on there will be the younger groups joining. There are a lot of people coming in [such as the shin-ijuusha and younger sansei], so they'll be joining [the society as well]. (Inose, Interview, 16 August 1996)

The elders discussed change as an inevitable process in the community, viewing it in relation to the change in leadership that occurred when they themselves took over from the first generation. Mrs. Takahara recalled:

> Well, when ... the Kyowakai Society changed over to the second generation there was a pow-wow too. The first generation were really good, they could write and read all our Japanese. [As the first generation was getting old] and the [leadership was] changing to the second generation – just like us changing [to] the third [generation] ... [It is like] ... they don't know ... [just like we didn't know]. It's just the same. Turn it over to the third generation and to you people, and we are still hanging on to the first-generation ideas, but the third generation doesn't know anything of those ideas. Oh, they don't know. (Takahara, Interview, 23 August 1996)

She concluded with what might seem like resignation: "We can't do anything anymore, so we just let them go on with it" (ibid.). But if we consider the context, it is as if she is throwing up her arms, shaking her head at the inability of the sansei to understand things properly. At the same time, she recalled how her own generation went through the same process. She conceded that, however frustrating it might be for the elders, it is time for the next generation to step forward. Moreover, as she constantly pointed out, the elders are getting "tired and old" and would prefer not to constantly have to "take care of things," emphasizing that it was time for the sansei to step in and become responsible for running the community.

Exclusions

The way in which the plans to publicly memorialize the internment camp in New Denver changed reflected the changes in the community's leadership. Mrs. Takahara described what the elders envisioned:

> Well, we just wanted to keep all these artifacts and didn't want to expand like this, really big, nationally. We use[d] to talk about [ways to publicly commemorate the camp] quite a bit, but since the younger generations wanted to do this and get bigger and bigger, well, we couldn't argue [against their plans] because we didn't know how to argue with them, and so we just let it go. (Takahara, Interview, 23 August 1996)

Then she added, in a rather matter-of-fact manner that brushed the issue aside: "We'll be going pretty soon [i.e., dying], so it's up to them now!" (ibid.).

The decision to proceed with the sansei's plans involved changing the technology and dominant language used by the elders to run the Kyowakai Society. This facilitated the change in leadership during the construction of the NIMC. For instance, without training in computer-based technology, which was now used to record the Kyowakai Society's business, it was difficult for the elders to participate in the organizational aspects of the NIMC, which is now the Kyowakai Society's main activity. The elders were acutely aware that the leadership was in transition, although, as mentioned earlier, they realized that this was both inevitable and necessary. As Mrs. Inose stated,

> Now that we have started using the computer at the NIMC and things like that, which we are not used to ... it makes it a little harder for us to go down and help. So that's one reason why we haven't been able to get involved. I suppose we should try to get used to a bit of that, like the cash register and things. But I think if there are younger people who can do that, they should do it. (Inose, Interview, 16 August 1996)

During the construction of the NIMC, the sansei made most of the decisions on the NIMC committee. In part, this reflected differences in language. The sansei converse in English, and while the elders speak English and Japanese, most are more comfortable communicating in their style of Japanese.[10] Since the NIMC committee meetings included the non-Japanese Canadian project manager and a representative for the village, the meetings were conducted in English. After the completion of the NIMC, these changes continued to affect the Kyowakai Society. The meetings continued in English, and the society relied on computer technology to record its business. Like Mrs. Inose, Mrs. Takahara described how these changes made it difficult to fully participate in meetings.

> We can't follow them. And we're kind of hard of hearing, and people are talking in low voices one after another. And before you know it, the meeting's over. And we don't know what it's about, but we can't say anything. So we just follow along, and we just do whatever we're being told to do. (Takahara, Interview, 23 August 1996)

Although the use of English made it difficult for the elders to participate fully, it is important to read these statements in the context of the interview. Mrs. Takahara was a prominent member of the Kyowakai Society speaking to me, a sansei. I was hired to work on their History Preservation Committee under one of the local sansei. Given my position, it would be expected that their concerns would undoubtedly press on my conscience and that I would discreetly communicate them to the other sansei.

Anxiety underlay the elders' criticisms. They were not certain whether the sansei understood how to run the community. As they became more elderly, they realized that they would be unable to take care of things as in the past. This was expressed, for example, in the following statements: "We are getting older and older. We can't do anything about it. It's up to you guys. I don't know what's going to happen when Nobby [an elder who takes care of the NIMC garden] dies. Who is going to take care of the [NIMC] garden?" (Takahara, Interview, 23 August 1996). These statements implore the sansei to be more responsible. They underline the importance of paying attention to the details of operating a community venue, in this case the NIMC.

The elders related to community venues primarily as members of a social group. The responsibilities and tasks required to operate a community venue situated each member in a network of relations to others. The coordination of responsibilities and tasks, which includes how the tasks are designated and performed, was not simply a matter of efficiency. They involved acts of inclusion, exclusion, recognition, status, obligation, and community face. The elders recognized that no matter how seemingly small a particular task might be – whether it is acknowledged or overlooked or whether it is facilitated or undermined by others – it affects community relationships.

The elders' anxiety about the ability of sansei to properly attend to what was necessary to "keep the place going" was evident in the following commentary. One elder explained that she and another elder had decided to find ways to become more involved in the operation of the NIMC. They decided to begin by helping with the garden. But she explains that "the last time we went to help, [Nobby, who does all the gardening on the site,] had taken all of his tools home. There was no place to keep them. So we just used the bucket and knelt on the concrete." This elder describes a situation in which a seemingly small detail – ensuring that there was a safe place at the NIMC for Nobby's tools – had repercussions. On the one hand, it meant that Nobby, who dedicated almost all his time to the garden, was not given a place where he could safely keep his tools: in other words, at a symbolic level he was not given "a place" in the NIMC. On the other hand, it also meant that those who wanted to become more involved in the Centre did not have access to gardening tools, which resulted in their exclusion. To make matters worse, no one noticed that two of their elders were on their knees on the concrete working with the most rudimentary tools to weed the garden.[11] These were all details to which the elders running the Kyowakai Society would have attended.

The NIMC precipitated a radical change in the operation of the Kyowakai Society. Their meetings were eclipsed by those of the NIMC committee meetings. The meetings became a forum to make decisions on the construction of the NIMC. As well, during this period, the contractors occupied their main community venues. They used the Centennial Hall as an office and the Kyowakai Hall as a work area. There was no place for the elders' meetings or activities. After the NIMC was completed, the elders had to adapt to the changed Kyowakai Society and to the fact that their community venues were now on display to tourists. They were thus forced out of their community venues and the decision-making positions on the executive committee of their organization.

In this context, weeding the NIMC garden was an initial attempt by the elders to reinvolve themselves in the NIMC. The fact that the people running the NIMC did not note their efforts was an oversight. But for the elders, who belonged to an interdependent network in which every person had an acute awareness of the others, the oversight represented a lack of care. In addition to a carefully targeted reprimand, these accounts express the elders' anxieties about the changing leadership and what they viewed as the ineptitude of the sansei. Another elder added: "Mrs. H.'s got a back ache. Mrs. T. too ... We're all – I'll be eighty soon. I was told off by my friend in Vancouver: 'You're not supposed to be doing all this work! ... You like to help but you can't keep on!' And there is nobody else to take our place."

Inclusions

The changes in the operation of the Kyowakai Society did not mean that the elders had no input in the design and construction of the NIMC. Mrs. Takahara describes how they were consulted for certain aspects of its design. She recalls,

> They put the three houses there like that, then the first house. I don't know how – they had a lot of meetings. Ken Butler wanted it the way we wanted it. I guess it was mostly Sockeye's idea to leave [the shacks] the way they were. The first one [was to be] an office with a bathroom ... Outside ... there was going to [be] just the boards, no shakes, [just like it was when we first came to the camp]; the second house would be the following year ... It was so cold in the first year ... [when the green wood we were given to build the shacks shrunk], you could see through [outside. So later, for insulation, we put cedar shakes and tar paper on the outside and layers of paper inside]. (Takahara, Interview, 23 August 1996)

Mrs. Inose also describes the elders' involvement in the NIMC committee meetings. I read this as an opportunity for her to acknowledge the contributions of the project manager.

> Oh, meetings all the time! And of course Ken Butler was our, uhm ... he was very considerate, and he wanted to do things the way we wanted. So naturally we were having meetings, and he wanted to ensure that [it was] the way we wanted it, not the way they wanted it. So he was very considerate and sensitive. (Inose, Interview, 16 August 1996)

Like Mrs. Takahara, Mrs. Inose describes how the elders were the main source of information for the restoration of the shacks.

> At each meeting it came about – the houses were brought in ... Ken would ask, How do you want it? One could be the first year, as it was originally, and [the next one could show] how people were living [in the following year], and ... the last one [would] be when people have put up their ceilings and started to fix up the walls, making it a little more comfortable. (Ibid.)

It seems that the project manager and his crew frequently consulted them. Mrs. Inose recalls,

> It certainly was [very busy], well yes, it sort of kept us going – really going – and it did sort of disrupt our daily lives a bit – for sure *[laughs]*! We couldn't get a lot of things done that should have been done around the place. But, well, I think that everyone just thought this is the time to go ahead when everyone is involved in it ... [It has slowed down a bit now], yes, because they are not constantly asking us questions. You know we always had to come up with something when they asked us to decide what we wanted to do. So yes, there [aren't] that many questions now. (Ibid.)

Records of the attendance of around eleven elders at the NIMC committee meetings, which involved a total of around twenty people, as well as a file with the short biographical notes the archivist made on various elders, suggest that the project manager and his crew consulted the elders frequently about the camp's living conditions. But, despite these consultations and the elders' attendance at NIMC committee meetings, there were difficulties in communication and gaps in understanding. The question here is not if the elders were consulted, but whether they were consulted on important decisions affecting their community. These decisions included, for example, whether their community buildings should be included in the public displays, how to publicly represent their history of internment, and what was an appropriate way to solicit accounts about their experiences in the camps. Part of the difficulty in communication stemmed from differences in language and cultural modes of interacting. But, in addition, the project manager was hired to construct the NIMC efficiently and quickly within tight deadlines set by the NIMC's funding bodies, making it difficult to develop more collaborative decision-making processes. Although he made efforts to include the elders, at the same time he was not hired to direct a community project geared toward facilitating collective remembrance of the past and healing.

To adequately include the elders, the project manager would have needed another process of decision making that included, for example, translators. But when Mrs. Takahara and Mrs. Inose spoke about the project manager and his staff, they expressed appreciation of the manager's efforts to include the elders and, more widely, his contributions to memorializing the internment camp. Again, for them, the NIMC was about their social relations with others in the community. Mrs. Takahara and Mrs. Inose emphasized the good intentions of the project manager. In this capacity, they continued to "take care" of the community, ensuring that relations with those outside the community were smooth.

Nevertheless, it is important to consider the consequences of the Kyowakai Society's decision to initiate a project in a manner that focused on efficiency rather than social process. For example, without an understanding of the community's historical and cultural background, it would have been difficult for the contractors to develop appropriate forums in which to solicit information about the history of New Denver (Kirmayer 1996). Mrs. Inose describes one of the meetings that the project manager arranged to learn about their experiences.

Kirsten McAllister (KM): And what happened in the meetings?
Mrs. Inose: A lot of the time [the project manager] would get us together, and Mory – Nancy Mory, [she lives] out in Hills now – she [would] record what [we'd] say. But they were very, very reluctant to keep pushing us and pulling it out of us. And at first no one really would talk. And it must have been very hard for those people trying to get the story out of us. But gradually ... gradually, as we met and met, and one of us would say something, and then someone would add something a little more, and [someone would] say, "Oh yes, it was like this" and "Oh yes, it was like that." And gradually, and gradually, it would come out. But it must have been very hard for them ... Nancy would say, "Well, if you really don't want to talk about it, it's all right. Maybe we can do it another time." And they never forced us to do it. But she had that recorder there, and somehow it seemed a little more

... even ... harder to ... I don't know why – you have a mental block just seeing [the recorder].

KM: I get that way too. But you are much better at interviewing than I am ... So that took place over a year? All the interviewing? All the talking?

Mrs. Inose: Two years.

KM: Wow. And then how did they use the material on the tapes that you shared?

Mrs. Inose: I don't know. I think Nancy said her tape wasn't working, so she was very disappointed about that.

KM: Oh dear.

Mrs. Inose: So she wasn't going to ask us all over again.

KM: So for the two years ...?

Mrs. Inose: No, she was [hired] just for the one year. And the other [year] was more or less just group talking.

KM: And then [the project manager] was there, taking notes?

Mrs. Inose: Someone was always taking notes. (Inose, Interview, 16 August 1996)

In this exchange, Mrs. Inose reflects on the meetings in which the elders were asked to disclose their experiences during the war. Given the conflicts that arose during the last phase of construction between an outspoken sansei and the contractors, Mrs. Inose is very diplomatic. She does not dwell on the loss of a year's worth of interviews, which would have been valuable for Japanese Canadians across Canada. Nor does she mention that the NIMC does not have records of the "notes" taken during the other year of interviews. Others had told me that the contractors had taken many of the NIMC records. Perhaps the notes were still in their possession.

It is notable that Mrs. Inose states that they were not "forced" to disclose their experiences. But her use of this term suggests that this is in fact how the interviews *felt*. By making this statement, she recognizes that she and the other elders could have, for example, decided not to participate. Yet it is likely that the elders felt obliged to attend the meetings, the NIMC was, after all, their memorial. Habits of formal decorum, especially with outsiders, would have made it very awkward to directly confront the interviewers, never mind the project manager. Moreover, the ability of elders to follow and thus also determine what happened in the meetings, as Mrs. Takahara and Mrs. Inose note, was limited because of language and cultural differences. Thus, it would seem that although they were not directly coerced, circumstances suggest that it was hard for the elders to do anything but comply. Yet, as Mrs. Inose noted on another occasion, "Of course, we couldn't expect them to understand a Japanese Canadian perspective." Here, she thought the Kyowakai Society was to blame, since it didn't set down any rules for the contractors and their work crew and left them to do what they wanted.

Although the elders had extensive experience being interviewed by journalists, and some had given public talks, they could not speak freely in the NIMC meetings. Numerous factors probably created discomfort. It did not help that local hakujin with little knowledge of Japanese Canadian history were hired to ask them questions about painful memories, with the project manager listening in. Their memories would have included the racism they experienced from local hakujin, making it very awkward to talk in this forum. Nonetheless, Mrs. Inose described how the elders eventually used the meetings as opportunities to overcome some of their feelings about the past. The presence of people from the region who lacked an in-depth understanding of Japanese Canadian history is especially notable. This is an example of how the NIMC as a collective form of remembering included people beyond the Japanese Canadian community, specifically those hired to construct the NIMC and living both in New Denver and in the wider region.

Community organizations assessing various models for building a memorial can learn from the NIMC about factors to ensure supportive conditions for elders to discuss their experiences, including attention to cultural protocols and linguistic differences and designing a process whereby the elders can determine and change the format of the information gathering. The agency of the elders must not be overlooked, as Mrs. Inose's comments underline.

KM: So it was sort of uncomfortable.

Mrs. Inose: Ah? you know, having put that Nikkei Centre together, and going through it – sort of – it wasn't as bad as people thought for us. Because having to work on the Nikkei Center [meant] a little of our feelings were brought out, and we were able to go down there [to the Centre to revisit the past] and see it all over again *[laughs]*.

KM: Hm, so people hadn't talked about their feelings or the past for quite a while? So the Centre was a way to ...

Mrs. Inose: ... It was a healing, a real healing experience for all of us. It is really surprising now, because a lot of people [who] wouldn't talk about it, will now talk about it. And when you can talk about things like that, you know ... things are out in the open, and you can feel ... better.

KM: You know, I think that's really important.

Mrs. Inose: Yes it is, to be able to talk.

KM: And for other Nikkei living elsewhere, to realize that it's important to talk. A lot of people don't know this until they start [talking]. I suppose it made a difference because you did it as a group together?

Mrs. Inose: Yes. It strengthened us ... one person possibly probably didn't want to [talk], but everyone else was talking about it. And then [the person would] sort of chime in and were able to tell what they felt, what they did. (Mrs. Inose, Interview, 16 August 1996)

When the contractors tried to turn the elders' community buildings into NIMC displays, Mr. Senya Mori and Mrs. Kamegaya stepped forward to intervene. They spoke directly or, in other cases, used old-style protocols, communicating through the grapevine and using oblique references. The old-style approach avoids confrontation, allowing the individual to keep face while modifying her or his decision so she or he can address the concerns expressed by others. Clearly, the contractors and the new Kyowakai president were not familiar with these formalities. Moreover, even if they did note the objections, it is not clear whether they would have changed their plans.

Mrs. Takahara noted that "things escalated when [the projector manager and Sockeye] wanted to put [a] video [display in the Centennial Hall]" (Takahara, Interview, 23 August 1996). Bob Inwood introduced this idea in his blueprint for the NIMC (Inwood 1992). Mrs. Takahara explained, "I think Sockeye wanted to have it like that. But Mrs. Kamegaya didn't want to have it ... If that [happened], we wouldn't have any place to have a meeting, have shows, or do origami sessions ... as long as there are Japanese here, we want that hall for ourselves" (ibid.). Today, the Centennial Hall is off limits to the public and continues to be the only building on site that is for the sole use of the Kyowakai Society.

There was also controversy over the use of the Kyowakai Hall, in particular with regard to the Buddhist shrine. Mrs. Takahara explained that originally "the hall was built for the Kyowakai members, and then we decided to have a church. So they extended the back part for a church. In Alberta too, there is a big building. Ordinarily the front part is used for entertainment and meetings and the raised part is for the church, but it is all closed in. During the church time, it is all opened up" (Takahara, Interview, 23 August 1996).

While the site was under construction, the contractors used the main floor of the Kyowakai Hall as a workspace for cleaning and organizing donated artifacts and documents. In the proposal written by Inwood, the hall was supposed to be used as a display area for Japanese Canadian history. This proposal included plans to incorporate the community's Buddhist shrine into the public displays as an artifact (Inwood 1992). Mr. Senya Mori, as well as Mr. Oda, another prominent community figure, strongly disapproved. Mr. Senya Mori pointed out that

Sockeye was involved there. Mrs. Kamegaya, she's the one! [She's the one] that started all that. I disagreed – at the time. But that's why I don't belong to the

4.4 Katherine Shozawa's memory box project for Senya Mori *(with Tad Mori on the left)*, 1995. *Courtesy of the artist, Katherine Shozawa.*

Kyowakai Society now. That's why they didn't invite all the past executive [to the opening ceremony]. *[He chuckles].* After all, now, if we weren't there, there's no Buddhist or Kyowakai Society. Three people came to us – Oda, me, and Sawada. They asked us, why don't we return? If not, [the society is] going to die out. We say, we want to do it this way, then we'll return. But no. (Mori, Interview, 5 September 1996)

This was a controversial issue. Mrs. Takahara acknowledged the position of Mr. Senya Mori and Mr. Oda, but she had another view:

Well [for] Mr. Mori and Mr. Oda – it's still alive, see. He didn't want it museumized. So Senya thinks that now that our members are getting fewer ... we should send that church to somewhere else, and be done with it. But without [the shrine], it's nothing. And I don't know what the BC Buddhist Church would think about it. I am not supposed to be saying those things. The church is only for the men members ...

The inner temple there. One person is responsible for it, and he and only he is supposed to do the flowers and decorating, no one else goes in and touches things like that. So Mr. Senya Mori and Mr. Oda are strict about it. But sometimes, if a busload or Japanese group comes, [Tad and I] open it and show them ... I asked the president of the Buddhist Church about this – it's okay to show them [as long as] we don't go up [into the shrine area]. Other places in Alberta or Vancouver, the church is open, but the inner [space behind the door] is closed ... People can not go up into the shrine ... I wanted the whole two panels [that close off the shrine from view] taken off and have the Plexiglas there so you can see through. But instead of that [the project workers] opened the place and made the Plexiglas [barrier] low. (Takahara, Interview, 23 August 1996)

In the end, the Kyowakai Hall was used as a display area, although the shrine was kept behind panels, out of the tourists' view. Despite his strong disapproval, when Mr. Senya Mori reflected back he did not completely dismiss the NIMC. When I asked what could be improved at the NIMC, he affirmed, "Well, in the first place, it's nice to have it all right" (Mori, Interview, 5 September 1996). Then he described some of the problems: "The hall itself, I thought it was too small. I didn't want all those things [the old junk, those photographs, that tent] in that building. Every time you have a meeting, you have to move everything out. I didn't like that" (Mori, Interview, 5 September 1996).

As was the case with the other elders, Mr. Senya Mori's concerns and criticisms involved anxieties about the changing leadership. He felt that the decision to use the Kyowakai Hall and the Centennial Hall did not take into consideration their significance for the community. Instead, these buildings, the social venues and spiritual centre of the community, were put on exhibit for outsiders. His underlying concern about "who is going to take care of the community" was stressed in his identification of details that had been overlooked. For example, he was particularly concerned about the failure to keep track of community records. He also wondered, "who's going to look after the books. Sawada used to be secretary [of the Kyowakai Society] and used to keep track of everything. I don't know where that book [with his records] went." (Mori, Interview, 5 September 1996).

As the mayor of New Denver, the president of the Kyowakai Society, and a lay priest – a role that required him to keep the Buddhist records of the dead – Mr. Senya Mori was aware of the importance of precise records. His concern over the record book is not trivial. Like the other elders who kept careful records going back to the war years, Mr. Senya Mori especially understood the importance of accurate records after his experiences during the war, including the loss of his family's property. He recalled:

I [knew this] Occidental girl, A. Robinson, through the business [in Vancouver before the war]. She was by herself. [I told her], "We'll give you title [for our house]." There are three bedrooms ... upstairs, and [the] kitchen, living room, dining room, [and] bathroom in the bottom. [The agreement had] one thing, [I told her] "I want you to use one bedroom and rent the rest." And that was the agreement. She [didn't] have to pay rent. She just collects the rent and maybe uses [the] kitchen facilities combined [with the others]. That was my agreement. She said okay. [So I said, we'll] give the title to the house [at] Fifth and Main. As soon as we moved out, she sold the whole thing ... We [were only permitted to] carry 150 pounds [to the internment camp]. So ... our Japanese stuff, we can't pack [it with us, so] we packed it [up] and locked it [in Vancouver]. I bet I had two hundred [musical] records, and they are worth money now! And she sold everything! I went [back] to Vancouver [after the war], and there are apartment buildings standing there *[laughs]*. (Mori, Interview, 5 September 1996)

Like thousands of other Japanese Canadians who were forced to leave their homes along the coast, Mr. Senya Mori later discovered that the agreement he had made to have the "Occidental girl" take care of the property in exchange for housing was not, in the end, legally binding. But, years after, records of these losses helped activists negotiate a settlement for redress with the Canadian government (Price Waterhouse 1986).

Thus, working with a community whose members have undergone persecution is a complex, involved process. Matters such as the importance of keeping precise records or the discomfort of being asked in public meetings about the racism might not be understood by those working with them, especially if they are unfamiliar with the group's history and cultural modes of interacting. It is not clear whether the project manager or his staff were initially aware of the deeply problematic nature of using community buildings, especially the Buddhist Hall, for tourists. The controversy resulted in the alienation of three prominent members of the community. Heated criticisms of plans became public just before the NIMC's grand opening, as I will discuss in the next section.

In Transition

During the construction of the NIMC, a transfer in leadership occurred not only between the generations but also between men and women. The chair of the History Preservation Committee brought this fact to my attention (Takana 1996, Discussion, 18 August). In part, this change reflected a change in the community's demographics: elderly men were passing away before the women. Men had conventionally taken public leadership roles in community organizations. Mrs. Kamegaya became an extraordinary exception when she assumed the presidency of the Kyowakai Society. This was a controversial development. Several powerful male figures publicly announced that they would not continue as members under a woman. Yet, despite this criticism, Mrs. Kamegaya's leadership was strongly supported by most Japanese Canadians in New Denver.

Women have always had prominent roles in the Japanese Canadian community. But, as Audrey Kobayashi claims, although Japanese Canadian women made significant contributions to family incomes, businesses, households, and community organizations in the pre-war period, few documents remain that record these contributions because of the patriarchal order of the community (1994b).[12] Thus, while Japanese Canadian women were influential, they did not receive the same public recognition as men.[13]

With the exception of Mrs. Kamegaya, most of the elderly women in New Denver did not have publicly recognized leadership roles in the Kyowakai Society. Like other pre-war Japanese Canadian women, they worked behind the scenes to facilitate and support certain goals and various projects over others. In New Denver, many had formidable skills gained from their experiences before the internment, whether as accountants for family businesses, teachers in Japanese-language schools, domestic workers for hakujin employers, or cooks in remote logging camps. Kobayashi (1994a, 62-63) describes how

issei women remained relatively insulated from the direct consequences of racism, not because they were not affected but because they shut themselves away, confined themselves to their own activities where possible and normally allowed their husbands to represent the family publicly. A vast network of community organizations provided an institutional bulwark against the difficulties of Canadian life and responsibility for public negotiation was clearly vested in the leaders of those organizations. Of course, large areas of Canadian life – social status, education, the professions, participation in most public activities – were completely inaccessible to them. But in order to recognize this inaccessibility, much less challenge its authority, they would first have had to break past the patriarchal conditions that denied such activities to them in any context. They were inhabitants of a double ghetto. Ghettoized, they were abused and protected.

In the camps, women were forced into the leadership roles that the male members of their households had usually assumed. The government initially removed the able-bodied men from their households and sent them to road camps or prisoner-of-war camps. In other cases, these men died or were debilitated from illnesses that resulted from a combination of the physical and emotional stresses of struggling to find ways to provide for their families in the impoverished conditions of the camps. Other men were killed or maimed in accidents. For example, many men in the camps filled labour shortages in local logging industries. Many had little training to work with logging or lumber mill equipment, and some paid the price with the loss of a limb. Others, unable to secure work nearby, were forced to find employment elsewhere. As a result, the women had to develop both the autonomy and the skills required to support their households.[14] These households usually included children and sometimes younger siblings and aging parents. In some instances, these women also helped support the households of dependent relatives. Women also provided home care to elderly Japanese Canadians with no families in the camps.

From the elders, I learned how the women found innovative ways to deal with hardship. They created home-based businesses, for example, as seamstresses. After 1945, they found work through camp connections as cooks or nurses' aides in the sanatorium. They set up kindergarten classes, sewed choir costumes for local churches, and taught technical classes to provide others with work skills to support their families. Their work in the larger New Denver community with churches and schools also gave them some independence from the Japanese Canadian community. Through their working relations with non-Japanese Canadian individuals and organizations, they secured new contacts, learning opportunities, prestige, and opportunities to take on leadership roles.

After Mrs. Kamegaya and, later, Mr. Senya Mori passed away, the sansei looked to the remaining elders, who were predominately women, for guidance. Mrs. Inose described their realization that the sansei now expected them to take up leadership roles. Somewhat modestly, she expressed their hesitancy about doing so.

We sort of expected our directors to do all that thinking for us. And since Mrs. Kamegaya has been gone, it has made a difference for us, and we have not really been able to get our act together. We should be thinking a little more to see what it will be to make it a little easier for our employees and making it better for the Japanese Canadian centre ... but I don't know whether, on our own, if we are going to be able to do that. We are going to need a little more – advice and a little more meetings, or whatever – and really get down to brass tacks. We haven't been doing that. We've been using the excuse that, after that grand opening, we're tired, and that has been tiring ... Now we feel, a few of us anyway, feel we should go down there and be a little more involved, but somehow we are not just able to do that for some reason. (Inose, Interview, 16 August 1996)

Mrs. Inose's reflections reveal that the elder women did not feel quite ready to take up the prominent leadership roles left by their peers. She was being quite modest, however. Their hesitancy reflected, in part, that they were tired after the big upheavals of constructing the NIMC and their roles in the television film, *The War between Us*. But, in addition, the operation of the Kyowakai Society had radically changed. Although the elders no doubt had the knowledge and skills to advise the sansei and take on official roles, they were familiar neither with the new organizational structure of their society nor the operation of the NIMC. They did not have the training to use the society's new communication technologies, and the administrative and funding practices of the NIMC. This made it difficult for them to immediately step into new leadership roles.

Yet, clearly, the elder women have taken initiatives. As mentioned above, Mrs. Takahara felt that the splendour of the shrine should be shared. She had the Kyowakai Society install a small Plexiglas window in the panels that close off the shrine from the public display area (Truly, Personal correspondence, 18 October 1998). Her initiatives reflected her social position in relation to the Buddhist Church. Because her father had been involved in the church, she has hosted visiting Buddhist dignitaries. This role involves responsibility and status. When necessary, it has also meant that she can consult the Buddhist offices on matters concerning the local Buddhist Church. So, despite her observation that Buddhism is "a society for men," the Plexiglas viewing window shows that her position in the Buddhist Church was recognized nonetheless (Takahara, Interview, 23 August 1996).

At another level, the elder women have groomed and directed younger women to take on prominent positions in community affairs.[15] Although Sakaye Hashimoto is the president of the Kyowakai Society, sansei women have a strong presence in the community both formally and informally. They are members of the executive of the Kyowakai Society. They have initiated community projects. The leadership of women in the community is part of a larger trend within the Japanese Canadian community.[16] In New Denver, it is also closely tied to changing demographics. In all generations, women are more involved than men in community affairs. In part this is because more sansei women have chosen to live in New Denver. Of the six living in New Denver in 1996, some grew up and stayed there, some had returned, and others were planning to build summer homes so that they could be close to their aging parents. There were also the newcomers who chose to settle in the valley. Those who grew up in New Denver offer stability and a knowledge of the community, while the newcomers, with their artistic careers and extensive travels, offer experience with creative and politically innovative projects. Through their work, the sansei women along with the elders have drawn younger sansei to work on a number of different projects in New Denver; these sansei include Katherine Shozawa, a multimedia artist, and myself.

Many initiatives were taken during and after the construction of the NIMC to reappropriate the NIMC as a community institution. Whenever sansei initiated projects, they sought out the elders and found ways to collaborate with them. Although I will discuss two of these projects in more detail in the next chapter, to provide an example, I will describe one of the smaller initiatives that was taken during my stay in New Denver.

In the summer of 1996, Katherine Shozawa was the NIMC's administrator. She noted that visitors tended to be distracted by the postcards and tourist paraphernalia on display. She proposed removing the tourist brochures and placing the souvenirs in a less prominent place. At this time, Takana, the chair of the History Preservation Committee, and Tsuneko Kokubo, a performance and multimedia artist, were working with elders to translate lists of the internees in New Denver. The Kyowakai Society made the lists in 1945. Unable to find the government documents with the names of the internees, the society used these lists like a census to identify the families who remained in, or were brought to, New Denver in 1945. The sansei worked closely with Mr. Senya Mori and other elders to translate the names and find the lists for other years. The chair and Shozawa prominently displayed translations of the lists as well as a photograph of the New Denver camp in the reception centre. Visitors began to gravitate toward these lists, searching for names – sometimes the names of families that they knew, and sometimes those of their own family members. According to Shozawa, changing the position of the souvenirs and posting the lists shifted the atmosphere of the NIMC away from a consumer-oriented tourist site. Working with the elders made this change possible. They had the records

4.5 Katherine Shozawa, Mrs. Pauli Inose, and Mrs. Kay Takahara *(left to right)* outside the Kyowakai Society's Centennial Hall, New Denver, ca. 1995. *Unknown photographer. Courtesy of Mrs. Pauli Inose.*

as well as the knowledge about the internees, which was significant to visitors who had personal ties to the camp.

Continuity and Change

Mrs. Takahara's and Mrs. Inose's accounts trace the transfer of leadership from one generation to the next. They saw this transfer initiated by Mrs. Kamegaya, along with the resulting difficulties, not simply as the end of their era, but as something inevitable. It was similar to what happened when leadership was transferred to them from the older issei. It thus embodied continuity. But it also embodied change. It could be argued that this change has involved a loss of values, a loss of a language, and a loss of experience. This loss marks their own passage, their own mortality. But, insofar as their passage involves the movement from one generation to the next, it embodies continuity in living relations and thus a form of what Robert Jay Lifton calls "immortality" (1979, 17). According to Lifton, immortality is the symbolization of continuity, "an individual's experience in some form of collective life-continuity" (ibid.). Our sense of immortality does not exclude the notion of death. Lifton claims that we "require symbolizations of continuity – imaginative forms of transcending death – in order to confront genuinely the fact that we die" (ibid.). Thus, the loss also signals transformation and change in the community, not simply its end.

For both women and men, the transfer of leadership between the generations and genders involved a change in ingrained habits, understandings, and investments in maintaining male leadership. For the women in particular, it also involved changing the roles they performed behind the scenes, with complex mediation and power negotiations. To be comfortable on centre stage as a leader, like Mrs. Kamegaya and Mr. Senya Mori, for example, an individual needs to develop a public persona that can withstand public scrutiny and instill confidence and trust, while occasionally acting against the will of group members and enduring skepticism and dissent as particular projects and decisions come to fruition or move in unexpected directions.

The transfer of leadership in New Denver from elders to the younger generations and from men to women is in progress. While I was in New Denver in 1996, there were men who continued to take on prominent public roles. This included elders, such as Mr. Senya Mori as the lay Buddhist priest, and sansei, such as Sakaye Hashimoto, who became the president of the Kyowakai Society after Mrs. Kamegaya.

The form of leadership that will develop next in the Japanese Canadian community of New Denver is still undetermined. Clearly, there is a change from the old hierarchy in which women stayed in the background. Yet another form of hierarchy could develop. For example, the involvement of the village and various funding agencies in the NIMC could result in a more corporate form of leadership. Yet when I conducted research in New Denver, there seemed to be a return to a consensus model of decision making. More local sansei had become involved in the community. They looked to the elders for their views and direction. As mentioned, the elders in the 1990s were increasingly women. As a result, the contributions of women, whether they worked behind the scenes or took on public roles, were more explicitly recognized.

Facing their own passage, the elders were anxious about the ability of the next generation to lead. The NIMC was a project that "got bigger and bigger" to include an externally hired project manager, funding agencies, and organizations outside the community. The elder members of the Kyowakai Society were well aware that the sansei did not weigh the implications of these changes. For those in charge of the Buddhist Church, it threatened to "museumize" their place of worship. Mr. Senya Mori stated that the shrine was still "alive" and that as long as there are Buddhists in New Denver it must be kept alive. He threatened to shut the shrine down and send it elsewhere rather than see it effectively turned into a museum artifact. As well, transferring the land where the community halls sit to the village has grave implications. Japanese Canadians will be allowed to occupy the land as long as they continue to use it. Aware of their own nearing deaths, it is difficult for them not to wonder what will happen once all the Buddhists have gone and once there are no longer enough members to use the land on which their halls sit. Their death could then also mean the death of the Japanese Canadian community in New Denver. What sort of passage does their death entail? The end of a community or its transformation? From Mrs. Inose's account, I understood that by working collaboratively with the sansei, while relinquishing their formal leadership positions, the elders were able to ensure that the community in New Denver would continue for another generation. And, as I will discuss in Chapter 6, by building the memorial, they also have ensured another form of continuity: that the history of the internment camps will be remembered by generations of people living in the region and across Canada.

CHAPTER FIVE

Making Space for Other Memories in the Historical Landscape

One by One

through thick-falling snow

comes the deer family: backs so white

– KAMEGAYA CHIE (1994)

The Historical Landscape

From a distance, it is easy to be entranced by the Nikkei Internment Memorial Centre (NIMC). Amid the ongoing clamour of daily life in this small village, there sits a peaceful Japanese garden that sweeps gracefully around weathered wooden buildings, all enclosed within a fortress-like cedar post fence.

Before even seeing the NIMC, the passing traveller most likely has already been introduced to the Centre as part of the network of historical sites criss-crossing the region. Tourist publications and free road maps with colourful images of historical museums, campsites, art galleries, parks, heritage walking tours, scenic drives, hotels, and restaurants along the traveller's route.[1]

In this economically depressed region, history has become a business sup-ported by government grants and employment projects. Most of the tourist sites in the Kootenays, like the Silvery Slocan Museum and the restored SS *Moyie* sternwheeler, are dedicated to the history of primary industries, in particular, the development of silver-lead mining in the late 1800s (Butler et al. 1995, 2-3). Mining opened up the area to white settlers. "Prospectors and entrepreneurs, mainly from the United States, swarmed to the area in 1892 ... New Denver was populated quickly. By April of 1892, 500 men were camped there and 50 build-ings existed" (ibid., 48). As in other regions in British Columbia, the economy went through a series of booms and busts with the rise of ore prices on the world market during the First World War and the fall of prices during the De-pression. After the Second World War, logging became the region's main eco-nomic activity.

Books, brochures, and websites recount how the fates of miners rose and fell with the world market for ore, their dreams lost in abandoned mine shafts, untended grave markers, and the ramshackle remains of once grand hotels.

5.1   Slocan Lake, 1968. *Shoichi Matsushita. Courtesy of the Matsushita family.*

What we do not hear about are the high alpine lakes saturated with poison from mining: crystal clear pools of death (Pamesko, Interview, 6 September 1996). Nor is the fact that the entire Slocan Valley was logged: what tourists might believe to be pristine forests are in fact second growth, far from the "supernatural British Columbia" promoted by the provincial government.

The NIMC is now featured in many tourist brochures as part of the historical landscape. The term "landscape" refers to views. As Jonathan Smith explains, "Whether depicted in paint, or rolled out as a tableau vivant below a scenic overlook, a landscape situates its spectator in an Olympian position, and it rewards its spectator with the pleasures of distance and detachment and the personal inconsequence of all that they survey. Thus, in ... landscape as scenery the spectator is transformed into a species of voyeur" (Smith 1993, 78-79). Brochures such as *Go and Do* inform the traveller that the NIMC tells "the painful story" of thousands of Japanese Canadians who were interned in New Denver by the Canadian government (1996, 37). In the history of this region, the story of Japanese Canadians has become one of many that circulate alongside the dreams and nightmares of the miners and loggers who came to this valley in the late 1800s seeking their fortunes in the earth's ore. In the tourist literature, the magnificence of panoramic mountain ranges crowned with glaciers and alpine meadows high above the forested slopes becomes a powerful setting for the painful story of Japanese Canadians. Amid such magnificence, the NIMC draws the traveller into a space of reflection. Inside the gates of the memorial, the cultivated simplicity of the traditional Japanese garden mirrors the powerful forces of nature, translating them into terms that humans can understand. According to *Go and Do* (1996), the garden presents metaphors of "past, present and future," allowing us to place the tragic stories in a continuum of time, where the passage of time has transformed experiences of pain, loss, and humiliation so that the traveller can look back upon them from the present, as something that now belongs to the past. The garden offers a soothing space to reflect on past wrongs and suffering. The memorial garden reflects the "painful story" of Japanese Canadians back into the surrounding landscape, investing the mountains and lake with a tragic beauty, turning the entire valley into a space of contemplation. In this space the repercussions of the history of racial hatred in the province of British Columbia become part of the distant past.

This view of the NIMC in the historical landscape of the Slocan Valley is from a distance, from the point of view of a passing traveller. It is from a position affected neither by the aftermath of political violence nor by the stakes and struggles of building a memorial to mark the small village with its dark history of incarceration camps. From this vantage point, it is easy to view the NIMC as one of the many local museums advertised in publications for tourists that recount tragic events that occurred in the region's past, where history is a colourful set of tales that lose their power to warn Canadian citizens that they must continue to be vigilant against the racial hatred that can drive governments to abuse their power. However, the longer one stays, the more one realizes that Slocan is not the idyllic valley it seems. The mountains and waterways might be stunningly beautiful, but they are not benign. Over the course of my stay, falling trees, cougar attacks, storms, and accidents along the narrow, snaking highway left numerous people maimed, crushed, or dead. Every year there is a drowning. The lake is known for its sudden storms: serene and glassy one moment, it can throw up a nightmare of massive waves the next, blasted by the torrential winds that smash across the lake, swallowing unsuspecting boaters into its depths. Nor does the past lie dormant. It tiptoes across domestic spaces and shudders through scarred bodies; it hovers on the lilt of a tongue or the taste of a pie and seethes in antagonisms that seem to have no basis.

The internment camps are only one of the histories that haunt the Slocan Valley. The dreams and downfall of the Doukhobors, for instance, were dredged from the recent past by younger members of the community during the 1970s. Evidence of their prosperity lies amid the remains of the huge abandoned communal farmhouses that are now surrounded by rusting ploughs and overgrown brush near Castlegar. The Doukhobors came to Canada, fleeing persecution in the old country, with the hope of building a peaceful society inspired by what they understood as God: the "power of love, the power of life, which is the source of all being" (Mealing, 1977, 1). There are however reports that, like other settlers in the region, they took over large tracts of land, violating the Sinixt Nation's rights to their territory, which the provincial and federal governments have also refused to recognize (Pryce 1999, 65-67). In turn, the Doukhobors lost their land when the provincial government foreclosed their loans in 1940.

There are accounts by Japanese Canadians about Doukhobors bringing them vegetables and other foodstuffs in the camps (Sumie Matsushita, Interview, 15 August 1996). However, the only official records I could find documenting the Doukhobors' relations with the thousands of incarcerated Japanese Canadians were RCMP reports and letters in Library and Archives Canada. But, rather than recording their attempt to relieve hunger in the camps, the reports make derisive references to shifty-looking Doukhobor men lingering around the perimeters of the camps (RCMP 1944) or express concerns about them trespassing to sell vegetables to the internees.

> It appears to the writer that unless we exercise strict control over people such as the Doukhobors in visiting our camp we are liable to be overrun both day and evening by them ... [It] is easy to visualize what might transpire such as sabotage by fire and stealing, as it is a well-known fact that [they] ... are given to both of these actions ... [If] we lower the gates and allow them to come in indiscriminately, their attitude will be ... unbearable as most of them are of a bullying and dominating nature if allowed to get away with it. (Burns 1944)

This letter, in response to courteous requests from a Mr. Pookachow from Winlaw to sell "farm and poultry products to the Japanese camps" (Pookachow 1944), reveals the hostile views of the government toward the Doukhobors.

The Doukhobors began to lose their language a decade after the government foreclosed their land; this is when the province took away their children and interned them in the former sanatorium in New Denver. Today, the Brilliant Cultural Centre marks the region with their history. Their beliefs live on through their involvement in the local peace movement. The Brilliant Cultural Centre and Kyowakai Society have maintained ties; they invite representatives to each other's formal events. But in the Slocan Valley, there are no longer prominent signs of the Doukhobors' presence.[2]

Even more strangely, when I arrived in the valley, there appeared to be an absence of any First Nation communities, in particular the Sinixt First Nation, which had numbered three thousand in the early nineteenth century and had played a major role in the fur trade and in securing the Hudson's Bay Company's hold on the Columbia District. Their people were devastated by the introduction of smallpox by white traders and by development on rivers, including the Columbia, which destroyed once-abundant Chinook, sockeye, and coho salmon runs, one of their main food sources. With a diminished population, and unable to maintain control over the development of their homeland as thousands of miners flooded into the Slocan Valley, they retreated to their southern territories across what is now the United States–Canada border to land shared with the Colville People (Sinixt Nation; Pryce 1999; Pearkes 2002). It was when Mr. and Mrs. Matsushita showed their photographs of the fading ochre paintings drawn onto the porous rock cliffs rising from the cold depths of Slocan Lake that I first saw any sign of their presence in the region. Mr. Matsushita had photographed these paintings during boat excursions up the lake decades before. As the local lore goes, for thousands of years the Sinixt followed the growing season of berries and roots and the migration of cariboo and salmon north up the lake. Locals professed to know little about them until 1987, when the Sinixt stopped the Ministry of Highways from constructing a highway at Vallican through a burial ground (Sinixt Nation; Pryce 1999; Pearkes 2002). As mentioned in the last chapter, it was only when I returned to Ottawa that I learned about their more recent efforts to protect another burial site from the government's plans for highway development.

During my stay in 1996, I saw only one news story about the Sinixt who remained in Castlegar, fighting the government's classification of them as extinct, which was the basis for denying them their rights to their land (*Valley Voice* 1996a). With the recent involvement of the provincial government in treaty negotiations, their presence has become more prominent. *Valley Voice* includes reports of meetings where the proceedings of the BC Treaty Commission are criticized (Murray 2007, 1).

Like the Sinixt Nation and the Doukhobors, the Kyowakai Society wanted to write a history of persecution into the valley. Until the redress movement in the 1980s, as far as the Canadian government was concerned, the plan to remove Japanese Canadians from British Columbia was justified as a necessary measure during a time of war (Adachi 1991; Miki and Kobayashi 1991).[3] It was the redress activists who used the government's own documents to demonstrate that the government knew there was no basis for categorizing all people "of Japanese descent" as security threats. Using this information, they proved that the government had violated their rights and turned the persecution of Japanese Canadians into a national issue concerning social justice.

The Kyowakai Society wanted the NIMC to continue addressing the issue of social justice, but as it is related to cultural memory in the Slocan Valley. In this regard, the Centre has been part of a larger movement to transform the terrain of memory in the province. Starting in the 1980s, many municipalities and districts sought to memorialize Japanese Canadians who had either lived in their communities before the war or had been incarcerated there from 1942 to 1945. For example, there are plaques in Chemainus, where there is also a public mural depicting the town's pre-war Japanese Canadian community (*Bulletin* Staff 1991). Kaslo (*Bulletin* 1992a; Ibuki 1993), Schrieber (Shimizu 1996), and Port Alberni (*Bulletin* 1992b) also have commemorative projects. There are landscaped interpretation sites at, for example, Yard Creek Provincial Park (*Bulletin* Staff 1995). Towns and cities have built public memorial gardens such as the Kohan Gardens in New Denver (Quirk 1991) and the Momiji Garden at the Pacific National Exhibition in Vancouver (Suzuki 1992).[4] Small history museums in districts where there were pre-war Japanese Canadian communities or internment camps often dedicate one part of their exhibit to the experiences of Japanese Canadians in their region; examples include the museums in Greenwood, Mission, New Denver, and Kaslo.[5] In many cases, museum curators have asked Japanese Canadians to participate on committees for constructing memorials, plaques, or exhibits.[6] When the Japanese Canadian National Museum was established in 1999 at the Nikkei Heritage Centre in Burnaby, BC, with funds from the Redress Foundation, a particularly active period of public exhibitions followed under Grace Eiko Thomson, the museum's director at the time. Exhibits such as "Asahi," on the legendary Japanese Canadian baseball team, and "Shashin: Japanese Canadian Photography to 1942" toured in British Columbia and across Canada (Thomson 2005).

With the transformation of the terrain of memory in British Columbia that followed the successful negotiation of redress with the Canadian government, one would expect that museums would not hesitate to critically interpret the government's plans to remove all people of "Japanese racial origin" from British Columbia. This was not the case with the NIMC. The fact that the displays in the NIMC today are critical of the government's actions, drawing on the redress narrative as described in Chapter 4, is a result of a struggle over the interpretation of history.

As discussed in Chapter 4, the contractors hired by the Kyowakai Society had their own ideas about the design of the NIMC, viewing it as a historical centre that would attract tourist revenue. The company that designed the memorial, as well as the project manager, had strong views on how the history of the community should be presented. The title they gave the Centre was "Nikkei *Evacuation* Memorial Centre" (emphasis added). But, in order to receive funding from the Japanese Canadian Redress Foundation, the National Association of Japanese Canadians required that they change the name to "Nikkei *Internment* Memorial Centre" (emphasis added). As anyone familiar with the history of Japanese Canadians from a human rights perspective would know, the term "evacuation" is one of the many euphemisms the government and its apologists have used to obscure the fact that Japanese Canadians were interned and not simply evacuated – a word that suggests temporary relocation from a dangerous situation (Miki 2004, 50-51).

The message that the contractors wanted the memorial to communicate balanced the hardships endured by Japanese Canadians with the government's reasons for interning Japanese Canadians. The contractors did not recognize the fact that the government had already officially acknowledged that it had acted on exclusionary racist notions of citizenship (Redress Agreement, in Miki and Kobayashi 1991, 138-139). The contractors set up an interpretive team to create the historical displays. Their draft outlining the historical displays included plans to present the "yin and yang" of internment and included sketches of the Taoist yin-yang symbol, a Chinese motif, to balance the negative and positive aspects of the internment. When it was installed in the Kyowakai Hall, local sansei were taken aback and presented the problems with this interpretation.

Balancing the yin and the yang – the negative and the positive – operates as a narrative device that simply neutralizes the negative. In this case, the negative was the violation of citizens' rights on the basis of their "racial origin;" being categorized as enemy aliens by their own government; liquidation of the properties and assets of over twenty-one thousand Japanese Canadians; the separation of families; forced labour; removal from British Columbia and, in many cases, Canada; and the social damage that has played itself out over several generations. The notes of the interpretive team that I found in the NIMC office, much like the work of recovery scholars, further underlined how they strove for a "neutral" perspective. This is documented in a draft of the historical displays. The introduction states: "It is not our intention to make political or social judgments nor to draw conclusions. We believe that historical facts and events, presented clearly through the use of artefacts, archives and on site re-creation will speak for themselves" (NIMC, n.d.). The intention to balance the negative and positive was further evident in a discussion about the ironies of the internment in the Nikkei Evacuation Memorial Centre proposal.

> [There] were elements even in this grim scenario which served to add a "Canadian" nuance. The locations chosen ... for the relocation camps were all in places of spectacular physical beauty, and even in social structures as rudely conceived as these, a comradeship arose with typical Japanese stoicism, which created valuable human experiences and positive outcome from an inherently negative situation. (Inwood 1992, 12)

The "Canadian nuance" of "spectacular physical beauty" hardly seems to be an ironic element in the "grim scenario." To read the accounts of Japanese Canadians in oral histories, biographies, novels, and personal letters – the "prison of mountain ranges," the burned-out muddy grounds, the freezing ice in their shacks, the snow collapsing their tents – is to understand that these conditions were not viewed as "stunningly beautiful." The emphasis on "comradeship [which] arose with typical Japanese stoicism" is inaccurate and ignores the conflicts and antagonisms that remain deeply embedded in the community today. Moreover, it seems misplaced for the authors to conclude *on behalf* of Japanese Canadians that the camps resulted in "valuable human experiences" that had a "positive outcome," especially as the authors appear to have little knowledge about the community. The very need to conclude that there was a positive outcome recalls those Japanese Canadians who defensively insist that the internment, the liquidation of all their property, and their expulsion from British Columbia was "a blessing in disguise" (Miki 1998c, 29-33). These Japanese Canadians argue that destruction of their pre-war community helped them integrate into the larger Canadian society. But they do not take into consideration the costs, which were extremely high. Moreover, the blessing-in-disguise argument assumes that, without the destruction of their pre-war community, Japanese Canadians would not have been able to participate successfully in the wider society. But if other racialized groups have managed to succeed outside the boundaries of their communities after the war, without internment camps, forced dispersal, and dispossession, why not Japanese Canadians? If Japanese Canadians had retained their community infrastructure, their property, and their support networks, they might have accomplished so much more. Redress activists argue that the blessing-in-disguise view is rooted in a denial of losses and of emotional pain (Miki 2004).

The interpretive team's effort to be neutral, to balance the bad with the good, possibly arose from their lack of familiarity with the community's history and, notably, with the Japanese Canadian movement for redress. But, perhaps more specifically, as the project manager suggested in an interview, the effort to understand rather than criticize the government's actions reflected the manager's personal situation. His father and his father's friends were war veterans who believed that the government's wartime actions were justified. They strongly criticized his involvement in the NIMC. He was also confronted by other residents in New Denver who were uncomfortable about the construction of the NIMC. But the project manager believed the NIMC was an important project. He stressed this importance to his father and his father's friends and tried to convince the uneasy residents that the NIMC would generate revenue for New Denver (Butler, Interview, 19 September 1996).

It was thus the project manager who revealed the tensions in New Denver that surrounded the memorialization of the internment camp. Even the president of the Kyowakai Society, who knows almost everyone in the village, had not been approached directly by people opposed to the Centre, although he knew they existed.

The need to neutralize and balance the impact of internment and emphasize the revenue it would generate for the village thus reflected the project manager's efforts to contend with the criticisms and discomfort of people he knew. The neutral approach to representation and the use of motifs such as the yin-yang symbol were not well received, especially by one particular sansei who had recently moved to the Kootenays to research local history. Apparently, there were arguments and heated disagreements. Most likely in the eyes of the manager and his employees, it did not help that this sansei was a newcomer to the valley. As a newcomer he would lack credibility. He had also disagreed with the president of the Kyowakai Society on a number of occasions, making him seem combative. But as Mrs. Takahara noted, things had already escalated when the president and manager wanted to turn the Centennial Hall into a display area for tourists. There were rumours that one of the employees had threatened a sansei with a lawsuit after this sansei wrote the elders with concerns about how the interpretive team planned to represent their history. Soon after, the project manager stepped in. A decision was made to transfer responsibility for the historical displays to a newly formed History Preservation Committee. Drawing on the extensive work already accomplished by the interpretive team – enlargements of archival photographs, the selection of archival documents and artifacts for display, a floor plan, display boards – the new committee remade the historical display for the quickly approaching grand opening.

But it was not until two years after the opening of the NIMC in 1996 that the chair of the History Preservation Committee completed the explanatory text for the displays (this is one of the projects I worked on). Visitors who had been to the Langham Cultural Centre in Kaslo to see the Japanese Canadian exhibit described to me how it evoked tears and feelings of sadness. They found the personal recollections of Japanese Canadians powerful. In contrast, the distanced human rights angle of the NIMC and the lack of personal testimonies had less emotional impact for them.

The History Preservation Committee was aware that their interpretation would not necessarily be shared or appreciated by all visitors and former internees. But they were committed to presenting an interpretation that would be acceptable to all of the elders in New Denver. It required a consensus among the elders who wanted to have input. Consensus building requires work and sensitivity. What one person considers to be representative of the losses Japanese Canadians experienced might be irrelevant to another; what might be a painful personal topic for one person might be considered important for public education by someone else. As well, the elders knew that their interpretation would affect their relationships with other residents in New Denver, family members, and visiting Nikkei. As a result, changes they have made to the displays have been done slowly. The committee recognizes that the interpretation will constantly undergo changes as community members rework the past, as well as their relationships with one another, visiting Japanese Canadians, and members of the public. In the words of the chair of the Kyowakai Society's History Preservation Committee, the NIMC aims to be an "interpretive centre":

We discovered that our interpretation had to be shaped by the decision of the senior members to focus on their experiences from this area ... [The] interpretive committee worked hard to provide a context that does not "speak for all Nikkei" but is more a sharing of one Nikkei community's history ... Interpreting the incarceration is very complex. The incarceration holds different meanings for each Nikkei generation and is further complicated by our small society's ambitious attempt to represent a part of the experience to the general public [many of whom do not know about the internment]. It became clear to the membership ... that it required ongoing work. The more we transformed the [hall where the displays are located], the more we understood that what we were doing was a kind of cultural ecology – and the insight to our people's history changed, not only with the addition of new information, but with the action of placement and replacement of that information within the building ... It is as if every time those items of our struggle are re-placed, a new language is created, different from the one before but with similarities that are perhaps more visceral and emotional than intellectual. It is the relationship of those items that tells the story, and that relationship is not confined by time. (Takana 1996)

The chair of the History Preservation Committee approached the challenge of working with disturbing memories as an ongoing process, "a kind of cultural ecology." As a member of the local Japanese Canadian community with a background in collaborative theatre and art projects, she felt that, rather than framing memories in terms that others would find palatable, her main objective should be to facilitate the ongoing process of transforming the past for the elders.

Small-Scale Memory Projects

To understand the significance of the NIMC for the elders, it is important to know that it is just one of many memory projects undertaken by local Japanese Canadians over the years. As I have mentioned, some of the projects were spurred by national events, such as the 1977 centennial anniversary of the arrival of the first Japanese immigrant to Canada and the movement for redress in the 1980s. Other memory projects, such as the annual Obon ceremony, in which the dead are welcomed back each year, are ongoing traditions. And then there have been projects such as planting the cherry trees sent by Japanese Canadians whom the government shipped to Japan after the war. The trees, when they blossomed each spring, bring back memories of these Japanese Canadians. Most recently, the Kyowakai Society built the NIMC to mark the valley with its members' history of internment and dispossession.

From this perspective, the NIMC has contributed to the Japanese Canadians' ongoing effort to transform the valley's terrain of memory. To gain insights into how they used the NIMC in this ongoing transformation, I now turn to a number of the small-scale memory projects at the NIMC in which the elders stepped forward and took active roles.

Restoring the Shacks

The three shacks on display at the NIMC show the living conditions of the internees. To restore the shacks, it was necessary to research their original structure, the material and fixtures used in their construction, and the improvements made by internees. The results of this research are documented in the *New Denver Japanese Internment Camp Restoration Assessment* (Scopick 1991), a preliminary assessment of the technical and financial aspect of the construction of the NIMC. This assessment was used by the authors of the 1992 funding proposal, Robert Inwood and Associates, who provided architectural advice throughout the construction of the NIMC.

Drawing on the technical knowledge of the site supervisor and the project manager's experience in restoration projects, the NIMC construction crew moved the shacks from their original sites in the Orchard into the NIMC's compound. The crew stabilized and then restored the shacks. To re-create the internees' living conditions, it was necessary to consult with the elders about household goods, personal belongings, fixtures, and improvements made over the years. As discussed in Chapter 4, the project manager and the carpenters consulted the elders – Mrs. Takahara and Mrs. Inose in particular. They recalled the process as straightforward but a little time-consuming: there was always someone "knocking on their doors," wanting information about the interiors of the shacks or wanting them to inspect their work.

Restoring the shacks was a means for the elder women to remember their experiences in the camps in their own terms. When I asked them, the elders readily gave descriptions of their role in advising the carpenters and finding items with which to furnish the shacks. From what I could discern, their working relations with the carpenters were informal one-on-one exchanges in which the elders approved or corrected the carpenters' work. The exchanges between the elders and carpenters were task-oriented. Mrs. Takahara gives the following description:

> We took things over to display ... chairs, bedding ... We just took our old stuff over there and displayed what we needed, like those cooler boxes ... [We told them] this belongs to the first house ... Dan the carpenter was working over there [at the second house,] and they had [it] built with the sink ... [We had to tell them], "Oh, the sink wasn't like that, it was all wood. The houses were all black, and we had to build shelves and make the sinks and everything like that." The sink was just wood with a hole; we had to bring the water from outside. There were no taps. The shelves were – we had to bring lumber from the [old skating] rink and build [shelves] for each family, one for that side and [one] for this side [of the shack]. My dad – we couldn't get the lumber. We were in Harris Ranch [which was a steep half-hour walk uphill from New Denver. And we had no car, no one had a car], so dad would go to the bush and cut these small trees, take off their bark, make a patio, or floors on the outside, [even] railing ... Nails were free – people had to build the buildings [for the internment camp,] so whatever was on the ground [we'd] pick it up ... [We had to keep reminding the project workers,] "Oh, that wasn't there, we never had luxury like that" ... Even now, the second house, the sink [in there] was even prettier now than it was. (Takahara, Interview, 23 August 1996)

Mrs. Takahara's description shows how the elders focused on the material details of the internment shacks, which gave them concrete topics to discuss with the carpenters. The discussions were not limited to the design of kitchen sinks or a shelving units. The discussions also provided a space in which the elders could recollect events associated with the objects and rooms under construction. It is also likely that the quiet, kind mannerisms and respectful attitude of the main carpenter, Dan Pamesko, made the elders feel comfortable working with him.

The elders were also involved in furnishing the shacks with household items such as bed linen, cooking utensils, dry goods, and clothing. The elders emphasized the importance of working with other elders to find items for the shacks. It was clear that furnishing the shacks was not simply a matter of pulling out a box or two and donating it to the NIMC. Below, Mrs. Takahara explains the process of finding these items.

> *Kirsten McAllister (KM):* So do you feel the [shacks] portray [the camp's living conditions] now?
>
> *Mrs. Takahara:* I think that was the best we could do. [We had to recall] whether that was [the] curtain or whether [those were the] mattress covers [we used then] – we had a hard time finding them. [But someone would always pipe in], "Oh maybe I have one of those." People threw out a lot of things [over the years that] we could have [used]. But anyway, someone would say, "Maybe I've got [that]." And we started searching our things, [looking in our] wood sheds ... And then there were these boxes [people had] brought from Vancouver, you know, [when] they moved out here [to the camps.] So they said, "Donate [it all] to the [project]." So we managed to get the [shacks] sort of looking like the way [they were]. But we did a lot of looking around for those things ...
>
> *KM:* I know whenever I ... go through my boxes even from five years ago, it ... brings up memories.
>
> *Mrs. Takahara:* Yes.
>
> *KM:* So what was that like?
>
> *Mrs. Takahara:* [We'd say], "Remember this? Remember what happened? How did we use to use this or that?" Some of the artifacts [are displayed] in the Kyowakai Hall now. [In the camp,] they used to have concerts and [other events in the Kyowakai Hall] in the fall ... There were so many real actors [who were in plays from] Vancouver. In the early days, when everyone was still here [before they were sent to central Canada and Japan], they would put on these concerts and things. They were really good. (Takahara, Interview, 23 August 1996)

Mrs. Takahara emphasizes how the furnishing of the shacks was accomplished as a group. The elders were the only ones who knew how the interior of the shacks looked, what they contained, and how internees lived in such restricted spaces. They were also the only ones who still possessed household items from the internment shacks. The women were more involved than the men, in part because they were more familiar with the domestic organization of the shacks and also knew where the items had been stored in cupboards, boxes, and sheds after the camp closed and their lives began to improve. The men participated more in the search for wartime photographs and in gathering documents from community organizations to use in the historical displays in the Kyowakai Hall, suggesting that they were the ones who kept official records of the community.

During the restoration of the shacks, the process the elders used to remember the past was not imposed on them. Mrs. Takahara describes how the women organized themselves as a group to reconstruct the shacks' interiors and share their findings. They recalled events in a flow of social exchanges, with the items they gathered acting as memory prompts. They remembered events, people, emotions, and activities. Even the very manner in which items were stored, whether neatly folded, wrapped in protective paper or tucked into the corner of box, triggered memories of when or why the elders or their parents or relatives had kept the items. Brought before the group, the items prompted other memories from different women. Thus they generated not only personal memories but also memories of the experiences they shared both in the camp and after the government closed the camp in the 1950s. Because they shared cultural protocols, forms of expression, and personal histories, they were also able to recognize when someone was struggling as they remembered a painful experience. They were not made anxious by the need to find appropriate and sensitive ways to explain their feelings to people who might misunderstand or feel uncomfortable about their experiences of discrimination. In contrast to the interview sessions with the NIMC committee, the process of searching for items to furnish the shacks facilitated the elder women's ability to collectively remember their experiences as a group, drawing on familiar modes of interacting and on shared cultural meanings.[7]

But did the memorial encourage the elders to "museumize" their lives as they removed items from their homes to furnish the restored shacks? Were they turning their personal possessions into artifacts and their past into history? Their activities must be seen in a broader context. All the elders I visited had personal archives. And the first time I visited the Matsushitas' home, I learned that their archives were not simply collections of documents of personal importance.

Mr. Matsushita was waiting for me on his doorstep with a big smile. This was my first visit to their home. He made a wide gesture, "Yes, this is my house, the one with the poppies!" And there they were, long green stalks sailing above the garden in clouds of tissuey red, rose, and salmon pink. Beyond the poppies, on the edge of the garden, there was a crazily painted wooden garage with bold, swirling, white psychedelic waves. Mr. Matsushita explained, "Years ago, I asked my son to paint it. And well, I suppose, he is sort of like me." I was soon to discover that the Matsushitas did not restrict their creative ventures to gardens and garages.

Mrs. Matsushita was there waiting on their doorstep, and they both welcomed me into their home, out of the intense summer heat into the coolness of their living room. Mr. Matsushita made a wide welcoming gesture. "Welcome to my museum!" I had entered a magical world. Their living room was artfully arranged with photographs, pictures, books, and mementos, each with its own place on a shelf, the wall, or in a drawer. A large tree branch festooned with brightly coloured origami balls was the centrepiece. Each item was an entranceway into a story about another place and another time. And, thus, I was introduced to the Matsushita family. (BASED ON FIELD NOTES, 21 JULY 1996)

Like the Matsushitas, the other elders had their own innovative systems to organize and display the items from their personal archives. They used the items to represent aspects of their experiences to others, including researchers like myself. As a result, these items already had the quality of being artifacts, representing the past. Some were autobiographical. Others were mementos of significant events, and yet others were invested with knowledge and memories of places. For example, one elder I was visiting disappeared into another room and reappeared with a kerosene lamp. She explained that, in the internment camp, she would leave it outside the door every morning, and they would fill it up.[8] She deftly lit it, placed the glass top back on, and adjusted the flame. There was a warm glow of light. She said the Tashme camp had kerosene lamps too. Her family was in Tashme first, but didn't like it. She shook her head and wrinkled her nose. I asked why she didn't like Tashme. After a bit, she said, "So many people!" and then continued, explaining that they shared the shack with an older couple. Each family had one room, and they shared the kitchen and stove. She wrinkled her nose again, remembering. The older man was overweight and, so, when they heated up the place, he would say it was too hot and he'd be sweating, even though it was cold. It was winter, and they had "the little child." So they were moved and ended up in the camp at Harris Ranch. As for the lamp, she told me, she still used it, especially if there was a power failure.

When I visited another elder, she presented a large sheet with handwritten haiku, each written by a different person. Presenting the haiku to me, she described the haiku club they had had in the Kaslo internment camp before she came to New Denver and told me about the haiku they had been inspired to write as a huge forest fire illuminated the skies for days with glowing orange smoke. On another occasion, while preparing tea and *sembei*,[9] another elder opened her kitchen cupboard to display an amazing array of homemade wine – made from wild berries and plants. I learned about how the Japanese Canadian internees had developed culinary knowledge of local plants, literally incorporating the valley into the seasonal rhythms of their everyday lives.

Most of the items that the elders showed visitors – whether they revealed autobiographical information or details about the social life in the camps – were part of their domestic spaces. In contrast, the items they donated to the NIMC to furnish the shacks belonged to another category. The elders had more distance from the items donated to the NIMC, although it is true that some donated items were subsequently retrieved, showing that the difference between the two categories was not always clear. They chose not to donate items from their archives that were part of their everyday lives, which suggests that the items they donated did not result in the museumization of their personal lives.

Moreover, the ability of the elders to search their homes for items to donate to the NIMC showed that they already had a certain degree of distance from their past experiences, in contrast to some Japanese Canadians who continue to be deeply torn apart by what happened to their families during the war. Wartime events do not haunt every aspect of their lives today; for instance, these events do not make them suspicious of the intentions of every person who approaches them. At the same time, this distance does not mean that their current lives are severed from what happened during the war. Their distance from the past is reflected in the extent to which their lives have changed over the years. The changes in their lives have been reflected in the transformation of their homes from small, thin-walled plank shacks to comfortable spaces built around their changing needs and aspirations.

The process of restoring the shacks to their original condition had great significance for the elders. Although restoring and furnishing the shacks was a safe group process, publicly displaying the shacks was different. The shacks carried personal memories about the families who had lived in them. One of the shacks on display at the NIMC had been inhabited by an elder until "quite recently," when she passed away. It stood in bleak contrast to the homes of the other elders. Within the compound of the NIMC where it is preserved, it stands as a visceral measure of the transformation of their lives. Although it was inhabited until the mid-1980s, the NIMC uses it to show typical living conditions in the period from 1945 to 1957. When I asked the elders about this shack, they responded a little forlornly, explaining that an elderly woman had lived there. She had had no local family members to take care of her. She had not renovated the shack. She had not updated its electrical systems or plumbing, and so it remained cramped, dimly lit, and damp. The pipes would often freeze and usually burst several times during the winter. She had refused to let government workers in, including those who wanted to assess her situation to determine what level of government assistance she could receive. Perhaps she had remembered the intrusion of other government agents during the war. Or dignity might have been the reason. She had let very few local Japanese Canadians into her home. Mr. Senya Mori and Mr. Oda were among the few members of the community she had allowed inside. They would visit regularly in the winter to melt and clean up burst water pipes. Others would bring her food, knowing that she depended on "canned food and raw vegetables" because she did not know how to cook, which is unusual for a Japanese Canadian woman who was probably an adult in her thirties when she was interned. She had insisted on being independent. Eventually, when she was unable to care for herself, Mr. Senya Mori had arranged for a rented room in the basement of one of the local hotels that provided housekeeping services.

Her living conditions were familiar to the elders: they themselves had endured similar conditions through the 1940s and 1950s. But most elders had managed to improve their living conditions over the years as they slowly re-established themselves. The permanently displayed shack at the NIMC provided a perspective on the distance they had travelled over the years; at the same time, it represented what they had endured. For the elders, this shack was not just an artifact from the internment: it displayed the living conditions of one of their own, showing that she had never been able to recover from the persecution Japanese Canadians underwent during the 1940s. The public display of this shack was a recognition of the fact that the government's actions had permanently damaged the lives of some.

"A Time Gone By"

Working Relations

The slide show "A Time Gone By" was produced by an elder, Mr. Matsushita,[10] in collaboration with one of the sansei from the Slocan Valley, Ruby Truly. Mr. Matsushita was known as New Denver's unofficial photographer through to the 1980s. He took photographs of community-wide events such as high school graduation ceremonies and May Day celebrations as well as Japanese Canadian events such as Obon. Ruby Truly, a multimedia sansei artist who works with video, performance art, and installations, was interested in his work.

5.2   Mr. and Mrs. Matsushita in the Orchard, New Denver, 1994. *Courtesy of the photographer, Katherine Shozawa.*

When Truly inquired if Mr. Matsushita might be interested in presenting a slide show, Mr. Matsushita was enthusiastic. In the context of old-style cultural practices, this was a member of the younger generation seeking out the knowledge of an elder. And, because Truly was a member of the contemporary art community, Mr. Matsushita was interested in her angle on his work. He had confidence in her knowledge of the format for such an event and agreed to put together a slide show if she collaborated with him. He entrusted her with selecting and organizing the images. He let her set up the event, which she framed as a slide show for the "old-timers" in New Denver. But he did not simply hand over the slides.

Over the period of several weeks, Mr. and Mrs. Matsushita invited Truly and myself to their home to view the slides. We would visit for hours, viewing the slides and chatting over tea and treats. During these sessions we learned that Mr. Matsushita had a narrative for each of the series of images he had taken over thirty years ago. The ease with which he delivered the narratives demonstrated his knowledge of the events and people. Mrs. Matsushita occasionally intervened, elaborating on his account or correcting points he had made. He often turned to her to confirm information. Together they had produced a well-scripted narrative.

For "A Time Gone By," Truly could have selected individual slides that she found appealing and imposed her own order on them. Instead, she used the structure that the Matsuchitas had taken the time to introduce to us, which they had developed over the years.

The Show, "A Time Gone By," 21 August 1996

At dusk, the hot summer afternoon dissolves into a cool evening indigo. The Nikkei Internment Memorial Centre is now closed to the public. Inside the protective cedar fence, low-lying lamps tucked amid the rhododendrons and crouching maples light the pathway to the Centennial Hall. Local residents begin to arrive. Tonight, the Kyowakai Society is presenting "A Time Gone By," a slide show of the work of New Denver's unofficial photographer, Mr. "Spud" Matsushita. The hall is packed. Tickets were sold out yesterday. Latecomers pull up benches under the evening stars in an arc just outside the entrance. For many New Denver residents, this is the first time they have visited the NIMC since it opened in 1994.

It is one of those events where everyone from artists, retired dentists, environmentalists, and store clerks to old hippies and nurses along with mill workers come together. Of course, not everyone from New Denver came; rather, mostly those who were close to the Nikkei community. Mostly everyone there had been in the valley for the last thirty, if not seventy, years, some living in the area for several generations. Old neighbours, friends, co-workers, relatives, everyone is chatting, talking. Some of the newer residents come as well, like the new baker's family, who moved here from Alberta.

Finally, the din settles. After an introduction by Ruby, Mrs. Inose cuts the lights. Magically, images of life in New Denver from thirty years ago reappear before us. The vibrant imprints of light from this bygone era illuminate the rows of intent faces in the audience, remembering, recalling, reminiscing ... Amid excited recollections and reflective pauses, Mr. Matsushita's gentle voice navigates through these luminous moments frozen by his camera's eye so many years ago. Occasionally, Mrs. Matsushita offers clarification and insights, just as she did when they showed us the slides in their living room. I am aware of her constant presence, whether inside the frame, where she looks back at the photographer while posing for a family snapshot or community picture, or just outside the frame, looking from her own line of vision at the scene about to be captured.

Everyone "oohhs" and "ahhs" at the close-ups of fragile spring buds, the soft whiteness of deep winter snow, the sunlit waterfall with its aura of mist moistening dry, rocky bluffs. All recognize the ancient paintings drawn on the rock walls lining Slocan Lake. The slide show starts with these images, as if a reminder: imprints from some other time, etched by other people, of whom now only a few remain.

The slides of community events cause much hubbub. Both Japanese Canadians and the other residents shout out the names of people and events. One of the favourites is the series of confectionery creations from a memorable cake-decorating course: results ranging from creamy white cakes covered in rosebuds to a sturdy looking (and, perhaps, tasting) chocolate log cake. There is a May Day celebration featuring fanciful floats. The floats swirl with the long dresses of the May Day queens, bright green billowing against windswept spring skies.

There are also the records of the Matsushita family. These are personal records of the photographer's own life [see Figure 5.3]. The camera captures this handsome man with his life-long partner, Sumie, his son, Masaye, and his daughter, Elaine (now Elaine Lett). In these photos we see the man who captured these unique lines of sight into the everyday world of New Denver. Truly selected shots of Mr. and Mrs. Matsushita's mod-looking dinner parties

5.3 Mr. and Mrs. Matsushita, their daughter Elaine, and a friend *(left to right)*, New Denver, 1968. *Shoichi Matsushita. Courtesy of the Matsushita family.*

with the local teachers: a worldly Nikkei couple and hip young hakujin. There are also photos of Christmas tea at the Pavilion, the extended-care facility for elderly residents where Mr. Matsushita as well as many other local Nikkei were employed over the years as it changed from a TB sanatorium to a care facility for "emotionally disturbed boys" to a detention centre for Doukhobor kids and, finally, to the Pavilion.

Another series of vivid shots are photographs of a cool, damp Remembrance Day. Young cadets – local boys decked out in berets and smart khaki wool uniforms – jauntily march, tapping their assortment of drums past vacant fields and the occasional building. Much noted are the shots of teenagers (a number of whom are now adults in the audience) posing for their high school graduation, beaming in their prom attire: beetle-ish glasses, fitted gowns, swank suits.

Then there are the events that are either predominantly Nikkei or hakujin. Bridging each moment are the Matsushitas. As Ruby Truly says, Mr. Matsushita, a Nikkei man, thought it was important to document these events as part of the life in New Denver: one community. Each group in the audience takes turns recollecting the occasion, naming the people, many of whom have passed on. Images of the Kyowakai Hall appear. This is before the hall was transformed into an exhibition area for the NIMC. We see countless social events. On every occasion, the hall is filled. Nikkei line the tables. The tables are laden with food and drink. On stage, talented members of the community entertain the rest with *odori*, singing, plays. The hall seems so barren now. A shell for memories. But it is easy to get carried away with nostalgia.

Mr. Tad Mori and Mr. Matsushita call out above the excitement, "With all these parties, it looks like it was just a good time – but you don't see the dirty times." "It wasn't all so easy. You see those smiling faces, but it was a real struggle." (BASED ON FIELD NOTES, 22 AUGUST 1996)[11]

Creating the Venue

The venue Truly created for the slide show made it an event that had significance for New Denver residents. In contrast, I had envisioned the slide show as an event that would draw in Japanese Canadians from other regions, presuming that its success would be measured by the number of audience members and by the distance they had travelled to see the show. I suggested that we place an advertisement in *The Bulletin*, a Vancouver-based monthly for Japanese Canadians. The ad would reach Japanese Canadians in other regions. If people from other regions were going to consider travelling to New Denver to see the event, we needed to submit the ad at least one and half months before the show to ensure it would appear in the next month's issue.

Advertisements in *The Bulletin* would have made the slide show a big event. It would have been necessary to host visitors travelling from other centres. It would have changed the event from one in which the participants remembered their past to one in which others became informed about New Denver. The arrival of visitors from other regions might have created anxiety both among the New Denver residents. They might have wondered how visitors from urban centres would view their lives in this small, underemployed, rural community that was once the site of an internment camp. Local Japanese Canadians had already seen how people from larger urban centres could misrepresent their lives. There had been a number of Japanese Canadian and Japanese reporters who had represented their lives inaccurately. In particular, Japanese reporters had written articles presenting them as impoverished old people, living in shacks and working in occupations suitable only for the lower castes in Japan. One Japanese reporter had even snapped a photograph of an elder in his bare feet and published the unflattering photograph. These images were misleading and, most of all, embarrassing for local Japanese Canadians as well as their relatives.

After some consideration, Truly thought it would be more appropriate to make it a local event: a photo-documentary retrospective of New Denver from the perspective of one community member, Mr. Matsushita. On behalf of the Kyowakai Society, Truly invited the larger New Denver community. For the elders, simply the idea of inviting other New Denver residents to their Centennial Hall was enough.

To ensure that the show was aimed primarily at local residents rather than tourists, Truly scheduled it outside the NIMC's regular hours of operation. Truly personally invited old-timers who knew the local Japanese Canadians. She advertised the event in the weekly New Denver newspaper and placed posters in hangouts such as the Apple Tree Restaurant and the Eldorado Grocery Store, but she avoided tourist venues. Timing was key. She announced the event a week and a half before the event, making it feasible primarily for local residents to attend. Given the isolation of New Denver, it would be an effort for anyone living elsewhere to come for the evening on such short notice.

Truly's careful planning ensured that the community's social life would not be turned into entertainment or a curious display of small-town life for outsiders. It is easy to assume that drawing large numbers of people to an event makes it successful. But it could result in an exhausting workload as streams of visitors approach the community instrumentally, wanting information and documents with no sense of reciprocity. For Truly, it was important that the slide show be for the local community.

A Collective "We"?

Holding the slide show at the Centennial Hall was a way to reclaim it from the NIMC and show that it continued to be part of the community. Although the slide show was a community event organized by Japanese Canadians, it was open to everyone living in the village of New Denver. By gathering everyone together at the Centennial Hall, the event initiated a new set of interrelations among groups that ranged from newcomers to Japanese Canadian elders. It should be said that interaction among different groups in New Denver is nothing new. There are all sorts of ongoing interrelationships between Japanese Canadians and other residents in New Denver. They include relationships based on friendships and marriage; exchanges between store clerks, waitresses, bakers, postal workers, and customers; and attendance at funerals and weddings. They included relationships formed in workplaces, on committees for the village council, and at cultural events such as art gallery openings. But bringing everyone together in the Centennial Hall for an event hosted by the Nikkei community was something unusual.

As community buildings, the Kyowakai Hall and the Centennial Hall have typically held events for Japanese Canadians, not the larger New Denver community. If non-Japanese Canadians attended these events, they usually had a formal relation with the community as a government official, a close family friend, or a son- or daughter-in-law. The apprehension of the elders at the beginning of the show, which was organized by Truly, a younger member of the society, was therefore understandable. They were present as honoured guests: "the stars" the audience would see in the slide show. But the elders, especially the women, were used to being the hosts rather than the guests at Japanese Canadian events and, moreover, they were not used to having so many non-Japanese Canadians in their community venues. Many refused to sit until all the non-Japanese Canadians were seated; others wanted to stand at the back of the hall rather than sit with the audience. Like Truly and me, they seemed a bit overwhelmed by the number of people who showed up.

This event also introduced a new activity. Japanese Canadians made an open invitation to other residents to come to their community hall to see the history of the village from the perspective of Mr. Matsushita, a man who had been branded an enemy alien during the 1940s. By bringing different people together to remember the past – presented as everyone's history in New Denver – the slide show recognized a community of people in New Denver that crossed social and cultural divides. The event was a forum through which these groups came together as *one group* and remembered what the slide show affirmed as *their* collective past, as was evident from the audience's response. For example, when a photo of a high school sports team appeared, someone called out, "Hey! Okay! can everyone name the people?" This does not mean that everyone saw or consented to the same version of the past. The point is that *everyone participated* in the process of remembering the past as one group. It didn't matter that the slide show did not include a photograph of everyone present. It was enough to recognize a building or a street. It was the shared knowledge of the buildings, streets, events, people, and places that made everyone's memories part of a shared past.

Heteroglossia in Action
Neither Truly nor the members of the Kyowakai Society were certain how "A Time Gone By" would be received. Not only was it the first time that a Japanese Canadian resident from the Orchard would be presenting the history of the village from her or his perspective, but the format of the slide show also made

Mr. Matsushita's portrayal of life in New Denver open to multiple readings. In many ways, this visually based event had the fluidity of what Mikhail Bakhtin (1981) describes as the heteroglossic characteristics of an oral utterance. An oral utterance is always formed in response to a particular situation. Whoever makes the utterance responds to the context of delivery which is shaped by various expectations, disciplinary knowledges, ambivalences, conflicts, and assumptions that are under constant negotiation by whatever ideological groups are implicated (ibid.). As a speaker makes an utterance, it becomes inflected with these heterogeneous dynamics, making it heteroglossic. The terminology that is used and the emphasis given to one point, rather than another, can reveal, for instance, the stake that the speaker has in being accepted in the context in which she or he makes the utterance while also resisting the ideological assumptions of the listeners. Thus, it is possible to examine the components of an utterance as well as how it is enunciated in order to gain an understanding of the heteroglossic context in which it has been formed.

Because utterances are generated in immediate interaction with others, there is an interactive fluidity in their formation. In contrast, rituals and prewritten speeches are more structurally rigid and have less fluidity, changing much less in response to the presence of others. Rituals and speeches thus have a tendency to impose the singular point of view of the institution that delivers them (Bourdieu 1991). Like Bourdieu's study of speech acts, Bakhtin's linguistic analysis is particularly attentive to the power dynamics of utterances and to how official culture tends to drive out the heterogeneous, what Bakhtin calls heteroglossic, dynamics to present a monolithic, or what he refers to as a "monoglossic," perspective.

The fluidity of an utterance is evident in how its meaning can be transformed through the use of a seemingly anomalous term, the tone of voice, the weight of a pause, the repetition of a phrase, the speed of delivery, the rounded soft rhythm of speaking English, or the intensity of the claim that "inter*marriage*" will lead to the "END" of the community. The fluidity of an utterance also makes its meaning a challenge to pin down as it transforms in a multitude of ways, depending on the listener's response or lack of response, with a shift in posture or the clench of a jaw.

Bakhtin was concerned with developing dialogic ways to represent "the living heteroglossia" of everyday life. To be dialogic entails representing without reifying or ideologically appropriating different worldviews, perspectives, opinions, and positions from the ongoing changing social world so that they are brought into "dialogue" with one another. The goal is to bring differences, similarities, silences, and conflicting views into engagement with one another so they will

5.4   May Day parade, New Denver, 1968. *Shoichi Matsushita. Courtesy of the Matsushita family.*

be mutually illuminating, bringing a new understanding to a situation or event (Bakhtin 1981).

In this way, Mr. Matsushita's slide show, "A Time Gone By," could be viewed as a heteroglossic event with dialogic possibilities. The format of the slide show was loosely structured rather than formally rigid. There was no authoritative voice-over that imposed a single interpretation. In contrast to the NIMC displays, there was no accompanying text that dictated the purpose of the show. During the presentation, different narratives with different points of view came spontaneously together or into conflict. For example, Mr. Matsushita's retrospective account of the slides as the photographer contrasted with Mrs. Matsushita's corrective insights as she recalled viewing the same scene standing beside him as he took the photographs. Then there was the implicit narrative based on Truly's choice and sequencing of the various sets of slides. At the same time, the perspective and composition of the slides both as individual images and as a series of images created yet other narratives, while the viewers spontaneously shouted out their recollections, quietly murmured, or sat in silence. Thus, the slide show did not impose one interpretation of the past: it generated multiple versions. The recollections of those in attendance worked to broaden not only

5.5 Remembrance Day parade with Masaye Matsushita *(first row of drummers, far right)* and Michael Mori *(left of M. Matsushita)*, New Denver, 1969. *Shoichi Matsushita. Courtesy of the Matsushita family.*

the details about various events, but also the terms through which various groups understood the past and one another.

The slides of events in which members of both communities worked, socialized, and celebrated together were particularly interesting. Documented from Mr. Matsushita's perspective, they captured dinner parties that he and Mrs. Matsushita had hosted for the local teachers, staff working at the San amicably posing together for group photos, teenagers dressed in gowns and suits for high school graduations, and May Day celebrations and Remembrance Day parades. These images showed how not only the economic but also the social lives of Japanese Canadians overlapped with the other villagers, especially after the war. Even if the wartime generation still maintained separate institutions and buildings for many of their community civilities, their lives became interconnected through their children.

The slides of Nikkei boys in the Remembrance Day parade are particularly striking, especially the slide taken close enough to see the identities of the cadets (see Figure 5.5). The boys march in remembrance of war. The war that most powerfully affected this generation would have been the Second World War, the war that brought Japanese Canadians to New Denver and also the war that the government used to strip Japanese Canadians of their rights and racially seg-regated them from the rest of the population. In the photograph of the parade that I have selected for closer examination, Mr. Matsushita captures his son, Mas, as well as Michael Mori in formation with, rather than separate from, the other cadets. Yet the photograph is not simply a proud testament to how the country now recognizes these two Nikkei boys as worthy members of its military order. Although the two boys seem to be just like the other cadets, smartly attired in their pressed khaki wool uniforms and polished boots, they also stand out. As the only Nikkei boys visible in the image, the camera focuses on them as they march in the first line of drummers toward the camera. While they follow their squad leader, who is taller and appears to be several years older, the leader moves toward the left edge of the frame, slightly blurred as he marches out of the camera lens's depth of field. In Mr. Matsushita's com-position, if you turn your attention to the two Nikkei boys, it appears as if the rest of the cadets are in fact following in step to the rat-tat-tat of their drums. While they are not leaders of their generation yet, in the photographer's frame, this is what could await them in a few years. This is an astounding view from a father who spent the war years in an internment camp branded as an enemy alien. He and the other Nikkei fathers would have never been in such a parade two decades earlier.

The war would have separated the parents of these cadets. Many of the surviv-ing war veterans in New Denver, with their horrific recollections of Japanese concentration camps, continue to find the divide unbridgeable and still view Japanese Canadians as enemy aliens. In contrast, through Mr. Matsushita's photographs of the Remembrance Day parade, the audience sees the postwar generation, marching toward us, together. Here, it is significant that Mr. Matsu-shita did not photograph the parade to emphasize the orderly lines and con-formity of the cadets. None of the cadets seem to move strictly in unison; rather, each boy retains his own sense of self. Berets and caps are all worn at slightly different angles. Yet they still march together through a village that was the site of a Second World War internment camp that they and their parents, Japanese Canadians and non-Japanese Canadians, had transformed into the community it is today. They march into the present, away from irreconcilable divisions of wartime racial hatred and fear into the warm summer evening of August 1996, when so many New Denver old-timers came to see "Spud's" slide show.

The heteroglossic dynamics of the slide show also presented new residents with an opportunity to gain insight into the village's past. Since the new residents had not lived in New Denver during the period when there was a large Japanese Canadian community in the village, it would have been easy for them to be unaware of the social significance of the local Japanese Canadians. But the way other long-term residents excitedly recognized various Japanese Canadians in the slides documenting the large community living in New Denver during the 1960s may have altered the new residents' impression and, hence, the terms through which they viewed the past and their Japanese Canadian neighbours. It might have made them more attuned to how different aspects of life in the village have become organized around the activities and needs of Japanese Canadians in the most subtle of ways. Consider the large array of Japanese food in the Eldorado Grocery. The fact that the store now permanently stocks this selection of Japanese food might seem at odds with the small number of local Japanese Canadian residents in the area, but it reveals the role Japanese Canadians have had in the economic and social life of the village over the years.

The simple presence or absence of elderly Japanese Canadian residents in the audience potentially had an effect as well. Consider an elderly Japanese Canadian sitting beside a new resident. The new resident's impression of New Denver might be based on its current image as a village with environmental groups, an independent bookstore, and a funky café. Before viewing the slide show, the new resident at most might have recognized the fact that the elder probably was a survivor from the New Denver internment camp. If the new resident recognized the elder thirty years younger in some of the slides, the new resident would be given a window into a period when this elder played an important role in a large, active Japanese Canadian community that was committed to transforming the remains of the internment camp, with all its dark reminders of the province's racist history, into a place where they could rebuild their lives and raise their children. The new resident also might realize that the records that the elders have made over the years, including the slides and the accounts they shared that evening, were some of the only remaining records of this unique period of the village's history. This realization would create more appreciation for elders' knowledge of the village.

While many elders in the audience were in the slide show, it was also notable that many individuals in Mr. Matsushita's photographs were missing. Now deceased, these individuals came alive in the images. But their absence was felt. When well-known figures appeared in the slides, many would utter their names, murmuring, for example, "and there she is ... Mrs. Kamegaya." Feelings of loss hushed the audience. These figures, captured in movement, whether in the swirling synchronized steps of odori or hammering the roof on the Kohan Gardens' new teahouse, illuminated the darkened Centennial Hall. In their absence, the slide show offered a moment to collectively remember, to commemorate, them.

It would be easy to romanticize this gathering of residents as an example of how the Nikkei Internment Memorial Centre fosters inclusive village life in

New Denver, bringing together Japanese Canadians and other residents. But this would simplify the complex relations that residents have with the Japanese Canadians. As noted, this was the first time that many of the non-Japanese Canadian residents had visited the NIMC since its opening two years before. Why had they not visited previously? Many had supported the NIMC as individuals and in official capacities. So why had some come to see Mr. Matsushita's slide show but had never visited the NIMC? Were they uneasy about how the NIMC publicly displayed their village's history of internment? Or were they critical of the way the contractors "museumized" the community? Takana told me about P.B., an old-timer in her seventies, "who hangs out with the seniors." She said that it would have been better if they had built a really nice old folks home for the "seniors" rather than the memorial. When Takana explained that the memorial brought Japanese Canadians from across Canada together, P.B. replied, "Look at what they've gone through – who cares about the others! What happens to them when they can't take care of themselves – what about their needs, language, food?" (Field notes, 27 July 1996).

Like P.B., many of these New Denver residents had close relationships with Japanese Canadians and had lived in the village for many years. They had already taken a position on the injustice of what had happened. Those living in New Denver no doubt also found the war years and the following decades difficult. So why visit the NIMC alongside the tourists who were seeking information about the internment camp? For them, it was friendship with the elders and their families that was significant. For them, the invitation from the Japanese Canadian community to be guests in the Centennial Hall to see the slide show was a way to celebrate and affirm their lives together in the same village over the years. Coming to Spud's slide show, hosted by the Kyowakai Society, was their way of affirming that the memorial continued to be a community space, rather than a museum or memorial that educated the public or served postwar generations of Japanese Canadians from other towns and cities.

At the same time, some Japanese Canadian elders were concerned that the slides misrepresented their lives and that the audience did not recognize the struggles Japanese Canadians had gone through after they were released from the camp. For example, when there was a ripple of exclamations and appreciative comments as the slides depicting large Japanese Canadian events in the 1960s appeared, Mr. Matsushita and Mr. Tad Mori tried to intervene. They tried to underline that, while it looked as if the Japanese Canadian community held "one fun party after another," this period was, in fact, very difficult for many Japanese Canadians. Their material and emotional struggles were evident in the slides if members of the audience turned their attention to the living conditions – for example, to the dilapidated buildings – or if they studied the signs of strain and tension in the bodies and faces of the community members. Both old-time New Denver residents and Japanese Canadian elders tried to make certain the audience did not become caught up in their nostalgia and overlook the struggles and difficulties of the postwar period. With so many older-timers and elders in their seventies and eighties, it was difficult not to wonder what would happen when they passed on and only these captivating images remained, removed from the living heteroglossia of New Denver.

A Dialogic Narrative

The dialogic interplay of memories elicited by the slide show made the NIMC's exhibitions seem lifeless by contrast. The vivid images showing the Kyowakai Hall filled with Japanese Canadians during the 1960s and 1970s revealed that, in contrast to the NIMC's story about these buildings, they were not just relics of the mythical years of internment. They were recently in use by an active community.

The profusion of imagery in the slide show in many ways split open the present scene of the NIMC. No longer was it self-evident as a museum. As a museum, the NIMC constructs the internment as a discrete event in the past. It presents the objects on display as evidence of internment and directs the visitor to reflect on the hardship and injustice of this period. It "museumifies" the internment camp. The imagery of the slide show spliced this trajectory, breaking open its temporal containment of the internment camp in the distant past. It relocated the objects on display in multiple relationships and events across different moments in the lives of the residents over the last thirty years. It became apparent that the internment camp was not simply part of the past but rather continued to be woven into the everyday lives of New Denver residents.

No single slide or exclamation broke open the museumizing trajectory. Rather, through the course of the slide show, out of the flow of images, recollections, and silences, the imagery began to coalesce, locating the remains of the camp (including the shacks, the Kyowakai Hall, the Centennial Hall, and also the Japanese Canadians themselves) in the valley's changing terrain rather than just confining them to the historical landscape of the past. Members of the audience related differently to the scenes in individual slides, bringing to their readings different points of view, experiences, and visions. The more a slide was contextualized, set in place (or rather multiple places) the more layered and heteroglossic its meanings became. Through this engagement, individual images generated imagery that challenged a monoglossic view of New Denver.

The imagery did not coalesce from a random set of images and recollections. Instead, the imagery formed as *memory nodes*. The term "node" suggests a site of growth, an intersecting point of movement, a fulcrum of energy. Memory nodes are the nexus of scattered traces from the past. The traces may be an photograph, an elder's powerful speaking voice, the skeleton of a wooden bucket entangled in tall summer grasses, or keepsakes nestled on the shelf in someone's living room. Memory nodes are resonant: as in the moment when a voice reverberates with the pitch of a tuning fork, a sensation of meaning opens up.

In some cases, what became a node in the slide show was highly specific to an individual's experiences. For example, in my case, a slide of women clearing a field on a late autumn day was filled with childhood memories: the time of year for clearing brush to prepare the grounds for winter (see Figure 5.6). The women working in motion, raking the burnt grasses and brambles, had an aesthetic reference to other childhood images of Japanese folk tales, wood-block prints, and my own Obaasan and mother working in their gardens and yards. The slide of the women in the field interconnected with my own childhood memories and formed the imagery in a prose piece I wrote. In this piece, I searched for a way to put into words what the elders and, I also realized, my own Obaasan and mother have done to transform the terrain of memory in British Columbia over the years.

> They burnt off the matted grasses suffocating new growth. sent down roots
> to break up the solidifying anguish, sorrow
> roots that drew out the bitter taste leached into
> the alluvial soil.
>
> Buried what they couldn't swallow. to rot deep in the earth.
> under the care of microscopic fungi, beetles and worms,
> creatures of the subterranean world.
> calloused hands.
> wind burnt faces.
> still breathing in the smoky residue
> of what-was
>
> — McAllister, 1998

In contrast, the 1960s images of the Kyowakai Hall acted like nodes that split open my perception of the space as simply an exhibition venue for tourists. Full of images of people and activities from the past, with everyone in the audience excitedly calling out the names of the people, the slides finally brought the hall alive.

Memory nodes are always transforming. Any remnant of the past can be drawn to any number of other remnants to form a node that in turn can resonate with other remnants. As the remnants interconnect, they move out of their

5.6 Clearing a field in the Orchard in preparation for building a tea house, 1967. *Shoichi Matsushita. Courtesy of the Matsushita family.*

familiar contexts. Now displaced from their temporally and socially specific contexts of meaning, they illuminate one another, each providing a new context of meaning that makes other's characteristics come into relief in new ways. In the moment when remnants are drawn together, condensing in new and sometimes disturbing ways, there is a dialogic potential for transforming how these remnants have been lodged, submerged, or excluded from viewers' own terrains of memory, which in turn can shift how the viewers relate to the past. Thus, the imagery from the slide show works as a memory node, insofar as it pulls together overlooked traces from New Denver's past. This imagery wrenches the Kyowakai Hall free from its current context, where it is simply a historical building on a tourist site and wards off the "museumification" that Mr. Senya Mori warned against.

In this manner, the slide show destabilized the hold that conventional historical trajectories had over the past in New Denver. It made a space for memory and, in particular, other memories that could not be seamlessly narrated into a historical narrative. In particular, this small-scale memory project shook loose the way the NIMC's museumizing discourses fit remnants of the past into the historical landscape of the Slocan Valley, presenting the stories of Japanese Canadians as a "painful story" that took place in the distant past. Its capacity to destabilize entrenched discourses lay in its open, flexible structure. As a dialogic narrative, it depended on the responses and interactions of those attending the slideshow.

An important aspect of this openness is that the narrative sequence of the slides did not reorganize the remnants and recollections of the past into another trajectory that pinned meaning down. The meanings that were generated relied on whoever came and their responses to one another as well as to the slides and the venue. It spun the images and the recollections into trajectories that were heteroglossic and fluid, never completely stated, developed, or rhetorically closed. This is because the imagery that coalesced from the slide show was not necessarily the same for each person in attendance. Although there seemed to be a general consensus about the what, where, and who, and even about the significance of certain locations, events, or people, for each person the slides and recollections undoubtedly touched different moments in their lives, relationships, and events. Without an authoritative narrative in place, it was possible for various memories to move into the foreground while others receded, and for certain images rather than others to gain significance and become weighed with inflections, reorganized around the concerns or feelings of those present, consolidating into powerful imagery.

The general banter and shared reactions, such as quiet moments of reflection or excited shouts of "Remember this?" reinforced a collective memory, making connections that resonated with meaning across the boundaries of the Japanese Canadian community and the other New Denver residents. It was through the responses and interaction of the audience that this collective memory came into play, rather than being directed by an imposed narrative. This memory was collective insofar as the audience remembered things as a group. But, again, this in no way meant that they remembered the same things the same way. Given the diversity of responses and the difficulty of sustaining one's particular interpretation of an event in the presence of others whose lives were intimately bound up in both the difficult and the celebratory aspects of the past, the slide show offered the dialogic potential to generate new understandings – whether for a new resident who did not know about the role of the Japanese Canadian community in New Denver, an old-timer who was troubled by the wartime racial divisions that continued to haunt the community, or an elder who had not realized the extent of other villagers' recognition of their role in making New Denver the village it is today.

CHAPTER SIX

In Memory of Others

Lake City, the warmth of fellow people
Uprooted, my body cries no more
Day by day my heart finds peace
New Denver, now my home

– N.A., TRANSLATION BY AYAKA YOSHIMIZU
OF POEM INSCRIBED ON THE PHOTOGRAPH
IN FIGURE 6.1

Establishing (the) History

A Tourist Site

The Nikkei Internment Memorial Centre (NIMC) transformed how the elders remember the internment camp in New Denver. Building the NIMC changed their relationship to the past and reconfigured their relationships to one another, to the younger generations, and to other residents in New Denver. But as a collective form of remembering, the NIMC involves more than the New Denver community. This chapter examines the NIMC as a site of memory for those who travel to New Denver to visit the memorial and reflects on how their visits affect the way the elders in New Denver relate to their history of internment.

When I began this study, I assumed that visitors with a family history of internment would approach the NIMC as a memorial where they could commemorate the losses of, mourn, and make tributes to the wartime generation. I discovered, however, that what shaped how they related to the Centre and how they interacted with staff, were much more complex. As my fieldwork revealed, discourses that construct the Centre as a tourist site and, in particular, as a museum where visitors can learn about Japanese Canadian history also shaped how visitors approached the Centre. As I have discussed in earlier chapters, promotional material advertised the NIMC primarily as one of the many tourist attractions in the Kootenays rather than as a memorial centre. Despite the name Nikkei Internment Memorial Centre, I found that a number of visitors did not approach the Centre as a memorial. In terms of its design, even the layout of the Centre focuses the visitors' attention on the historical displays rather than

湖水の都平民の情
進み来し身に涙を
日毎人に心もなごみ
住谷都止ニューデンバー

6.1   The New Denver tuberculosis sanatorium, ca. 1945. *Unknown photographer. Basil Izumi Collection. Courtesy of the Japanese Canadian Museum.*

on rituals of memorialization. Despite signage that suggests that it is a place to reflect and remember, the garden is designed as a setting for the museum rather than as a place where visitors can take time to meander in reflection.

However, given that the memorial was built by Japanese Canadians on the site where they were interned, the NIMC promises something more authentic than just a museum with informative displays and interesting artifacts. For some, it has become a pilgrimage site. Dean MacCannell (1989) and Erik Cohen (1996) argue that being a tourist and a pilgrim are not necessarily mutually exclusive. Although many tourists seek diversion and recreation, many others go on pilgrimages in search of spiritual centres where they can have deeply meaningful, authentic experiences (ibid.). Unlike the pre-modern pilgrim, MacCannell's and Cohen's tourist does not search for authentic experiences in her or his own society. MacCannell claims that the shallowness and in-authenticity of modern life drive the tourist to look for "reality and authenticity elsewhere: in other historical periods and other cultures and in purer simpler life styles" (1989, 3).

Yet, according to Chris Rojek and John Urry (1997), whether tourists are seeking distraction or spiritual discovery, their experiences are "produced." Tourist destinations sell experiences, investing capital in visually spectacular sights and culturally significant events as well as in transportation infrastructure and service industries. Traditional cultures and unspoiled pieces of paradise do not lie waiting in their pristine glory for crowds of tourists to discover (Urry 1996, 1997). "Paradise" in "tropical" countries, for instance, is usually a region where the "Natives" have been forced off their land, killed by local paramilitary, or turned into underpaid service workers on luxury retreats with pesticide-laden golf greens and dining halls filled with imported food. For Rojek and Urry (1997), tourism is a set of social discourses and practices that *produce various types of tourist experiences,* only one of which is the search for authentic experiences in so-called traditional societies.

Rojek and Urry (1997) and Urry (1995, 1996) outline a method for analyzing tourism that can be applied to the NIMC. They claim that tourism can be understood as a field of discursive activity that is not separate from but, rather, constituted in conjunction with other social practices and discourses (Urry 1996, 115). This chapter considers the range of practices and discourses that place visitors in relation to the NIMC, including the ethnographic gaze and personal journeys to discover, mourn, and make amends for the past. A textual analysis of the NIMC would be insufficient here. It would not provide details about the ways in which visitors articulated and negotiated the various discourses and practices while they were visiting the memorial. By working at the NIMC, I inadvertently became a participant-observer with the opportunity to see how visitors approached the NIMC, whether as a tourist site, an educational centre, a memorial, or a community venue.¹ I did not plan to become a participant-observer; in fact, while I was working on the History Preservation Committee projects, I tried to avoid the visitors at first. However, working on the projects at the memorial most week days and helping the NIMC staff when they needed an extra hand, I ended up greeting people when they entered the NIMC, answering questions and chatting with them as a way of welcoming them to the Centre. Some interactions provided detailed information, since some visitors wanted to talk about their reasons for coming to the Centre. Other interactions led to conflicts or uncomfortable encounters. In some cases, visitors felt the need to justify the incarceration of Japanese Canadians, and in other cases, they ignored signs prohibiting their entry when the Centre was closed. And then there were visitors who solemnly walked through the memorial, saying little to anyone. Here it is important to emphasize the sensitive nature of the memorial, making it inappropriate to directly approach people during their visits. One was never certain how visitors would react to the memorial, whether they wanted to talk about their personal experiences or if they wanted to be left alone to wander in their own thoughts. I did my best not to be intrusive, but there were occasions when I failed. This component of my research project allowed me to learn about how visitors approached the memorial on their own terms, without having to explain themselves or justify their views to an inquisitive researcher. I had the opportunity to see what visitors did at the memorial, who they brought with them, and their interactions with the NIMC staff. I learned how the memorial, a public venue run by the Kyowakai Society and visited by thousands of people, influenced how the elders remembered experiences of internment.

In this chapter, I present passages from my field notes that describe visitors. To understand the extent to which the practices of the visitors and their interactions with myself, the staff, and the members of the Kyowakai Society reproduce or depart from the discourses that constitute the NIMC as a tourist site, in particular, as a museum, I will first describe in more detail the way that museum discourses place visitors in relation to the exhibitions.

Museums: The Ethnographic Gaze

Museums were once elite institutions, but as Ivan Karp has argued in his foundational volume on museums (1992), they are now vested with the task of educating the general public. Yet they do not simply impart knowledge to members of the public about the world in which they live. They aim to educate the public about the characteristics of the ideal citizen (ibid., 6; Bennett 2004).

> [As] repositories of knowledge, value and taste ... [on which civil society is based] ... [museums] establish the social ideals of a society, the sets of beliefs, assumptions and feelings in terms of which people judge one another and which they sometimes use to guide action. Social ideas often set up hierarchies of moral values ... They embody notions people have about their differences and similarities and they are organized in terms of which is good and ... bad ... superior and ... inferior ... what is central or peripheral, valued or useless, known or to be discovered. (Karp 1992, 5-7)

According to Kreamer (1992), many of the discourses that remain central to what is regarded as the ideal citizen were established in museum exhibitions in the 1800s and were shaped by that period's scientific racism and colonialism. Exhibits in major museums were "intended to control the educational process and to guide the public to desired conclusions that served political ends" (ibid., 368). Drawing on the scientific racism of the late nineteenth century, museums reinforced colonial policies by constructing the "other" in an arrested state of development, encouraging the general public to support colonial domination. Tony Bennett describes how in Victorian England museums aided lower- and middle-class Britons to imagine a homogenous nationalistic identity "counterpoised to a racially different and exotic 'other'"(in ibid., 369).

Barbara Kirshenblatt-Gimblatt (1991) and Sveltana Alpers (1991) describe how the contemporary Western museum goer has been produced through the articulation of scientific and ethnographic discourses. They argue that museums utilize practices of viewing derived from these institutionalized systems of knowledge. Exhibitions of exotic cultures dissect and then reassemble the components of these cultures in a logic of classification that attempts to explain what distinguishes them from supposedly superior Western nations. Following an evolutionary timeline, these exhibits conventionally contrast the "primitive" and "aberrant" with the "developed." Practices of viewing in museums also draw on residues of practices from older systems of knowledge that still inform current exhibitions, such as the collection of curiosities (Kirshenblatt-Gimblatt 1991, 393). Throughout the nineteenth century, proponents of the scientific approach complained that collections of curiosities continued to be displayed without systematic arrangement. By their very definition, these collections were at odds with both Charles Darwin's evolutionary and Carolus Linneaus' hierarchical systems of classifying species. Curiosities were defined as chance occurrences and exceptions to the rule, freaks of nature, amazing events, or natural wonders that were in and of themselves unique rather than instances of a category (ibid., 392-393). As abnormal occurrences, they engendered fascination, horror, titillation, and wonderment.

Over the twentieth century, as mainstream museums became established scientific institutions, they dispensed with displays of curiosities. But exhibitions of live specimens, especially performances by humans from "primitive" societies, continued to appeal to visitors' morbid curiosity and to arouse fascination. These exhibits often used theatrical techniques drawn from popular entertainment, including the circus and the chamber of horrors. To grant exhibitions the guise of respectability, particularly in the early nineteenth century, when conservative Protestants in the United States and Britain were critical of theatre, performances were reframed in terms of science, nature, and education (Kirshenblatt-Gimblatt 1991, 397-398).

Today, many ethnographic museum exhibits continue to frame the "exotic other" through the conventions of the early nineteenth-century gaze. These conventions affirm the West's evolutionary distance from (neo)colonized people. They draw on a way of looking characteristic of those ethnographers, military agents, and colonial administrators who mapped resources, populations, and transportation routes in "uninhabited lands" and colonial territories. These agents observed and documented the behaviours of indigenous people for their colonial projects and as objects of fascination, fear, and fantasy. They reduced them to objects of their gaze rather than viewing them with the respectful regard one grants to another human subject, recognizing their dignity and value (Green 1984; Gilman 1986; Todorov 1987; Maxwell 1999). Social conventions regarding if, how, and when it is appropriate to look at another person were of no relevance.

Kirshenblatt-Gimblatt explains how the gaze – "the power to look" – structures contemporary ethnographic displays. These displays invoke "the power to open up to sight differentially, to show with respect to others what one would not reveal about oneself – one's body, one's person, and life" (1991, 415). The displays are arranged to reveal intimate details, stripping away the protection of privacy from the lower orders of humanity.[2]

But over the last three decades, many museums have begun to change their exhibition practices after being publicly criticized for their dehumanizing exotification of others. In Canada, especially since the 1990s, coalitions of racialized communities have publicly criticized and protested exhibitions as well as theatre performances that reproduce denigrating images of their communities (Gagnon 2000; Gagnon and Fung 2002; Butler 2008 [1999]). In response, many major museums and galleries are now housing exhibits that deconstruct colonial imagery, for example, of indigenous people, such as "The Cowboy/Indian Show" curated by Gerald McMaster, which was exhibited at the Museum of Civilization in Ottawa. There have also been solo shows by contemporary indigenous artists such as Rebecca Belmore and Brian Jungen at the Vancouver Art Gallery over the last decade. Yet, at the same time, many of these museums still carry permanent exhibits that trace the evolution of indigenous and "ethnic" cultures and program traditional dance and music performances that powerfully appeal to colonial discourses. Thus, while Karp notes that as early as the 1980s prominent museum historiographers such as Neil Harris observed that museums were undergoing a phase of deconstructing established systems of knowledge and authority (Karp 1992, 10), he hesitates to celebrate museums as sites of deconstruction. Yet he recognizes that if museums are "places for defining who people are and how they should act," they are also key sites for challenging these definitions (ibid., 4). This provides a context for examining how visitors are discursively positioned in relation to the NIMC.

Although the NIMC's exhibits interpret the history of Japanese Canadians from a human rights perspective, established racial discourses are difficult to strip away from their representations. Racial discourses frame all representations of Asians in Canada under the rubric of "Orientals," "the Far East," and "the Yellow Races." As Gina Marchetti argues with respect to Hollywood films, "these discourses create a mythic image of Asia that empowers the West and rationalizes Euroamerican authority over the Asian other" (Marchetti 1993, 6).

Under the lexicon of "the Oriental," Japanese Canadians lose all particularities that mark them as individual human subjects. They lose the differences that defy stereotypes. As Orientals, Japanese Canadians become sites for a shifting mélange of contradictory qualities drawn from Japanese, Korean, Vietnamese, and Chinese caricatures (Said 1979, 62). These qualities are no longer directly traceable to historical incidents in particular geographic regions (McAllister 1992a, 9). The Oriental becomes a category that, as Edward Said argues, "allows one to see new things, things seen for the first time, as versions of a previously known thing. In essence such a category is not so much a way of receiving new information as it is a method of controlling what seems to be a threat to some established way of viewing things" (1979, 58-59). The codes for looking at Orientals are widespread in British Columbia's museums, where reconstructions of stereotypical Chinatowns are especially popular.³ Marchetti argues that "any act of domination brings with it opposition, guilt, repression and resistance, which also must be incorporated into these myths and silenced, rationalized, domesticated, or otherwise eliminated" (1993, 6). Physically removed from the social landscape in 1945 through an extension of orders-in-council passed by the federal cabinet under the War Measures Act, official discourses no longer needed to negotiate the presence of Japanese Canadians as labourers living in segregated nihonmachis or as members of lobby groups demanding the right to vote. Until the redress movement in the 1980s, Japanese Canadians were predominantly absent from the province's official history, whether in museums or school textbooks.

In contrast, exhibitions of reconstructed Chinatowns have had a prominent place in British Columbia. I remember as a child seeing reconstructed Chinatowns in the Royal British Columbia Museum and in heritage sites such as Barkerville, a town dating from the 1862 Cariboo gold rush. In these exhibits, exterior walls that shield the lives of the inhabitants from prying eyes were removed. Like a cross-section that cuts a snail shell in half in a scientific study, revealing pulsating internal organs, the exhibits exposed the mysteries of interior life. The removal of the walls gave viewers intimate access to activities that are normally shielded from outsiders. The exhibits played on an element of exoticism, drawing on references to opium, prostitutes, and secret clan societies. The experience was titillating, reinforcing voyeuristic relations of looking. The lighting was dim as we peered into cramped gambling dens or medicine shops lined with collections of odd glass vials holding concoctions used, we imagined, to heal all sorts of strange ailments. We saw impoverished living conditions so different from what most of us knew, along with rice bowls and chopsticks, Chinese-language newspapers, and strange clothing and footwear. And high on a small shelf was usually an altar for an unknown deity.

The NIMC resists the curious ethnographic gaze that turns Japanese Canadians into Orientals and instead shows archival photographs showing them in typical Canadian activities as pioneers, war veterans, baseball players, performers in jazz bands, and concerned citizens writing letters to decry the abuse of democratic principles. The NIMC belongs to a movement of local museums run by communities with mandates to reinterpret the ways that they have been constructed by established discourses (Simpson 1996). Many African American museums, for example, strive for a "positive education" and are guided by "the principle that museums can be the vehicle for social change" (Kreamer 1992, 376). Museums and cultural centres with mandates to reinterpret experience from a critical community-based perspective are sites where groups who are devalued by or deleted from official history can affirm "a heritage" and claim contemporary identities (ibid., 374; Simpson 1996). Likewise the NIMC also operates against the grain of established historical discourses. Until the NIMC was built, there was little public recognition of Japanese Canadian history in the region. In this context, the NIMC offers them a place to reclaim their presence in the historical terrain of the province.

But to what extent does the NIMC challenge the visitor's construction of Japanese Canadians as Oriental objects of the ethnographic gaze? As Rojek and Urry (1997) argue, visitors are not positioned only through discursive practices specific to tourism, museums, and official history. How visitors relate to the NIMC depends on their negotiation of these discourses and on whatever else compels them to visit the Centre.

Visitors: Negotiating or Reproducing Established Discourses

The NIMC Staff: Duty and Burnout

My purpose in reviewing the literature on tourism, museums, and the ethnographic gaze is to make evident that NIMC visitors are not simply propelled by innocent curiosity or the search for authentic culture. The ways we view museum exhibits are shaped by predispositions and practices from established discourses. I now turn to the visitors, describing how they approached the NIMC, their interactions with staff and local residents, and their responses to the Centre as a tourist site or a memorial. Most descriptions are from my field notes, which include daily entries about my activities and reflections. I also include observations made by NIMC staff and members of the Kyowakai Society.

When I was working at the NIMC, I had many opportunities to meet visitors, although the staff, many of whom were not Japanese Canadians, interacted with them on a daily basis, greeting them, directing them through the exhibits, giving guided tours, and answering questions. The Kyowakai Society carefully selects the staff to ensure they can appropriately represent the society. Because most of the staff grew up in New Denver, the Kyowakai Society knows them and their families well. As I worked alongside the staff, many described their enthusiasm about working at the NIMC. They explained that working there was not just a summer job to gain experience and earn wages. They viewed their work as a service to the New Denver community. With family relationships and friendships linking the lives of Japanese Canadian and non-Japanese Canadian residents over several generations, the staff, whether or not they were Japanese Canadian, regarded Nikkei history as an important part of their own past.[4]

The staff observed that most visitors approached the NIMC as a historical museum. Because, until quite recently, British Columbia's official history had left out its Japanese Canadian "pioneers," the staff assumed that most non-Japanese Canadian visitors would know little about the history of internment. Assumptions about the visitors' lack of knowledge were affirmed by the terminology that many non-Japanese Canadian and sometimes Japanese Canadian visitors used. Terminology is significant. As Trinh Minh-ha claims, "Power ... has always inscribed itself in language ... [Language] is one of the most complex forms of subjugation, being at once the locus of power and unconscious servility" (1989, 53). For example, many visitors referred to Japanese Canadians as "Japanese," not realizing the significance of using "Japanese Canadian." A common question asked by visitors was whether the government caught any spies during the 1940s or whether any "Japanese" were loyal to Japan, drawing on the same wartime rhetoric used to sway the general public and justify their removal from British Columbia. It was similar rhetoric that war veterans used forty years later to oppose granting redress to Japanese Canadians.

NIMC staff found the visitors' terminology and questions distressing. They were also unprepared for visitors who expressed a confused mixture of guilt and anger, suggesting unresolved psychological trauma. The NIMC administrator reported the following to the Kyowakai Society:

> There is a fatigue/"burn-out" factor involved in working at the N.I.M.C. which stems directly from the emotionally, intellectually, and politically offensive nature of the internment and its post-traumatic effects. This can be true for both Japanese

Canadian and non-Japanese Canadian employees. Both [my] co-employee and I have discussed the matter. The responses and political perspectives of visitors who come to the N.I.M.C. vary greatly: from the aggressive to the emotionally riveted; from the indifferent to the elderly Japanese Canadian survivor and his/her family. It is the responsibility of the employer to train, prepare, equip, fore-warn, and support future employees. [My co-employee] has mentioned that often the most difficult situations arise when she cannot answer a question posed by a visitor, whether that visitor is benignly inquisitive or, in the worst scenario, challenging the very injustice of the internment. (Shozawa 1996, 1)

The report documents the psychological distress experienced by those working at the NIMC and, more generally, what community-based museums that challenge established historical discourses likely undergo on a regular basis. This was and continues to be the general context for NIMC staff working with visitors.

Like the staff, I was defensive and cautious when faced with intrusive or argumentative tourists. The defensiveness is evident in some of my field notes. In some cases, my tone is judgmental, and I present the tourists as caricatures. I still cringe when I read these passages. Writing late at night or early in the morning, I resorted to vivid language and character types to quickly capture my impressions and convey what I experienced, feelings and all. Why include this material? As discussed in Chapter 1, like ethnographers who insert themselves in their texts as characters interacting with local inhabitants,[5] I have constructed myself as a character working at the NIMC. The ethnographic character operates like a literary device. The character's attitudes and misunderstandings function to reveal the fallacy of the researcher's objectivity and authority and, also, her worldview. Given that I am from the same culture as my research "subjects," the readers might view the ethnographic character as a mirror, making evident cultural attitudes (that readers may or may not share) and the limitations of academic knowledge. The readers might find my character obnoxious, naive, sympathetic, perplexing, or uninteresting. The goal is not to present a likeable character. Typically, the ethnographic character goes through a transformation as the limitations of her or his cultural attitudes and disciplinary knowledge become evident (though sometimes this does not happen until after she or he leaves the field). This is inherently an uncomfortable, conflict-ridden process.

In my account, I start with descriptions of the difficult tourists, giving my initial (often irritating) attitudes and responses. I then turn to visitors who made me reflect on the limitations of my assumptions and behaviour. The point is not to make conclusions about who is right and who is wrong. In addition to showing the range of visitors who visited the NIMC, the purpose of including descriptions of my encounters with them is to show the powerful discourses and emotional dynamics still rooted in the process of remembering Japanese Canadian internment camps. These dynamics place visitors and Japanese Canadians, as well as local residents working at the NIMC, sometimes in conflict and sometimes, as I will discuss, in mutual relations of understanding and learning. In this light, this chapter highlights the concerns expressed in the administrator's report regarding the challenges faced by members of persecuted communities working on public education projects.[6] The conflicted emotional responses of some visitors have a cumulative impact, making staff defensive, which can make it difficult to remember that many other visitors come to centres like the NIMC to learn about Japanese Canadian history, show support for Japanese Canadian friends, or discover what happened to their families during the war.

I made several methodological choices regarding the categorization of visitors. Because non-Japanese Canadians and Japanese Canadians have different relationships to the history of internment, I separated them into two groups. I then divided non-Japanese Canadian visitors into those who approached the NIMC as a tourist site and those who approached it as a memorial. I divided the Japanese Canadian visitors into those who objectified the local community and those who approached it as a pilgrimage site or community venue. These categories are based on my field notes as well as on discussions with NIMC staff and elders before and after my research visit in 1996. I ordered the categories, moving from visitors who displayed touristic behaviour to those who had nuanced, complex relations to Japanese Canadian history. In doing so, I also mapped my growing awareness of the complexity of the visitors' relation to Japanese Canadian history.

The Non-Japanese Canadian Visitors

The Tourists

The first group of visitors I discuss are "the tourists." Like Kirshenblatt-Gimblatt's ethnographer, the group I call the tourists enacted the power to look: "the power to open up to sight differentially, to examine details of an individual's life that one would never reveal about oneself" (1991, 415). The power to look – the gaze – strips away the social conventions that would normally govern how and when to look at another person. The disregard for these social conventions reflects the social distance between the person who looks and the person whom is looked at. The social distance between the tourists and the NIMC workers was compounded by gender, race, age, and class. In the tourist industry, service jobs are characterized by low wages, unskilled labour, and seasonal or part-time employment. Like other service workers in the tourist industry, most of the staff at the NIMC are women. Most are either recent high school graduates from New Denver or university students. Most were Japanese Canadian.[7] Judging from the accounts of the workers, a number of tourists appeared to expect the workers – as young women from "racial minorities" working in the service industry – to be subservient and cater to their needs. According to John Urry, this is a common expectation among tourists (Urry 1997, 70-89). For example, these tourists treated these workers authoritatively, demanding they answer their questions and then sometimes emphatically disagreed with their answers, as if attempting to demonstrate their superior knowledge. In contrast, the same tourists tended to defer to the older sansei, in particular, the president of the Kyowakai Society and the chair of the History Preservation Committee. The male president received more deference than the female chair. The tourists kept their distance from the elders, as if they were uncertain about how to approach them, perhaps assuming a language barrier. The formal comportment of the elders might have also dissuaded them, which I will discuss in more detail below.

To give an example of authoritative treatment, I include field notes describing a tourist who ignored the basic social proprieties that normally govern exchanges between strangers. The interaction between the tourist and NIMC worker (myself) began when he indicated he was interested in the NIMC because of his fondness for Japanese culture. When I defensively underlined that the Centre was dedicated to educating the public about the violation of Japanese Canadian rights, he asserted his authority by asking intrusive questions about my personal history.

Field Notes #1: An Interrogation – Just How Japanese Are You?

Today, a very difficult man came to the Centre. He approached me in the Visitors' Reception Centre. He initially asked about the gardens, explaining that he was building his own Japanese garden. I inquired about how he became interested in Japanese gardens. He explained that he went to Japan about five years ago. He became fond of the architecture. He was also taking Japanese-language lessons. Uncomfortable with his association of Japanese culture with Japanese Canadian internment camps, I reflected, "Well, I guess the buildings here aren't very Japanese. They are just internment shacks."

He immediately reacted by asking me if I was born in New Denver. I said no. Where was I from then? Was one of my parents "Japanese"? I felt as if I was suddenly being interrogated about my status as a Japanese Canadian, as if that was somehow related to my right to work at the NIMC: Was I a fake? And if I was authentic, just how authentic was I? But most of all, it felt as if he was determined to assert his authority over me.

To deflect his onslaught of questions, I acted as if I did not quite understand what he was asking, while at the same time waving my status as a true-blue British Columbia resident at him: "Huh? Oh – I'm from Vancouver Island." Having rural roots in itself is a testament to authenticity in BC. But he persisted, trying to trace the effects of internment into my personal history: "How did your family get there?" Despite my indignation, I felt compelled to answer him. I tried to answer in a nonchalant manner: "Jobs." Attempting to turn the inquiry around, I asked where he was from. "Abbotsford." Trying to deflate his probing, with a subtle counter that underlined how he was the one passing through the area, I nonchalantly mused, "Oh ... so you're *visiting* here." He returned to his interrogation about my credentials, retorting: "So how long have you been here?" Me: "I was here this year and visited last year too."

Refusing to acquiesce in his interrogation, I persisted, trying to turn the gaze back on him but never getting further than sniping over who is more familiar with New Denver: "Have you been here before?" Him: "Passed through, but I have never been to New Denver." I felt myself losing my composure as I thought: "Ha, a point." I wanted to find a way to exit the conversation and replied with a noncommittal, "Oh." Then, to my horror, he punched out a phrase in Japanese. [When I lived in Vancouver during the 1980s, non-Asian men – often naval crewmen, martial arts students, or American tourists – would regularly approach my friends and me with phrases in Cantonese or Japanese. There is little that is more disconcerting than Japanophiles and Chinaophiles trying to speak to you in what they assume is your "native language" or testing your comprehension to see how "Asian" you are.][8] Given that he had already determined that I was not a pure-blooded Japanese, it was as if he was demonstrating who in fact was the expert in Japanese culture. Rather huffily, I pronounced, "Well, you are encountering the cultural decimation of the incarceration. We never learned Japanese because of the war."

I pointed to some of the publications on the bookstand and stated, "That one is a good introduction to the Japanese Canadian redress movement."

He picked it up. I was called to the phone by one of the elders working at the NIMC. The man was still at the bookstand when I finished on the phone. He turned as if he expected me to want to continue talking with him. I marched off to the Centennial Hall. When I was in the hall's kitchen, I saw him charging by. When I slipped out of the hall, trying to sneak back to the office, he intercepted me and asked if there was a "Galapagos Island effect" with "the Japanese." I suppressed my urge to criticize the use of Darwin and said, "No." I explained that the community has continued to change over time. To emphasize this fact, I added, "Anyway, most of the issei [the original sources of Meiji-era Japanese culture in Canada] are *dead* now."

He reflected, "Fifty years is such a short time for a language to stay still anyway." This seemed to be his gesture toward understanding something about Japanese Canadian culture. I offered, "Well, look at Japan. Over the last fifty years, the language has rapidly changed." I remained a bit defensive, but managed to say, "Well ... I hope you find what the NIMC has to say interesting." (FIELD NOTES, 6 SEPTEMBER 1996)

This is a typical example of the exchanges that occurred between tourists and NIMC staff. I initially assumed that the man simply demonstrated how the ethnographic gaze constructs Japanese Canadians as racial others. Consider the tourist's avid interest in Japan. The NIMC is dedicated to educating the public about the internment of Japanese Canadians during the Second World War. By introducing himself with the statement that he had developed an interest in Japanese culture, he seemed to see the NIMC primarily as an example of Japanese culture. Initially, I was taken aback, viewing his statement as akin to introducing himself at a public inquiry into the abuse of Aboriginal children at residential schools by stating he was fond of Native art. Did he not recognize the purpose of the NIMC: its political critique of the Canadian government's actions? Did he not understand it was a memorial for generations of people affected by the internment camps?

Yet, given that I was so critical and defensive, it was easy to overlook more nuanced aspects of the exchange. I did not consider the difficulty of discussing histories of persecution. Perhaps the reference to Japanese culture was the most comfortable way for him to begin a conversation about the internment. Moreover, it is important to recognize that after I "marched off to the Centennial Hall," he looked for me, wanting to continue the discussion. On the one hand, feeling that this tourist relished asserting his authority, I was annoyed by his determination to find me. On the other hand, when he found me, he seemed to want me to know that he had considered some of the particularities of

Japanese Canadian experience. He asked if there was a "Galapagos Island effect," whereby Japanese Canadians isolated from contemporary Japan developed differently. Unfortunately, this again suggested to me that he regarded Japanese Canadians as "Japanese" rather than "Canadian." He believed the dynamic forces of change that shaped Japanese Canadians must emanate from Japan rather than Canada. Yet it is important to note that in this exchange he asked what I, the worker, thought and considered my response, making a gesture to enter a dialogue. At another level, caught up in the power dynamics, I had clearly forgotten that the NIMC was designed to be "educational." Japanese Canadian history was not well known, and so it was wrong to expect all visitors to speak in an informed manner about Japanese Canadian history.

At the same time, this interchange is an example of how numerous tourists attempted to assert their authority over NIMC staff. Like other tourists, this man asserted his authority by asking about personal details of a site worker's life, in particular, about my family's history of internment, in essence making me part of the exhibit. Like any experience of victimization, the internment is a sensitive topic. Yet some visitors felt no compunction about asking workers to reveal personal information, even if they were not comfortable talking about themselves. They invoked the power to look, ignoring social rules of conduct that specify it is inappropriate to ask relative strangers about what could be painful personal experiences.

The fact that the tourist became defensive when I attempted to reverse the gaze by asking him similar questions is further evidence that he was invoking the power to look. As Kirshenblatt-Gimblatt argues (1991), the power to look involves examining details of someone's life that one would never reveal about oneself – "one's body, one's person, and life." Other tourists who asked personal questions were also uncomfortable when they were asked similar questions, such as why they were interested in Japanese Canadian history, whether they knew anyone in the Japanese Canadian community, their views on social justice, their ethnic background, or whether they had lived through the Second World War.

Some tourists tried to be empathetic but also deployed the power to look. Wanting to understand how Japanese Canadians felt, they asked the workers about the intimate details of their lives. When workers became uncomfortable, they sometimes politely changed the subject or answered with impersonal examples. Some tourists would stop asking questions. Other persisted, treating the workers' social manoeuvres like annoying roadblocks. Their initial concern over the plight of Japanese Canadians sometimes made it difficult to recognize the nature of their interest until they gained entry into the intimate zone of a worker's feelings. Tourists would then begin to frame their questions in ways that, for example, constructed Japanese Canadians as resentful victims. For example, some wanted to know if the Japanese Canadians were "still bitter" or "angry." To be *still* bitter or angry suggests someone who is trapped in a hostile or resentful emotional state. It also suggests someone who is fixated on events that happened in the past and are no longer relevant. Using negative terms to describe the strong feelings that Japanese Canadians might have about their treatment during the war negates the validity of their feelings about, for example, racist government policies, their sadness about the humiliation the issei underwent, and their frustration about the fact that many Japanese Canadians have no interest in human rights issues. There is no satisfactory answer to this question. "No, Japanese Canadians are not bitter" suggests they have moved on and that the violation of their rights is no longer an issue. "Yes, Japanese Canadians are still bitter" suggests they are full of feelings of resentment.

Returning to the passage above, the tourist's queries into the personal details of my life challenged my "authenticity" as a Japanese Canadian. He presumed that he knew the criteria for such authenticity, and that authenticity was relevant. When the Kyowakai Society hires workers, it decides the relevant criteria for working at the NIMC. As I mentioned earlier, all workers are associated with the Japanese Canadian community, and it is New Denver's youth in particular who have an investment in the history of the camp. Is the expectation that all workers should be bona fide "Japanese" Canadians based on the desire to see authentic Japanese Canadians as part of the NIMC experience? Other tourists also asked about the authenticity of the workers. They asked whether the workers' parents were Japanese Canadian and whether they spoke Japanese. If the answers were affirmative, the next question usually was whether the workers were from New Denver: in other words, if they were authentic descendents of the New Denver internees. If the workers did not fit the tourists' criteria, the tourists suggested or sometimes directly stated that the workers did not have the right to work at the NIMC.

Other tourists were concerned about the politics of representation. They felt that only Japanese Canadians should represent what happened to this group of citizens during the 1940s. Sometimes this expectation led to unpleasant exchanges. In the first year of the NIMC's operation, several members of staff were local happa sansei. Unable to recognize them as Japanese Canadians, some non-Japanese Canadian tourists abruptly questioned their right to work at the NIMC (Takana, Personal correspondence, 12 August 1995). They felt that "white people" had no right to tell the story of Japanese Canadians. Although well-intentioned, these tourists had problematic assumptions about what defined individuals as Japanese Canadian. Inadvertently, they seemed to be imposing dominant definitions of ethnic identity based on physiological traits.[9] For Japanese Canadians in New Denver, whom to include as members of their community and under what circumstances is a complex matter. Over the years, Japanese Canadians have built friendships and families as well as social and political networks with other residents, including the family of the (non-Japanese Canadian) NIMC administrative assistant in 1996.

But the visitors' sentiments were complicated, as one of the staff noted. She noted that visitors always deferred to a new worker who had a physical disability. While he was "learning the ropes" and visitors asked him questions he couldn't answer, she would pipe in to help out her co-worker and friend. Some visitors would either glare at her or ignore her, as if she were being patronizing. Of course, the visitors did not know that the two co-workers had grown up as the best of pals who enjoyed a friendship full of laughter and playful teasing. Perhaps visiting the NIMC made some especially attuned to human rights issues and quick to make judgments; or perhaps, as another New Denver resident suggested, the visitors came to the NIMC already feeling guilty about something and wanting to prove that they were conscientious.

Ignoring Social Conventions: Gaining Access to the Backstage

The tourists were not only interested in the authenticity of the workers, they also sought access to the "backstage" areas of the community, where authentic events supposedly occurred. Dean MacCannell argues that "[sightseers] are motivated to see life as it is really lived, even to get in with the natives" (1989, 94). They seek to go beyond what Goffman refers to as the "front stage" regions where people enact social performances for outsiders. Performances are self-conscious and calculated, and actors do not reveal what they really think or their actual cultural beliefs or practices. The backstage is where one supposedly sees the actual cultural practices and beliefs: it is where the "props" and motivations for the front-stage performances are revealed (ibid., 92-93). False backstages are produced for tourists, both as a protection against intrusion and for profit. Yet, if they are willing to "take risks," tourists can move progressively from front stage to authentic backstage areas (ibid., 101).

In the passage that follows, I describe three sets of visitors who attempted to gain access to the backstage of the NIMC while it was closed during Obon. Obon is a Buddhist ritual that takes place in August to guide the spirits of ancestors back to their homes. Although some of the local Japanese Canadians are Christians and others are Buddhists, everyone participates in Obon. For the community, this ritual is a gathering to remember the many members of their community who are no longer living among them. In New Denver, Obon is always held in the Kyowakai Hall, where the Buddhist shrine is located. The hall is now situated in the NIMC's compound.

The Kyowakai Society closes the NIMC during Obon. NIMC workers post signs on the NIMC's gates indicating that no visitors are permitted during the event. The region's Buddhist priest, who was at the time a young married man from Japan living in Kelowna, travels with his wife to New Denver to conduct the ritual every year. To prepare the Kyowakai Hall for the ceremony, younger members of the community remove the historical displays under the guidance of Nobby Hayashi, a nisei from New Denver. They sweep the floors and arrange chairs in rows facing the shrine. Mr. Senya Mori, a prominent elder in the community, is responsible for preparing the shrine in his capacity as the lay priest.

Field Notes #2: Two Buddhisms

The local sansei and the NIMC workers arrived at the NIMC early in the morning to prepare the Kyowakai Hall for the Obon ceremony. I was invited to help, but I was not going to attend the ceremony. A few days before the ceremony, one of the local sansei made it clear to me, with some offhand muttering about how it wouldn't be right to have some anthropologist scribbling notes during the ceremony, that it would not be appropriate for me to attend Obon. The sansei noted, though, that during the ceremony it would be helpful if I could watch the gates with the administrator's assistant to make sure tourists did not wander in.

While we waited for Nobby to instruct us about how to prepare the Kyowakai Hall, the first tourist arrived. One of the NIMC workers came running toward me. She told me that an angry male tourist had yelled at the administrator's assistant. The worker asked me to talk to the assistant to ensure that she was okay. The assistant was shaken, but as she recounted the incident she composed herself. The tourist had insisted on seeing the NIMC even though workers had posted signs stating that the Centre was closed that day for a community event. Apparently, the man was very sarcastic and very angry. He explained that he had decided not to leave New Denver at 7 a.m. as he had planned so that he (and, we supposed, his family, who were sitting in his truck) could visit the Centre. They were from Hope, a town on the edge of the coastal mountains in the Lower Mainland. The tourist concluded the exchange by slamming the door of his truck and yelling, "Well thank you very much!" Reviewing the incident, the assistant said that she wasn't happy with her response. She had sarcastically responded to the tourist, "Well, thank *you*." When she came back into the garden, she meekly told me that she began to cry. Later, I wondered if the man was crying too.

That is when Nobby called us to help him prepare the Kyowakai Hall. Under his guidance, we dismantled the historical displays and arranged neat rows of folding metal chairs. On each chair, we placed a flat square cushion made from scraps of material, similar to the cushions found in Japanese Canadian community centres with nisei and issei members. Nobby seemed nervous about us younger folks creating a mess in this carefully organized space. He tried to be patient. Mr. Senya Mori arrived with the other members of the Buddhist Church. They removed the screen walls protecting the shrine from view. The shrine was magnificent – transforming the hall with the splendour emanating from the golden light that illuminated it.

After we finished preparing the hall, two tourists, a man and a woman, slipped past the closed gates and began madly snapping photos of the site. I politely indicated that the Centre was closed. The man smiled dismissively and kept snapping photos. In one smooth line, as if to cover the time he needed to take his photos, he purred on about how his friend was interned in a shack "just like one of these shacks" and how he would want to see them. Finally, they left. Next, a nisei couple walked up to the Centennial Hall. I apologetically said, "Oh ... it's Obon today, and the place is closed. I am terribly sorry." They apologetically started leaving. But then one of the local sansei intervened. This sansei said, "But if you'd like to join us for the service, please do ..." I smiled, feeling like a stupid rule-bound cop. The nisei man said, "But we are not dressed for the service." He made a gesture to indicate his short sleeves, shorts, and runners. The sansei said, "That's okay!" The couple asked for the bathrooms so they could "tidy up." They reappeared transformed in neatly pressed trousers and proper shoes ... The sansei later explained to me that he saw them chatting with the Buddhist minister and the minister's spouse. He invited them to join the ceremony because he had ascertained they had some sort of connection to the Buddhist Church.

I returned to the Kyowakai Hall after the ceremony was completed and helped reassemble the historical displays. The sweet scent of incense lingered in the hot dry air. There were still a few small gatherings of people chatting, their voices wafting around the hall. Nobby instructed us about where to place each photograph and artifact. One of the local sansei suddenly signalled to me. A woman – clearly a tourist – was standing at the entrance to the hall staring in, her mouth hanging open. A young girl of about eleven or twelve stood beside her. I nodded to the sansei and gave the photo I was about to hang on the wall back to Nobby. "Here! You do it!" Everyone laughed, and off I went.

I approached the tourist, explaining that because of the community event the NIMC was closed to the public that day. She was maybe fifty-five. With her short hair and amber earrings, she exuded an earthy middle-class aesthetic, suggesting that she was educated and well travelled. The tourist ignored my firm but polite indication that the ceremony was a private event. She ignored me when I said: "So thank you very much for your interest. You will have to come back another day." It felt like she had an insistent hunger to stay and look. Her eyes hooked onto the brilliant splendour of the shrine. She clung to the site. Pleasant words poured from my mouth, but through the stiff formality of my body movements, it was clear that I was attempting to escort her out of the NIMC. She kept throwing out questions as if to stop her exit: "So how many people were interned?" "How many of you were there here?" I repeated, "So, thank you very much for your interest, and this is the way to the gate."

The young girl tagged along. The tourist seemed unperturbed by her exposure to what must have seemed like a rather unpleasant "native." She kept repeating, "Yes, I know, *we are leaving.*" I tried to loosen her determination to find a way to stay on the site by changing the subject. "So you are travelling through the valley?" She could see through my thinly veiled strategy. Her response was affirmative. "*Yes* – we are travelling through the valley." When we reached the gate, she suddenly asked her daughter for her camera. As she pulled it out, I felt a wave of horror. Her gesture emphasized how she was determined to "capture" the site. I cautioned, "Oh, as I said, it is a very spiritual day here. We need to respect it, so please –" She retorted, "Well I want to tell you I am a *Buddhist* so *I know this.* And the way the minister responded to me was much more spiritual and respectful than the way you are talking to me, which is hardly respectful." I took a deep breath and replied, "Well, I accept your commentary. And will consider it." Probably expecting me to become angry, she paused and then wheezed out a deflated "Oh." At the NIMC's exit, I repeated, "So, thank you very much. We appreciate your interest. I hope you enjoy the rest of your trip." They left.

I turned around and realized that one of the elders was sitting in the shade of the Visitors' Reception Centre. He was relaxing on a lawn chair, chatting with the other elders. My rush of determination to escort the woman off the site turned into a rush of embarrassment. Maybe I had been too insistent? Had I been coercive? How could I have assumed it was appropriate to apply such force on behalf of the elders when I did not yet know them very well? Maybe I embarrassed them.

I slowly walked up to the elder. Feeling like an oaf, I tried to explain. "I hope I was not rude. I am terribly sorry. I hope I did not embarrass you, but one of the sansei told me that it was a very special day today and that there were to be no tourists, no people to snap photos of this place for their photo albums. It is a spiritual day and the sansei said it must be respected, a day for the community. So, I am terribly sorry if I embarrassed you with my insistence." He listened to my apologetic muttering for a bit. Then looking a bit perplexed by my befuddled behaviour, he shrugged his shoulders and said, "Oh, that's okay!" Then he continued chatting with the other elders. I felt even more embarrassed. I was overdoing everything: I was too insistent when escorting the tourist off the site, and my apologies were excessively formal and self-deprecating.

Later, to my embarrassment, I discovered that the minister and an elder had let the woman enter the NIMC with them. There were also some elders who shook their heads and exclaimed, "Why can't they understand? Didn't they read the sign? The Centre was closed!" Others seemed nonchalant. Some seemed pleased that visitors saw the splendour of their Otera.[10]
(FIELD NOTES, 13 AUGUST 1996)

From my perspective as a designated "gatekeeper," when I first encountered the three sets of non-Japanese Canadian tourists, I simply assumed that they refused to respect the local community's private space. They violated social boundaries, ignoring the signage indicating that the NIMC was closed and then dismissed or challenged workers who asked them to leave the site. I will first discuss the two sets of tourists who wanted access to "the forbidden backstage" area designated for community members and personal guests. For these tourists, it appeared that the social conventions of the local Japanese Canadians were irrelevant.

It could be argued that the woman who identified herself as a Buddhist displayed characteristics similar to intrusive ethnographers. Like MacCannell's tourist, she sought the backstage area of the community where there was authentic culture. A power struggle ensued when she was told she could not view the event. She became even more determined to view it when she was told it was out of bounds. Perhaps the exotic "Oriental" features – especially the ornate shrine enveloped in the scent of incense – changed this zone from simply out of bounds to "forbidden," something with an erotic air. There is pleasure in moving into forbidden zones, prying back the protective shell and peering at the exposed mysteries of a living community.

But the tourist could have simply regarded the ceremony as a public event. It is true that in other places Obon is a public event that is celebrated with special foods and festive activities such as *odori*.[11] But, in New Denver, Obon is not a public event, as the signs and closed gates indicated. When she was initially asked to leave the site, she could have mentioned she was given permission to walk around by the Buddhist priest. Did she feel affronted being asked to explain herself? It seemed as if she assumed the right to be there and that she did not recognize that she was intruding. The tourists taking photographs for their friend who was interned in a shack "just like one of these shacks" also ignored the signage and the worker. Unlike the other tourists, they did not display anger or indignation. The woman and especially the man reacted with indifference when I intercepted them. Of all the tourists who tried to enter the NIMC during the Obon ceremony, the man with the camera displayed the most extreme form of the power to look. His indifference showed that he was unaffected by the worker, as if he considered the worker completely insignificant. He did exactly what he wanted to do. He entered the NIMC and took as many photographs as he pleased, completely unperturbed that he was trespassing and showing disrespect to the community.

All three sets of tourists differed from the nisei couple. When told that the NIMC was closed, this couple immediately responded by apologizing for being inside the NIMC – even though they knew the Buddhist minister and his spouse. They felt obliged to observe the local Japanese Canadian community's social conventions. In contrast, the non-Japanese Canadian tourists dismissed or resisted the workers who informed them that the NIMC was closed. The tourists reacted by displaying anger, indignation, or complete indifference. This seems strange insofar as they were the ones who were trying to force their way into the NIMC. In terms of power dynamics, perhaps it was disconcerting to be given directions by a young-looking woman who refused to defer to them. Yet such situations are always difficult to fully understand. The woman with the child might have felt an even greater need to retain her authority or dignity in front of her child, to provide her with a sense of security when faced with an obnoxious member of the staff.

Was the tourists' anger and indignation triggered by my tone of voice and mannerisms? I must admit that my tone was more apologetic with the Japanese Canadian couple than with the other tourists. My manner likely suggested that the non-Japanese Canadian tourists had intentionally violated community boundaries. Perhaps I did not leave room for them to gracefully withdraw from their faux pas. But not every visitor who was turned away that day or on subsequent days responded with anger and indignation. Moreover, if they found me abrasive, was this sufficient reason to continue to trespass? It is too simplistic to view all visitors who become angry when refused entry in this light.

I now turn to the tourist from the town of Hope. It is easy to dismiss the tourist from Hope, especially from the hermetically sealed vantage point of a group in which everyone shares a similar perspective. In my case, this group included NIMC staff who, as the administrator's report claims, were burned out from dealing with "the emotionally, intellectually, and politically offensive nature of the internment and its post-traumatic effects." One could conclude that the tourist's display of anger was an inappropriate reaction to being told that the NIMC was closed. Yet just because he reacted with anger does not mean he should be dismissed.

Although the elders often offered insights that challenged my presuppositions, in this case it was Meg Seaker, one of my aikido teachers, who did so. When I arrived in New Denver, I began to train at an aikido dojo at Mirror Lake, a small settlement over the Selkirk mountain range in the next valley. This space offered a reprieve from the emotional intensity of fieldwork as well as a place to reflect on incidents such as the one involving the tourist from Hope. In the dojo, I was also a stranger and had a chance to reflect on the generous welcome of Meg, her partner, Jean-René, and the students who regularly trained at Mirror Lake. I recounted the incident to Meg using hostile war-like terms, describing how tourists could be like intruders, invading community spaces. She did not try to correct me, moralize, or dissect my argument. Nor did she readily agree with my views. Instead, she wondered whether the man from Hope was upset because he was disappointed. She recounted her travels through France. She had decided to make a pilgrimage to a tiny museum dedicated to a French artist and writer. When she arrived, it was closed. There was no schedule indicating its hours of operation. After several days waiting for it to open, she left, disappointed. She reflected that perhaps visiting the NIMC had personal significance for this man, just as the visit to the tiny museum in France had personal significance for her.

Without defending or condoning the tourist's anger, Meg made me reflect on his reaction. The tourist originally planned to leave New Denver at 7 a.m., but he changed his plans so he could visit the NIMC. He underlined how he had *changed* his plans, emphasizing how he had deliberated over his decision to delay his departure by four hours. What did the four-hour delay mean? Perhaps he had work obligations; maybe he had to arrange child care commitments, or perhaps returning to Hope late would have meant he would get little rest before starting work the next morning. Because it is at least an eight-hour drive through mountainous terrain to reach Hope, it would not be easy to return on another weekend. Why would someone from Hope, BC – a small town at the foot of the coastal mountains, a town with a reputation as a rough loggers' town – be so intent to visit the NIMC? Why was he so upset? If I had paused to reflect, I would have remembered that the Tashme internment camp for

Japanese Canadians was located just east of Hope. Did he or his family have personal connections to members of the Japanese Canadian community? Or was there another reason he felt determined to stay in New Denver to visit the NIMC? I could not know the answer to these questions now that the man was gone. I felt remorseful for all the occasions when I had jumped to conclusions. The incident began to make me question my assumptions. It marked a pivotal point during my stay in New Denver; I began to consider the complexity of visitors' reactions to the Centre.

Personal Connections, Personal Responsibility

I now turn to non-Japanese Canadian visitors who I could not categorize as tourists or museum-goers who deployed the power to look. I present examples of visitors with personal connections to either Japanese Canadians or the events surrounding their removal from British Columbia during the 1940s. Some had Japanese Canadian friends, and others felt implicated in the uprooting and internment of Japanese Canadians. It was not always possible or appropriate to ask visitors about their relation to Japanese Canadians. I start with an incident described in my field notes that seriously shook my presuppositions and demonstrated the complex and fragile connections that some non-Japanese Canadian visitors have to the NIMC.

Meaningful Gestures

Reflecting back to the summer of 1996, I now realize that when I arrived in New Denver I viewed the NIMC primarily as a community venue. Over the previous year I had heard criticisms about the way the contractors had designed the NIMC as a tourist attraction rather than as a community memorial. I aligned myself with the sansei on the History Preservation Committee, especially Takana, my mentor, agreeing that as a community-run project the NIMC should prioritize preserving local history and cultural knowledge rather than being part of a sightseeing tour. Thus, I was overly critical of visitors who approached the NIMC as tourists, despite the fact, as I have argued, that most of the local discourses and even the design of the Centre presented the NIMC as a tourist site rather than as a memorial or community venue. Even worse, I took a defensive stance and made the assumption that most visitors approached the NIMC simply as a tourist attraction.

The reasons that brought visitors to the NIMC were not always immediately apparent. Working at the NIMC on an almost daily basis, I learned that many non-Japanese Canadian visitors had personal connections to either Japanese Canadians or the events surrounding their removal from British Columbia during the 1940s. I was struck by the vulnerability of some visitors. They were cautious about exposing their feelings and hesitant about unburdening their personal histories. Their vulnerability reminded me that the past does not belong to one group. But it took an encounter with an older man that I still find shameful to recount that made me rethink my assumptions. The incident I describe in the following passage took place while I was in the Centennial Hall working on one of the History Preservation Projects with another sansei. We were discussing the merits of developing a cataloguing system based on the elders' organization of their social worlds, using place names, family lines, events, and institutions rather than implementing the order used by established institutions such as museums, libraries, and archives.

Field Notes #3: Fragility

An older white woman walked by the doorway of the Centennial Hall, her gauzy presence illuminated in the bright light of the July sun. As she passed by, she smiled in a knowing, almost familiar way into the darkness of the hall. Following her gauzy presence, like a shadow, if that were possible on this hot July day, was a very white, very elderly man. Delicate, pale, and quite frail, he hesitated at the doorway. He peered into the building. We stopped. He smiled and stepped, shoes on, over the threshold into the dark space of the hall. Probably not seeing us completely because of the transition from the bright sunny day to the darkness of the hall, he began to inquire about whether we were interested in Japanese dolls. He pointed to a small doll in a glass case sitting by the entranceway. He explained that he had a Japanese doll that he would like to give to the NIMC.

Our bodies tensed. We were tired, in part by the sensitive, engrossing project we were working on and in part by visitors who ignored the "do not enter" and "private entrance" signs, intruding with a demanding ruckus of enthusiastic questions in the midst of our work. This was the only building on site that was off limits to the public. It was where the Kyowakai Society conducted meetings and held social events. It was not on display. And so it was easy to become irritated when visitors ignored the signs and pulled at the locked doors, interrupted meetings, wandered in, and asked questions.

One of the workers leapt up. "No, we are not interested in Japanese dolls." Unsaid but said in this short statement was: "We are not interested in Japanese things and all the paraphernalia of the exotic Orient. We are concerned with the history of internment in New Denver." The worker continued in a war-moat voice, from a solid, fortified position loaded with years of training, and curtly stated that we were busy at present. With that, the man was dismissed. He raised his hand in apology, backing out of the door, "Sorry, please excuse me ..." His voice trailed off as he exited.

My heart cracked as I saw him withdraw. We looked at each other, wide-eyed, not sure what we had done. This elderly man, so frail that a breeze could crack his bones. Such a small spontaneous gesture, so obviously taken by what he saw that day at the Centre, stepping blindly across a threshold a little awkwardly into the dark hall, but with good will, good intentions ... Oh, what did we know about what his gesture meant, meant to him, meant at a bigger level. (FIELD NOTES, 18 AUGUST 1996)

This man immediately realized we regarded his gesture as inappropriate. This, combined with his fragile appearance, had a strong effect. It was as if we gave a huge shove to what we thought was an intruder moving into our space. But instead of resistance, we encountered an open space – space left by his departure – a space that we fell into with the energy of our own shove. Although we did not discuss this incident until much later, at the moment it was obvious that our assumptions were wrong. Caught up in our own stereotypes, we assumed that he was just another tourist who had confused Japanese Canadians with the Japanese, failing to recognize the political and social significance of the NIMC. When he withdrew rather than trying to persuade us to accept his offer, we realized our assumptions were dreadfully wrong. He had approached us with sensitivity and courtesy. We realized how easy it was to negate visitors and misread their gestures.

The man's gesture was filled with historical resonances, especially his offer to donate a Japanese doll to the Centre. The doll may have had no connection to the Japanese Canadian community. But, given the man's age and interest in the NIMC, there was a chance there was a connection. The man had probably been in his thirties when the government removed Japanese Canadians from British Columbia's coast. If he had been living in British Columbia during the 1940s, and depending on his class and occupation, he could have known Japanese Canadian workers, students, clients, domestic servants, shopkeepers – or even friends. He could have witnessed or been implicated in removing them from the coast in 1942. If he had Japanese Canadian friends he might have had contact with them while they were in the camps or on sugar beet farms. Alternatively, he might have been involved in projects to relocate Japanese Canadians in Ontario through the government or church organizations.

How did the doll connect him to the past? There are many stories circulating in the community about Japanese doll collections. When women came to Canada to join their husbands, some had the means to bring their belongings with them across the Pacific Ocean, including their doll collections. When the government implemented its plan to remove Japanese Canadians from the one hundred-mile strip along the coast, they were ordered to hand over their properties and possessions to the Custodian of Enemy Alien Property, which was to hold everything in trust. Everything was disposed of, including the dolls. Belongings left in storage were ransacked, and items left with friends or neighbours were in most cases sold or never retrieved.

Years later, some Canadians who had "inherited" the dolls or purchased them at government sales became determined to return them to their rightful owners. But it was not clear who the rightful owners were. Nor did they know how to find the original owners. Moreover, many of the issei who owned the dolls have died. When Japanese Canadians set up their own archives in the 1990s, some of these people began to come forward to return the belongings of Japanese Canadians in their possession. Was this elderly man trying to return one of the dolls that once belonged to an issei woman? How had he acquired the doll? Did he buy it? Maybe it was given to him or his family? Left in his care? His sensitivity as well as the familiar warmth exuded by his female companion suggested that they had a meaningful personal connection with the community. Who were they? What stories could they have told us? Rigidly positioned in an inflexible discourse of community self-determination, we were unable to extend ourselves to this man, to receive his gesture.

Recognizing the Social Significance of the NIMC

After this encounter, I started to reflect more on the significance of the NIMC for visitors. I will present examples of an array of visitors who regarded the NIMC as a memorial for Japanese Canadians, with links to other victimized groups, and in some cases their own communities. Many of these visitors had personal connections to Japanese Canadians, whether a spouse, family friend, co-worker, or college friend. Others had a pre-war or wartime association with the community through schoolmates, neighbours, or employees. Some felt compelled to visit the NIMC because of these connections. For others, discovering these connections at the memorial made their visit more meaningful.

I begin and end this section with visitors who felt indirectly implicated in the government's removal of Japanese Canadians. They demonstrate that, as Robert Jay Lifton argues, the psychological effects of violent events are not confined to the victimizer and the victims.[12] Guilt radiates through a population. Guilt, here, is understood as anger turned inward "precisely because [the person] cannot but help accept and internalize the world in which [she or] he has been victimized [or seen victimization], including in some degree the motivation and behaviour of the victimizer" (Lifton 1967, 497). A number of visitors to the

NIMC felt tainted by their association with the removal of Japanese Canadians from British Columbia, even if they were not directly involved in the government's plan. Visiting the Centre became part of their process of working through these feelings. The president of the Kyowakai Society recounted stories about some of these visitors to me.

Field Notes #4: To Be Just ...

The president told me about a hakujin man who was about sixty years old who came up to him and said he felt really bad. The man explained that his parents had taken advantage of the Japanese Canadians' situation and bought things really, really cheaply, so he and his siblings had things in their possession to this day that they did not properly come by. The president guessed that seeing the context and the history at the NIMC made this man reflect. He said that most people make some sort of connection – makes them think – though, he added, there are of course some tourists. (FIELD NOTES, 18 JULY 1996)

Perhaps the NIMC provided a place where the man could dedicate a moment to reflect about the things that he and his siblings had in their possession that "they did not properly come by." It seemed as if these possessions had always made him uncomfortable. The NIMC thus seemed to offer a public place for such people to address what they experienced as guilt. These visitors were not trying to be empathetic, like the tourists described earlier. Rather, they saw themselves as somehow implicated in the uprooting and internment of Japanese Canadians – in some cases, simply because as children they had witnessed what happened. Whether they quietly visited the site, told one of the workers about their past, or offered to make a donation, it was a way to publicly acknowledge their regret about past events and to make a gesture toward making amends. They approached the NIMC as a memorial.

Other visitors recognized the significance of the NIMC for the Japanese Canadian community. They expressed their support for the effort to heal from their traumatic wartime experiences.

Field Notes #5: Recognizing the Healing Process

A woman was standing outside talking to one of the elders who takes care of the NIMC garden. She asked, "Are the Japanese who went through this angry?" He said, "Some." She replied, "Oh, so this is part of the healing process ... Was there any apology?" He stated, "Redress." She responded,

saying, "The site was meaningful, and thank you very much." (FIELD NOTES,
6 SEPTEMBER 1996)

Comments written by visitors in the NIMC guest book also showed a recognition of the significance of the site for other members of the public. These
comments typically described the treatment of Japanese Canadians as "sad"
and "disgraceful." There were statements about how "this episode in history
should not be repeated." But because of the conventions of writing, and especially those for writing short entries in guest books, their comments were often
in the form of platitudes and disclosed little about their personal views and
feelings (Langer 1991, 17-20). In contrast, in person, they tended to respond
more spontaneously, revealing their own complex relations to the past. A
number of the visitors spoke directly about their concern for social justice. In
the comment presented below, the visitor makes a connection between the
treatment of Aboriginal peoples and the experience of Japanese Canadians.
She shared what she learned from the NIMC with the workers and told them
that the NIMC had been effective in conveying the political and social impact
of the internment.

Field Notes #6: Making Connections to Other Persecuted Groups

"I knew about how badly [the] British Columbia [government] treated the
Aboriginal peoples – but didn't realize how badly they treated the Japanese."
(FIELD NOTES, 6 SEPTEMBER 1996)

Given the extreme forms of racism against Aboriginal peoples expressed by
many members of British Columbia's populace, her open criticism at this time
is notable. Her use of the term "Aboriginal peoples" rather than "Indian" suggests
that she was well versed in social justice issues.

Not all visitors were as attuned to these issues and to non-racist terminology.
But they were open to rethinking how they conceptualized Japanese Canadians
as a "racial minority."

Field Notes #7: Changing Perspectives

Today, a man asked if Japanese Canadians caught tuberculosis in New
Denver, or if they had it when they arrived. His question recalled the
reasoning that the Canadian government used to justify interning Japanese
Canadians after 1945: to introduce them to hygienic practices and cure them
of the diseases they caught while living in their substandard housing.[13] One

of the elders who works at the NIMC on a regular basis simply answered: "When they came up." Nervous that this answer would reinforce the stereotype that pre-war Japanese Canadians were a diseased and uneducated people by nature, I added, "Well, TB was widespread among all working-class communities, not just Japanese Canadians!" The man reflected, "Oh, I hadn't thought of it like that." (FIELD NOTES, 9 SEPTEMBER 1996)

Unlike some tourists, this visitor did not respond defensively when his assumptions were questioned. He accepted the new perspective offered by the worker without excusing his misconceptions or trying to show he was not as uninformed as his question suggested. This interaction shows both the educational dimension of the NIMC and the openness of some visitors to understanding history in new ways.[14]

Many of the visitors walked through the garden and viewed the exhibits, saying little to workers or the other visitors. When visitors did not approach us it felt invasive to ask them about their interest in the NIMC. Other visitors commented on the exhibits, saying to one another, for example, "These shacks aren't so bad! My grandparents lived in shacks like this" or "How could two families live together in such a small room?" Some would try to recognize the locations depicted in the archival photographs, exclaiming, "I've been there ..." or "I didn't realize that there was an internment camp there!" Others quietly walked through the NIMC as if in deep thought. Many visitors lingered in the Visitors' Reception Centre and were riveted to the lists of the names of Japanese Canadians interned in New Denver that were posted by the entrance. Visitors searched the lists, looking for an old friend, someone they knew in school, or a colleague from work. Sometimes they would just quietly trace the names with a finger, slowly drawing a line connecting all the names.

Some visitors stopped to chat with the NIMC workers about the weather and the local scenery. This was a way for them to introduce themselves and shyly share their own experiences relating to the internment.

Field Notes #8: The Park Next Door

Today, I met an interesting older woman at the NIMC. A male friend accompanied her. After musing about how many people did not know about the history of Japanese Canadians, she mentioned that she had grown up in East Vancouver, out by the Pacific National Exhibition grounds: what previously had been Hastings Park. She confessed that her parents had lived near Hastings Park when hundreds of Japanese Canadians had been detained there before they were transported to internment camps. Neither her parents nor their neighbours – no one – said anything about "it." She tried to recall when she had heard about the internment. "It was the time when people began to talk about it, in the fifties or sixties?" I offered, "The sixties and seventies ... more the seventies." "Yes." She confirmed that it was only then that she had heard about it [that thousands of women, men, and children were brought to Hastings Park and held in livestock stalls before they were shipped out to internment camps]. Her soft-spoken friend reflected, "Yes, so much happens ..." His great-grandfather had been incarcerated as an Italian national in Petawawa for two years, although he added that this experience wasn't anything near the magnitude of what had happened to Japanese Canadians. I asked where his grandfather was located: "Hamilton." I then continued, "Oh, there must be lots of stories ..." He nodded. I asked if his grandfather was still alive. "No ..." But he had interviewed an older man who was interned there. (FIELD NOTES, 13 AUGUST 1996)

It seemed that this woman felt implicated in the removal of Japanese Canadians from British Columbia because she had lived near Hastings Park when she was a child. She was shocked by the silence of her own parents and neighbours. She was amazed that she did not learn about what happened to Japanese Canadians until the 1970s. This meant that for over twenty years her parents and their neighbours had never directly discussed the events that took place in their own neighbourhood across from Hastings Park, where over thirteen thousand up-rooted Japanese Canadians were "processed" before being transported to internment camps, sugar beet farms, and road camps. Up to four thousand Japanese Canadians at a time were held in Hastings Park for as long as four months or more while the government finished building internment camps and finalizing its plans about what to do with them (Sunahara 1981, 56). Her use of general terms such as "it" to refer to the confinement of Japanese Canadians in Hastings Park suggested that she was still working through how to articulate what had been structured into the lives of her family and neighbours as a shameful secret.

Her friend's recollections about his grandfather were also significant. He offered his grandfather's internment as a parallel experience. He was not trying to argue that the internment of Italian nationals was as traumatic as the internment of Japanese Canadians. He was careful not to compare and to make claims about whose experience was worse but rather mentioned this history to show his support. In this, he actively demonstrated his recognition of the NIMC as a site that memorializes the experiences of Japanese Canadians and that has meaning for other groups in Canada.

Like this man and woman, many other visitors approached the NIMC as if it were a repository for uneasy memories and unresolved feelings surrounding the disappearance of childhood friends, schoolmates, and neighbours or feelings of being implicated in or tainted by the government's removal of Japanese Canadians from their neighbourhoods. It was also a place where they could acknowledge the isolation and pain that reverberated through the life of a Japanese Canadian spouse, friend, or colleague. Having a public place, a memorial, to acknowledge the impact of political violence is important. In a context where many histories of persecution have been erased from the terrain of memory, the NIMC marks one such history and offers a place where people can come with unresolved feelings, fading memories, and stories they want to share. They come with feelings, experiences, and memories that are out of place in their everyday lives. At the memorial, these feelings, memories, and experiences have meaning. Others who have travelled long distances to visit the NIMC recognize their significance. The memorial thus creates a collective space for people affected by the history of internment.

Searching for a Collective Past

A Significant Site

How do Japanese Canadian visitors relate to the NIMC? As a community-based museum, the NIMC works against the grain of official historical discourses. Like other community-based museums, it has a mandate to reinterpret the historical experiences of Japanese Canadians from a critical perspective. It is a site where members of the community can claim "a heritage" and affirm their identities (Simpson 1996).

A significant proportion of the visitors to the NIMC are drawn from the approximately seventy thousand Japanese Canadians in Canada today. During the summer of 1996, for example, several Japanese Canadian groups visited the Centre each week, at least two groups visiting each day, especially through July and August. Some travelled specifically to visit the NIMC from other towns in British Columbia or the nearby province of Alberta. Others visited the NIMC on their way to see relatives living in the region. Still others journeyed to the NIMC from locations scattered across Canada and, in some cases, the United States and Japan. A few were postwar Japanese immigrants, though most were Japanese Canadians who had been interned or whose families had been interned.

As discussed in previous chapters, Japanese Canadians had travelled to New Denver searching for their roots even before the Centre was built. The search for connections to pre-war and wartime experiences is part of a larger discursive field of activity that has contributed to the formation of a post–Second World War Japanese Canadian identity. As has been the case with other historically persecuted groups who have sought redress, the nature of Japanese Canadians' search for connections to the past has changed over time: from the grassroots activism of the 1970s to the redress movement of the 1980s to the exploration of personal experiences in the 1990s.

For Japanese Canadians, it is significant that the NIMC is located on the site of a former internment camp that the internees themselves subsequently transformed into a community. The NIMC marks a site of continuity of knowledge, social relations, cultural practices over the generations. In a context where Japanese Canadians are still trying to re-imagine themselves as a community, every representation of the community is invested with powerful significance. The Kyowakai Society was sensitive about how other Japanese Canadians would respond to their interpretation of the internment. They decided to represent only their camp, the New Denver camp, and were careful not to presume to represent the experiences of all Japanese Canadians who were interned. Representing just one camp would be challenging enough.

It is easy to romanticize New Denver. This is especially the case for younger Japanese Canadians who were not interned or forced to leave British Columbia after the war. For those searching for their roots, the Japanese Canadians community in New Denver might represent what a settlement of issei, nisei, and sansei would have been like had they not been forced to disperse. But this view fails to recognize the years of impoverished conditions faced by those the government left in New Denver "to die." Many Japanese Canadians left as soon as they had saved enough to move. As a researcher, I could also romanticize the Japanese Canadian visitors, seeing them as a movement of individuals on a pilgrimage in search of their collective identity and heritage. But, as this section shows, although many Japanese Canadians sought a connection to their past, that connection was sometimes troubled and always complex.

Advice from an Expert
Some Japanese Canadian visitors attempted to assert their authority when they interacted with NIMC staff, lecturing or instructing them about historical facts or the memorial. In one case, a middle-aged shin-ijuusha man and hakujin woman arrived at the NIMC just after closing time. We apologized, informing them that the Centre was closed for the day. The woman assured us that they were not upset, noting that the workers must be tired after a long day of work. After the man introduced himself, he began to instruct us – two female staff

members – about what the Kyowakai Society should do to preserve the internment shacks. He told us that the society should get the village to change the bylaws so that residents living in the remaining internment shacks would not be able to renovate them. This would preserve the local history. When we tried to explain the Kyowakai Society's approach to preserving history, he brushed our points aside. He did not register our growing discomfort. For him, it was not adequate that the Kyowakai Society had already preserved three internment shacks at the NIMC. He did not recognize that the bylaws he proposed would force mostly elderly Japanese Canadians who had lived in impoverished and humiliating circumstances during the war to live in leaky, small shacks. Was he suggesting that the Kyowakai Society should preserve poverty? As well, by forcing residents to keep the internment shacks in their original state, the society would have turned the entire neighbourhood into a living museum. Perhaps the residents would not want to become museum objects.

This man assumed that the Kyowakai Society needed and wanted advice. He also assumed that he was in a position to give it, without asking about the NIMC's mandate or guiding principles. His approach differed from others who offered critiques of the NIMC's exhibits or asked about the inclusion or exclusion of information and events. Rather than sharing his impressions and interpretations, the man felt the need to instruct us. He was not sensitive to the social signals indicating that we were increasingly unreceptive to his advice. He surveyed the site and appraised it according to his own system of knowledge (Todorov 1987), oblivious to the community that had lived there for over fifty years.

Object(ional) Research

It was researchers (and, from what I had heard, some of the Japanese journalists in particular) who most blatantly displayed the power to look. These researchers usually stayed in New Denver from two to four days, coming individually or in groups. Like many Japanese Canadian visitors, they were drawn to New Denver in search of information about the community's past. But, in numerous cases, they reduced local residents to objects of research. In contrast to the tourists, the researchers recognized social conventions and protocols as visitors. In fact, this knowledge as well as their community membership helped them acquire research data. These researchers used social protocols at times in a superficial and instrumental manner, though arguably unconsciously so.

Despite their busy schedules and the stream of guests and family members who visited them during the summer, the elders graciously welcomed the researchers into their homes for lunches and dinners. The sansei working at the NIMC also invited the researchers to their homes, looking forward to discussing community news. But the researchers did not approach these visits as an opportunity for mutual exchanges. They turned the visits into interviews, asking streams of questions about the topics they wanted to investigate. After the first series of exchanges, some of the NIMC sansei became uncomfortable, feeling as if the researchers regarded them simply as sources of data rather than as hosts and members of the same community.

The following passage recounts the visit of one group of researchers. It was a large group composed of Japanese Canadians, Japanese Americans, and hakujin. To me, a researcher, their behaviour acted like a mirror and made me reflect on my own research practices.

Field Notes #9: The Search for Information

We were initially enthusiastic about their visit and the chance to exchange ideas about community projects. But soon, not only did I but also a few other NIMC workers (though not all the Japanese Canadians in New Denver) began to try to avoid them. As the days passed and the researchers' scheduled departure approached, they became more frenzied in their search for information. They dropped their social veneer in discussions, which degenerated into what felt like interrogations. Everything we said seemed like it was "potential material" or a "potential lead." They seemed oblivious to the social cues made by their hosts that with increasing bluntness indicated, "Enough! I am tired." "Enough! That is not your business!"
(Field notes, 19 August 1996)

The researchers seemed to have little consideration for the hospitality that was offered and were not interested in discussing the challenges of running the Centre or other community issues that troubled us. Since we knew them socially, primarily as members of the community, we were taken aback by their behaviour. But since the researchers had only five or six days to conduct their research, they clearly felt pressed to gather as much material as possible. As a researcher, I knew how difficult it is to conduct research involving people you know socially. It requires careful negotiation. The passage above demonstrates that the researchers were insensitive to some not-very-subtle signals to stop the relentless questioning. It is the researcher's responsibility to ensure mutual agreement about whether, when, and in what manner research is conducted. As I learned during my own research, this agreement must be renegotiated constantly, and there can be situations in which, suddenly and with little forewarning, your presence as a researcher is not welcome. It is true that sometimes people are willing (or are not willing) to talk to a researcher openly simply because he or she is a member of their community. Membership can grant rapid access to the community. In the case described here, the NIMC staff at first willingly answered questions. But when the researchers persisted, turning every encounter into a one-way stream of questions that disregarded all social protocol, NIMC sansei actively avoided them. Here, the researchers related to the NIMC and the staff like the non-Japanese Canadian tourists.

Bus Tours

Many Japanese Canadian visitors travel to New Denver, like Cohen's tourist (1996), in search of a centre of meaning that does not exist in their everyday lives. Their journeys to the NIMC are in many ways like pilgrimages. In this section, I discuss visitors on pilgrimages searching for a connection to the past and in some cases an understanding of events that cataclysmically changed their families and communities. Insofar as they are charged an entrance fee to the NIMC, must pay for accommodations and travel, and very likely purchase souvenirs, their experience, to use Rojek and Urry's terms (1997), is produced and commodified. But, as Urry (1996) argues, their travel is articulated with other cultural and community practices. I begin with Japanese Canadians who travelled to the NIMC on bus tours of the internment camps.

Two Japanese Canadian bus tours visited the NIMC in the summer of 1996 with approximately forty participants each. Bus tours are typically arranged by community organizations such as Tonari Gumi, a seniors' social service organization in Vancouver, or in conjunction with reunions for former internees from particular camps. The National Association of Japanese Canadians organized one of the first bus tours in 1987 to motivate the redress negotiating team during negotiations with the Canadian government (Kobayashi and Miki 1989, 7-8). The participants on most of the subsequent tours had been interned in the camps, linking the tours to reunions. The tours were especially popular in the early 1990s, just after the redress settlement in 1988 (McAllister 1993).

An essential component of the experience on bus tours is its collective nature. As reunions, the tours can be an opportunity to meet others who have memories about the pre-war or wartime community; in other cases, they provide a excursion for members of a social organization. Although the participants do not necessarily know one another, they have a common point of reference: they or someone in their family underwent internment, forced labour, dispersal, loss of property, and being stripped of their rights in the 1940s. Participants socialize with one another, chatting about their recollections and mutual acquaintances, where they were interned, and where they lived before 1942 (McAllister 1993).

In addition, and just as important, they discuss what happened after 1945 when they were dispersed across Canada or shipped to Japan.[15] Because tour participants are usually Japanese Canadian, there is some assurance that each member of the group will be sensitive to what the others are experiencing. As pre-war nisei, they will know the conventions for interacting during what could be an emotional experience. At the same time, the formality of old and new acquaintanceships offers a degree of social distance that ensures that others will not pry into sensitive areas. Insofar as bus tours call for a light and congenial mode of interacting, they provide a safe distance from confusing or strong emotions that might be difficult to control in the company of, for example, family members (ibid.). Yet the camaraderie of the tour also means that participants will not be alone in their memories or in their inability to remember. The reunions are somewhat self-selecting in that participants are Japanese Canadians who *want* to remember the past and who have the financial means, time, and interest to join a tour. Nevertheless, among participants there is a range in status, class, age, education, and past or present occupation (ibid.).

Adhering to social conventions on the bus tours reinforces the collective nature of the experience (McAllister 1993). When the participants arrive in New Denver, the Kyowakai Society greets them. The nisei and issei members of the Kyowakai Society have a prominent place on these occasions. They greet the participants of the bus tour as visitors to their community. The president of the society or another representative guides them through the site. After the tour, lunch or tea is usually served, providing an opportunity for individual interaction with members of the Kyowakai Society (ibid.; McAllister 1994).

Because most participants are nisei, they show respect for the elders, who would have been adults when they were children or adolescents in the camps. Thus, the nisei recognize their status and use formalities in conversation with the elders (McAllister 2003). The nisei also look to the elders for assurance, as if they are uncertain about what they will undergo during their return visit. In a sense, the participants are returning as the children and youth they were during the war, positioning the elders as the adults who were responsible for their well-being.[16] On these occasions, the elders are also very formal, invoking a ceremonial air that the nisei, positioned as guests of the Kyowakai Society, would recognize. The visit ends when the group thanks the elders, showing their appreciation by giving a formal speech and presenting a donation (ibid.).

Like the tourist-pilgrims described by Cohen (1996) and MacCannell (1989), the participants are seeking meaning that can not be found in their everyday lives. At a romantic level, it could be argued that New Denver symbolizes the cohesive community that the participants lost: a world that the government destroyed during the war. The purpose of the pilgrimage is to seek a connection with that lost world. But, in contrast to Cohen's and MacCannell's tourist-pilgrims, who must leave their societies to find meaning, by participating in the reunions, the nisei rebuild relations with other Japanese Canadians and create new memories about the tour itself that can be incorporated into their lives when they return home. Thus, rather than seeking a spiritual connection that will affirm, rejuvenate, or reveal higher truths, the tours expand the social networks and activities of the participants.

As reunions for former internees, the tours are also an opportunity to witness the changes their lives have undergone. They do not seek to nostalgically re-create the lost world with *ofuros* (Japanese-style baths) and nihonmachis. Returning to the sites of pre-war communities and overgrown internment sites makes it evident that little is left of the pre-war and wartime worlds. But there is also a sense of reassurance in that they can see that individuals and community organizations, whether the Kyowakai Society or the National Association of Japanese Canadians, have taken it upon themselves to recognize the devastating wartime losses while creating new possibilities and new futures (Herman 1992).

Building Intergenerational Bridges

In the summer of 1996, most Japanese Canadians who visited the NIMC came as families or couples. Visiting as a family can build intergenerational links between wartime and postwar generations. Older generations often used the NIMC as a means to share their experiences during the war with postwar family members. Given the demographic shift in the community, these excursions also had a bicultural dimension.

Many bicultural families and couples visited the NIMC during my stay: Japanese Canadian grandparents with small happa grandchildren, bicultural couples, and families with happa children. Visiting the NIMC as a bicultural family or couple shows a change in the community's notion of the Japanese Canadian family as "genetically Japanese" (McAllister 1991; McAllister and Medenwaldt 1992). Introducing a non-Japanese Canadian spouse to Japanese Canadian history is part of the process of introducing her or him into the community. This is not a straightforward process. One can encounter community members who might criticize or reject one's non-Japanese Canadian partner. The non-Japanese Canadian partner might be unfamiliar with social proprieties and sensitive community issues. As a result, he or she might appear as uncouth, offensive, or unreceptive. In the following passage, I describe a sansei woman introducing her bicultural family to her mother's history during their visit to the NIMC.

Field Notes #10: Extending the Family

Another happa family visited the Centre today. The hakujin grandmother and grandfather walked in first and asked, "Where are pictures of [the camp]?" Their Japanese Canadian daughter-in-law followed with her husband and young boy. The daughter-in-law talked to one of the non-Japanese Canadian members of the staff. Her mother's family name was Nakashima, and her father's was s. I exclaimed, "Oh – my mum was also Nakashima!" I knew that, of course, we were not related, but still ... she looked at me in a blank sort of way. She seemed impatient and perhaps a bit disconcerted by what I realized was my intrusive attempt to identify with her. She seemed to want to get on with the business of showing her new family around – on her own terms. The grandfather turned to another worker and me, "So, Rosebery would have shacks like they have here ..." We chimed, "Oh no, they've been ploughed down!" We made a rough map to show them the location of the old camp. The grandparents seemed so warm. They wanted to find out about the internment camps, it seemed, not to authoritatively gain knowledge about their daughter-in-law, but rather it was as if the grandparents welcomed the opportunity to be introduced to what was important to her – her family's history. This was now important to their son, their grandson, and themselves. (FIELD NOTES, 13 AUGUST 1996)

It is significant that the sansei introduced herself to the non-Japanese Canadian worker rather than sansei staff or myself. In community venues, members often introduce themselves with their parent's family names as well as the camp or prairie town where they were interned. The sansei's cautious response to my attempt to identify with her suggested that she was not familiar with the community space of the NIMC.

Introducing oneself to other Japanese Canadians is not straightforward, especially if their families have refused to discuss the past, investing the topic with tension and ambivalence. Presenting oneself by identifying family names and wartime locations can inadvertently suggest an alignment with old political factions, embarrassing tragedies, an elite or low status, and so on. But the sansei woman freely identified her parents' family names. She also did not seem uncomfortable about talking about her family's history, having clearly discussed it with her in-laws.

But she was uncomfortable talking to the sansei and happa workers. For some members of postwar generations, entering a community venue is awkward because they are unaccustomed to socializing with Japanese Canadian peers.

Also, some have dealt with the emotionally charged conflicts in the contemporary community. First-hand experience working with community organizations has made some wary of other Japanese Canadians. If either situation were applicable, the sansei woman would probably keep her distance from other sansei. But, more likely, introducing her new family to her mother's history was a very personal matter, and she did not want others to interfere or take over. This was an instance where, positioned as one of the NIMC staff, I was intrusive and assumed an inappropriate amount of familiarity, as a happa sansei, perhaps overidentifying with this visitor's bicultural family.

Disconnected Pasts

For some sansei, visiting the NIMC was part of an uncertain emotional journey. They had travelled to the NIMC to understand why their families refused to discuss the past. In the next passage, I describe a man facing this situation. His visit reveals that there are still Japanese Canadians who continue to be haunted by the internment, despite the success of the redress movement.

Field Notes #11: A Shadow

A motorcycle carrying two passengers circled the Centre, pulling up outside the gates. A travel-weary man and woman in their late thirties, clad in protective black leather gear, approached the Visitors' Reception Building, where another worker and I were talking. Both looked thin and worn. The man meekly said, "Hi." He was pale – too many cigarettes, too many worries, too much of something or perhaps not enough ... He had that look, like he might be Japanese Canadian – a shadow of movement softening his angular Anglo comportment. But I wasn't sure. He drifted off toward the exhibits. The woman lingered behind. After looking at the books on display, she commented on what we had been discussing as they came in, something about how it is difficult not to be filled with grief whenever you reflect on the internment.

Tentatively, the woman began to ask if we knew anything about Kaslo. She asked if there were any maps. She made a gesture toward the man who had accompanied her and explained that her husband's family had been in Kaslo during the war. She told us that his family had lived in one of the houses, but they weren't sure which one.

The other worker said that the government had placed a lot of people in the local hotels. The woman replied, "Isn't it odd? That they were in a house?" The worker explained that the British Columbia Security Commission used whatever buildings were available in Kaslo. Although the NIMC did not have much information on Kaslo, we suggested that they could ask some of the old-timers. She immediately responded by stating that his family never talked about the internment. His family was resolutely silent about what had happened during the war. It was a forbidden subject. We suggested that there were other old-timers from Kaslo who would probably be pleased to talk about the internment. She said that her husband felt uncomfortable prying. He felt that people didn't want to talk about it. After we gave her the addresses of some organizations that might have more information, she drifted off as well, catching up with her husband. (FIELD NOTES, 26 JULY 1996)

If the man was trying to find information about the Kaslo internment camp, the way he drifted past us, barely meeting our eyes, suggested that he was not comfortable approaching members of the community. The woman, rather than the man, came forward to talk to us. As his wife, she seemed committed to helping him find clues to what happened to his family. Yet she was cautious. Only when it was apparent that the staff were comfortable answering questions did she share more information about his family. She presented information she thought was important: his family had lived in a house, which possibly distinguished them from other internees. Was there something about the house that had placed his family in a contentious position with other internees or with other members of the family? Given that the woman was not familiar with the names of the community organizations we gave her, probably neither her husband nor his family were members of Japanese Canadian organizations. It is likely that they did not receive any of the community newspapers that have many articles and announcements about events, art exhibits, and projects examining pre-war and wartime experiences. If so, the man must have been disconnected from many others trying to come to terms with the aftermath of internment. The woman seemed to confirm their lack of contact with other Japanese Canadians when she mentioned her husband's belief that others did not like to discuss the internment.

The fact that he was a happa in his late thirties was also significant. His Japanese Canadian parent likely met a non-Japanese Canadian partner in the early or mid-1950s.[17] This would have been just after the government lifted restrictions on the rights of Japanese Canadians in 1949. It was not a period of widespread "tolerance" in the province. Moreover, in the 1950s and 1960s, intermarriage was still considered wrong by issei, and happa children and bicultural couples were not always fully accepted. He could thus have had an awkward relationship with the wider Japanese Canadian community, especially if he lived outside an urban centre where happa such as Jay Hirabayashi (Kokoru Dance) and Audrey

Kobayashi (university professor) are well known.[18] In contrast to the sansei woman described earlier, for this man the effects of the internment were still raw: he was not at ease talking about his family. This suggests how visiting the NIMC and the need to find information about Kaslo was not a matter of positively affirming his identity and heritage. It was a matter of helping him cope with whatever haunted his family.

But it is not only sansei who can become disconnected from the community, as the next example shows.

Field Notes #12: Left Behind

On Thursday, a group of elderly men visited the Centre under the guidance of a younger woman. The woman turned to one man who looked like he could be Japanese Canadian and pointed to the list of residents in New Denver, saying, "Oh, is that a relative?" When we gave them brochures, I pointed to the brochure's cover design and said, "That's a fuki, a Nikkei artist, Kokoburo, designed it." The man shyly gave me a curious, sidelong look, and then looked down again. When the men went to see the exhibits, the woman lingered behind. Katherine and I asked her about the man and she began by explaining that the men were from a facility for the mentally ill in Vernon. She then spoke about Mr. Y, the Japanese Canadian man. Just before "the evacuation," at eighteen, Mr. Y had been committed to Riverview, a mental hospital in Vancouver. He was from Cumberland on Vancouver Island and was a great baseball player (she inquired about the book on the famous Asahi baseball team in Vancouver). His family was interned, then shipped to Japan after 1945. They ended up making it back to Canada but moved to central Canada. He was left behind in Riverview. The woman hadn't realized he had a family until one day when she asked him what he would do if he won a million dollars. He talked about how he and his brother would buy a car. Thus she discovered he had a brother. She made some unofficial inquiries and found out that he had family in Canada via the redress office. Since then, the brother, who is now in Toronto and hadn't seen Mr. Y for over fifty years – has visited several times. The woman made sure Mr. Y got his redress payment, and he used it to visit his brother in Toronto. (Field notes, 20 July 1996)

Only occasionally do stories surface about individuals who disappeared during the war, either because they simply went missing or because the government put them in mental asylums or prisons. For their families, the feelings of helplessness as well as shame and guilt would be difficult to bear. Perhaps in the years after the war, once the families had finally managed to reunite almost everyone and to re-establish some material security, they could not bring themselves to search for those who had been taken away by the government, fearing that their final fate would be too painful to face. But from Mr. Y's visit, there is an opportunity for Japanese Canadians to learn that not all stories end tragically. There are people like the young woman who have looked out for individuals who lost their families. Some have found other communities of support and, in some cases, have found ways to reconnect with their families.

Part of the Community

Some Japanese Canadians visited the NIMC on a regular basis. They had turned visiting the centre into a regular practice. Their trips were part of the process of maintaining a community. They were comfortable being in community venues, warmly interacting with other Japanese Canadians. These visitors often brought their own Japanese Canadian guests and proudly showed off the Centre. They freely extended themselves to others, chatting and seeking social connections. I recall one group of nisei from Kamloops who merrily burst into the Visitors' Reception Centre, exclaiming that this was their annual visit to the Centre.

Field Notes #13: A Small World

One of the women brought her mother's old leather suitcase and Brownie camera. She wanted to donate them to the NIMC. Cleaning out her mother's place, she had planned to throw away "this old stuff," when it occurred to her that perhaps the NIMC could use them. Her friend jumped up and exclaimed, "Are you Kirsten McAllister?" She had just seen my parents last week in the Greek restaurant in Nanaimo! Then I met her husband, who was talking to the president of the Kyowakai Society. The husband told the president, "I met her Ojiisan after the war – he was a fisherman." The president noted, "Just like our family!" (FIELD NOTES, 6 SEPTEMBER 1996)

The enthusiasm of these nisei was infectious. Their donations and the way they freely identified with other Japanese Canadians showed an inclusive understanding of community. They reminded me of my mother's friends and of many of the nisei working at community organizations in cities and towns across Canada. Rather than retreating from the social networks that knit together their pre-war communities, they tugged at worn threads from the past, knitting them together into what might become a new social fabric.

At the same time, it is important to emphasize that, for some nisei, affirming connections with community members is not necessarily comfortable. I recall an account of an elderly nisei man who came to New Denver with his grown children. He quietly mentioned that he thought he knew someone who had lived in New Denver, someone he knew while he was interned. His children inquired at the Centre and discovered that the man still lived in New Denver. The father seemed enthusiastic, and so his children urged him to knock on his old friend's door. The father approached the house, walked up the steps, and then froze. Despite the encouragement and urging of his children, he could not bring himself to knock on the door. He turned and walked away from the house.

Ambivalent Feelings

Some Japanese Canadian visitors expressed ambivalence about the NIMC. In the next passage, I describe a nisei woman who made me wonder what it was like to have one's history on public display. On the one hand, she seemed proud of the Centre and wanted the staff to know she had grown up in New Denver. On the other hand, she also asked them pointed questions. Because the description of the visit shows the complexity of interactions between staff and visitors, I include the entire passage.

Field Notes #14: Whose History

Yesterday, a very fit woman in her early sixties, with a bob haircut and wearing Birkenstocks, sporty shorts, and a T-shirt, visited the site. Her tall, relaxed-looking hakujin husband must have been in his mid-sixties. She marched into the office building and stated that she recognized some of the people in the photos in the Kyowakai Hall's displays. She informed us that she was related to A.S., one of the former residents in New Denver. Her authoritative manner indicated that she wanted us to know that she was a bona fide New Denver-ite. This was her hometown, and the NIMC was portraying her history. She turned to speak to me, bypassing the administrator and other members of the staff. I deferred to the administrator, as she was the one in charge. The administrator asked if the woman wanted to identify some of the people in the photos. She consented. I piped in, "Oh, I'll come along!" I hesitated, sensing that I had been a little too spontaneous in my assumption that I was welcome. Then I thought, oh well, I am working with the History Preservation Committee, and she will undoubtedly share important information.

As we walked past the Kyowakai Hall, she suddenly turned to me. Glaring, she asked pointedly, "And *who are you*?" I pretended not to take in the full force of her implied accusations. Was she saying, you don't look Japanese Canadian, so what is your business here? Or perhaps she was saying, how is it that *you* presume that you can accompany us? I replied, quizzically, "My name is Kirsten?" She continued, sharply asking, "Do you live here?" I read her statement to mean, if you are not from New Denver, what right do you have working at the NIMC? I explained that I was working for the History Preservation Committee and doing some independent research. Then, she replied casually, "Oh, you just *never know* who is who here." We went into the hall. She skimmed over the photographs, identifying various people. Further underlining her credentials, she also cited the names of various elders in New Denver, advising us that we should consult with them about the people in the photos. As if to indicate just how familiar she was with the elders, she asked the administrator if the elders still lived here or there, at this or that address.

Then she again turned toward me and, as if trying to repel me like some annoying mosquito, demanded, "And *where* are you from?" Rather than receiving the blow of her words, I again tried to look slightly puzzled: "Well, I grew up on Vancouver Island but am now studying in Ottawa."

Rather than cowering, I was getting a little annoyed with what felt like her accusatory tone. I decided to try to change the exchange into something more positive. When she again advised us to ask the elders about the photographs, I explained, "Well, when the NIMC initially collected the photographs, there was not enough care taken to identify the people and places, so we often just have the photos. Any identification or source we can get is very useful." I continued, "You also mentioned that you are connected with the S. family. There are some documents that refer to the S. family in our historical collections. We might need references for this material. This will be very useful for the History Preservation Committee."

Her husband, who had been quietly tagging along, noted, "Yes, without information, they are not of much value." He pointed to the ofuro in the back room of the hall and commented about how he'd love to have a Japanese bathtub because they are made so well. "The water just comes right up to your chin." I responded, joking that, yes, the Japanese have figured out all the qualities of displacement.

Deferring to her show of expertise, I asked if we could get her address so we could ask for further details if necessary. She hesitated. Was she surprised that we showed no (at least visible) signs of intimidation? Instead, we chose to enthusiastically accept her expertise, recognizing her as someone whom the Centre would find knowledgeable. But she did not leave her number or address. As they left, we both went "Byeee," waving our hands. She turned to the administrator and said in a more relaxed, friendly way, "Oh, and what was your name again? I have such a bad memory, getting old I guess!" It was hard to tell whether she was relaxing a little and being sociable or letting us know she had our names for future reference. (FIELD NOTES, 27 JULY 1996)

The interaction with this visitor and her husband was complex. As my description in the passage indicates, when I wrote the passage I read her response as hostile. I discussed her response with another sansei, wondering if the woman had responded to me negatively because I was a happa. But the worker said that the woman had initially reacted to her in a similar manner the day before. This made me consider what I interpreted as hostility. Her reaction differed from that of the tourists. She was not trying to access the backstage activities of the community, annoyed at "natives" who refused to give her access. She had grown up in New Denver. It was *her* past that was on display. By questioning my background and my relation to the NIMC she was, like the tourists, asserting her authority over me. But she herself was an insider who had lived in New Denver, and I was clearly the outsider and intruder. Perhaps she was uncomfortable having her life on display at the NIMC with strangers like myself now the custodians of her past. Yet she also seemed proud of the Centre. By informing the NIMC workers that she knew people in the photographs, she emphasized her relation to the community in New Denver. But when we responded by acknowledging her knowledge of the community, asking if we could contact her for more information, she did not give her address or phone number. She was not trying to assert herself as an authority figure whom we must consult; instead, she showed ambivalence about how to position herself in relation to the NIMC and New Denver's history.

After this incident, I reflected on the difficulty of presenting "living histories" in which the people depicted are still alive. Perhaps the woman was trying to claim ownership of the history that the NIMC presented. It was *her* history. She had grown up in New Denver, and she knew the people in the photographs. The interned Japanese Canadians in the images were family friends, playmates, and so on. Strangers such as myself, with uncertain connections to New Denver, now presided over the presentation of this history to the general public. Just as much as I felt that some tourists peered at the staff as if they were living Japanese Canadians on display, the staff at the NIMC, including myself, peered at other Japanese Canadians visiting the centre as potential sources of information.

Remembering Difference

Japanese Canadians do not necessarily share the same memories or have the same investments in what happened to them during the war. The NIMC can never affirm everyone's recollections or answer everyone's questions. In some cases, the Centre challenges how visitors want to remember the past. NIMC staff members told me stories about Japanese Canadians who were upset when they saw the Centre. They claimed that it did not accurately portray the conditions of the camp. The garden was too pretty. The shacks should have been set in muddy fields with burnt-out stumps, just as they had been when they were interned in New Denver. They wanted the NIMC to portray the desolate, barren state of the camp. There was nothing pretty about what they experienced. It was as if these visitors felt that the NIMC should immerse the visitors in the misery and depression experienced by the internees. As the administrator stated in her report to the Kyowakai Society, the lack of signage at the NIMC was the problem. Without adequate signage, it was not evident that the garden was meant to be a place to peacefully reflect. The report stated that some visitors "are misled to believe that a beautiful garden such as this one actually existed during the war" (Shozawa 1996).

At the Centre, Japanese Canadians can also be confronted by other Japanese Canadians with different memories of the past or memories and associations that make them uncomfortable. In the following passage, one of the New Denver Japanese Canadians, a nisei who some hinted had the reputation of being a "bad boy" in his younger years, is approached by a visitor. This encounter shows that one can never be certain who will reappear from the past at the NIMC.

Field Notes #15: Out of the Blue

Another notable visitor today was Mr. Takanaka and his wife. He reminded me of Norm Tsuyuki, with his solid build and solid movements. He came into the reception Centre and took one look at Harold Kono[19] and exclaimed: "HARRY KONO! Your brother was Frank Kono." Harry looked down and replied, "Nope, nope, no, not my brother ..." Though he was a big, athletic man even into his seventies, Harry seemed to back away from this short man with an incredible booming presence. "Okay, RON? Or was it Rick? We were in House 1, and you were right behind us." Harry looked like he was freaking out, backing away, trying to hide. So I said, "Okay, Harry, what are your brothers' names?" He kept backing away and then finally said, "George ..." Mr. Takanaka drew up closer to Harry and exclaimed "YES! THAT'S RIGHT!"

Then Mr. T. started going down the list of internee names on the wall, naming people and filling in what they were doing. "Enomoto – he was a chef in France. He had two well-known restaurants; just retired." It was amazing. When it became clear that Mr. T. wasn't going to spring any past stories about Harry, Harry relaxed and began to chat. (Field notes, 16 August 1996)

Harry was apparently trying to avoid being recognized by Mr. Takanaka and was very likely worried that he would recall stories that he would rather leave in the past. In New Denver, people still uneasily remembered the fast cars, girlfriends, and way he treated his parents. Even though they ended up chatting amicably, the incident demonstrates that reunions are not always comfortable. It was also a reminder to sansei like myself not to idealize all older Japanese Canadians as kind, wise elders.

Mediated Relationships

Most of the interactions between elders and visitors were buffered through the NIMC staff. The elders heard about the visitors' reactions through the administrator, the president of the Kyowakai Society, the chair of the History Preservation Committee, or others working on the site, such as myself. Hearing about the many people who travelled to the Centre underlined the importance of sharing their history of internment. The appreciation shown by the visitors, as well as the personal connections visitors made to the history of internment, was meaningful. Rather than being isolated by their experiences of internment, the NIMC made the elders realize that many people, not just Japanese Canadians, felt a connection to the community and recognized that their rights had been violated.

I want to emphasize the importance of mediating the connection between the visitors and the elders through those working on the site. There is no need for people who have been the direct target of political violence to face the confused emotional baggage of the general public. The fatigue and burn out of staff that the administrator reported to the Kyowakai Society attests to the challenges of dealing with visitors to a centre that educates the public about the wartime experiences of Japanese Canadians. Making a public statement about a historical event that implicates a large number of individuals, organizations, businesses, and government departments and officials is an onerous task. It is difficult to bear the unpredictable reactions and inevitable denials and criticisms of those who feel implicated. As I found, it is also challenging to withhold judgment – which, as I see it now, was ultimately about my own fears and my inability to accept the different ways that other people related to Japanese Canadian history. From a distance, it has been possible to learn from the visitors' reactions, particularly their criticisms and what I initially regarded as their angry outbursts. The visitors' reactions have shown the elders that it is not just Japanese Canadians who struggle with the aftermath of the internment, labour camps, and forced dispersal. Although the elders might have found some of the reactions troubling, they did not feel threatened. Otherwise, it would have been uncomfortable to keep the NIMC open, especially since it is located within blocks of many of their homes. But clearly, even the elders like Mr. Senya Mori, who was opposed to the NIMC's display of the Buddhist shrine, saw its benefits.

Elders accepted the fact that many visitors had accounts that differed from their own. This is remarkable, since it is not uncommon for victims of persecution to feel threatened by divergent accounts: they have a strong investment in keeping their version of reality intact. For example, in other contexts I have met Japanese Canadians who described their childhood years in the internment camps as "fun," "carefree," and full of adventure. They dismissed others' claims that the internment had "ruined their lives." It was as if they could not accept – or needed to deny – that the internment had had a severe impact on others. It would be exhausting to be driven to constantly correct, dismiss, or deny the accounts of others, though this demonstrates the powerful emotional investment in protecting their version of reality. The elders in New Denver accepted that others felt discomfort, sadness, anger, and defensiveness, as well as indifference. They were aware that they could not control how others would react. To accept others' differences, to find ways to accept that it is valid for others to have their own unique responses and versions of events, is necessary in the process of rebuilding the capacity to have mutually respectful relationships with others (Herman 1992). It means others are not viewed as threats that need to be controlled.

When the elders heard how some visitors had treated the NIMC staff, especially younger non-Japanese Canadians, they were very concerned. For instance, there were instances where visitors questioned the right of white people to work at the NIMC. The administrator reported these incidents to the Kyowakai Society. The administrator indicated that one of the unrecognized challenges of working with visitors was contending with their emotional responses, which ranged from anger to complete indifference. The workers were put in a position where they had to bear some of the burden of a history of racism (Shozawa 1996). Yet, in response, the workers made it clear that they considered the internment part of *their* history. Their commitment to the Centre expanded the elders' realization of who was affected by the consequences of the persecution of Japanese Canadians. It revealed that others were committed to educating the public about the injustice they had endured: it shifted the elders' sense of who was encompassed in a sense of "we." In 1996, two years after building the NIMC, the elders felt strongly about the importance of educating others about their experiences of injustice. They also had an increasingly nuanced conception of what was important for visitors to learn. Mrs. Inose describes ways in which the NIMC could be improved.

> *Mrs. Inose:* I would certainly like [the NIMC] to be more educational ... so people could come and learn what discrimination is really like for ... minority people. And it should be more ... that the experience will be [the] education. I think people could learn a lot by coming here and knowing that discrimination is a very – what would you say – something that could happen quite easily and that if people realize what does happen and could happen, perhaps that will be an education that will stop a lot of discrimination. As we have [set it up now], I don't like those artifacts. Well, I suppose even they could [provide some] education because we don't [use those items anymore. They are useful] for those who want to study the past. Yes, it has to be more [oriented toward] education, for people to understand what discrimination can do to people.
>
> *Kirsten McAllister (KM):* So that could be something to work on? So it talks about that history more?
>
> *Mrs. Inose:* Yes, and what it can do to *human beings*. Some people are strong enough to overcome and get stronger from discrimination. Like in our case, our people picked up and really went ahead and bettered themselves ... *despite* all ... they went through ... To be able to overcome these things. But a lot of people aren't strong enough.
>
> *KM:* So you saw that around you as well?
>
> *Mrs. Inose:* ... in one sense, as devastating as it was, [we were able to make it do] some good for us as well. And yet there are those people who never really overcame the misery, [never overcame] what happened. It helped the younger people more – the older people, they lost everything they worked for and their children. And it was too late to start over again. (Inose, Interview, 6 August 1996)

Sharing what happened to Japanese Canadians can show others what discrimination "can do to people." Mrs. Inose makes the argument that, to understand discrimination, it is necessary to understand what it does: the damage, the devastation, the humiliation that some never overcome. It is also something that can happen rapidly: hatred and fear can be mobilized quickly and transform into government policies that destroy the lives of thousands of people. She points out that in order to protect society against future acts of political violence, it is vital to underline the fundamental humanity of those who are targets of hatred. This is something that she very strongly feels the NIMC needs to underline: the humanity of the victims. While acknowledging the devastating affects of political violence, she also makes it clear that the victims have the capacity to survive and rebuild their lives in new ways. This is evident in the act of building the NIMC. In building the NIMC, New Denver Japanese Canadians have rebuilt a sense of a future that recognizes the potential for violence as well as the possibility of intervention.

The large volume of visitors to the NIMC demonstrated the importance of sharing the elders' history. The range of visitors' reactions, whether appreciative, angry, or contemplative, shows the elders how people have been affected in different ways by the government's plan to remove Japanese Canadians from British Columbia during the 1940s, and that many are still working through its aftermath.

Points of Departure

While everyone slept, snow dusted the massive ridges towering over Slocan Lake. Even at night, peering up from the darkness of the valley, I could see their white forms glowing eerily in the moonlight, now part of the celestial world.

The insect life that survived the first frost, notably an odd assortment of spiders, plump and spindly, tiny and large, scuttled indoors. At the village post office, an elderly woman nodded her head knowingly – this was a sign that winter was coming. Everyone was preparing for the deep snow and freezing temperatures. As they restocked their firewood, dug up their dahlias, and finished their canning, it was as if the world were moving inside, drawn to the warmth emanating from wood stoves, inside into the quiet contemplation of winter.

I wanted to stay. The beginnings of a new life were gently tugging me into the valley. But instead I prepared to leave. I swept the rough floorboards of the huge creaking house that had been my home over the summer, now even more empty than when I arrived. Returning the array of cooking pots, blankets, and bicycle pumps that people generously lent me, I began to disassemble my life in the valley.

So many goodbyes. I promised I would return, not knowing that this would be my final farewell to so many.

The elders were so much more knowledgeable about the act of departure than I. They understood that in every act there are possibilities not to repeat the past but to transform it into something beyond the limits of what was. As I drove west, across damp grey savannah and over the bare mountain ranges, with boxes of field notes, photographs, documents, and the memory of their words, I trusted what the elders had taught me, that this departure was yet another starting point.[1]

In July 1996, I travelled from the coastline of British Columbia nine hours into the interior of the province to the village of New Denver. I travelled there to learn about a memorial that Japanese Canadian elders had built to mark the site where the government interned them during the Second World War. As members of the Kyowakai Society, they envisioned a memorial that would remind Canadians just how quickly popular sentiments of fear and hatred can spiral out of control and become discriminatory legislation that violates the fundamental rights of targeted groups. As elders in the Japanese Canadian community, they envisioned a place where future generations haunted by the past could return.

When I first arrived to conduct research on the memorial, all I could see was a community project that local contractors had turned into a tourist attraction. Against the wishes of the elders, the contractors had made the community buildings where the elders held their meetings, social events, and religious ceremonies into public exhibits, literally turning the elders' lives into museum displays. The appropriation of their community buildings echoed what had happened during the war, when the government, as well as friends and neighbours, had taken over the homes, properties, and community holdings they had promised to keep in trust. But what I initially saw, using a sociological framework and entrenched in my position as a cultural activist, was limited. I had reified the memorial. I viewed it as a project that began with an "original plan," which then underwent phases of development, with various sources of funding and struggles over its final design. I did not understand how the memorial fit into the lives of the elders and the history of the region.

By writing myself into this book as a character, a character that was at times irritating and judgmental, I presented how I struggled to position myself in relation to the community, aware of my own internalized sociological gaze and my status as an outsider. Then came the necessary crisis of identity, in which my assumptions about the New Denver community began to unravel. Over time, working closely with the elders, I began to recognize that they had a different way of understanding and ordering their worlds. I learned that the memorial was just one of many projects they had undertaken to transform the site of an incarceration camp in an isolated mountain valley into a home village where they would continue to live over the next fifty years. The elders continued to transform the site over the years, including an agreement community leaders made with the government in 1957 to deed much of the land in the Orchard to the remaining Japanese Canadians. Finally, with the completion of the Nikkei Internment Memorial Centre (NIMC) in 1994, the Kyowakai Society turned the site into a place of remembrance for those who had been interned in New Denver from 1942 to 1945.

The design of the NIMC is not remarkable. It is not a countermonument (Young 1993) designed to resist the monumental forms of remembrance characteristic of fascism and reactionary forms of nationalism. As a community initiative with limited resources, the NIMC is like many community-run centres in rural regions across the province. It is a multi-purpose centre that serves both the community and the public. It will continue in its current form only as long there is a living community to run it. The tax-free agreement with the Village of New Denver specifies that it will revert to village property if Japanese Canadians are no longer able to operate it. This raises questions about the eventual fate of the memorial if it becomes village property. The agreement was not something that all elders supported. It raises questions about what is entailed in the stewardship of public memory, especially the memory of historically persecuted groups whose presence has been erased from the social landscape. Who will tend to the remembrance of these groups once the last survivors have died, leaving only the remains of their once vibrant communities?

Centres like the NIMC, which disrupt the historical landscape by laying bare sites of racial violence, can easily be incorporated into networks of tourist sites. This has happened in the Kootenays, where tourism is replacing the region's primary industries. Yet, if one goes beyond a textual analysis of tourist discourses and the design of the memorial centre, as I learned from working at the NIMC and meeting many visitors, these centres can also function as repositories for troubling memories. There are few places where people haunted by the aftermath of what happened to Japanese Canadians and other groups can go with their unresolved guilt, their anger and sorrow, and their gestures of remembrance. That being said, in many ways it has been the presence of the living community in New Denver that has made the NIMC so significant for many visitors. For some, the need to authenticate their experience – as I now realize from the visitors' queries about whether the staff were members of the New Denver community – arose partly because they wanted to ensure that their gestures of remembrance were made to people from the community. Of course, this was not the case for all visitors. Some related to the Centre and staff as if they were part of an ethnographic museum display and, in so doing, revealed the extent to which colonial discourses with a differential "power to look" still structure so-called intercultural encounters. They objectified the Centre and workers, feeling no compunction about demanding personal information about the staffs' racial backgrounds and family histories. They ignored social boundaries, pushing past signage indicating the Centre was closed for community services, and refused to leave when they were informed that the Centre was closed.

To counter the colonial and wartime discourses that reduce Japanese Canadians to sinister Orientals who threaten national security, the Centre uses the narrative of the redress movement to frame the internment camps in terms of the violation of the rights of thousands of loyal Canadian citizens. Although the redress narrative is an important component of the NIMC, in some ways it is the site itself and the remains of the camp that have the most potency. From records written by internees, we have glimpses of what happened to them. There are the remaining letters stored in the national archives, for example, with inky handwriting that captures the confusion and chaos of the camps and the inhuman living conditions on the prairie sugar beet farms. There are boxes and boxes of typewritten letters, composed in the gloom of the camps. Each letter manages to muster a commanding voice, requesting the return of husbands and sons in work and prisoner-of-war camps, protesting their living conditions in makeshift quarters and questioning the sale of the properties and homes they had left in the trust of the Custodian of Enemy Alien Property. Because the national archives has neither the resources nor priority to make inventories of individual documents, Japanese Canadians cannot easily access these letters stored in Ottawa. Weeks if not months are needed to conduct research in the archives. And there remains so much that internees did not write down, so much that was censored, lost, or left behind when they were forced to leave British Columbia with restricted baggage allowances.

With only a limited number of surviving documents, and as the tangible memories of the internees fade, the site of the New Denver camp itself, scattered with the remains of the war years, grows in significance. But what will become of it over time? The NIMC does not have the resources to install the technology to control humidity and temperature to preserve the artifacts, documents, and restored shacks from the erosion of time. Thus, everything is in the process of disintegration. This disintegration defies the chronotope of the immemorial that removes space from the forces of everyday organic time. Their decomposition could be viewed in terms of the loss of what remains of our history, which will inevitably lead to a forgetting. But it is also possible to view the disintegration of the remains, salvaged as reminders of the internees' lives, in terms of their potential transformation. Brought together in the memorial, the fragmented remains are recognized and honoured – in a sense, given a burial. The memorial is where the fragments of the past, both literal and figurative, can come to rest and, through the rituals of remembering, become incorporated into memory and transformed by the many people who come to visit, some whose families were interned and others who never knew about the camps.

The process of building the memorial, the act of making a public statement about the violation of their rights in the very village where they were interned during the 1940s, was transformative for the elders. They excavated the painful past from the social landscape. They struggled against local contractors who refused to represent the interment camps in ways that criticized the Canadian government and named the racism that motivated its policies. The elders did not give in. They ensured that their history of internment was presented as they wanted it to be presented: as the violation of the rights of thousands of innocent Canadians.

In building the memorial, the elders reworked the last of their buried shame and pain into something that was not theirs alone to bear. Building the memorial transformed their relations with one another, with younger generations, and with other residents in New Denver. It also transformed their relationship with strangers from across Canada as well as the United States and Japan. They realized the extent to which others were burdened by the after-effects of the internment camps. These after-effects continue to haunt generations not only within but also outside of their community. As they learned from the visitors, the history of internment has worked itself through people's lives in diverse and unpredictable ways. There were visitors who adamantly argued that the government was justified in using the War Measures Act to strip the rights of Japanese Canadians and intern them in camps. There were others who felt guilt simply for not knowing about the history. The NIMC thus does not function like a conventional memorial, unifying the visitors as they remember the deeds of the past in a collective position of sorrow and regret. Instead, it is a place where different memories, discourses, and experiences intersect, showing that this history of political persecution in Canada is still part of an unresolved, contested terrain of memory.

As I write my final words in this Conclusion, the celebrations for the twentieth anniversary of the 1988 Japanese Canadian redress settlement negotiated by the National Association of Japanese Canadians with the federal government are coming to a close. Redress was the political movement that made not only research projects like this study but also memory projects like the NIMC possible. The funding from the settlement has enabled individuals, artists, writers, and community groups to create, re-imagine, and build what we envision we might be as contemporary Japanese Canadians. At another more profound level, redress relocated Japanese Canadians back into the world of politics and dynamic social change. Redress broke open the fear that froze many Japanese Canadians in the present, as if we had no history. We can now trace how this history has contributed to the political and psychic formation of Canada. Rather than "cleansing" the population in British Columbia of people with undesirable "racial origins," the sudden disappearance of thousands from small towns, fishing ports, and city neighbourhoods has left deep scars. Although there remains much work to do in documenting the losses, the violations and humiliation, as the elders in New Denver have demonstrated, it is important to attend to the impact on those living today. How we document, recount, and

7.1 Rock arrangement by Mr. Matsushita, 1970. *Shoichi Matsushita. Courtesy of the Matsushita family.*

represent the past – our stories – can embalm our history in the past or explore the potential for transformation.

Part of the potential of our stories, as Roy Miki writes, lies in their power to both compel and confound us.

> I'm rummaging among archival boxes on redress in my study: boxes stuffed into closets with mounds of papers, newspaper clippings, essays, notes, memos, press releases, the whole frenzy of the years of daily involvement in that, now, historic movement called "redress." Despite that dazzling accomplishment by our community, the past shimmers with the unknown. Our history still remains baffling as we continue to construct stories that evade completion. (Miki 1998b, 15)

In writing an account of the memorial, what I consider one of our community's "dazzling accomplishments," I have attempted to keep the elders' teaching "alive." Rather than museumizing them, as Mr. Senya Mori warned might happen, I have tried to keep their words, their lives, their past "shimmering with the unknown." For what would happen if we were to somehow complete these stories? Would the compulsion to search news clippings, memorandums, and photographs, the boxes and landscapes overflowing with mounds of meaning, condensing and dissipating with the passage of time, simply cease?

Yet I wonder if the compulsion to gather everything into words, into a story, stems from the hope that we can somehow transcend their disappearance into temporal oblivion and is, in the end, a commitment to another type of memorial, in memoriam. Is there a fatalistic desperation in the urge to preserve, to give shape to all that is gone? Does this urge suggest that one lives in continual loss, unable to live in the present and instead driven to recover what can no longer be? Is this a desperate search for an origin, a beginning, a home?

> Home coming, or speaking more actively, coming home, as if home were a place, like Powell or Gore, or a house one can stroll into, toss a hat on the rack, and say hello to one and all. As if home were the completed story.
> If only it could be that translucent. (Miki 1998b, 15)

New Denver can never be such a home. It can never be so translucent. As long as it "evades completion" and remains "baffling," whether we chase its mysteries into the past or make it present, the stories will remain alive in the present.

New Denver is both the site of loss *and* the site of continuity. But continuity is too often what is forgotten. Many of the elders have now passed on. I have also heard that the bonsei in the Hei-wa Tei-en garden are mysteriously dying. Mortality.[2] But again, this is what they tried to help me understand in so many ways: that death can be a passage. Through letting go, easing one's grip, there is a possibility for transformation. To hold on too tightly is to freeze, locked in stasis, in a death where there is no possibility for life. It is through the act of representing, with all of my misunderstandings, the way I have tripped over ideas and become tangled in repetitions that I have been able to let go. To let go, though, is not too sever. For it has been only through working with the elders, through facing the limits of my own assumptions, through living in the Slocan Valley and working at the memorial under the guidance of Takana, and through writing and rewriting this work that I have been able to let go of my own stories that held me in a form of stasis.

It is here, as I suggested at the beginning of this work, that I am not alone. Returning to Vancouver in 2003, with my untouched dissertation packed among my papers in my boxes of belongings, I feared that the return to the Pacific Coast, to this terrain of memory, would return me to that stasis, locked into one story of what it meant to be a sansei, a Japanese Canadian in Vancouver. But here on the coast, writers such as Roy Miki, Hiromi Goto, and Mark Nakada; artists and performers such as Cindy Mochizuki, Katherine Shozawa, Leslie

Komori, Baco Ohama, and Jay Hirabayashi; and cultural activists and curators such as Grace Eiko Thomson and those across the rest of Canada, including Audrey Kobayashi, Mona Oikawa, Michael Fukushima, and Midi Onodera, to mention only a few, have continued to explore the poetics of multiple forms of being, as they look not only to the past in Canada but also to migrations across the Pacific to contemporary Japan, to Europe, and elsewhere that reconfigure the terrain of memory. With other writers and artists, with a new generation of scholars, there is the hope that the stories will keep transforming, in movement, interconnecting with the histories of others as well as exploring the injustices in and possibilities of the contemporary world. The moving migratory stories of these writers, artists, and activists have shown me, like the elders, that while stasis is always a threat, working with the potent remains of history does not have to trap one in the past. It is not a choice between being frozen in the present or trapped in the past. Movement is possible. Thus I come to the end of the story I have rendered here. It is one of many possible stories that could have been written, one that I hope "evades completion," evades finality, and thus continues to be open to life.

Notes

Introduction: The Drive to Do Research

1 For an analysis of removing the hyphen from "Japanese-Canadian" (whether adjective or noun), see studies on the cultural politics of Asian Canadian nomenclature by Miki (1998a), Wah (1999), and Kamboureli (2000). I use the term "elder" to refer to those who have taken on roles dedicated to the public good, whose work transcends individual interest and is in accordance with spiritual and living principles that affirm the interdependence of that which is different (in New Denver, Japanese Canadians refer to themselves modestly as seniors, as in "senior citizen"). "Elder" is a term used in indigenous communities, and I use the term in acknowledgment of their example. My use of the term is also intended to recognize their supportive relationships with Japanese Canadians over the years, which are often unacknowledged. (Mona Oikawa has started a SSHRC-funded study that examines these relationships.) For example, in 1942, indigenous leaders offered a number of Japanese Canadians the option of becoming members of their bands rather than being incarcerated by the government. During the movement for redress, Japanese Canadian activists and indigenous leaders entered into a dialogue to strategize about their respective cases and, as well, indigenous communities have always provided the example of their own work in rebuilding intergenerational relationships in the aftermath of persecution.

2 A total of 21,164 Japanese Canadians were removed from their homes. Of these, 12,029 were sent to government-run internment camps, and 1,161 were sent to camps directly financed by the internees themselves. The government-run camps were financed by liquidating the properties, investments, and possessions of Japanese Canadians left in trust under the temporary care of the Custodian of Enemy Alien Property. In addition, just under 4,000 women, men, and children were sent to work as labourers on sugar beet farms in the Prairies, 945 men worked on road construction, and 699 men were interned in prisoner-of-war camps in Ontario (Miki and Kobayashi 1991, 31).

3 Ironically, many Japanese Canadians were infected by unsanitary conditions in camps and internment centres such as Hastings Park (Matsushita, interview, 15 August 1996; Takahara, interview, 23 August 1996).

4 Teresa Takana is a pseudonym. As the chair of the History Preservation Committee, she read a number of preliminary drafts and later I sent her the new sections in which I wrote about our working relationship. With generosity, Takana recognized the importance of writing these sections and including them in this study.

5 "Sansei" refers to the third generation of Japanese Canadians.

6 Life histories can be rich, insightful dialogic records for full-length studies. See Rak (2004), Cruickshank (2005), and Cruickshank et al. (1990). Recognizing the significance of the elders' accounts, I gave copies of their interviews to the Japanese Canadian National Museum, where they are now, with the elders' consent, available to the public.

7 See Ayukawa (1995, 2005), Geiger-Adams (2005), Izumi (2005), Makabe (1995), Roy (2005), and Roy et al. (1990).

8 For Canadian historians who examine questions of cultural memory, see Opp and Walsh (2010).

9 In Canada, the Asian Canadian Studies Association and the Japan Studies Association (which includes Japanese Canadian topics) have regular conferences.

10 For example, at the 2005 Association for Asian American Studies conference in Los Angeles, two panels on Asian Canadian topics were organized by researchers trained in the United States or affiliated with US academic networks. A good number of those who attended identified themselves as US-educated Canadians, including expatriate Canadians working in the United States. The discussions that followed the panels focused on what they assumed to be a lack of Asian Canadian scholarship in Canada. There seemed to be a consensus among the forty or fifty scholars about the need to help Canadians establish Asian Canadian Studies units in Canadian universities. It seemed that the underlying goal was to increase the recognition of Asian Canadian Studies as a legitimate field in the United States, which would help increase the legitimacy of their own research. Mona Oikawa and I were two of the Canadian-based academics invited to present on one of the panels. We raised questions about two assumptions: (1) that research concerning Asian Canadians in Canada was lacking and (2) that Canadian universities needed their help. There was no response to requests for clarification about these assumptions. No one in attendance responded to the argument that Asian Canadian research in Canada has its own history, methodologies, issues, and visions, making it problematic for US-based scholars to conclude that this research does not exist just because it does not conform to their criteria. During the discussions following the panels, Mona Oikawa and I pointed out what have been some guiding principles for many Asian Canadian scholars over the years, including praxis, grassroots activism, coalitions with other movements and communities, and creative work, which, ironically, have been important for many Asian American scholars in different periods over the last forty years. No one responded, and the other researchers returned to their plans about how to set up Asian Canadian studies in Canadian universities. In fact, there are US scholars who are critical of the disciplinary assumptions of Asian American studies who, for instance, also argue that dividing research on the Asian diaspora into separate fields of ethnic specialization, each with their own university institutes and programs, can result in the production of the racialized, regional, class-based subjects that many Asian American scholars aim to critique (Chow 2002). Here, it is interesting to note that after the panel discussion, a few individuals expressed their support of our critique, though they did not publically state their position.

11 In the book *Mutual Hostages* (1990), Roy, Granatstein, Lino, and Takamura, in contrast, claim these policies were justified. Like the government in 1942, they fail to recognize that most Japanese Canadians were Canadian citizens and different from Japanese soldiers fighting overseas under the command of the Japanese military.

12 In Canada, this is most evident in the publishing process (rather than in debates in journals, for example, which hopefully will follow), especially in referees' reports. Many of my colleagues have discussed how their work is categorized in part like my own, by the subject matter, Japanese Canadian history. This makes sense, but many area experts in Canada working in the social sciences are disciplinary recovery scholars, rather than cultural studies scholars specializing in Asian Canadian studies. Although it is important to ensure factual accuracy, in many cases the use of positivist criteria means that these scholars do not recognize the validity of analyses that draw on postcolonial studies, feminist theory, or cultural studies.

13 Fourth-generation Japanese Canadian.

14 Makabe has made generalizations about sansei across Canada, even though most of her participants are from Ontario and she did not include sansei activists, community workers, artists, or writers.

15 See Okano and Nutley (2002) and Nutley (1992) for work by the Human Rights Committee of the Vancouver JCCA on internalized racism. For an example of recent incidents of racism against Japanese Canadians, see Murakami (2005).

16 Examples of such work include Gunn (1979), Wong (1990), Miki and Wah (1994), Miki (1998a), Lowry and Kong (2001), Lowry (2001), Gagnon and Fung (2002), Gagnon (2000), and Wong and Lee (2008).

17 See Lowry's essays on Miki's poetry (Lowry 2002, 2003). Also note organizations such as Direct Action Against Refugee Exploitation (DAARE) (http://www.harbour.sfu.ca/freda/reports/daare.htm) and the Asian Society for the Intervention of AIDS (ASIA). Some key cultural events included the 1991 "Invisible Colours" film and video festival organized by Zainub Verjee and others; the "Writing Thru Race" conference in 1994; exhibitions curated by Henry Tsang and Scott Taguro McFarlane in the 1990s, including "Self Not Whole"; magazines such as *Rhung,* which was run by Zool Suleman; and research and organizing by Yasmin Jiwani when she was at the Feminist Research, Education, Development, and Action Centre (FREDA).

18 On returning to Vancouver in 2003, I began discussions with Glen Lowry about the notion of a West Coast School of Cultural Studies rooted in the cultural politics of and the questions raised by racialized and (post)colonial artists, writers, and activists in the 1970s (note early publications such as Gunn's *Inalienable Rice* and journals such as the *Powell Street Review*).

19 There are many powerful examples of this collective remembering. For just a few, see Alanis Obomsawin's film, *Richard Cardinal: Cry from a Diary of a Métis Child* (1986); Suzanne Fournier and Ernie Crey's *Stolen from Our Embrace: The Abduction of First Nations Children and the Restoration of Aboriginal Communities* (1998); Richard Van Camp's stories, such as "Mermaids" (2000); and the poetry of Marilyn Dumont, such as the collection *Green Girl Dreams Mountains* (2001). There is also, obviously, the extensive writings of Jewish authors, such as Elie Wiesel's 1961 novel *Night.*

20 In 1988, Japanese Canadians' redress settlement included the following terms: an "acknowledgment that the treatment of Japanese Canadians during and after World War Two was unjust and violated principles of human rights as they are understood today"; a "pledge to ensure, to the full extent that its powers allow, that such events will not happen again"; the recognition "with great respect the fortitude and determination of Japanese Canadians who, despite stress and hardship, retain their commitment and loyalty to Canada and contribute so richly to the development of the Canadian nation"; as well as symbolic redress, which included funds granted to eligible individuals, funds for activities that promote educational, social, and cultural activities, including the promotion of human rights, in addition to funding for a Race Relations Foundation (Miki and Kobayashi 1991, 138-139).

21 The National Association of Japanese Canadians (NAJC) established local branches throughout Canada during the 1980s. Today, most NAJC branches focus on issues concerning community development, although some have history preservation and human rights committees. Most communities have social and cultural organizations, such as churches and Buddhist temples, elder-care facilities, community centres, flower-arranging clubs, Japanese language schools, and shin-ijuusha support networks. With the funding from the redress settlement, individuals and community organizations can apply for funding that adheres to the NAJC's mandate to contribute to the development of the arts, education, historical research, social services, and social infrastructure.

22 Although social movements can become communities, they do not necessarily start as communities.

23 The film work by indigenous activists and artists in Canada is exemplary. See, for example, Christian (2007), Claxton (2001, 2004), Todd (2001, 2003), Obomsawin (1986, 1993, 2006), Cheechoo (1997, 2005), and the work of newer generations, including Hopkins (2004) and Barnaby (2004).

24 This is evident in the case of Japanese Canadians. For example, the effects that the government's measures had on issei differed from the effects on young nisei children. Most issei lost the homes, livelihoods, social networks, and communal buildings they had attained before the war. The prospect of rebuilding their lives elsewhere in Canada was daunting, especially for those who were not fluent in English or French and were unfamiliar with regions outside of British Columbia. In contrast, young nisei children were usually protected from the harsh realities of camp life by their parents and older siblings. In many cases, the older siblings gave up their own aspirations to support their parents and siblings, ensuring that there were funds for their younger siblings' education.

Chapter 1: A Necessary Crisis

1 Rather than counting only the main administrative centres – for example, Slocan and New Denver – I have included the adjunct camps in each centre, such as Harris Ranch, Rosebery, and Trite Ranch.

2 These projects included coordinating the Oral History Project of the Japanese Canadian Citizens' Association as well as running workshops on intermarriage, women's experiences, research, and human rights.

3 For example, in addition to working on NIMC projects while I was in New Denver, I gave a draft of my doctoral dissertation to the chair of the History Preservation Committee, which used it as the basis for one of its education projects. I also gave the committee copies of all of the archival documents I had collected from Library and Archives Canada.

4 Archivists from the Simon Fraser University Library introduced us to the very helpful *Manual for Small Archives* by Lillian Bickerton et al. (1988).

5 Takana's Kyowakai Society projects were funded by the National Association of Japanese Canadians (NAJC) Redress Foundation. My research was funded by the NAJC Redress Foundation and the Social Science and Humanities Research Council of Canada.

6 All people continually negotiate their identities in their everyday lives. Each has a different level of vulnerability. Some take for granted that others will affirm their social identities by responding as expected, while others must constantly manage negation and suspicion, constantly warding off a crisis of identity. In some cases, groups create new spaces and communities of affinity (not necessarily progressive, as neo-Nazi groups demonstrate) for ways of being otherwise not generally recognized or valorized.

7 This applies to studies of socially (rather than legally) marginalized groups with relative amounts of autonomy, living to some degree according to terms they have collectively determined and by which they can freely reject the researcher without direct consequences. Researchers are responsible for making their objectives and temporary status evident and for moderating their engagement accordingly so that they do not deceptively cultivate emotional, social, or material expectations from the participants. Other sets of identity practices are needed for studies of elite groups, violent gangs, and studies of vulnerable groups, such as asylum seekers as well as powerful institutions such as asylum courts (see Guterson 1993 and Good 2007).

8 Matsutake is a prized wild mushroom that grows in well-drained acidic soil, usually on mountain slopes under hemlock, Douglas fir, or pine. The elders have many stories about matsutake harvests in the Slocan Valley. Gohan is steamed Japanese rice. Matsutake gohan is a sushi-rice dish made with matsutake.

9 Manju is a Japanese sweet. It consists of azuki, a sweetened pulverized bean paste, wrapped with thick soft dough made from rice flour.
10 Buddha's house.
11 I kept in regular correspondence with four elders over three years. I sent the Kyowakai Society and the chair of the History Preservation Committee a draft of the project to review and sent copies to individual elders, highlighting excerpts from their interviews and asking for corrections. Before submitting the final draft to my PhD committee, I checked a third time to see if the elders I interviewed wanted to be identified with a pseudonym. They all wanted their full names used.
12 During this period, the work of Jeanette Armstrong (in Anderson 1997) and Roy Miki (1998a) in British Columbia would have offered guidance, but I read their work only after I had finished.

Chapter 2: Mapping the Spaces of Internment

1 A type of seaweed.
2 The idea of the pilgrimage developed through separate conversations with Mona Oikawa and Wendy Larner. Both discussed the ironies and difficulties that members of historically persecuted communities in Canada and New Zealand face as they enter government buildings and navigate dominant codes of conduct and classification systems to piece together their histories.
3 The government also ensured that little remained to mark their material presence in settlements along the coast. The hastily boarded-up houses, businesses, and community buildings, the fleets of fishing boats, deserted cannery housing, motor vehicles, and the untended fields of produce – left behind when everyone was sent to the camps or to sugar beet farms – did not stand idle for long. Japanese Canadians were instructed to leave their properties and businesses under the care of the Custodian for Enemy Alien Property during what the government promised was going to be a "temporary evacuation." (I've come across archival documents describing huge vats of miso found in the Amano miso factory. The government, unable to find any use for the miso, distributed it among Japanese Canadian internees.) But rather than keeping those belongings in trust, the government swiftly sold almost everything for below market value, often letting buildings deteriorate beyond repair and giving prime property and farmland to returning war veterans. Thus, rather than marking their absence – the vacated shells of their lives – the deserted buildings, vacant lots, and unused fleets of fishing vessels were quickly reincorporated into the hungry wartime economy as it headed toward postwar prosperity (Adachi 1991; Kobayashi 1992a, 1992b, 1994a).
4 For analyses of mapping with regard to epistemological questions of coding and ordering space and constituting subjects, see Pickles (2004), Cosgrove (1999), Duncan and Ley (1993), Harley and Laxton (2002).

Chapter 3: The Chronotope of the (Im)memorial

1 See Takashima (1991 [1971]), Knight and Koizumi (1976), Nakano (1980), Kogawa (1983, 1992), Kitagawa (1985), Miki (1991, 1995, 2001, 2004), Goto (1994, 2001), Kiyooka (1997b), Watada (1997), Kamegaya (1994), Ito (1998), Sakamoto (1998), and Ohama (2001).
2 See Adachi (1991), Japanese Canadian Centennial Project (1978), Sunahara (1981), Takata (1983), Ito (1984), Oikawa (1986), Kobayashi (1987, 1989, 1992a, 1992b, 1994b), Miki and Kobayashi (1991), and Murakami (2005).
3 See Marlatt (1975), Nakayama (1984), Oiwa (1991), Okano (1992), Kiyooka (1997a), Oikawa (2002, forthcoming), and Sugiman (2004, 2006).

4 See Onodera (1987), Fukushima (1992), and Ohama (1993, 2001).

5 See the work of artists such as Aiko Suzuki, Nobuo Kubota, Baco Ohama, Bryce Kanbara, Jay Hirabayashi (Kokoru Dance), Tamio Wakayama, and Cindy Mochizuki as well as *taiko* (drumming) groups such as Katari Taiko, Uzume Taiko, and Sawagai Taiko. Also see Aiko Suzuki's directory of Japanese Canadian artists (1994).

6 Even what would seem to be the most apolitical memorials can cause controversy. For example, the placement of the memorial to commemorate Terry Fox, a young man with cancer who attempted to run across Canada to raise funds for cancer organizations, caused a heated debate in Ottawa. Its location was debated because it would denote Terry Fox's national significance in relation to other memorials and statues.

7 See Mealing (1977) and Rak (2004) for a discussion of the efforts of Doukhobors to recall their history as a persecuted group in the region.

8 There are also atrocities that are internationally condemned. The Auschwitz and Birkeneau death camps, for example, have become so powerful symbolically to populations across the world that the Polish government made them into a state museum by an act of Parliament on 2 July 1947. See the Auschwitz Museum website. For critiques of this international narrative, see Huyssen (2003).

9 I also used the chronotope to examine the space-time dimension of a video documenting a pilgrimage of nisei back to the site of their internment camp (McAllister 1994).

10 Bakhtin maintains a strict division between the actual world as "a source of representation and the world represented" in an artistic work (Bakhtin 1981, 253). He also claims that they are "indissolubly tied up with each other and find themselves in continual mutual interaction ... similar to the uninterrupted exchange of matter between living organisms and the environment that surrounds them. As long as the organism lives, it resists a fusion with the environment, but if it is torn out of its environment it dies" (ibid., 254). Likewise, cultural creations with designs invoking their own temporality are both inspired by, yet differ from, the world as it is lived. As cultural creations, they mediate the world as it is lived – its space and materiality – but the extent of the mediation was limited, depending on the tractability of living subjects, their imaginations, their social habits and routes of travel, already established designs, and so on.

11 In addition, chronotopes have a series of subcategories, such as the chronotope of meeting and the chronotope of adventure (Pearce 1994, 67).

12 This should probably be matsutake, not shitake.

13 By recounting their history in terms of the familiar story of immigrants who left their homeland to build a new life in Canada, Japanese Canadians are constructed as pioneers who became contributing members of society, embracing their new country despite legislated and popular racism (McAllister 1999).

14 This is also something Ruby Truly, a video artist who has worked with the elders, mentioned. She said that we tend to document the "good times," not the grim moments.

15 The most formal systems of Japanese writing.

16 Subjugated groups whose sense of self is constantly denigrated within the dominant order typically develop ways to negotiate and build other relations and spaces of trust as well as tactics that elude and usurp negating discourses.

Chapter 4: Continuity and Change between Generations

1 There was some sensitivity about the NIMC files. Later, after local Japanese Canadians became more familiar with me, some explained that the Kyowakai Society did not have all the documents pertaining to the NIMC since the project manager still had a large number of these documents in his files.

2 In contrast, the Sinixt Nations' presence, notably their efforts to protect their ancestral burial grounds, are not noted in tourist brochures and promotional materials.

3 The autobiographical narrative in the Japanese Canadian community is powerful, replicating the narrative of the development of settler societies: the arrival of the first (male) immigrants; their role as pioneers clearing land and working in primary industries; the social and cultural development of communities with marriage and the birth of children; the education and maturation of the second generation. In this narrative, their incarceration and violation of their rights halts the normal development of the community. The results include assimilation into the dominant population, with large numbers marrying individuals from outside the community (Kobayashi 1989).

4 For example, in my field notes I describe reading a 1982 article from the *Nelson Press* in which Mr. Matsushita is interviewed about the internment camps. He expressed very strong views about the violation of human rights and how younger generations should learn about what happened (Field notes, 10 August 1996).

5 See note 6 in the Introduction.

6 When I used sections of their accounts that I thought might be sensitive or cause embarrassment, I simply referred to the speaker as "one of the elders." I also showed these sections to the elders and asked if I could publish them and if there were any corrections.

7 Mrs. Kamegaya was born in Japan in the early 1900s. She met her husband while she was teaching in Tokyo. They came to Canada, and both taught in a Japanese-language school in New Westminster, BC. Her refined sense of decorum, peaceful nature, generosity, wry sense of humour, adventurous nature, and leadership qualities reflected not only her education and family upbringing but also her innovative approach to what was, from the viewpoint of a cultured Samurai family, a roughly hewn world with little sense of tradition. The government sent her to Kaslo in 1942 and her husband to a road camp. In 1965, they moved to New Denver. Here, she was an active member of the local community. She taught Japanese and also worked with the "disturbed children" in the old sanatorium. In 1988, she received the Order of the Chrysanthemum, one of the highest honours granted by the Japanese emperor to expatriate Japanese for their contribution to the development of Japanese culture overseas.

She was an artist with connections in different communities. She encouraged and collaborated with many young artists but had a special warmth for younger Nikkei. There are stories of her hitchhiking down the dusty gravel Slocan highway to the next village hours away so that she could participate in that community's haiku club. As well, there are accounts of her finesse at the koto, jamming with musicians visiting from Japan (Truly 1992a, 1995; Hartog 1994; Hoshino, Personal correspondence, 1996).

8 The bus tours were often part of the "camp reunions" organized by nisei. For documentation of the tours, see "Sentimental Journey," a booklet compiled by Bob Nimi et al. for the reunion and bus tour organized for Japanese Canadians interned in Bridge River, Devine, Lillooet, and Minto during the 1992 Homecoming Conference in Vancouver; also, Ruby Truly's 1991 video documentary, *With Our Own Eyes: A Trip to Lemon Creek*, records the reunion and bus tour of Japanese Canadians interned in the Lemon Creek camp.

9 There are many stories that circulate among Japanese Canadians about how issei parents vigorously disapproved of marriages between their children and non-Nikkei during the 1950s and 1960s. A few anecdotal accounts have been recorded (Truly 1992b; Hirabayashi 1997; Takata 1998).

10 Before the war, many Japanese Canadian children grew up in households and communities where Japanese was primarily spoken. In contrast to younger nisei, many of these older

nisei are less comfortable speaking English in a formal capacity in public and institutional settings.

11 That being said, the NIMC staff might not have known enough about gardening to realize the elders were doing perhaps what they might consider the equivalent of wiping cold, misty windows with their bare hands to ensure visitors inside the shacks could see the gardens (in which case, no doubt, the staff would have run to give them towels).

12 Previously, the relative power of men was based, for example, on their facility in English, their ability to secure higher wages and a more regular income, and their membership in a network of male-run community organizations.

13 There were exceptions to this and, especially among the nisei, there are notable cases where women had a public presence, notably Muriel Kitagawa (1985).

14 In the camps, women were required to directly contact government social services for clothing, schooling for their children, or welfare. With the absence or weakening of male control, women also made more independent decisions about the welfare of their families.

15 Although there is little research on Japanese Canadian mentorship, I have observed (and experienced) mentorship especially between sansei and nisei as well as issei women. Whether there is a sense of "extended family" (many born before the war can identify familial or social connections to other pre-war families) or not, this mentoring has encouraged many sansei to pursue careers in education and the arts as well as to accept positions of responsibility and initiate projects in the Nikkei community. As well, in contrast to men, the fact that many pre-war Japanese women who immigrated to Canada had high levels of education may have had an impact on the aspirations and interests of the next generation of women.

This is not to say that male authority has been completely overturned in Japanese Canadian organizations and families. Nor are all Japanese Canadian women professionals and community leaders groomed by mentors. But there are numerous women who are well regarded for their professional achievements, public service, and artistic careers in local and national forums. Significant, here, are also postwar immigrants from Japan, on whom Audrey Kobayashi has a forthcoming publication.

16 This was not just part of the general impact of feminism in North America. In Meiji-era Japan, industrialization and the adoption of Western ideologies resulted in the increasing confinement of women to households in positions with decreasing autonomy (Uno 1991). Thus it could be argued that asserting more autonomy was a return to "tradition."

Chapter 5: Making Space for Other Memories in the Historical Landscape

1 See for example, *The Silvery Slocan Heritage Tour: A Scenic Drive in the West Kootenay* (Butler et al. 1995), Raven Creations' *Vacation Guide Map of the West Kootenays* (1995), and *Welcome to Slocan Lake: New Denver, Silverton and Sandon* by the New Denver and Silverton's Chamber of Commerce (n.d.).

2 Photographs of the Doukhobor impoundment in New Denver can be found in the British Columbia Archives; for example, see "Visiting Day at New Denver Institution for 'Sons of Freedom' Children," acc. 193501-001 (also see Rak 2005).

3 Before the redress movement, several films and books by non-Japanese Canadians sympathetically and/or critically documented the history of Japanese Canadians. See La Violette (1948), Marlatt (1975), Ashworth (1979), Broadfoot (1979), Berger (1982), and Ward (1990 [1978]).

4 The Pacific National Exhibition (PNE) board of directors first rejected the idea of a plaque to mark Hastings Park, which "housed nearly 8,000 Japanese Canadians en route

264 Notes to pages 168-179

to forced exile." There was a "bitter battle" because the directors did not want to "sully" the reputation of the modern PNE. The battle finally went to city hall, but the PNE board was not swayed; therefore, the plaque was installed on city land just outside of the PNE. That was in 1989. In 1992, the garden and the plaque were accepted on the grounds of the PNE (Suzuki 1992).

5 Individuals have also taken initiatives; one example is Stephen Nemtin, who restored abandoned charcoal pits built by early Japanese settlers on Galiano Island. See Nemtin (2001) and Nemtin, Ohara, and Yesaki (2001).

6 This is the case for the Kohan Gardens in New Denver, the permanent exhibit at the Langham Cultural Centre in Kaslo, the temporary exhibit, "Rites of Passage," in the Mission Museum in 1992 and, more recently, "Leonard Frank: the BC Security Commission Photographs," curated by Bill Jeffries in consultation with Grace Eiko Thomson at Presentation House Gallery in North Vancouver in 2003.

7 Bringing people together to remember experiences they shared, whether of persecution or not, can also have other less generative results. As discussed in Chapter 4, during the group interview sessions at NIMC committee meetings, the elders found it very difficult to answer the detailed questions put to them by people who did not necessarily understand much about their experiences of persecution, especially because these individuals had also lived in the same valley for years and might have been implicated in the wartime events. But individuals might be just as uncomfortable discussing their experiences with other members of their own community. This might, for instance, make them vulnerable to criticism or compromise someone else's privacy. This again shows how our lives in the present, our social relations, are shaped by how the past is recounted.

8 She was probably referring to British Columbia Security Commission (BCSC) employees.

9 Japanese crackers.

10 Mr. Matsushita was the oldest son of a large family that, before the war, lived in the crowded, cramped, flimsy wooden cannery row housing piled onto wooden wharves in the fishing village of Steveston, located south of Vancouver along the Fraser River. When his father died, although he was young, he became responsible for supporting his mother, grandmother, and nine younger siblings, whose ages ranged from four to fifteen years. Life was a struggle. He had few chances to pursue his own dreams or opportunities. At the point when the government stripped the rights from Japanese Canadians and ordered them to vacate their homes for internment camps, Mr. Matsushita had just managed to invest his years of incremental savings into a fishing boat that would have ensured more financial security for his family. His family was sent to Kaslo. He stayed behind in the deserted cannery housing to tend to a brother who was in a nearby tuberculosis hospital.

Finally, the RCMP sent orders for him to report to Hastings Park, the grounds for the region's annual agricultural exhibition. This is where hundreds of Japanese Canadians outside Vancouver were confined in a vast maze of stalls for livestock, in some cases for months, until the internment camps were ready to receive them. This is where Mr. Matsushita became sick with tuberculosis. The BCSC sent him to the New Denver camp, where the government had built a sanatorium. One has the sense that he refashioned his life in New Denver. No longer positioned as the oldest son of a family living in the cannery buildings of Steveston, he explored his creative side as he recovered from his illness in New Denver and took on an identity as an artist, adopting, as he notes, an "Italianate style." Interestingly, his documentation of life in New Denver reveals a view at the intersection of the Japanese Canadian community and the local residents. His account suggests that, as a nisei with an adventurous and artistic flair, he would have had a worldview quite distinct from the issei in New Denver who adhered to more traditional conventions. His father had also decided that there was no reason to teach his children Japanese, for they were living in Canada. Without the same fluency in Japanese as, say, Mr. Senya Mori, he would have been positioned even more between the worlds of the issei, nisei, and local residents (Matsushita, Interview, 15 August 1996; Matsushita, Personal correspondence, 21 July 1996).

11 This description of the slide show is based on my field notes, but I also integrate subsequent reflections to provide a more vivid description of the imagery.

Chapter 6: In Memory of Others

1 A conservative estimate of the number of visitors who came to the Centre while I worked there would be twenty people a day; multiplied by eighty days (again, a conservative estimate, taking into consideration that I was not on the site every day), the total number would be approximately 1,600.

2 Exhibits of deceased members of the upper classes, by contrast, usually present the individual as an exemplar of moral fortitude, genius, and so on. Icons in popular culture are exceptions. But, in contrast to the racial other, they are usually not abject and have qualities that are desired or revered. Peering into the privacy of their lives offers proximity and intimacy or, in the case of the fallen icon, insight into their tragedies (and thus the human qualities that we share, even if they are weaknesses).

3 See Anderson (1991) for more discussion on the construction of stereotypical Chinatowns.

4 To protect the identities of the NIMC staff I do not refer to them by name and sometimes refer to them as local sansei and at other times as staff. I also have increased their numbers and randomly changed their gender to further protect their identities.

5 Derek Smith, who was one of my academic advisors, encouraged me to read extensively in this area. He provided a constant stream of ethnographic studies, classic and contemporary. He spent many hours discussing these texts with me, pointing to yet more readings, reflecting on the dynamics of fieldwork and at times offering marvellous accounts from his own research experiences in British Columbia and the North.

6 When I visited the museum and memorial for Auschwitz in 2005, I noted the defensive position taken by our Polish guide, who was probably even more than I a target for visitors' anxieties, hostilities, and guilt.

7 For example, among the three workers hired to operate the NIMC each summer, usually there has been not more than one non-Nikkei worker.

8 All information added after the field notes were first written is enclosed in square brackets. I include extra details in sections of my field notes where it seemed that more contextual explanation was needed.

9 This demonstrates the difficulties of having any control over defining the terms of their identities and community membership.

10 Buddhist temple or place of worship.

11 Traditional Japanese dance.

12 Lifton describes the way in which guilt radiated outward from the bombing of Hiroshima: "survivors feel guilty towards the dead; ordinary Japanese feel guilty towards survivors; and the rest of the world (particularly but not exclusively) feels guilty towards the Japanese" (Lifton 1967, 499).

13 See the propaganda film *Of Japanese Descent* produced for the Department of Labour (Canada, Department of Labour 1945).

14 In addition to field trips from local schools, a number of educators asked the staff about resources on the history of Japanese Canadians, explaining that their curriculum was inadequate in the area of social justice.

15 I am basing my description on others' accounts of bus tours as well as a tour I took in 1991, during which I worked for a video-documentary artist to record the participants' accounts. The video documentary was produced primarily for the participants on the tour (McAllister 1994).

16 Adults were under incredible duress in the camps but attempted to provide emotional security, especially for the younger children, and often expected their oldest children to take on responsibility for them. See Mona Oikawa's 2011 *Cartographies of Violence.*

17 If we assume, conservatively, that the man was in his mid-thirties, then his Nikkei parent would have been born at the latest in 1944 (the parent would be seventeen), but more likely in the mid- to late 1930s (the parent would be twenty-two to twenty-six). According to census data, for this demographic group the intermarriage rate was 18.3 percent for Japanese Canadian men and 26.8 percent for Japanese Canadian women (Kobayashi 1989, 32).

18 Participation of happa in community organizations became widespread in the 1990s (see McAllister 1991).

19 The names of Harry and his family have been changed.

Conclusion: Points of Departure

1 This passage is compiled from descriptions in the field notes that I produced for this research project.

2 The use of this term echoes a comment made by Roy Miki one morning during his visit to New Denver about the fragility of life as he observed blue bottle flies, dead, lying on their backs, scattered along the window sills of the mansion.

References

Interviews, Personal Correspondence, and Meetings

Butler, Ken. 1996. Interview by author. New Denver, BC. 19 September.

Hashimoto, Sakaye. 1996. Interview by author. New Denver, BC. 23 August.

Hoshino, Hisako. 1996. Personal correspondence with author. New Denver, BC. 9 September.

Inose, Pauli. 1996. Interview by author. New Denver, BC. 6 August.

Matsushita, Shoichi. 1996. Interview by author. New Denver, BC. 15 August.

–. 1996. Kyowakai Society. Discussion during History Preservation Meeting, New Denver, BC. 20 August.

–. 1996. Personal correspondence with author. 21 July.

–. 1996. Slide show commentary. New Denver, BC. 21 August.

Matsushita, Sumie. 1996. Interview by author. New Denver, BC. 15 August.

Miki, Roy. 1993. Personal correspondence with author. Vancouver, BC. 12 June.

Mori, Senya. 1996. Interview by author. New Denver, BC. 5 September.

Mori, Tad. 1996. Interview by author. New Denver, BC. 23 August.

Pamesko, Dan. 1996. Interview by author. New Denver, BC. 6 September.

Takahara, Kiyoko. 1996. Interview by author. New Denver, BC. 23 August.

Takana, Teresa. 1996. Discussion during History Preservation Committee meeting. 18 August.

–. 1995. Written correspondence. New Denver, BC. 12 August.

Takasaki, Mayu. 1990. Interview by author. Vancouver: Japanese Canadian National Museum and Archives Society. 15 July.

Truly, Ruby. 1998. Personal correspondence with author. 18 October.

Films and Videos

Barnaby, Jeff. 2004. *From Cherry English*. Montreal: Nutaaq Media Inc.

Canada. Department of Labour. 1945. *Of Japanese Descent*. Ottawa: Film Board of Canada.

Cheechoo, Shirley. 1997. *Silent Tears*. Montreal: Spoken Sound Productions and the National Film Board of Canada.

–. 2005. *Johnny Tootall*. Vancouver: Brightlight Pictures.

Claxton, Dana. 2001. *The People Dance*. Toronto: V tape.

–. 2004. *The Hill*. Toronto: V tape.

Christian, Dorothy. 2006. *A Spiritual Land Claim*. Vancouver: dpagan Productions.

de Valk, Mark. 1992. *The Pool: Reflections on Japanese Internment*. Vancouver: Falcon Films.

Fukushima, Michael. 1992. *Minoru: Memory of Exile*. Montreal: National Film Board of Canada.

Hopkins, Zoe Leigh. 2003. *A Prayer for a Good Day*. Toronto: V tape.

Lehrman, Jeanette. 1975. *Enemy Alien*. Ottawa: National Film Board of Canada.

Obomsawin, Alanis. 1986. *Richard Cardinal: Cry from a Diary of a Métis Child*. Montreal: National Film Board of Canada.

–. 1993. *Kanehsatake: 270 Years of Resistance.* Montreal: National Film Board of Canada.
–. 2006. *Waban-Aki: People from Where the Sun Rises.* Montreal: National Film Board of Canada.
Ohama, Linda. 1993. *The Last Harvest.* Harvest Productions Ltd.
–. 2001. *Obaachan's Garden.* Montreal: National Film Board of Canada.
Onodera, Midi. 1987. *Displaced View.* Toronto: Onodera Production and McAno Inc.
Todd, Loretta. 2001. *Today Is a Good Day: Remembering Chief Dan George.* Vancouver: Eagle Eye Films with Nimpkish Winds and Four Force Productions.
–. 2003. *Kainayssini Imanistaisiwa: The People Go On.* Montreal: National Film Board of Canada.
Truly, Ruby. 1991. *With Our Own Eyes: A Trip to Lemon Creek.* Vancouver: Datazoo Productions.
–. 1992a. *Homecoming Conference: Before the Uprooting – The Community Remembered.* Winnipeg: National Association of Japanese Canadians.
–. 1992b. *Homecoming Conference: The Intermarriage Workshop.* Winnipeg: National Association of Japanese Canadians.
–. 1995. *Nikkei Internment Memorial Centre.* Nelson: Datazoo Productions.
Wheeler, Anne. 1996. *The War between Us.* Toronto: Canadian Broadcasting Corporation.

Articles, Books, and Other Documents

Achebe, Chinua. 1988. An Image of Africa: Racism in Conrad's *Heart of Darkness.* In *Hopes and Impediments: Selected Essays, 1965-1987,* 1-19. Oxford: Heinemann International.
Adachi, Ken. 1991 [1976]. *The Enemy that Never Was: A History of the Japanese Canadians.* Toronto: McClelland and Stewart.
Alpers, Svetlana. 1991. The Museum as a Way of Seeing. In *Exhibiting Cultures: The Poetics and Politics of Museum Display,* edited by Ivan Karp and Steven D. Lavine. Washington: Smithsonian Institute.
Anderson, Kay J. 1991. *Vancouver's Chinatown: Racial Discourse in Canada, 1875-1980.* Montreal and Kingston: McGill-Queen's University Press.
Anderson, Kim. 1997. Reclaiming Native Space in Literature/Breaking New Ground: An Interview with Jeannette Armstrong. *West Coast Line: A Journal of Contemporary Writing and Criticism* 31/2: 49-65.
Anthias, Floya, and Nira Yuval-Davis. 1989. Introduction to *Woman-Nation-State,* edited by Floya Anthias and Nira Yuval-Davis, 1-15. London: MacMillian.
Ashworth, Mary. 1979. *The Forces Which Shaped Them: A History of the Education of Minority Group Children in British Columbia.* Vancouver: New Star Books.
Augé, Marc. 1995. *Non-Places: Introduction to an Anthropology of Supermodernity.* London: Verso.
Ayukawa, Michiko. 1995. Good Wives and Wise Mothers: Japanese Picture Brides in Early Twentieth-Century British Columbia. *BC Studies* 105 (6): 103-18.
–. 2005. Yasutaro Yamaga: Fraser Valley Berry Farmer, Community Leader, and Strategist. In *Nikkei in the Pacific Northwest: Japanese Americans and Japanese Canadians in the Twentieth Century,* edited by Louis Fiset and Gail M. Nomura, 71-94. Seattle: University of Washington Press.
Bakhtin, Mikhail. 1981. *The Dialogic Imagination: Four Essays.* Translated by Caryl Emerson and Michael Holquist. Edited by Michael Holoquist. Austin: University of Texas Press.
Bal, Mieke, Jonathan Crew, and Leo Spitzer. 1999a. Introduction to *Acts of Memory: Cultural Recall in the Present,* edited by Mieke Bal, Jonathan Crew, and Leo Spitzer, vii-xvii. London: University Press of New England.

–, eds. 1999b. *Acts of Memory: Cultural Recall in the Present*. London: University Press of New England.

Balibar, Etienne, and Immanuel Wallerstein. 1991. *Race, Nation, Class: Ambiguous Identities*. London: Verso.

Bannerji, Himani, ed. 1993. *Returning the Gaze: Essays on Racism, Feminism and Politics*. Toronto: Sister Vision Press.

–. 2000. *The Dark Side of the Nation: Essays on Multiculturalism, Nationalism and Gender*. Toronto: Canadian Scholars' Press.

BCSC (British Columbia Security Commission). 1942. *The Removal of Japanese from Protected Areas*. Ottawa: Government of Canada.

Ben-Amos, Avner. 1993. Monuments and Memory in French Nationalism. *History and Memory* 5 (2): 50-81.

Benjamin, Walter. 1985. The Work of Art in the Age of Mechanical Reproduction. In *Illuminations*, translated Harry Zohn, edited by Hannah Arendt, 217-251. New York, Schocken Books.

Bennett, Tony. 1995. *The Birth of the Museum: History, Theory, Politics*. New York: Routledge.

–. 2004. *Past Memory: Evolution, Museums, Colonialism*. London: Routledge.

Berger, Thomas R. 1982. *Fragile Freedoms: Human Rights and Dissent in Canada*. Toronto: Irwin Publishing.

Bickerton, Lillian, Leonard DeLozier, Linda Johnston, Donald A. Baird, and Laura M. Coles. 1988. *Manual for Small Archives*. Vancouver: Association of British Columbia Archivists.

Bischoping, Katherine, and Natalie Fingerhut. 1996. Borderlines: Indigenous People in Genocide Studies. *Canadian Review of Sociology and Anthropology* 33 (4): 481-506.

Blackmore, Michael. 1986a. Cartography. In *The Dictionary of Human Geography*, edited by Tom Bottomore, Laurence Harris, V.G. Kiernan, and Ralph Miliband, 41-44. Oxford: Blackwell.

–. 1986b. Maps and Map Images. In *The Dictionary of Human Geography*, edited by Tom Bottomore, Laurence Harris, V.G. Kiernan, and Ralph Miliband, 277-278. Oxford: Blackwell.

Bodnar, John. 1992. *Remaking America: Public Memory, Commemoration and Patriotism in the Twentieth Century*. Princeton: Princeton University Press.

Boggs, Carl. 1986. *Social Movements and Political Power: Emerging Forms of Radicalism in the West*. Philadelphia: Temple University Press.

Bourdieu, Pierre. 1991. *Language and Symbolic Power*. Oxford: Basil Blackwell.

Brandt, Susanne. 1994. The Memory Makers: Museums and Exhibition of the First World War. *History and Memory* 6 (1): 95-122.

Briggs, Jean L. 1970. *Never in Anger: Portrait of an Eskimo Family*. Cambridge, MA: Harvard University Press.

Broadfoot, Barry. 1979. *Years of Sorrow, Years of Shame: The Story of the Japanese Canadians in World War II*. Don Mills, ON: Paperjacks.

Brown, Wendy. 2001. *Politics Out of History*. Princeton and Oxford: Princeton University Press.

Brunner, José. 1997. Pride and Memory: Nationalism, Narcissism and the Historians' Debates in Germany and Israel. *History and Memory* 9 (1/2): 256-300.

Bulletin. 1991. J-C Cemetery Memorial Monument Planned for Port Alberni. *The Bulletin: A Journal for and about the Nikkei Community* 33 (11): 16.

–. 1992a. Kaslo Commemorates Internment. *The Bulletin: A Journal for and about the Nikkei Community* 34 (7): 9.

–. 1992b. Plaque Remembers Exiled Japanese Canadians: J-C Cemetery Memorial Monument Planned for Port Alberni. *The Bulletin: A Journal for and about the Nikkei Community* 34 (9): 13.

Bulletin Staff. 1991. Chemainus Revisited. *The Bulletin: A Journal for and about the Nikkei Community* 33 (9): 20-23.

–. 1995. BC Parks and Langham Society Interpret Road Camps. *The Bulletin: A Journal for and about the Nikkei Community* 37 (2): 10.

Burns, J.S. 1944. Correspondence to Mr. W.A. Eastwood, General Manager of the BC Security Commission, 8 June. Library and Archives Canada, Records of the Department of the British Columbia Security Commission, RG 36/27, vol. 26, file 1100.

Butler, Ken, Dan Nicholson, Jan Murray, and Rodney Huculak. 1995. *The Silvery Slocan Heritage Tour: A Scenic Drive in the West Kootenay*. New Denver, BC: The Word Publishing.

Butler, Shelley Ruth. 2008 [1999]. *Contested Representations: Revisiting into the Heart of Africa*. Peterborough, ON: Broadview Press.

Canada. n.d. The Details of Information and Instructions to Internees' Family. Library and Archives Canada.

–. 1996. *The Royal Commission on Aboriginal Peoples, Volume I*. Ottawa: Government of Canada.

Canada. Department of Labour. 1947. *Re-establishment of Japanese in Canada, 1944-1946*. January.

–. 1978. The Administration of Japanese in Canada, 1942-1944. In *Two Reports of Japanese Canadians in World War II*. New York: Arno Press.

Carroll, William K., ed. 1992. *Organizing Dissent: Contemporary Social Movements in Theory and Practice*. Toronto: Garamond Press.

Caruth, Cathy. 1995. Capturing the Past: Introduction. In *Trauma: Explorations in Memory*, edited by Cathy Caruths, 151-157. Baltimore: Johns Hopkins University Press.

Chow, Rey. 2002. *The Protestant Ethnic and the Spirit of Capitalism*. New York: Columbia University Press.

Clifford, James. 1988. *The Predicament of Culture: Twentieth-Century Ethnography, Literature, and Art*. Boston: Harvard University Press.

Clifford, James, and George E. Marcus, eds. 1986. *Writing Culture: The Politics and Poetics of Ethnography*. Berkeley and Los Angeles: University of California Press.

Cohen, Erik. 1996. A Phenomenology of Tourist Experience. In *Theoretical and Empirical Investigations*, edited by Yiorgos Apostolopoulos, Stella Leivadi, and Andrew Yiannakis, 90-114. London: Routledge.

Comaroff, Jean, and John Comaroff. 1992. *Ethnography and the Historical Imagination*. San Francisco: Westview Press.

Connerton, Paul. 1989. *How Societies Remember*. Cambridge: Cambridge University Press.

Cosgrove, Denis, ed. 1999. *Mappings*. London: Reaktion Books.

Crapanzano, Vincent. 1972. *The Fifth World of Forster Bennett: Portrait of a Navaho*. New York: Viking Press.

–. 1980. *Tuhami: Portrait of a Moroccan*. Chicago: University of Chicago Press.

Creef, Elena Tajima. 2004. *Imaging Japanese Americans*. New York: New York University Press.

Crosby, Marcia. 1991. Construction of the Imaginary Indian. In *Vancouver Anthology: The Institutional Politics of Art*, edited by Stan Douglas, 267-294. Vancouver: Talon Books.

Crownshaw, Richard. 2000. Performing Memory in Holocaust Museums. *Performance Research* 5(3): 18-29.

Cruickshank, Julie. 2005. *Do Glaciers Listen? Local Knowledge, Colonial Encounters, and Social Imagination.* Vancouver: UBC Press.

Cruickshank, Julie, in collaboration with Angela Sidney, Kitty Smith, and Annie Ned. 1990. *Life Lived Like a Story.* Vancouver: UBC Press.

Davidson, R.A. 1944. Memorandum to Geo. Collins, Commissioner of Japanese Placement, Re: Change of Policy – Japanese, August 31. Library and Archives Canada, Records of the Department of the British Columbia Security Commission, RG 36, vol. 16, file 622, part 3.

Desbrisay, F. E. In F.W. Jackson, W.R. Bone, Mary Sutherland, and George F. Davidson. 1944. Report of the Royal Commission to Inquire into the Provisions Made for the Welfare and Maintenance of Persons of the Japanese Race Resident in Settlements in the Province of British Columbia, 12 January. Library and Archives Canada, Records of the Department of the British Columbia Security Commission, RG 36-27, 22.2.

Dumont, Marilyn. 2001. *Green Girl Dreams Mountains.* Lantzville, BC: Oolichan Books.

Duncan, James, and David Ley, eds. 1993. *Place/Culture/Representation.* New York: Routledge.

Eastwood, W.A. in F. W. Jackson, W.R. Bone, Mary Sutherland, and George F. Davidson. 1944. Report of the Royal Commission to Enquire into the Provisions Made for the Welfare and Maintenance of Persons of the Japanese Race Resident in Settlements in the Province of British Columbia, 12 January. Library and Archives Canada, Records of the Department of the British Columbia Security Commission, RG 36-27, 22.2.

Eng, David L. 2001. *Racial Castration: Managing Masculinity in Asian America.* Durham: Duke University Press.

Fanon, Frantz. 1967. *Black Skins, White Masks.* New York: Grove.

Farmer, Paul. 1996. On Suffering and Structural Violence: A View from Below. *Daelalus,* 125 (1): 261-283.

Folch-Serra, M. 1990. Place, Voice, Space: Mikhail Bakhtin's Dialogic Landscape. *Environment and Planning D: Space and Society,* 8: 255-297.

Foote, Kenneth E. 2003. *Shadowed Ground: America's Landscapes of Violence and Tragedy.* Austin: University of Texas Press.

Foucault, Michel. 1979. *Discipline and Punish: The Birth of the Prison.* New York: Vintage Books.

Fournier, Suzanne, and Ernie Crey. 1998. *Stolen from Our Embrace: The Abduction of First Nations Children and the Restoration of Aboriginal Communities.* Toronto: Douglas and McIntyre.

Gagnon, Monika Kin. 2000. *Other Conundrums: Race, Culture, and Canadian Art.* Vancouver: Arsenal Pulp Press/Artspeak Gallery/Kamloops Art Gallery.

–. 2006. Tender Research: Field Notes from the Nikkei Internment Memorial Centre, New Denver, BC. *Canadian Journal of Communication* 31: 215-225.

Gagnon, Monika Kin, and Richard Fung. 2002. *13 Conversations about Art and Cultural Race Politics.* Montreal: Artextes Editions.

Geddes, Jennifer L., ed. 2001. *Evil after Postmodernism: Histories, Narratives, and Ethics.* London: Routledge.

Geertz, Clifford. 1973. *The Interpretation of Culture.* New York: Basic Books.

–. 1983. *Local Knowledge.* New York: Basic Books.

Geiger-Adams, Andrea. 2005. Writing Racial Barriers into Law: Upholding B.C.'s Denial of Vote to Its Japanese Canadian Citizens. In *Nikkei in the Pacific Northwest: Japanese Americans and Japanese Canadians in the Twentieth Century,* edited by Louis Fiset and Gail M. Nomura, 20-43. Seattle: University of Washington Press.

Gilman, Sander L. 1986. Black Bodies, White Bodies: Toward an Iconography of Female Sexuality in Late Nineteenth-Century Art, Medicine and Literature. In *Race, Writing, and Difference,* edited by Henry Louis Gates Jr., 223-261. Chicago: University of Chicago Press.

Go and Do. Centre Tells of Struggles of the Japanese. *Go and Do: West Kootenay's Visitor Magazine.* 1996. Fall/Summer: 137.

Goldberg, David Theo. 1993. *Racist Culture: The Philosophy and the Politics of Meaning.* Cambridge: Blackwell.

Good, Anthony. 2007. *Anthropology and Expertise in the Asylum Courts.* Abingdon (Oxon), UK: Routledge-Cavendish.

Gordon, Avery. 1997. *Ghostly Matters: Hauntings and the Sociological Imagination.* London: University of Minnesota Press.

Goto, Hiromi. 1994. *Chorus of Mushrooms.* Edmonton: NeWest Press.

–. 2001. *The Kappa Child.* Calgary: Red Deer Press.

Green, David. 1984. Classified Subjects: Photography and Anthropology, the Technology of Power. *Ten 8* 14: 30-37.

Greenaway, John Endo. 1995. Katherine Shozawa: Looking at History from Inside Out. *The Bulletin: A Journal for and about the Nikkei Community* 37 (4): 17-21.

Gunn, Sean. 1979. *Inalienable Rice: A Chinese and Japanese Canadian Anthology.* Vancouver: Intermedia Press.

Guterson, Hugh. 1993. Exploding Anthropology's Canon in the World of the Bomb: Ethnographic Writing on Militarism. *Journal of Contemporary Ethnography* 22 (1): 59-79.

Haig-Brown, Celia. 1988. *Resistance and Renewal: Surviving the Indian Residential School.* Vancouver: Tillacum Library.

Halbwachs, Maurice. 1980. *On Collective Memory.* Translated by Francis J. Ditter Jr. and Vida Yazdi Ditter. New York: Harper and Row.

Hall, Stuart, Dorothy Hobson, Andrew Lowe, and Paul Willis, eds. 1980. *Culture, Media, Language.* London: Hutchinson University Library in Association with the Centre for Contemporary Cultural Studies at the University of Birmingham.

Harley, J.B., and P. Laxton, eds. 2002. *The New Nature of Maps: Essays in the History of Cartography.* Baltimore and London: Johns Hopkins University Press.

Harrison, Faye V., ed. 1997 [1991]. *Decolonizing Anthropology: Moving Further towards an Anthropology of Liberation.* Washington, DC: American Anthropological Association.

Hartog, Diana. 1994. Biography in Chie Kamegaya. In *Seasons in New Denver: Haiku by Kamegaya Chie,* edited by Diana Hartog, 3-4. Silverton, BC: Laughing Raven Press.

Herman, Judith Lewis. 1992. *Trauma and Recovery: The Aftermath of Violence – From Domestic Abuse to Political Terror.* New York: Basic Books.

Hirabayashi, Gordon. 1997. Children of Intermarriage. *The Bulletin: A Journal for and about the Nikkei Community* 34 (6): 15.

Hirsch, Marianne. 1997a. *Family Frames: Photography, Narrative and Postmemory.* London: Harvard University Press.

–. 1997b. Mourning and Postmemory. In *Family Frames: Photography, Narrative and Postmemory,* 17-40. London: Harvard University Press.

Hirsch, Marianne, and Leo Spitzer. 2006. There Was Never a Camp Here: Searching for Vapniarka. In *Locating Memory: Photographic Acts,* edited by Annette Kuhn and Kirsten Emiko McAllister, 135-154. Oxford: Berghahn Books.

Holloway, Julian, and James Kneale. 2000. Mikhail Bakhtin: Dialogics of Space. In *Thinking Space,* edited by M. Crang, and N. Thrift, 71-88. London: Routledge.

Hunt, Alan. 1999. The Purity Wars: Making Sense of Moral Militancy. *Theoretical Criminology* 3 (4): 409-436.

Huyssen, Andreas. 2003. Present Pasts: Media, Politics, Amnesia. In *Present Pasts: Urban Palimpsests and the Politics of Memory*, 1-29. Stanford, CA: Stanford University Press.

Ibuki, Norm. 1993. Langham Display of Wartime Japanese Canadians Opens. *The Bulletin: A Journal for and about the Nikkei Community* 35 (5): 16-17.

Inwood, Bob. 1992. *Nikkei Evacuation Memorial Centre Proposal*. New Denver, BC: Robert Inwood and Associates.

Ito, Roy. 1984. *We Went to War: The Story of Japanese Canadians Who Served during the First and Second World Wars*. Stittsville, ON: Canada's Wings.

Ito, Sally. 1998. *Floating Shore*. Toronto: Mercury Press.

Izumi, Masumi. 2005. Reclaiming and Reinventing "Powell Street": Reconstruction of the Japanese Canadian Community in Post-World War II Vancouver. In *Nikkei in the Pacific Northwest: Japanese Americans and Japanese Canadians in the Twentieth Century*, edited by Louis Fiset and Gail M. Nomura, 308-333. Seattle: University of Washington Press.

Jackson, F. W., W.R. Bone, Mary Sutherland, and George F. Davidson. 1944. Report of the Royal Commission to Enquire into the Provisions Made for the Welfare and Maintenance of Persons of the Japanese Race Resident in Settlements in the Province of British Columbia. January 12. Library and Archives Canada, Records of the Department of the British Columbia Security Commission, RG 36-27, 22.2.

Jacobs-Huey, Lanita. 2002. The Natives Are Gazing and Talking Back: Reviewing the Problematics of Positionality, Voice, and Accountability among Native Anthropologists. *American Anthropologist* 104 (3): 791-804.

Japanese Canadian Centennial Project. 1978. *A Dream of Riches: Japanese Canadians, 1877-1977*. Vancouver: JCCP Redress Committee.

Jordan, Winthrop. 1968. *White over Black: American Attitudes towards the Negro, 1550-1812*. Baltimore, MD: Penguin.

Kamboureli, Smaro. 2000. *Scandalous Bodies: Diasporic Literature in English Canada*. New York: Oxford University Press.

–. 2005. Disciplining Asian Canadian Studies: Method, Diaspora, Nation. Paper presented at Virtually American? Denationalizing North American Studies conference, University of Siegen, Germany, October 6-7.

Kamegaya Chie. 1994. *Seasons in New Denver: Haiku by Kamegaya Chie*. Edited by Diana Hartog. Silverton, BC: Laughing Raven Press.

Karp, Ivan. 1992. Introduction to *Museums and Communities*, edited by Ivan Karp, Christine Mullen Kreamer, and Steven D. Lavine, 1-18. Washington: Smithsonian Institute.

Ketelaar, Eric. 2002. Archival Temples, Archival Prisons: Modes of Power and Protection. *Archival Science* 2: 221-238.

Khalili, Laleh. 2005. Places of Memory and Mourning: Palestinian Commemoration in the Refugee Camps of Lebanon. *Comparative Studies of South Asia, Africa and the Middle East* 25 (1): 30-45.

Kirmayer, Laurence. 1996. Landscapes of Memory: Trauma, Narrative, and Dissociation. In *Past Tense: Cultural Essays in Trauma and Memory*, edited by Paul Antze and Michael Lambek, 173-198. Routledge: New York.

Kirshenblatt-Gimblett, Barbara. 1991. Objects of Ethnography. In *Exhibiting Cultures: The Poetics and Politics of Museum Display*, edited by Ivan Karp and Steven D. Lavine, 386-443. Washington: Smithsonian Institute.

Kitagawa, Muriel. 1985. *This Is My Own: Letters to Wes and Other Writings on Japanese Canadians, 1941-1948*. Edited by Roy Miki. Vancouver: Talonbooks.

Kiyooka, Roy. 1997a. *Mothertalk: Life Stories of Mary Kiyoshi Kiyooka*. Edited by Daphne Marlatt. Edmonton: NeWest Publishers.

–. 1997b. *Pacific Windows: Collected Poems of Roy Kiyooka*. Edited by Roy Miki. Burnaby, BC: Talonbooks.

Knight, Rolf, and Maya Koizumi. 1976. *A Man of Our Times: The Life-History of a Japanese-Canadian Fisherman*. Vancouver: New Star Books.

Kobayashi, Audrey. 1987. The Uprooting of Japanese Canadians after 1941. *Tribune* 5 (1): 28-35.

–. 1989. *A Demographic Profile of Japanese Canadians and Social Implications for the Future*. Ottawa: Department of the Secretary of State, Canada.

–. 1992a. The Japanese-Canadian Redress Settlement and Its Implications for "Race Relations." *Canadian Ethnic Studies* 24 (9): 1-19.

–. 1992b. *Memories of Our Past: A Brief History and Walking Tour of Powell Street*. Vancouver: NRC Publishing.

–. 1994a. Colouring the Field: Gender, "Race," and the Politics of Fieldwork. *Professional Geographer* 46 (1): 73-80.

–. 1994b. For the Sake of the Children: Japanese/Canadian Workers/Mothers. In *Women Work and Place*, edited by Audrey Kobayashi, 45-72. Montreal: McGill-Queen's University Press.

Kobayashi, Cassandra, and Roy Miki, eds. 1989. *The Spirit of Redress: Japanese Canadians in Conference*. Vancouver: JC Publications.

Kogawa, Joy. 1983. *Obasan*. New York: Penguin.

–. 1992. *Itsuka*. Toronto: Viking.

Kondo, Dorinne K. 1986. Dissolution and Reconstitution of Self: Implications for Anthropological Epistemology. *Cultural Anthropology* 1 (1): 74-88.

Kracauer, Siegfried. 1995. *The Mass Ornament: Weimar Essays*. Translated and edited by Thomas Y. Levin. Cambridge and London: Harvard University Press.

Krauss, Rosalind. 1999. Photography's Discursive Spaces. In *Visual Culture: The Reader*, edited by Jessica Evans and Stuart Hall, 193-210. London: Sage.

Kreamer, Christine Mullen. 1992. Defining Communities through Exhibiting and Collecting. In *Museums and Communities*, edited by Ivan Karp, Christine Mullen Kreamer, and Steven D. Lavine, 367-381. Washington: Smithsonian Institute.

Kugelmass, Jack. 1996. Landscapes of Memory: Trauma, Narrative, and Dissociation. In *Past Tense: Cultural Essays in Trauma and Memory*, edited by Paul Antze and Michael Lambek, 199-214. New York: New York.

Kuhn, Annette. 1995. *Family Secrets: Acts of Memory and Imagination*. London: Verso.

La Violette, Forrest. 1948. *The Canadian Japanese and World War II*. Toronto: University of Toronto Press.

Laclau, Ernesto, and Chantal Mouffe. 1992. *Hegemony and Socialist Strategy: Towards a Radical Democratic Politics*. London: Verso.

Langer, Lawrence L. 1991. *Holocaust Testimonials: The Ruins of Memory*. London: Yale University Press.

Lansberg, Alison. 2004. *Prosthetic Memory: The Transformation of American Remembrance in the Age of Mass Culture*. New York: Columbia University Press.

Lee, Robert G. 1999. *Orientals: Asian Americans in Popular Culture*. Philadelphia: Temple University Press.

Lifton, Robert Jay. 1967. *Death in Life: Survivors of Hiroshima*. New York: Random House.

–. 1979. *The Broken Connection: On Death and the Continuity of Life*. New York: Simon and Schuster.

Lowry, Glen. 2001. After the Ends: CanLit and the Unravelling of Nation, "Race," and Space in the Writing of Michael Ondaajte, Daphne Marlatt, and Roy Kiyooka. PhD dissertation, Simon Fraser University, Burnaby, BC.

–. 2002. Surrender by Roy Miki. *Cross-Cultural Poetics* 11: 163-172.

–. 2003. "i missed you in the past tense": An Introduction to the Poetry of Roy Miki. *Ellipse* 70: 10-19.

Lowry, Glen, and Sook C. Kong, eds. 2001. *In-Equations:* "Can Asia Pacific." Special issue, *West Coast Line* 34 (3).

MacCannell, Dean. 1989. *The Tourist: A New Theory of the Leisure Class.* New York: Schocken Books.

Mackinnon, J.F. 1947. Re: Analysis of New Denver Project, 12 February. Library and Archives Canada, RG 36/27, vol. 24, file 1005, pt 1.

Makabe, Tomoko. 1995. *Picture Brides: Japanese Women in Canada.* Translated by Kathleen Chisato Merken. Toronto: University of Toronto Press.

–. 1998. *The Canadian Sansei.* Toronto: University of Toronto Press.

Mamdani, Mahmood. 2004. From When Victims Become Killers: Colonialism, Nativism and the Genocide in Rwanda. In *Violence in War and Peace,* edited by Nancy Scheper-Hughes and Philippe Bourgeois, 468-474. Oxford: Blackwell Publishing.

Manganyi, Noel Chabani. 1977. *Alienation and the Body in Racist Society: A Study of the Society that Invented Soweto.* New York: NOK Publishers.

Marchetti, Gina. 1993. *Romance and the Yellow Peril: Race, Sex, and Discursive Strategies in Hollywood Fiction.* Berkeley: University of California Press.

Marcus, George E., and Michael M.J. Fischer. 1986. *Anthropology as Cultural Critique: An Experimental Moment in the Human Sciences.* Chicago and London: University of Chicago Press.

Marion, Jean-Luc. 1991. *God without Being.* Chicago: University of Chicago Press.

Marlatt, Daphne, ed. 1975. *Steveston Recollected: A Japanese-Canadian History.* Victoria: Aural History, British Columbia Archives.

Marx, Karl. 1963 [1884]. Economic and Philosophical Manuscripts. In *Karl Marx: Early Writings,* edited and translated by Tom Bottomore, 69-219. New York: McGraw-Hill Book Company.

Mass, Amy Iwasaki. 1986. Psychological Effects of the Camps on Japanese Americans. In *Japanese Americans: From Relocation to Redress,* edited by Roger Daniels, Sandra C. Taylor, and Harry H.L. Kitano, 159-162. Salt Lake City: University of Utah Press.

Massey, Doreen. 1993. Power-Geometry and a Progressive Sense of Place. In *Mapping the Futures: Local Cultures, Global Change,* edited by Jon Bird et al. London: Routledge.

Maxwell, Anne. 1999. *Colonial Photography and Exhibitions: Representations of the "Native" and the Making of European Identities.* London: Leicester University Press.

McAllister, Kirsten Emiko. 1991. The Changing Face of the Japanese Canadian Community: Children of Intermarriage – An Ambivalent Issue? *The Bulletin: A Journal for and about the Nikkei Community* 33 (5): 7.

–. 1992a. Asians in Hollywood. *CineAction* 30: 8-13.

–. 1992b. Issue of Injustice Reveals Different Perspectives. *The Bulletin: A Journal for and about the Nikkei Community* 34 (6): 15, 21.

–. 1993. Cultural Production and Alternative Political Practices: Dialogic Cultural Forms and the Public Sphere in the Japanese Canadian Community. MA Thesis, Simon Fraser University.

–. 1994. Confronting Official History with Our Own Eyes: Video Documentary in the Japanese Canadian Community. In "Colour, An Issue," edited by Roy Miki and Fred Way. Special issue, *West Coast Line* 13 (14) Spring-Fall: 66-84.

–. 1998. The Hum ... : Locating the Video Documentary of Ruby Truly. *Interior Motives: Part II*, 8-10. Exhibition catalogue. Kelowna, BC: Alternator Gallery.

–. 1999. Narrating Japanese CanadiansIn and Out of the Canadian Nation: A Critique of Realist Forms of Representation. *Canadian Journal of Communication* 24: 79-103.

–. 2001. Captivating Debris: Unearthing a World War Two Internment Camp. In "Testimonial Cultures," edited by Jackie Stacey and Sara Ahmed. Special issue, *Cultural Values* 5 (1): 97-114.

–. 2002. Held Captive: The Postcard and the Icon. In "Photography, Autobiographical Memory, Cultural Literacy," edited by Jerald Zaslove and Martha Langford. Special issue, *West Coast Line*. 35(1): 20-40.

–. 2006a. Stories of Escape: Family Photographs from World War Two Internment Camps. In *Locating Memory: Photographic Acts*, edited by Annette Kuhn and Kirsten Emiko McAllister, 81-110. Oxford and New York: Berghahn Books.

–. 2006b. Photographs of Japanese Canadian Internment Camps: Mourning Loss and Invoking a Future. *Visual Studies* 21 (2): 133-156.

McAllister, Kirsten, and Scott McFarlane. 1992. Reflections on the Pool: Interning Japanese Canadian History. *The Bulletin: A Journal for and about the Nikkei Community* 34 (12): 25.

McAllister, Kirsten, and Mari-Jane Medenwaldt. 1992. Intermarriage/Coupling in the Japanese Canadian Community. *The Bulletin: A Journal for and about the Nikkei Community* 34 (9): 25.

McAllister, Kirsten, and Mona Oikawa. 1996. Research: Re-search. Search. Searching, Sear-ch-ing. *Nikkei Voice: A National Forum for Japanese Canadians* 10 (2): 1, 11.

McFarlane, Scott Toguri. 1995. Covering Internment and the Narrative of Internment. In *Privileging Positions: The Site of Asian American Studies*, edited by Gary Y. Okihiro, Marilyn Alquizola, Dorothy Fujita Rony, and K. Scott Wong, 401-411. Pullman, WA: Washington State University Press.

McLaren, Angus. 1990. *Our Own Master Race: Eugenics in Canada, 1885-1945*. Toronto: McClelland and Stewart.

Mealing, F. M. 1977. Preface and Chronology. In Toil and Peaceful Life: Portraits of Doukhobors, compiled and translated by Marjorie Malloff and Peter Ogloff. *Sound Heritage*, 6 (4): 1-8.

Memmi, Albert. 1965. *The Colonizer and the Colonized*. New York: Orion Press.

Merleau-Ponty, Maurice. 1994 [1962]. *The Phenomenology of Perception*. London: Routledge.

Miki, Roy. 1991. *Saving Face: Selected Poems, 1976-1988*. Winnipeg: Turnstone Press.

–. 1995. *Random Access File*. Red Deer, AB: Red Deer College Press.

–. 1998a. *Broken Entries: Race, Subjectivity, Writing*. Toronto: Mercury Press.

–. 1998b. Redress: A Community Imagined. In *Broken Entries: Race, Subjectivity, Writing*. Toronto: Mercury Press.

–. 1998c. "Shikata Ga Nai": A Note on Seeing/Japanese Canadian. In *Broken Entries: Race, Subjectivity, Writing*, 29-53. Toronto: Mercury Press.

–. 1998d. Sliding the Scale of Elision: "Race" Constructs/Cultural Praxis. In *Broken Entries: Race, Subjectivity, Writing*, 125-159. Toronto: Mercury Press.

–. 2001. *Surrender*. Toronto: Mercury Press.

–. 2004. *Redress: Inside the Japanese Canadian Call for Redress*. Vancouver: Raincoast Books.

Miki, Roy, and Cassandra Kobayashi. 1991. *Justice in Our Time: The Japanese Canadian Redress Settlement*. Vancouver: Talon Books.

Miki, Roy, and Fred Wah, eds. 1994. "Colour, An Issue." Special issue, *West Coast Line* 13 (14) Spring-Fall.

Minh-ha, Trinh T. 1989. *Woman, Native, Other*. Bloomington: Indianapolis Press.

Mochizuki, Cindy Naomi. 2006. Kanashibari, Shadow Archive. Masters of Fine Arts Documentation, Simon Fraser University, Burnaby, BC.

Murakami, Rose. 2005. *Ganbaru: The Murakami Family of Salt Spring Island*. Salt Spring Island: Salt Spring Garden Society.

Murdy, Justine. 1992. Nikkei Evacuation Memorial Centre: A Contextual History. NIMC Records, New Denver, BC. April.

Murray, Jan. 2007. Treaty Commission Hears Sinixt Concerns. *Valley Voice* 16 (17) 29 August: 1.

Myerhoff, Barbara. 1980. *Number Our Days*. New York: Simon and Schuster.

Nagata, Donna K. 1993. *Legacy of Justice: Exploring the Cross-Generational Impact of the Japanese American Internment*. New York: Plenum Press.

Nakano, Takeo Ujo, with Leatrice Nakano. 1980. *Within Barbed Wire Fence: A Japanese Man's Account of His Internment in Canada*. Toronto: University of Toronto Press.

Nakayama, Gordon G. 1984. *Issei*. Toronto: NC Press.

Narayan, Kirin. 2003 [1997]. How Native Is a "Native" Anthropologist? In *Feminist Postcolonial Theory: A Reader,* edited by Reina Lewis and Sara Mills, 285-305. New York: Routledge.

National Association of Japanese Canadians. 1984. *Redress for Japanese Canadians: Community Forum Proceedings*. Vancouver: NAJC.

–. 1985. *Democracy Betrayed: The Case for Redress*. Winnipeg: NAJC.

–. 1988. *Justice in Our Time: Redress for Japanese Canadians*. Vancouver: NAJC.

Nemtin, Stephen. 2001. Japanese Charcoal Pit Kilns on the Gulf Islands. *British Columbia Historical News* 43 (2): 2-3.

Nemtin, Stephen, Mary Ohara, and Mitsuo Yesaki, panelists. 2000. Japanese Charcoal Pits of Galiano Island. *Nikkei Images* 5 (3): 10.

New Denver and Silverton Chamber of Commerce. n.d. *Welcome to Slocan Lake: Map of New Denver, Silverton and Sandon*. New Denver, BC: New Denver and Silverton Chamber of Commerce.

Nikkei Voice Staff. 1997. Mixed Blessings: Intermarriage in the Japanese Canadian Community. *Nikkei Voice* 11 (3): 1, 11.

NIMC (Nikkei Internment Memorial Centre). n.d. Nikkei Internment Memorial Centre Interpretive Team's Notes. Kyowakai Society files in the Nikkei Internment Memorial Centre. Accessed 1996. New Denver, BC.

NIMC (Nikkei Internment Memorial Centre). 1992. Agreement with the Langham Cultural Centre. NIMC Records, New Denver, BC.

Nimi, Bob, Leah Weiss, Kel Lambright, and David Nimi, eds. 1992. *Sentimental Journey: A Booklet Published for the 50th-Year Anniversary Reunion of the Japanese-Canadians Relocated to Bridge River, Devine, East Lillooet, and Minto*. n.p.

Nora, Pierre. 1989. Between Memory and History: Les lieux de mémoire. *Representations* 26: 7-25.

Nutley (Hanazawa), Judy. 1992. Internal Racism in the JC Community #3. *The Bulletin: A Journal for and about the Nikkei Community* 34 (4): 26-27.

Ohama, Baco. 2001. *Miyoshi: A Taste that Lingers Unfinished in the Mouth*. Lethbridge, AB: Southern Alberta Art Gallery.

Oikawa, Mona. 1986. "Driven to Scatter Far and Wide": The Forced Resettlement of Japanese Canadians to Southern Ontario, 1944-1949. MA Thesis, University of Toronto.

–. 2002. Cartographies of Violence: Women, Memory and the Subject(s) of Internment. In *Race, Space, and the Law: Unmapping White Settler Society,* edited by Sharene Razack, 71-98. Toronto: Between the Lines.

–. 2011. *Cartographies of Violence*. Toronto: University of Toronto Press.

Oiwa, Keibo, ed. 1991. *Stone Voices: Wartime Writings of Japanese Canadian Issei*. Montreal: Véhicule Press.

Okano, Haruko. 1992. *Come Spring: Journey of a Sansei*. North Vancouver, BC: Gallerie Publications.

Okano, Haruko, and Judy Nutley (Hanazawa). 1992. Internal Racism in the JC Community: The Enemy Within, #1. *The Bulletin: A Journal for and about the Nikkei Community* 34 (2): 10-11.

Opp, James, and John Walsh. 2010. *Placing Memory and Remembering Place in Canada*. Vancouver: UBC Press.

Oxford Modern Dictionary. 1996. 2nd ed. Oxford: Oxford Univerity Press.

Parker, Andrew, Mary Russo, Doris Sommer, and Patricia Yaeger, eds. 1992. *Nationalisms and Sexualities*. New York: Routledge.

Pearce, Lynne. 1994. *Reading Dialogics*. New York: Routledge.

Pearkes, Eileen Delehanty. 2002. *The Geography of Memory: Recovering Stories of a Landscape's First People*. Nelson, BC: Kutenai House Press.

Penguin English Dictionary. 1979. New York: Penguin Books.

Pickersgill, T.B. 1945a. Correspondence to Mr. A. MacNamara, Deputy Minister of Labour, Canada, Library and Archives Canada, Records of the Department of the British Columbia Security Commission, RG 36 vol. 16, file 622, part 2.

–. 1945b. Re: Carrying Out Segregation, June 12. Library and Archives Canada, Records of the Department of the British Columbia Security Commission. RG 36, vol. 16, file 622, part 1.

Pickles, John. 2004. *A History of Spaces: Cartographic Reason, Mapping and the Geo-coded World*. London and New York: Routledge.

Pookachow, N. 1944. Correspondence to the BC Security Commission, 22 May. Library and Archives Canada, RG 36-27, vol. 26, file 1100.

Potter, Jonathan. 1996. *Representing Reality: Discourse, Rhetoric and Social Construction*. London: Sage.

Price Waterhouse. 1986. *Economic Losses of Japanese Canadians after 1941*. Winnipeg: National Association of Japanese Canadians.

Pryce, Paula. 1999. *"Keeping the Lakes' Way": Reburial and the Re-creation of a Moral World among an Invisible People*. Toronto: University of Toronto Press.

Quirk, Eleanor. 1991. Japanese Canadian Garden. *The Bulletin: A Journal for and about the Nikkei Community* 33 (8): 12.

Rabinow, Paul. 1977. *Reflections on Fieldwork in Morocco*. Berkeley: University of California Press.

Radstone, Susannah, ed. 2000a. *Memory and Methodology*. Oxford: Berg.

–. 2000b. Working with Memory: An Introduction. In *Memory and Methodology*, edited by Susannah Radstone. Oxford: Berg.

Rak, Julie. 2004. *Negotiated Memory: Doukhobor Autobiographical Discourse*. Vancouver: UBC Press.

Ram, Uri. 1995. Zionist Historiography and the Invention of Modern Jewish Nationhood: The Case of Ben Zion Dinur. *History and Memory* 7 (1): 91-124.

Raven Creations. 1995. *Vacation Guide Map of the West Kootenays*. Crescent Valley, BC: Raven Creations.

Razack, Sherene. 1998. *Looking White People in the Eye: Gender, Race, and Culture in Courtrooms and Classrooms*. Toronto: University of Toronto Press.

–, ed. 2002. *Race, Space, and the Law: Unmapping a White Settler Society*. Toronto: Between the Lines.

RCMP (Royal Canadian Mounted Police). New Denver Division. 1944. Conditions among Japanese, Lemon Creek, BC. Library and Archives Canada, Records of the Department of the British Columbia Security Commission, RG 36-27, 213.

Rojek, Chris, and John Urry. 1997. Transformations of Travel and Theory. In *Touring Cultures: Transformations of Travel and Theory,* edited by Chris Rojek and John Urry, 1-22. New York: Routledge.

Rosaldo, Renato. 1989. *Culture and Truth: The Remaking of Social Analysis.* Boston: Beacon Press.

Rowlands, Michael. 1996-1997. Memory, Sacrifice and the Nation. *New Formations* 30 Winter: 8-17.

Roy, Patricia E. 2005. Lessons in Citizenship, 1945-1949: The Delayed Return of the Japanese to Canadian's Pacific Coast. In *Nikkei in the Pacific Northwest: Japanese Americans and Japanese Canadians in the Twentieth Century,* edited by Louis Fiset and Gail M. Nomura, 254-277. Seattle: University of Washington Press.

Roy, Patricia, J.L. Granatstein, Masako Lino, and Hiroko Takamura. 1990. *Mutual Hostages: Canadians and Japanese during the Second World War.* Toronto: University of Toronto Press.

Said, Edward. 1979. *Orientalism.* New York: Vintage Books.

Sakamoto, Kerri. 1998. *The Electric Field.* Toronto: Alfred A. Knopf Canada.

Scharf, Rafael F. 1999. *Poland, What Have I to Do With Thee ...: Essays on Prejudice.* Kraków: Fundacja Judaica.

Scheper-Hughes, Nancy. 2004. From Undoing: Social Suffering and the Politics of Remorse in South Africa. In *Violence in War and Peace,* edited by Nancy Scheper-Hughes and Philippe Bourgeois, 459-467. Oxford: Blackwell Publishing.

Scopick, Ken. 1991. *New Denver Japanese Internment Camp Restoration Assessment.* Kamloops: Mainstreet Designers, October 1: 1-29.

Sedgwick, Eve Kosofsky. 2003. *Touching Feeling: Affect, Pedagogy, Performativity.* Durham: Duke University Press.

Sekula, Allan. 1999. Reading an Archive: Photography between Labour and Capital. In *Visual Culture: The Reader,* edited by Jessica Evans and Stuart Hall, 181-192. London: Sage.

Semujanga, Josias. 2003. *Origins of Rwandan Genocide.* Amherst, NY: Humanity Books.

Shields, Rob. 1991. *Places on the Margin: Alternative Geographies of Modernity.* London: Routledge.

Shimizu, Henry. 2008. *Images of Internment: A Bitter-Sweet Memoir in Words and Images.* Toronto: T-Jean Press.

Shimizu, Kay. 1996. Schreiber Plaque Dedication. *The Bulletin: A Journal for and about the Nikkei Community* 38 (10): 22-24.

Shozawa, Katherine. 1996. *Administrator's Report,* Calendar. NIMC Records, New Denver, BC.

Silverton Chamber of Commerce n.d. Welcome to Slocan Lake: New Denver, Silverton and Sandon.

Sinixt Nation. http://www.sinixt.bc.ca/history.html. Accessed 9 January 2006.

Simpson, Moira G. 1996. *Making Representations: Museums in the Post-Colonial Era.* London and New York: Routledge.

Smith, Dorothy. 1990. *The Conceptual Practices of Power.* Toronto: University of Toronto Press.

Smith, Jonathan. 1993. The Lie that Binds: Destabilizing the Text of Landscape. In *Place/Culture/Representation,* edited by James Duncan and David Ley, 78-92. London and New York: Routledge.

Smith, Linda Tuhiwai. 1999. *Decolonizing Methodologies: Research and Indigenous Peoples.* London and New York: Zed Books.

Sobchak, Vivian. 2004. *Carnal Thoughts: Embodiment and Moving Image Culture.* Berkeley and Los Angeles: University of California Press.

Soyinka, Wole. 2004. From the Burden of Memory: The Muse of Forgiveness. In *Violence in War and Peace,* edited by Nancy Scheper-Hughes and Philippe Bourgeois, 475-477. Oxford: Blackwell Publishing.

Spitzer, Leo. 1998. *Hotel Bolivia: The Culture of Memory in a Refuge from Nazism.* New York: Hill and Wang.

Stacey, Jackie. 1997. *Teratologies: A Cultural Study of Cancer.* London: Routledge.

Stewart, Kathleen. 1996. *A Space on the Side of the Road: Cultural Poetics in an Other America.* Princeton, NJ: Princeton University Press.

Sturken, Marita. 1997. *Tangled Memories: The Vietnam War, the AIDS Epidemic, and the Politics of Remembering.* Berkeley: University of California Press.

Sugiman, Pamela. 2004. Memories of Internment: Narrating Japanese-Canadian Women's Life Stories. *Canadian Journal of Sociology* 29 (3): 359-388.

–. 2006. "These Feelings that Fill My Heart": Japanese Canadian Women's Memories of Internment. *Oral History* 34 (2): 69-84.

Sunahara, Ann Gomer. 1979. Historical Leadership Trends among Japanese Canadians: 1940-1950. *Canadian Ethnic Studies* 11 (1): 1-16.

–. 1981. *The Politics of Racism: The Uprooting of Japanese Canadians during the Second World War.* Toronto: James Lorimer.

Sunahara, M. Ann, and Glen T. Wright. 1979. The Japanese Canadian Experience in World War II: An Essay on Archival Resources. *Canadian Ethnic Studies* 11 (2): 78-87.

Suzuki, Aiko. 1994. *Japanese Canadians in the Arts: A Directory of Professionals.* Toronto: SAC/rist.

Suzuki, Nancy. 1992. Commemorative Garden Planned for the PNE. *The Bulletin: A Journal for and about the Nikkei Community* 34 (9): 17-19.

Sweet Wong, Hertha D. 1998. First-Person Plural: Subjectivity and Community in Native American Women's Autobiography. In *Women, Autobiography, Theory: A Reader,* edited by Sidonie Smith and Julia Watson, 168-178. Madison: University of Wisconsin Press.

Takana, Teresa. 1996. Appendix. In *Kyowakai Society Japanese Canadian History Preservation Committee Project Proposal: Application to the NAJC Redress Foundation Special Projects Fund.* March 1996: 1-5.

Takashima, Shizuye. 1991 [1971]. *A Child in Prison Camp.* Montreal: Tundra Books.

Takata, Toyo. 1983. *Nikkei Legacy: The Story of Japanese Canadians from Settlement to Today.* Toronto: NC Press.

–. 1998. Life Partner for 60 Years. *Nikkei Voice* 12 (8): 7.

Tanaka, George. 1979. To What Lies Buried Deep. *The New Canadian,* December 28, Section 3: 1.

Taylor, Diane. 2003. *The Archive, the Repetoire: Performing Cultural Memory in the Americas.* Durham and London: Duke University Press.

Thomson, Grace Eiko. 2005. *Shashin: Japanese Canadian Photography to 1942.* Burnaby: Japanese Canadian National Museum.

Todorov, Tzetan. 1987. *The Conquest of America.* New York: Harper and Row.

Turnbull, Elsie. 1988. *Ghost Towns and Drowned Towns of West Kootenay.* Surrey, BC: Heritage House Publishing.

Ulysse, Gina. 2002. Conquering Duppies in Kingston: Miss Tiny and Me, Fieldwork Conflicts and Being Loved and Rescued. *Anthropology and Humanism* 27 (1): 10-26.

Uno, Kathleen S. 1991. Women and Changes in the Household Division of Labour. In *Recreating Japanese Woman: 1600-1945,* edited by Gail Lee Bernstein, 17-41. Berkeley: University of California Press.

Urry, John. 1995. *Consuming Places.* London: Routledge.

–. 1996. Tourism, Culture and Social Inequality. In *The Sociology of Tourism: Theoretical and Empirical Investigations,* edited by Yiorgos Apostolopoulos, Stella Leivadi, and Andrew Yiannakis, 115-153. London: Routledge.

–. 1997. *The Tourist Gaze: Leisure and Travel in Contemporary Societies.* London: Sage.

Valley Voice. 1996a. First Nations People Gather for Picnic in New Denver, *Valley Voice* 5 (17) September 5: 7.

–. 1996b. McCory Warns Denver Flats Logging Will Be "Sure Devastation." *Valley Voice* 5 (17) September 5: 1, 14.

van Alphen, Ernst. 1997. *Caught by History: Holocaust Effects in Contemporary Art, Literature, and Theory.* Stanford: Stanford University Press.

Van Camp, Richard. 2000. Mermaids. In *Skins: Contemporary Indigenous Writing,* edited by Kateri Akiwenzie-Damm and Josie Douglas, 33-43. Wiarton, ON: Kegedonce Press.

Wah, Fred. 1999. *Faking It: Poetics and Hybridity: Critical Writing, 1984-1999.* Edmonton: NeWest Press.

Ward, Peter W. 1990 [1978]. *White Canada Forever: Popular Attitudes and Public Policy towards Orientals in British Columbia.* Montreal and Kingston: McGill-Queen's University Press.

Watada, Terry. 1997. *Daruma Days: A Collection of Fictionalized Biography.* Toronto: Ronsdale.

Wiesel, Elie. 1961. *Night.* New York: Hill and Wang.

Williams, Paul. 2007. *Memorial Museums: The Global Rush to Commemorate Atrocities.* Oxford and New York: Berg.

Winter, Jay. 1996. *Sites of Memory, Sites of Mourning: The Great War in European Cultural History.* Cambridge: Cambridge University Press.

Winter, Jay, and Emmanuel Sivan, eds. 2000. Setting the Framework. In *War and Remembrance in the Twentieth Century,* edited by Jay Winter and Emmanuel Sivan, 6-39. Cambridge: Cambridge University Press.

Wong, Paul, ed. 1990. *Yellow Peril Reconsidered.* Vancouver: On the Cutting Edge.

Wong, Rita, and Jo-Anne Lee, eds. 2008. "Active Geographies: Women and Struggles on the Left Coast." Special issue, *West Coast Line* 58 (42): 2.

Yamamoto, Grayce. 1974. Reminiscences of Slocan: Then and Now. *The New Canadian,* December 27, Section 3: 1-6.

Yasui, Roy. 2006. Remembrances of New Denver, 1942-1946. *Nikkei Images* 11 (3) Autumn: 20-25.

Young, James E. 1990. *Writing and Rewriting the Holocaust: Narratives and the Consequences of Interpretation.* Bloomington and Indianapolis: Indiana University Press.

–. 1993. *The Texture of Memory: Holocaust Memorials and Meaning.* New Haven: Yale University Press.

INDEX

Note: Page numbers in *italics* refer to illustrated material. NIMC stands for Nikkei Internment Memorial Centre.

Brunner, José, 14
Buddhism: Buddhist temple (*otera*), 5,
107, 111, 123, 137, 138, 142-143, 152-155;
Alberta church 131, 134; and internment
camp deaths, 56; New Denver church,
41, 56, 115, 123, 156, 158-159, 162, 214-218,
265n10; Obon festival, 122-123, 137, 173,
213-220; shrine, 107, 152-154, 214-218,
265n10; wall scrolls, 115
The Bulletin (periodical), 184
Burns, J.S., 166
bus tours, 232-234, 262n8, 266n15
Butler, Ken, 125, 138, 147, 148, 163, 171
Butler, Shelley Ruth, 202
butsudan, 40, 259n10

Canadian Department of Labour, 60-61,
64, 67, 265n13
Canadian government: racist policies, 4,
66, 251; repatriation plan, 63-66; War
Measures Act, 7-8, 203; wartime policies,
101, 167-168, 169, 171
Carroll, William K., 16
cartography, 68-70, 82
Caruth, Cathy, 17, 118
Castlegar, 32, 72, 127, 136, 166, 167
censorship, 67-68
Centennial Hall: description, 103, 106, *107*,
137-139; Japanese Canadian visitors, 136;
NIMC construction headquarters, 147;
public/private use, 106, 136, 152, 171,
184-186; "A Time Gone By" (slide show),
183-186, 193
Centennial Park, 3-4, 50-51, 134-135
children, impact of internment camps on,
44, 62, 65-66, 88-90, 135, 224, 227-228
Chow, Rey, 257n9
chronotopes: artistic expressions, 261n10;
auratic quality, 112, 113, 116; Bakhtin on,
69, 97-100, 261n10; camp remains, 112-
114, 117-118, 121; cultural space, 98; defined, 98; empty time, 69-70, 97, 99, 101,
119; ethnographic research, 98; gardens,
120, 121; Greek literary texts, 98-100, 117;
of the immemorial, 97-102; in literature,
97-99; metaphysics, 69, 98, 100, 113, 117,
122; organic time, 69, 251; political violence, 92-97, 117-119; Rabelaisian, 97, 99,

119-122; subcategories, 261n11; temporality, 98-102, 251, 261n10
citizenship: ideal citizen, 200-201; racist
notions of, 59, 169
Clifford, James, 22, 39, 112
Cohen, Erik, 198-99, 232, 233-234
collective identity, 16-17, 228-229, 232-234
collective memory, 6, 12-15, 101, 196, 197,
258n18
colonial discourse, 22-23, 27, 39, 201-202,
218, 250, 257n11, 258n17
Commissioner of Japanese Placement,
60, 65
countermonuments, 95-96, 119, 249
Crapanzano, Vincent, 34-35
Creef, Elena Tajima, 13
crematorium, 56
Crewe, Jonathan, 6-7
Crosby, Marcia, 70
Crownshaw, Richard, 113, 116
cultural identity, destruction of, 12-13
cultural memory, 6-7, 8, 12-15
cultural studies, 11, 22, 23, 37-38, 257n11,
258n17
Custodian of Enemy Alien Property, 223,
251, 256n2, 260n3

Davidson, R.A., 65
death: elders' approaches to, 10, 122, 161,
254; funerals, 12, 61; immortality, 10,
161; internment camp deaths, 56; of
Japanese Canadian community, 9-10;
Obon festival, 122-123, 137, 173, 213-220;
public place for mourning, 43
Desbrisay, F.E., 3
dialogic method, 187-188, 193-196
discrimination, 4, 64, 178, 245-247
Displaced View (Onodera), 135
Doi, George, 68, 69, 76-78, 79-80
dolls, 90-91, 221-223
Doukhobors, 32-33, 52-53, 86, 127, 136,
165-167

Eastwood, W.A., 3
elders: accounts of internment camp life,
83-91; acts of memory, 58; approaches
to death, 122, 254; bus tours, 232-234;
defined, 256n1; museumification, 249,

Kaslo/Kaslo internment camp: commemorative projects, 168; history, 1; internees, 65, 87, 178, 262n7; Langham
Cultural Society, 126, 172, 264n6
King, MacKenzie, 16, 59
Kirshenblatt-Gimblatt, Barbara, 201-202,
207, 211
Kitagawa, Muriel, 109, 260n1, 263n11
Kitsilano Buddhist church, 107
Kneale, James, 97-98
Knight, Ralph, 63, 64
Kobayashi, Audrey: Asian Canadian
scholarship and activism, 7, 8, 21, 47;
autobiographical narratives, 261n3;
biographical data, 237-238, 255; evacua-
tion process, 260n3; intermarriage,
266n17; mentorship roles, 263n15; pre-
war Japanese Canadian communities,
16, 85; role of women, 156-157
Kobayashi, Cassandra: Emergencies Act,
8; evacuation, 256n2; internee return
visits, 93, 135; redress movement, 15, 167,
169, 232, 258n19; repatriation, 2
Kogawa, Joy, 7, 92, 93
Kohan Reflecting Gardens, 51, 56, 131, 168,
191, 264n6
Kokoru Dance, 237, 260n5
Kokubo, Tsuneko, 29, 159
Kondo, Dorinne K., 18, 23, 35-37, 39, 45
Kracauer, Siegfried, 113
Kreamer, Christine Mullen, 200-201, 204
Kugelmass, Jack, 113
Kuhn, Annette, 22, 47, 58, 68
Kyowakai Hall: Buddhist shrine, 214;
community vs tourist use, 136, 152-154,
183-186, 214-218; description, 103, 106-
111, *107*; displays, 131, 175-176; NIMC
construction, 147; Obon festival, 122-
123, 213-218; renovation, 137-139; singing
in, 33; "A Time Gone By" (slide show),
183-184, 193, 194
Kyowakai Society of New Denver:
building/maintenance of NIMC, 5-6,
13, 103, 119-122, 125-127, 131-132, 138-139;
bus tours, 232-234; Centennial Hall, 152;
changing leadership, 132-135, 144-147,
155, 156-162; formation/transforma-
tion, 4, 48, 139-144, 159-162; funding
sources, 259n5; Historical Preservation

Committee, 24, 28, 30, 39, 128, 156,
171-173, 240-241; historical records, 51-
52; History Preservation Project, 221,
230; internee lists, 159-161; meetings/
membership, 106, 131, 134, 139-141, 143-
144, 152; missing files, 261n1; role of
women, 156-161; "A Time Gone By"
(slide show), 181-184. *See also* Nikkei
Internment Memorial Centre (NIMC)

labour shortages, 59-60, 109, 157. 256n2
landscapes, 17-19, 164-165. *See also* history/
historical landscape
Langer, Lawrence L., 118, 119, 225
Langham Cultural Society, 126, 172,
264n6
language differences, 148-149, 150
language/power dynamics, 205-206
Lemon Creek internment camp, 1, 31, 65,
136, 262n8
Lifton, Robert Jay, 10, 17, 118, 161, 223,
265n12
Lillooet internment camp, 95
logging industry, 55, 93, 109, 126-127, 157,
163-165

MacCannell, Dean, 198-199, 213, 217, 234
Mackinnon, J.F., 3, 67
Makabe, Tomoko, 10-11, 257n13
Malinowski, Bronislaw, 22
*A Man of Our Times: The Life History of a
Japanese-Canadian Fisherman* (Knight
and Koizumi), 63-64
Manganyani, Noel Chabani, 11
manju (Japanese confection), 39, 55, 136,
259n9
mapping, 57-58, 71-72, *71*, 80-83; scheme/
schemata, 68-71, 79-80; the space of
internment, 67-83
Marchetti, Gina, 203
Marcus, George E., 22, 39, 44
Marion, Jean-Luc, 117
Marx, Karl, 7
Mass, Amy Iwasaki, 11
Massey, Doreen, 58, 78, 83; identity of
place, 49, 57
Matsui, Elaine, *183*
Matsui, Ichiro Roy, 73, 74
Matsushita, Masaye "Mas," 183, *189*, 190

Printed and bound in Canada by Friesens

Set in Minion and Swiss 921 by Artegraphica Design Co. Ltd.

Copy editors: Ann Marie Todkill and Lesley Erickson

Proofreader: Lesley Erickson

Indexer: Lillian Ashworth

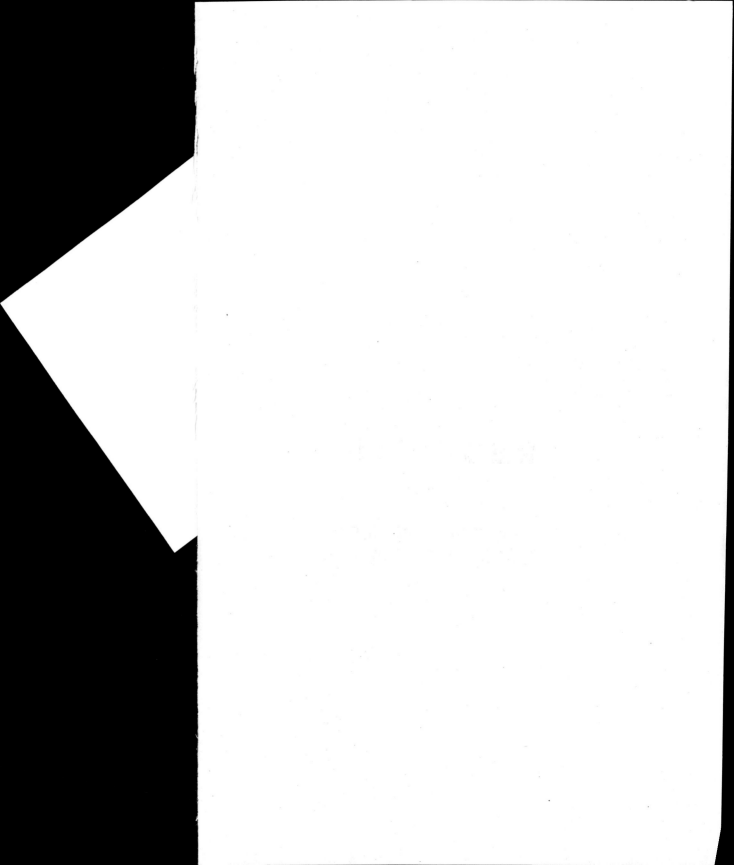

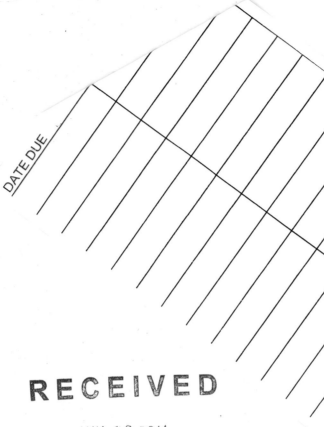